Chinese Heritage Sites and their Audiences

Chinese Heritage Sites and their Audiences provides a Chinese perspective on tourists' relationship to heritage. Contributing to ongoing debates within heritage and tourism studies, the book offers insights into how and why visitors engage with such sites.

Drawing on interviews with domestic tourists, local residents and heritage officials at the World Heritage sites of West Lake, Xidi and Hongcun, Zhang argues that tourists have agency: when they visit heritage sites, they are doing cultural, social and emotional work, whilst also negotiating cultural meanings. Providing an examination of the complex interactions between locals and tourists, the author then considers how tourists navigate and interpret heritage sites. Finally, Zhang examines whether the government or locally controlled tourism enterprises are more effective in facilitating meaningful cultural interaction between tourists and locals. Overall, the book demonstrates the interrelation between tourism and heritage, and the tensions that are created when the ways in which sites are used differ from the expectations of UNESCO and national or regional site managers.

Chinese Heritage Sites and their Audiences pays particular attention to ongoing debates about heritage performances, the importance of emotions and the agency of tourists, and will thus appeal to academics and students engaged in the study of heritage, tourism, landscape architecture and anthropology.

Rouran Zhang is a lecturer in the College of Tourism and Service Management, Nankai University, China. He is an expert member of ICOMOS-IFLA International Scientific Committee on Cultural Landscapes and ICOMOS International Scientific Committee on Cultural Tourism. He is a Chinese representative of the ongoing collaborative project of ICOMOS and IUCN entitled 'Culture-Nature Journey.'

Routledge Research on Museums and Heritage in Asia

Titles include:

Heritage Politics in China
The Power of the Past
Yujie Zhu and Christina Maags

A Representation of Nationhood in the Museum
Sang-hoon Jang

Chinese Heritage Sites and their Audiences
The Power of the Past
Rouran Zhang

Sacred Heritage in Japan
Edited by Aike P. Rots and Mark Teeuwen

www.routledge.com/Routledge-Research-on-Museums-and-Heritage-in-Asia/book-series/RRMHA

Chinese Heritage Sites and their Audiences

The Power of the Past

Rouran Zhang

LONDON AND NEW YORK

First published 2020 by Routledge

2 Park Square, Milton Park, Abingdon, Oxon OX14 4RN
605 Third Avenue, New York, NY 10017

Routledge is an imprint of the Taylor & Francis Group, an informa business

First issued in paperback 2021

Copyright © 2020 Rouran Zhang

The right of Rouran Zhang to be identified as author of this work has been asserted by him in accordance with sections 77 and 78 of the Copyright, Designs and Patents Act 1988.

All rights reserved. No part of this book may be reprinted or reproduced or utilised in any form or by any electronic, mechanical, or other means, now known or hereafter invented, including photocopying and recording, or in any information storage or retrieval system, without permission in writing from the publishers.

Notice:
Product or corporate names may be trademarks or registered trademarks, and are used only for identification and explanation without intent to infringe.

Publisher's Note

The publisher has gone to great lengths to ensure the quality of this reprint but points out that some imperfections in the original copies may be apparent.

British Library Cataloguing-in-Publication Data
A catalogue record for this book is available from the British Library

Library of Congress Cataloging-in-Publication Data
A catalog record has been requested for this book

ISBN: 978-1-138-62493-1 (hbk)
ISBN: 978-1-03-217292-7 (pbk)
DOI: 10.4324/9780429460333

Typeset in Bembo
by Newgen Publishing UK

Contents

List of figures viii
List of tables ix
Acknowledgements x
List of abbreviations xii

Introduction 1
Research background 3
Book statement 7
Fieldwork and data collection 9
Structure of the book 17

1 **International debate on heritage and tourism** 20
UNESCO World Heritage Programme, Eurocentric process 21
'Boundedness' of heritage 24
The authorised heritage discourse 27
Evolving of UNESCO World Heritage Programme 31
Community and heritage 34
Issue of heritage tourism 35
China's heritage tourism 38
The active sense of tourists 40
Heritage as a cultural process 41
Conclusion 45

2 **Heritage and tourism in China** 47
A context: China's history and its traditional philosophies 47
China's tourism development 51
China's heritage development 56
China's heritage management systems 63
Discussion 68
Conclusion 72

3 The Chinese sense of heritage: the nature–culture journey 76
Case study background 78
The authorised heritage discourse and harmony discourse of West Lake 81
Fieldwork 83
Tourists' and local people's discourses of World Heritage and cultural landscape 85
West Lake: cultural diversity and integrity 91
West Lake: a continually changing landscape 95
The emotional feeling associated with the notion of Ten Poetically Named Scenic Places *98*
Conclusion 101

4 Feeling a sense of place 104
Tourism as a problem: discourses from officials and experts 105
Tourists' active sense of heritage 111
Sense of feeling 117
Local people's attitudes to tourism and tourists 125
Conclusion 132

5 Cultural moments at heritage sites 136
Xidi and Hongcun – background and tourism development 137
Fieldwork 144
Tourists and cultural moments 146
Discussion – comparison of Xidi and Hongcun 155
Conclusion 158

6 Local people's reactions to heritage tourism 161
Local people's reactions to tourism 162
Local people's reactions to the government's policies and management mode 169
The local management policies – 'Keep Old, Keep Authentic' 178
Conclusion 185

7 Discussion: emotion, tourist agency and heritage 188
The influences of the authorised heritage discourse 189
Economic gain, cultural gain 192
Emotional engagement in cultural moments 193
Emotional expression of feeling 196
Emotional interactions between local people and tourists 202
Conclusion 210

Conclusion 212
Book summary 213
Some implications for World Heritage practice 216
Further research 218

References 220
Index 249

Figures

0.1	A view of South Lake (photo by Rouran Zhang)	2
3.1	The view of West Lake (photo by Rouran Zhang)	79
3.2	Longjing tea plantations (gardens) to the west of the lake (photo by Rouran Zhang)	93
3.3	The view of 三潭印月 *Three Pools Mirroring the Moon* (photo by Rouran Zhang)	100
4.1	Yue Fei's sculpture in West Lake Museum (photo by Rouran Zhang)	116
4.2	Tourists left poems and emotional messages on the message board (photo by Rouran Zhang)	120
4.3	The view of 花港观鱼 *Viewing Fish at Flowery Pond* (photo by Rouran Zhang)	122
4.4	Residential quarter '嘉绿苑 Jialvyuan' (photo by Rouran Zhang)	130
5.1	The view of Xidi (photo by Rouran Zhang)	138
5.2	The view of Hongcun (photo by Rouran Zhang)	138
5.3	Business street of handicrafts and special local products (photo by Rouran Zhang)	143
5.4	Poster posted on the wall about 'butchering a pig' in Xidi (photo by Rouran Zhang)	154
6.1	A resident was repairing his old house (photo by Rouran Zhang)	172
7.1	Message board in Hongcun's local hostel (photo by Rouran Zhang)	203
7.2	New handicraft shops in Hongcun (photo by Rouran Zhang)	209

Tables

2.1	Comparison of the original international documents with the Chinese version	67
3.1	What does World Heritage mean to you?	86
3.2	Do you understand the meaning of cultural landscape?	88
3.3	What categories of World Heritage do you think make up West Lake?	89
4.1	What are your reasons for visiting West Lake?	111
4.2	What experiences do you value on visiting this site?	114
4.3	Do tourists have any impact on your daily life?	126
5.1	Statement and inscription reasons of Xidi and Hongcun	139
5.2	What are your reasons for visiting Xidi?	147
5.3	What experiences do you value on visiting this site?	148
5.4	What messages about the heritage or history of the site do you take away?	152
6.1	Do tourists have any impact on your daily life?	162
6.2	What do you think about the tourism management of the site (for local people)?	170
6.3	What do you think about the tourism management of the site (for tourists)?	170

Acknowledgements

The National Natural Science Foundation of China (Grant No. 51908295) and Tianjin Philosophy and Social Science Planning Funds (Grant No.TJGLQN18-002) funded the research on which this book is based.

This book would not have been possible without the support of many people and organisations. First and foremost, I am grateful to Professor Laurajane Smith for her critical and encouraging support. Thank you for your enthusiasm about the topic of this book from the very beginning, and for helping me to understand the meaning of critical heritage and develop the argument of the book. I am also grateful to Professor Ken Taylor for his constant and illuminating encouragement, advice and support for this manuscript. I would also like to thank my friends Dr Steve Brown, Juliet Ramsay, Fergus Maclaren and Professor Robyn Bushell. Their comments on the earlier versions of this manuscript had significant impact on the development of my argument. I would also like to thank Gary Campbell for his professional editing of this manuscript.

I am extremely grateful for the people from the Ministry of Housing and Urban-Rural Development(MHURD), the State Administration of Cultural Heritage (SACH) and the China Tourism Academy; Rusheng Li, Xiaoping Zuo, Wei Tang, Yulin Shen, Zhenpeng Li, Jian Liu, Jin Fu, Xiaoru Yang and Yiyi Jiang; without their support and guidance I could not have finished the book so smoothly. I am also grateful for the people from the China National Commission for UNESCO, the World Heritage Institute of Training and Research for Asia and the Pacific, and the Institute of Architectural History, the Cultural Heritage Monitoring and Management Centre of West Lake, and the Xidi and Hongcun local governments. I also owe thanks to all the tourists and local residents I interviewed in West Lake, Xidi and Hongcun.

Special thanks to Guo Zhan, Rusheng Li, Jinlu Li, Panyan Wang, Zhaozhen Meng, Laili Yang, Xiong Li, Jianning Zhu, Zhenpeng Li, Hongcai Zhao, Fang He, Changhong Bai, Hong Xu, Hanqin Qiu, Yanbo Yao, Ye Chen and Feng Han. They have all been mentors to me since I was an undergraduate. I would also like to thank my colleagues Jieyi Xie, Cut Dewi, Chunxiao Li, Hui Li,

Xiaoyi Li, Shai Liang, Kun Zhang, Yujie Zhu, Alexandra Walton, Tzu-Yu Chiu, Kathy Chen, Megan Deas, Jennifer Clynk, Judith Downey, Laura Parker, Jane Smyth, Rachael Coghlan, Emma Wensing, Lachlan Dudley and Sulamith Graefenstein. I enjoyed my time talking with them in the Research School of Humanities and the Arts (RSHA) at the Australian National University and Nankai University.

Last but not least, I have dedicated this book to my family. To my parents, Biyun Sun and Jian Zhang, thank you for your unconditional love and support for my academic career. I am also grateful to my wife, Qian Sun. This book is my special gift to her.

Abbreviations

AHD	Authorised Heritage Discourse
CCP	Chinese Communist Party
CNKI	China National Knowledge Infrastructure
ICOMOS	The International Council on Monuments and Sites
ICCROM	International Centre for the Study of the Preservation and the Restoration of Cultural Property
ICHC	Convention for the Safeguarding of the Intangible Cultural Heritage
IUCN	International Union for Conservation of Nature
MHURD	Ministry of Housing and Urban-Rural Development
PRC	People's Republic of China
SACH	State Administration of Cultural Heritage
SPSS	Statistical Package for the Social Sciences
WH	World Heritage
WHL	World Heritage List
WHS	World Heritage Site
WHC	World Heritage Convention
WTO	World Tourism Organization
UNESCO	The United Nations Educational, Scientific and Cultural Organization

Introduction

How do tourists and local people interact with heritage sites and each other? I was pondering this question as I walked through the Hongcun World Heritage Site in China. I am a landscape architect, and my understanding of the meaning of heritage has been influenced and framed by official definitions from international authorities such as the United Nations Educational, Scientific and Cultural Organization (UNESCO) and the International Council on Monuments and Sites (ICOMOS). As with many other architecturally trained heritage practitioners, I privileged the physical importance of the site and stressed the idea that management and conservation had to ensure that non-renewable heritage resources (such as the traditional buildings and the street layout of Hongcun village) would be protected for the 'future.' I had, nevertheless, considered tourism to be one of the most significant threats to vulnerable heritage sites. However, as I conducted my fieldwork at two Chinese World Heritage sites, tourists talked about their experiences and feelings to me, and their comments reflected a greater sense of active engagement with heritage than I had assumed would be the case. I also observed an intimate link between local people and tourists. I started to rethink the interrelation between tourism and heritage and considered that this might be a more active and complex dynamic than I had been trained to assume. This was a particular 'moment' that enlightened me.

It was a winter season, and I lived in a locally run hostel located on the lakeshore of the 'South Lake' in Hongcun. I planned to finish my interviews in Hongcun on 27 December 2013. However, I fell ill with fever on the morning of Christmas Day. The woman who managed the hostel came to my room to turn off the air conditioning, as there was an unwritten rule that guests should turn off the air conditioning during the daytime to save power unless they paid extra money. She noticed that I was sick, and asked me whether I needed to take some traditional Chinese medication, which she would willingly make for me. I thanked her for her kindness and said I had already taken some medicine.

Then she walked out of my room, leaving the air conditioning on. About half an hour later, she told me to go downstairs to the courtyard. I struggled to put on my clothes and went downstairs to the courtyard. It was a sunny day. She prepared a bowl of egg noodles with a cup of hot ginger water and invited me to sit inside their traditional '火桶 Warm Barrel.'[1] She told me, 'Think of here as your home, and me as your family.' I was really touched by the empathy in that 'moment' of sitting in the 'Warm Barrel' in the traditional Hui courtyard, eating the hot food and looking at the beautiful view of the South Lake (Figure 1.1), and talking to my 'family' in Hongcun. I began to revise my assumptions about the relations between heritage and tourism. Heritage is a process constituted by countless, multi-layered cultural moments created by the combination of the activities and interactions between tourists and local people. For myself, the 'cultural moment' described above in Hongcun, the intimate interactions between myself (as a tourist), local people, and the physical heritage site created for me a sense of heritage, that is, a sense of belonging and well-being.

Can my experience as a tourist in that situation reflect anything about the interrelation between tourism and heritage more broadly? Is heritage tourism simply an 'inauthentic' leisure activity, as some heritage commentators argue (see for example, McCrone et al. 1995; Brett 1996; Choay 2001; Burton 2003; Mason 2005) or are tourists engaged with multi-layered social and cultural work? Is the tourism–heritage relationship simply negative, as much of the literature argues, as it changes or threatens the heritage values of World Heritage sites? It is often assumed that increased tourism results in the commodification

Figure 0.1 A view of South Lake (photo by Rouran Zhang)

and simplification of heritage values and meanings (see for example, Lowenthal 1985; Hewison 1987; Ap and Crompton 1993; Hall and McArthur 1998; Leask and Yeoman 1999; McKercher and du Cros 2002; Pedersen 2002; Kim et al. 2013). Alternatively, is heritage actually constructed by the cultural moments from each tourists' experiences, feelings and social performances and their interactions with local residents?

In responding to these complex problems and questions within heritage and tourism, this book draws on interviews with domestic tourists and residents at the World Heritage sites of West Lake Cultural Landscape of Hangzhou <https://whc.unesco.org/en/list/1334> and Ancient Villages in Southern Anhui – Xidi and Hongcun <https://whc.unesco.org/en/list/1002>. I argue that tourists have agency. By this, I mean that when they visit heritage sites, they are not simply touring, but are actively doing cultural, social and emotional work, displaying an active feel for the sites, and remembering and negotiating cultural meanings. There is a complex local–tourist dialogue which constructs the cultural moments evident at the two World Heritage sites. Local people gain pride, self-esteem and contentment through a process of sharing and communicating the values of the sites to domestic tourists.

In some cases, a sense of contentment emerges from both local people and tourists when they feel that bonds have been established with each other, no matter how fleeting or impermanent these bonds may be. This is more common when local people are able to participate in local tourism operations. This suggests that, to some Chinese people, the meaning of heritage is a social and emotional process of feeling and emotional engagement, as well as a dialogue between past and present, and communication between personal internal worlds and the outside world, constructed by the interplay of local people, tourists and official management. The book contributes to debates about the nature of heritage meaning-making, with particular regard to ongoing debates about heritage performances, the importance of emotions and the agency of tourists.

Research background

As Winter and Daly (2012) have identified, World Heritage has become a prestigious brand widely used by state parties in the promotion of tourism (see also Labadi 2007; Reichel et al. 2011). With the concomitant growth in the number of heritage tourists, the status of World Heritage sites acts as a catalyst for attracting tourists, particularly in developing countries (Shackley 1998). For instance, since Fanjingshan <https://whc.unesco.org/en/list/1559> – a high mountain landscape, notable for its topography and subtropical beech forest – was inscribed on the World Heritage List (WHL) in 2018, there has been a huge tourist impact. The site received about 1.2 million visitors in 2018, an increase of about 370,000 people over the same period in 2017, and the income from tourism reached 255 million renminbi (RMB; the Chinese currency), an increase of about 40% from 2017 (Cfi.cn 2019). Many other Chinese World Heritage sites (such as Fujian Tulou <https://whc.unesco.org/en/list/1113> and Old Town of Lijiang <https://whc.unesco.org/en/list/811>) have experienced similar increases in tourism revenue after being inscribed on the WHL (China National Knowledge Infrastructure website 2011). Local governments use this 'international brand' to make considerable profits after successful inscriptions (Li et al. 2008; Tao and Luca 2011). However, the newspaper *China Daily* (2007) reported in an interview with a UNESCO expert that we 'wish the local governments in China understand that being inscribed on the World Heritage List means more than enjoying tourist profits, but assuming more responsibilities and fulfilling promises.' The influence of World Heritage listing for Chinese World Heritage sites can be very different from similar sites in Western countries. China has the largest population of any country in the world, and World Heritage sites in China attract and serve a considerably higher number of domestic tourists than in other countries (Wu et al. 2002; Leng and Zhang 2009). With rapid economic development and massive investment in public transport infrastructure, mass domestic tourism has developed at a dramatic rate in China. Additionally, 'China has made a transition from being (a) centrally planned to a market-based economy' (Li et al. 2008: 309), which has given rise to a large middle-class population, who can afford to travel for leisure reasons. The China National Tourism Administration (CNTA) reports that the number of domestic tourists increased dramatically from 240 million in 1985 to 1610 million in 2007, while the domestic tourism revenue in the same period increased from 8 billion RMB to a staggering 777 billion RMB (CNTA 2008).

Tourist activities have had a variety of increasingly obvious social and environmental impacts, such as environmental degradation, overcrowding, excessive noise, and compaction from tramping, resulting in ecological damage and pollution. There is also the issue of cultural commodification, as well as the conflict between residents and tourists (see, for example, Harrison 1994; Swarbrooke 1995; Hall and McArthur 1998; Leask and Yeoman 1999; McKercher and du Cros 2002; Starr 2010; Fisher et al. 2008; Su and Teo 2009). In this sense, Wang (2007) notes that Zhang Tinghao, a representative to the 2004 National People's Congress, called for a new law for World Heritage site protection, stating that 'the masses of tourists are crowding the Forbidden City, Xian's Terracotta Warriors and the Dunhuang caves. All of these destroy the authenticity of World Heritage, and in some cases, the sites are now beyond saving.' The *China Daily* (2007) reported that during the World Heritage Committee's annual meeting in Christchurch, New Zealand, there were six

Chinese World Heritage sites, including the Forbidden City, the Summer Palace, Temple of Heaven, the ancient city of Lijiang in Yunnan Province and Three Parallel Rivers, that received 'yellow cards' from UNESCO that signal the possible removal from the list. Tong Mingkang, Deputy Director of the State Cultural Relics Bureau (in 2007), pointed out a significant problem in that local government in 'some sites are over profit-driven,' particularly in regard to tourism. He suggested that 'the "yellow card" warning helps China to understand the real meaning of World Heritage sites, "which might be a good thing"' (Li 2007).

The literature and media reports referred to above illustrate two issues. First, the focus of Chinese local governments on economic gains from tourism suggests that they do not understand the 'real meaning' of World Heritage. Secondly, they demonstrate the existence of a Chinese professional heritage concern with heritage tourism that is identical to, as Ashworth (2009) observed, the dominant Western heritage literature's concern that tourism 'destroys' fragile heritage, and that tourists are 'destroyers,' which can be accentuated in China due to its high number of domestic tourists. However, there is a need for further research to determine a clear causality between World Heritage listing and patterns of tourist visiting, and the influence this then has on the heritage values of such sites. Taylor (2012: 28) suggests that mainstream tourism concerns across the globe often focus on discussing 'marketing, facility management or growth statistics.' The majority of scholars in mainland China also focus on such 'mainstream' practical and management issues (see for instance, Wu et al. 2002; Lu and Zhou 2004; Deng 2005; Liang 2006; Huang 2006; and Zhang and Ma 2006; Luo et al. 2018; Zhang et al. 2018). In recent years, scholars such as Winter et al. (2009), Byrne (2012), Winter and Daly (2012), Winter (2009, 2014) and Aygen and Logan (2016), have examined the links between tourism and heritage in Asian contexts, 'within its wider social, political and cultural contexts, addressing an array of topics, including aesthetics … heritage … and nation building' (Winter et al. 2009: 6). Those scholars call for research about the interrelation between tourism and heritage within Asia and, as Winter (2014: 134) argues, 'lengthy, multidimensional study and important research still needs to be done in this area [Asia].'

As Graburn and Barthel-Bouchier (2001) demonstrate, a particularly negative image of the tourist can exist in public policy and tourism management planning, characterising heritage tourists as passive sightseers, with little or no agency in the meanings they construct at heritage sites (see for example Hewison 1987 for these assumptions at work). Contrary to this characterisation, Smith (2006, 2012), Ashworth (2009), Hall (2009), Waterton and Watson (2014), Zhang and Smith (2019) and Zhang and Taylor (2019), among others, argue that tourists may bring negative effects, but they may also be mindful and play active roles in constructing heritage meaning during their visits (see also Coleman and Crang 2002; Bagnall 2003, Poria et al. 2003; Palmer 2005; Byrne 2009; Sather-Wagstaff 2011; Smith 2012; and Waterton and Watson 2012). However, an active sense of tourists as cultural producers has not yet been addressed in a Chinese context (although see Zhu 2012; Zhang and Smith 2019; Zhang and Taylor 2019). Although an increasing number of studies have been concerned with the relationship between tourists and residents in Asia (see Oakes 1993; Cohen 2000, 2004; Winter 2007; Su and Teo 2009; Xie et al. 2014; Zhang et al. 2016), these have tended to focus on discussing the economic benefits/burdens that tourists bring to local communities (see Butcher 2003; Fisher et al. 2008; Su and Teo 2009; Hitchcock et al. 2010; Zou et al. 2014; Ribeiro et al. 2017). Alternatively, studies have focussed on local agency in adapting to global tourism influences (see Oakes 1993; Cohen 2000, 2004; Erb 2000; Winter 2007; Su and Teo 2009; Wu et al. 2014). The agency of tourists is not a topic that has yet been widely considered in Asia, and China in particular, nor have studies that explore the cultural and social (as opposed to the economic) interactions of tourists and local residents (although see Zhang and Smith 2019).

Ignoring the creation of touristic social and cultural value, and the social and cultural interaction that occurs between host communities and tourists, is largely a result of the naturalising effects of what Laurajane Smith (2006) has labelled the 'authorised heritage discourse' (AHD). The AHD refers to the professional discourse that frames the way heritage is understood and used internationally, and that maintains particular hierarchies of cultural expertise and understanding (Smith 2006). The AHD establishes and sanctions a top-down relationship between experts, heritage sites and tourists, in which the expert 'translates' the site and its meanings to tourists. Heritage tourists are then cast as passive consumers in this top-down system. A result has been the tendency for communities to resist the influence of experts, despite the widespread academic and practitioner calls for community participation in heritage management, interpretation and conservation work (see for example Hayden 1997; Newman and McLean 1998; Hodges and Watson 2000; Byrne et al. 2001; Smardz Frost 2004; Smith 2006: 35, Smith and Waterton 2009a; Waterton and Watson 2010; Little and Shackel 2014, among others). Although this literature has been important in identifying the interaction of stakeholder communities with expert communities, the literature has given little consideration to how communities and tourists interact. Nor has attention been paid to how tourists themselves engage in constructing the meaning of heritage in a Chinese context. This gap is largely a result of the naturalising effects of the AHD, which promotes the view that heritage as objects and places are frozen in time and space and displayed behind fences, rather than a changing process in which tourists and local people play an active role. Therefore, as I show in this book, it is necessary to examine the ways in which an active sense of tourists' agency exists in a Chinese context. It is also useful to consider if there are differences between Chinese studies and similar research in the Western contexts, such as Poria et al. (2003) and Smith (2006, 2012, 2015) have identified. What do tourists feel at and about Chinese heritage sites? What performances do tourists and local people engage in at Chinese heritage sites?

Book statement

The research presented in this book crosses disciplinary boundaries but is situated primarily within the fields of critical heritage studies and critical tourism studies. The book draws on the theoretical framework developed by Laurajane Smith (2006, 2012), which focusses on heritage as a social and cultural process (see also Harvey 2001 and Byrne 2009). In this volume I argue that the process of heritage is partly constituted by the use of heritage by individuals, for a range of personal, social, cultural and political purposes, and not primarily by 'official' heritage and management practices. Consequently, the book explores the active agency of tourists in a Chinese context. While the agency and diversity of tourists' interactions with a range of heritage sites have been explored in Western contexts (see for example, Bagnall 2003; Poria et al. 2003; Staiff 2003; Palmer 2005; Smith 2006, 2011, 2012, 2017; Byrne 2009, 2012; Sather-Wagstaff 2011), there is no such corresponding literature on East Asia.

I will argue that tourists at heritage sites are often neither passive nor accept official or authorised messages or interpretations, but display an active sense of their understandings of heritage, which are entangled with their personal, cultural and social identities and memories. My interviews with Chinese tourists demonstrate that they often draw on an aesthetic discourse that mobilises a poetic sense of the past, which in turn is linked to traditional Chinese philosophy and the 'harmony between culture and nature' (Lin 1935; Zhang 1986; Wang 1990; Xu 1996; Zhou 2003; Han 2006, 2012; Chen et al. 2012; Zhao 2018). This poetic way of experiencing heritage sites can also be found in the way local people talk about their own heritage which is being visited by tourists. Speaking with and observing Chinese domestic tourists reveal that they are enmeshed in multidimensional and complex 'cultural moments,' which are entangled with their feelings, memories, processes of remembering, places and performances. I find from my research that an active and self-conscious sense of genuine and sincere 'feeling,' or having an emotional response to heritage, is particularly prevalent in the Chinese context. The expression of emotional engagement appears to be quite different to the Western contexts that have been examined by researchers such as

Cameron and Gatewood (2000, 2003), Poria et al. (2003) and Smith (2006, 2011, 2015). As these researchers have identified, tourists in the Western contexts often displayed strong emotional engagements during their visits to heritage sites. However, they tended not to talk explicitly about feeling anything, and feelings were often not clearly articulated (see Smith 2011, 2015). I argue that the Chinese domestic tourists were explicitly aware of having or seeking an emotional response, and their sense of feeling was often expressed in or around encounters with the physical, and/or was connected to communicative encounters with local people associated with the heritage site being visited.

The book also documents the complex cultural moments constructed by the interactions of residents and tourists. In contrast to scholars such as Oakes (1993), Cohen (2000, 2004), Ying and Zhou (2007), Su and Teo (2009) and Nyaupane and Poudel (2012), who identified the agency of local people as being key for innovations in heritage site management, I suggest that this occurs through and because of the interactions local people have with tourists. The focus in tourism research tends to be on marketing issues and a concern with bringing tourists to heritage sites. There is an assumption common in this literature that the narratives promoted through marketing and site interpretation are the primary way tourists engage with heritage. This book, in documenting the in-depth cultural and social interactions that are constructed through local–tourist dialogue, argues that the interactions of tourists and local people need to be understood as underpinning marketing and economic issues. I will show that the local–tourist dialogue generated by World Heritage listing, and the presence of mass tourists, has in some instances elicited a sense of pride for local residents. Equally, however, there is a deeper dimension to the local–tourist dialogue, in which local people and tourists can form bonds, however fleeting, with each other that draw on deeper emotional and cultural registers and that are seen as both genuine and sincere. In addition, I argue that the process of official heritage management by governments can either constrain or facilitate such positive local–tourist dialogues.

This book contributes to current debates within heritage and tourism studies that aim to understand how and why tourists engage with heritage. It also demonstrates the interrelation between tourism and heritage, and illustrates the tensions that tourism can create between the way sites are used by audiences and publics and the expectations of UNESCO and national/regional site managers. Finally, as Winter (2007, 2014), Byrne (2012), Winter and Daly (2012) and Aygen and Logan (2016) have identified, there is a significant absence of non-Western understandings of heritage and tourism, and this research will provide Chinese perspectives of the interactions among tourists, local governments and communities and their understandings of heritage and tourism.

Fieldwork and data collection

This book adopts a qualitative mixed-methods approach, which includes case studies, documentary sources, structured interviews, semi-structured interviews and observation. The use of mixed methods in social research has a long history and has been actively promoted (Erzberger and Prein 1997; Greene et al. 2001; Moran-Ellis et al. 2006). For example, Sørensen (2009) argues that single methods may not deal with complex social science research agendas, such as those investigating heritage, and advocates employing complementary mixed-methods. Mason (2006: 9–10) argues that a qualitative mixed-methods approach can help researchers think creatively and 'outside the box' to deal with complex social research questions, and enhance and extend researchers' capacities for asking qualitative questions. In recent years, qualitative mixed-methods drawn from disciplines such as sociology and social anthropology have become a key methodology in the study of people in the field of heritage studies, 'and can be deployed productively to advance our understanding of the phenomenon we call heritage' (Filippucci 2009: 320).

The research that is the focus of this book adopts a qualitative mixed-methods approach, including interviews, archival and public policy analysis, centred on two case study sites. They are Chinese cultural landscape sites and ancient villages listed on the UNESCO World Heritage List. The first is the West Lake Cultural Landscape of Hangzhou (West Lake) and the second is Ancient Villages in Southern Anhui – Xidi and Hongcun (Xidi and Hongcun). West Lake, located in the city centre of Hangzhou, a relatively prosperous area in China, was listed on the WHL in 2011. As well as the changes to the built environment, the local government of Hangzhou has used 'World Heritage' branding to legitimise their huge urban regeneration effort, the 'West Lake Protection Project,' since 2001 (Xinhuanet.com 2011). After being successfully inscribed on the WHL, national and local social media reported the news with the header '让世界读懂西湖' (see Xinhuanet.com 2011; People.com 2011b; Hangzhou.com 2011), which in English means 'How to translate the meaning of West Lake to the world.' One of the most influential national newspapers, the *China Daily* (2011), interviewed a senior official in Hangzhou, who reportedly 'broke into tears' because the international experts finally 'understand the meaning of West Lake,' based on strenuous efforts to 'translate the meaning of West Lake to the world.' In this sense, during the process of World Heritage listing, Chinese governments adapted the value and meaning of West Lake to make them understandable to international authorities (Zhang 2017a). This modification process changed the locally understood values of West Lake, and added new values articulated in line with global heritage meanings, as well as influencing tourists' and local people's understandings of the site (Zhang 2017b).

However, how the Chinese government used the World Heritage 'brand' and policies to construct tourism narratives during and after the World Heritage listing has not been addressed. Local people's and tourists' responses to the listing have not been documented.

The Ancient Villages of Southern Anhui – Xidi and Hongcun – are located in the northern and north-eastern part of Yi County in southern Anhui. This region is historically called 徽州 Huizhou and is renowned for its traditional Hui landscape, 程朱理学 Cheng-Zhu philosophy, and 徽商 the Hui merchant tradition. The two villages are about 40 kilometres away from Huangshan Mountain, which is also a World Heritage site. They are about 15 kilometres apart. UNESCO inscribed the two villages on the World Heritage List, because they demonstrate 'a type of human settlement created during a feudal period and based on a prosperous trading economy; reflect the socio-economic structure of a long-lived settled period of Chinese history' and represent 'the traditional non-urban settlements of China, which have to a very large extent disappeared during the past century.' The site or property is listed on the basis of criteria (iii), (iv) and (v) (UNESCO, 2000b).

World Heritage listing has caused a dramatic increase in tourist numbers. It also brought local management policy changes that focus on strictly implementing the conservation of Outstanding Universal Value, as well as the authenticity and integrity of the site (see for instance Ying and Zhou 2007; Gao and Woudstra 2011; Xu et al. 2012, 2014). Xu et al. (2014: 805) observed that management changes have impacted on local people's sense of place, as Hongcun local people consider that they were being alienated from their houses. In this sense, listing changed both the governments' and local people's understanding of the site. However, the literature on Xidi and Hongcun attributed the alienation of local people' sense of place to both local governments and tourists. For instance, Xu et al. (2014: 805) argue that the local government in Hongcun fossilised the village for the 'convenience of administration and reflects the will of community elites and tourists with the power of discourse.' However, there is little literature that carefully analyses the interrelations among tourists, local residents and governments. Therefore, Xidi and Hongcun provide an excellent case study to explore the interrelation among tourists, local people and local governments.

Winter and Daly (2012: 16) note that the transformation from pre- to post-industrial society in Asia only took a short period of time compared to Western countries – from the late-twentieth-century to the early twenty-first century. In China, dramatic changes to economies and new forms of wealth accumulation have caused extremely uneven levels of development in different regions. Although the two selected World Heritage sites are located relatively close to each other geographically (about 280 km), West Lake is located in the city centre of Hangzhou, which is a relatively prosperous area in China, while Xidi and Hongcun are located in an area of relative poverty in Yi County.[2] West Lake is described as 'a classical master-piece and a national cultural icon ... [and] represents the Chinese philosophies of "oneness with nature"' (Han 2008: 1–2). It is a top-five tourist destination in China and was already nationally significant before being inscribed on the World Heritage list. Tourists are very familiar with the site because of history, stories, poetry and TV programmes etc., and I believe that their touristic experiences are varied and worth exploring. However, the majority of the literature discusses how to use WH to develop 'international tourism' (Fu 2004; Luo 2010; Li 2012; Wei 2012; and Zhang 2012) or analyses the appropriate tourism management policies and strategies to manage the expanding tourism market (see Chen 2005; Lv 2006; Wang 2008; Zheng 2008; Li 2012). There is very little research conducted on the experience of tourists and what they do and feel at heritage sites. Any consideration of local–tourist interactions is also absent from the existing literature.

WH listing of Xidi and Hongcun has dramatically boosted the number of tourists visiting the two villages since 2000, when the site was inscribed on the WHL. Tourism has resulted in changes to the local industries, which moved from being dominated by traditional farming to a focus on the hospitality industry. The majority of local people are currently engaged in some way with tourism businesses, including hostels run by local people. There is a common position in the literature which argues that tourism, when it causes substantial economic and social changes such as seen in Xidi and Hongcun, is a negative thing, particularly as it leads to the commodification of local culture (Greenwood 1977; Handler and Saxton 1988; McCrone et al. 1995; Brett 1996; Handler and Gable 1997; Waitt 2000; Choay 2001; Greenspan 2002). As MacCannell (1999) argues, the presence of tourists alters the authenticity of the heritage site, particularly for local people. However, as Sather-Wagstaff (2011) and Smith (2012: 210) maintain, 'little consideration is given to the interaction that occurs between host communities and tourists and what, ultimately, may be created by this interaction.'

This book aims to identify the interrelations of tourists, local people and local governments in the two villages. West Lake and Xidi and Hongcun villages have proved excellent case studies to explore the agency of tourists and their relation to local people, local governments and heritage sites.

Documentary sources

I conducted my fieldwork in China from November 2013 to February 2014, and in December 2017. I established a cooperative relationship with the Ministry of Housing and Urban-Rural Development (MHURD), especially the sections within the Heritage and Landscape Department. Based on this relationship, I have been able to acquire hundreds of official announcements, circulars, regulations, planning documents, relevant tourism data and tourism development strategies in both published and unpublished materials (some of these documents are confidential, and while they inform the research none is directly used or referenced). The purpose behind accessing and employing these resources is to identify, compare and analyse the ongoing policies, documents and nomination dossiers, as well as the current laws and policies for the case study sites. This method can help to analyse the difference between international and Chinese understandings of heritage and tourism at the policy level. This data assisted in elaborating and providing contextual background and helped to frame my qualitative interviews and observational work.

I also reviewed the relevant local newspapers, including *Hangzhou Daily*, *Zhejiang Daily*, *Anhui Daily*, *Chian Tourism News*, *Chinese Cultural Heritage News* and *Xinhua Daily Telegraph*. In addition, I analysed internet resources associated with the three case study sites, including UNESCO's archive. After the successful designation of the site (in the case of West Lake), millions of Chinese people have used weibo.com (similar to Twitter) to circulate the information on and experiences of the site. While the designation was widely celebrated by the public, they have also been concerned about tourism issues that WH listing has created. Newspaper, internet and weibo data has enabled me to investigate issues of public concern, and these sources were extremely useful in developing and focussing interview questions and analysing interview data.

Qualitative interviews

The analysis of qualitative interviews is one of the commonly used methods to elicit people's perspectives and attitudes in heritage research. Sørensen (2009: 164) notes that heritage researchers should consider interviews 'as a means of gaining information about complex and abstract relations, thoughts and feelings' and 'the method should be adapted to the needs of the specific research involved, rather than predetermined by its existing applications and formats.' Qualitative interviews have been used extensively in the field of heritage studies to explore the interaction between heritage and people. For instance, scholars such as Bagnall (2003), Poria et al. (2003), Selby (2004), Palmer (2005), Smith (2006, 2012, 2015, 2017), Byrne (2009), Cameron and Gatewood (2012), Waterton and Watson (2012) and Zhu (2012) have used qualitative interviews to research people's performances, feelings and attitudes as they engage or interact with designated heritage sites and places. However, in the literature on heritage, much less attention has been given to the interaction between tourists and local communities, and what may be created by this interaction (Smith 2012).

The research was conducted using both structured and semi-structured interviews. The questionnaire I created for my research drew on one designed by Smith (2006, 2012, 2015, 2017) and the findings of her research in Australia, England and the US. Firstly, I employed semi-structured interviews to analyse how Chinese officials and experts understood the relationship between heritage and tourism. Secondly, I conducted structured interviews with tourists and residents at the two sites. These aimed to explore the meanings and messages that tourists take away from the site, and to identify what tourists do and feel at heritage sites. I also wanted to investigate local people's reactions to mass tourism. I examined whether tourists were simply passive receivers of an 'authorised heritage discourse' (i.e. the 'official' meaning and narrative of the site constructed by World Heritage listing), or whether tourists played a more active and thoughtful role in understanding the meaning of their visit to the heritage sites. I also compared and analysed the interview data collected from tourists, local people, officials and experts to identify and discuss the differences and interactions among those stakeholders in the heritage process. All of the interviews conducted for this research were recorded by audio-taping and note-taking. All interviews were conducted in Mandarin and I then translated them into English.

Semi-structured interviews

Semi-structured interviews were undertaken to determine how Chinese government officials at both national and local levels, and experts: (1) define heritage and tourism; and (2) respond to their experiences of the World Heritage processes (discussed in Chapters 3–6). The range of groups interviewed included: (a) key officials from the national government; (b) key officials from the local government of Hangzhou; (c) key local government officials for the villages of Xidi and Hongcun; (d) heritage experts (such as historians and architects); and (e) tourism operators.

Interviews with the Chinese government officials, experts and tourist operators were done confidentially, and material from the interviews has been cited in such a way that interviewees remain anonymous. The people I proposed to interview were initially approached by phone or email. An information sheet and consent form detailing the research, its aims, the ways in which the information from the interview was to be used, the questions to be asked etc. were emailed to *each* interviewee prior to the interview. A transcript of the interview was provided to the interviewee. Any material quoted in research publications has been verified before publication with the participating interviewees.

The open-ended questions I asked in these interviews were:

1 How do you personally understand World Heritage?
2 What do you think about the UNESCO World Heritage programme?
3 What were the reasons given for encouraging the local governments at West Lake or Xidi and Hongcun to apply for World Heritage status?
4 Were there any challenges during the listing process?
5 Has World Heritage listing brought any changes to the site?
6 Did local communities participate in the listing process of West Lake and Xidi and Hongcun?
7 How important is tourism to local communities associated with the site?
8 What is your perspective on tourism and tourists?
9 How would you characterise the relationship between tourism and heritage at this site?
10 Has WH listing brought any changes of the management policies of the sites; and if so how?

Additional questions were asked during the interviews in response to issues raised by the interviewees.

The specific aims of interviewing officials, experts and tourist operators was to: (1) identify the interrelations among international authorities, national governments and local governments; (2) identify the interrelations between local governments and local communities; and (3) identify their attitudes towards tourists.

Interviews with domestic tourists and residents

I interviewed a total of 287 tourists and residents at West Lake, Xidi and Hongcun during my three and a half months' fieldwork (from 6 November 2013 to 22 February 2014), resulting in 2971 minutes (88.5 hours) of recorded data.

At West Lake, interviews with domestic tourists and residents were conducted from November 2013 to February 2014, with 133 people (64 tourists and 69 residents) interviewed at the site. Interviews with domestic tourists and residents at Xidi and Hongcun were conducted during December 2013, with 154 people (91 and 63 respectively) interviewed at the sites. These interviews were significant for this research project. The interviews were structured, consisting of several demographic questions to determine, among other measures, age, gender, occupation, education and how far they had travelled. These were followed by open-ended questions designed to explore the types of identity and memory work that tourists undertook during their visits and their understanding of WH and tourism. Open-ended questions were also designed for residents to identify local reactions to tourists. Fourteen open-ended questions were asked of tourists at West Lake, while 12 open-ended questions were asked at Xidi and Hongcun. I asked two more open-ended questions at West Lake than Xidi and Hongcun: (1) what categories of WH did respondents think made up West Lake? and (2) what do you understand the meaning of cultural landscape to be? The reason for these additional questions is that West Lake is listed as a cultural landscape (a sub-category of 'cultural site'), while Xidi and Hongcun are listed under the broader designation of cultural site only. One of the key issues I identify in Chapter 3 is the significant difference of how heritage is conceptualised in China and the West with regard to the dichotomy of nature and culture, and the concept of cultural landscape.

Based on the open-ended questions, a random sample of transcripts was read through to define thematic responses. I devised codes for each theme, and all transcripts were read through and coded. During the transcribing and coding processes, I was able to add new codes and alter codes as new themes emerged, and combine some codes where this could be beneficial to the research. To create descriptive statistics, the demographic data and the coded open-ended questions were entered into a Statistical Package for the Social Sciences 22 (SPSS 22) database, which was used to derive descriptive statistics, and cross-tabulations were undertaken against the demographic variables to determine if variables such as gender and age influenced the interview results. Given the small size of the database, such cross-tabulations returned no statistically significant results, nor were patterns in the variation of interview results significant for any of the interview demographic variables. As such the results of the cross-tabulations are not discussed in the following chapters.

The open-ended questions are as follows:

1 Do you come to West Lake frequently (question for locals)?[3]
2 What are your reasons for visiting West Lake (question for both)?[4]
3 Were your expectations met (for tourists)?
4 What experiences do you value on visiting this site (for tourists)?
5 What messages about the heritage or history of the site do you take away (for tourists)?
6 What does World Heritage mean to you (for both)?
7 What categories of World Heritage do you think make up West Lake (for both)?[5]
8 What do you understand the meaning of cultural landscape to be (for both)?[6]
9 Do you think it is important that this site is on the World Heritage List (for both)?
10 Is tourism important to you (for tourists)?[7]
11 What is the relationship between tourism and heritage (for both)?
12 What do you think of the tourism management of the site (for both)?
13 Did you come before it was a World Heritage site? If so have there been any changes to the site (for returning tourists)?

14 What do you think of those changes (for returning tourists)?
15 What aspects of West Lake/Xidi/Hongcun are most valuable in your opinion (for locals)?
16 Has World Heritage listing process brought about any changes in the way you use and understand the site (for locals)?
17 Do tourists have any impact on your daily life (for locals)?
18 What are the massages or experiences that you hope visitors take away from the site (for locals)?

The aims of the interview schedule were to: (1) determine the demography of tourists to the site; (2) determine the frequency of local people's use of the site; (3) determine how local people understand their site; (4) identify issues and themes relevant to tourists and heritage; (5) identify the affective memory and identity work undertaken by tourists during their visit; (6) identify the messages, if any, that visitors may take away from their visits; (7) identify the reactions of local people to tourists; (8) identify the reactions of local people to World Heritage listing.

Interviews with local people who had previously lived within the WH site boundaries from the West Lake World Heritage inscribed area were also conducted. All of the interviewees had been living in this area, which has now been in the World Heritage inscribed area of West Lake for over 40 years. The government migration project, which commenced in 2003, resulted in more than 3000 people being moved to a newly constructed, high-rise, housing settlement. The five open-ended questions asked are as follows: (1) Where did you live before you moved here? When did you move to this place? (2) What do you think of the differences between the two places? (3) What did local governments negotiate with you for migrating? Was there anything relevant to World Heritage application? (4) Do you think it is important that this site is on the World Heritage List? (5) What is the relationship between tourism and heritage from your perspective?

The aims of interviewing this group of local people were to: (1) identify concerns of the residents who migrated after their move; (2) identify the relationship between them and local governments; (3) identify their attitude to tourists; (4) identify their perspectives on the World Heritage Listing of West Lake.

The government officials from both national and local authorities that I interviewed were cautious, as well as thoughtful, in the responses they provided. As I transcribed the interview data, many of their responses gave me a feeling that they were concerned to formulate 'correct' answers. However, this style of response represents 'typical' thought process and responses from Chinese officials – as is likely for all government officials around the globe. While they sometimes expressed their personal understanding of heritage and tourism,[8] they were typically quick to return to 'official' and 'authorised' responses.

In contrast, my interviews with both tourists and local residents were generally sincere and honest. Although some tourists did not engage in dialogue, and provided formulaic responses or platitudes, many local residents and tourists became engaged in the conversation we were having. As I interviewed them, both local people and tourists seemed relaxed and, in some cases, highly emotional. Their direct language, body language and eye contact gave me a strong feeling that they were providing heartfelt answers.

Observation

Observations of visitors were undertaken in each case study to observe what tourists 'do' at these sites and to observe how local people and tourists interact. The data was recorded photographically and by note-taking. Observations were only undertaken in public open spaces at and around the heritage sites. This method was useful to map the interrelationship among different stakeholders. Observations were also undertaken of 11 residents at Longjin Tea Plantation Base, a significant landscape adjacent to West Lake Cultural Landscape, but rejected by the World Heritage Committee for inclusion within the listed boundary. The observation was not planned.[9] I was drinking Longjin tea in a local hostel, and the 11 tea farmers were informed by the host that I am a student in the area conducting heritage research, so we ended up sharing an informal talk. These local residents were not aware that the tea-growing area had been excluded from the boundary of the World Heritage site (discussed in Chapter 3 and 7).

In addition, I participated in three different tour groups in Xidi from 14 to 24 December 2013 (with 123 minutes of recorded data); and I also joined five different tour groups in Hongcun from 20 to 22 December 2013 (with 204 minutes of recorded data). This was done to observe what the main focus of interpretations from the tourism company were and to observe tourists' interests and performances during the tour.

Structure of the book

The book consists of eight chapters, excluding this introductory chapter and the concluding chapter. Chapter 1 locates this research in the international theoretical contexts of heritage and tourism through a review of scholarly literature. It analyses the contested literature on heritage and tourism and identifies the 'Eurocentric' process of heritage that dominates international policy and processes on heritage tourism. The chapter also discusses the theoretical framework I have applied in this book, including the 'authorised heritage discourse' and idea of heritage as process and performance (Smith 2006), 'the Chinese harmony discourse' (Yan 2015), the Chinese traditional concept of 'harmony with nature' (Han 2006, 2012) and the debates that reveal the agency of tourists (Poria et al. 2003; Smith 2006, 2012; among others). Chapter 2 explores the literature on Chinese history and traditional Chinese philosophy and their relation to and impact on tourism and the Chinese view of heritage. I also examine China's heritage management system, discusses China's role in the World Heritage Programme, and identifies the tensions between China and UNESCO's World Heritage Programme.

Chapters 3 and 4 present and discuss the findings for West Lake Cultural Landscape of Hangzhou. Chapter 3 analyses interviews with both local people and tourists, and argues that that the majority of those interviewed, whether tourists or locals, did not passively accept the authorised discourse that frames the management and interpretation of West Lake. This discourse stresses a dichotomy between the natural and cultural heritage embedded in the UNESCO/ICOMOS concept of 'cultural landscape,' expressing an active sense of the aesthetic or poetic idea of the heritage site based on a holistic understanding of Chinese landscape. Chapter 4 draws on my interviews with national and local government officials and analyses their understanding of heritage and tourism. I examine how they used 'World Heritage' as an icon, and how this influenced the development of policies to reshape the Chinese heritage system, as well as how this influenced the dissemination of 'official discourse' to tourists and local residents. Chapter 4 also explores what tourists do and feel at West Lake, and describes the sense of place, identity, feeling, memory and freedom that characterised many tourists' response to the site. It also identifies locals' reaction to tourists, with particular emphasis on the sense of pride that many local people expressed, while also acknowledging the tensions expressed by those locals forced to leave this landscape.

Chapter 5 and 6 investigate a second case study – the Ancient Villages of Southern Anhui – Xidi and Hongcun. Chapter 5 analyses what tourists do and feel at the two villages, while Chapter 6 explores the complex interaction among tourists, local people, local governments and the tourism companies in each village. I argue that when local governments and private tourism companies control tourism, as they do in Hongcun, the local people's sense of place and tourists' sense of feeling is constrained, and limits positive local–tourist interactions. On the other hand, the village-run tourism company at Xidi afforded local people and tourists with opportunities to interact and produced a positive cultural and social experience for both groups. Chapter 7 compares the two case studies. I identify three themes that emerge from the research: (1) active interactions that occur between locals and tourists; (2) emotional feeling in heritage visiting; and (3) active tourist agency in heritage visiting. I interlock these themes together by contrasting the two case studies and each stakeholder's understanding of heritage and tourism. In the concluding chapter, I draw out implications and discuss the nature of heritage and tourism in a Chinese context.

Notes

1 The traditional way to keep warm in Xidi and Hongcun province.
2 In 2014, the annual average per capita income in Hangzhou was roughly 16,000 USD, while the annual average per capita income in Yi County was only 4255 USD (Zhejiang Government: 2015; Yi County Government 2015)
3 The majority of local people in Hangzhou did not geographically live around West Lake, thus I asked the frequency and reasons they visit or use West Lake. As local people in Xidi and Hongcun live inside the villages, the two questions I asked in West Lake were not applicable.
4 Ibid.
5 West Lake was nominated as a cultural Landscape property, while Xidi and Hongcun were inscribed as a cultural heritage property. The questions are designed for West Lake.
6 Ibid.
7 I did not ask local residents this question.
8 See Chapter 4, pp. 107–109; the responses from GO001 and GO002 show discomfort or disjuncture with the UNESCO position on tourists
9 At the time I conducted my interviews, I only focused on places that were included in the WH listing boundary.

Chapter 1

International debate on heritage and tourism

Discussions about heritage value have become increasingly important in heritage debates and practice in recent decades (see, for example, Ashworth and Tunbridge 1990; Byrne 1991; Graham et al. 2000; Smith 2006; Labadi 2007; Labadi and Long 2010). Concerns about the heritage value of World Heritage properties have been a key aspect of heritage designation and valorisation for the UNESCO World Heritage Programme. Accordingly, this chapter has two broad aims. The first is to identify the current debates in heritage studies to which this study will contribute. Arising out of this, my second aim is to identify the key concepts that will be investigated in this study. Three core debates are identified as crucial for this study. The first of these is the ongoing criticism of the UNESCO World Heritage Programme as 'Eurocentric,' and in particular as 'Western Eurocentric,' in its perspective (Byrne 1991; Cleere 2001; Meskell 2002, 2015; Waterton 2010; Labadi 2007, 2013; among others). I will discuss the nature of the hegemonic 'Eurocentric' discourse which Laurajane Smith (2006) has labelled the 'authorised heritage discourse' (AHD). Thus, this chapter firstly explores the role of Western understandings of heritage that framed the World Heritage Programme in 1972 and continues to do so. In discussing this debate China's role in the World Heritage Programme is reviewed, and the tensions between China and UNESCO's World Heritage Programme and its advisory bodies are identified. The chapter explores the issues and events that triggered these tensions. Secondly, the chapter examines the debates around defining and analysing the meaning of heritage, a particular source of international tension. Finally, the chapter explores the role of tourism in heritage debates, yet another area of significant international tension within World Heritage site management. It further examines the interrelationship between tourism and heritage in an East Asian context, focussing on China. Additionally, I analyse the way much of the heritage and tourism literature has constructed the issue of tourism as problematic and tourists as inauthentic; and then I discuss an alternative discourse of the use of heritage concerning community and heritage visiting, and reconsider the agency of tourists. I am particularly concerned with inserting the idea of agency into the work of Chinese scholars' investigating heritage tourism. Finally, drawing on Smith (2006), Harvey (2001) and others, I define the concept of heritage used in this research as performance or cultural process.

UNESCO World Heritage Programme, Eurocentric process

The concept of 'World Heritage' and its associated ideas have, according to Askew, been destructive in its worldwide usage as an instrument which 'mobilises resources, reproduces dominant arguments and rationales, establishes programme agendas and policies, and dispenses status surrounding the conservation and preservation of the thing called "heritage"' (Askew 2010: 19). The 1960s and 1970s saw worldwide awareness and cooperative rescues to save endangered cultural properties and the natural world from loss and degradation (see Turtinen 2000; Askew 2010; Harrison 2013). In order to be consistent with the United Nations' mission to promote a 'culture of peace,' the United Nations Education, Scientific and Cultural Organization (UNESCO) adopted the *World Heritage Convention* (WHC) in 1972, which is arguably the most influential doctrinal text in the heritage conservation sphere (Di Giovine 2009; Buckley 2014). As Lowenthal (1998) observed, the promulgation of the WHC facilitates global discussions about the modern implications of heritage, and UNESCO state parties obsessively engage with the mechanisms of World Heritage designation (Meskell 2014). Since then, the usage of 'World Heritage' has become an integral part of the multi-faceted phenomenon of globalisation, and has received as much criticism as praise (Askew 2010; Buckley 2014).

Since the WHC was promulgated in 1972, over 191 states have become signatories to the WHC, making it one of the most powerful instruments of heritage recognition, not least because it proclaims itself politically neutral and objective, which is intended to give it a level of international scientific credibility (UNESCO 2019). There are currently 1121 sites in 167 countries (State Parties) listed on the World Heritage List (UNESCO 2019). State Parties to the WHC have also nominated 1650 sites to the 'Tentative List' (UNESCO 2018a). The mission of the WHC is to 'seek to identify, protect, conserve, present and transmit to future generations cultural and natural heritage of "Outstanding Universal Value"' (OUV) (UNESCO 2010a). In this sense, the WHC created a 'cosmopolitan law' to protect the past for future generations, an aspiration for a shared sense of belonging and global solidarity (Choay 2001: 140; Meskell et al. 2015: 424). OUV is central to and a fundamental concept within World Heritage nomination and other processes. To be considered for listing as a World Heritage site, properties must be demonstrated to be of 'outstanding universal value' (see Jokilehto and Cameron 2008; Labadi 2007, 2013; Meskell et al. 2015). A nominated property must also meet the conditions of integrity and/or authenticity and have sound protection and management system (UNESCO 2017).

The World Heritage Centre was established in 1992 in order to coordinate within UNESCO all matters related to World Heritage practice. The World Heritage Centre organises the annual meetings of the World Heritage Committee and provides advice to State Parties in the preparation of site nominations (UNESCO 2015). The Committee consists of 21 State Parties, each serving three year terms. The Committee, advised by the Advisory Bodies, is responsible for the implementation of the *World Heritage Convention*, and determines whether a property is inscribed on the World Heritage List (UNESCO 2015). The Advisory Bodies comprise three international non-governmental organisations which include the International Centre for the Study of the Preservation and the Restoration of Cultural Property (ICCROM), the International Council of Monuments and Sites (ICOMOS) and the International Union for Conservation of Nature (IUCN). The three Advisory Bodies are comprised of international experts such as archaeologists, historians, architects, planners and landscape architects, etc., each with their own disciplinary expertise, as well as national and personal priorities, conservation philosophies and attachments (Turtinen 2000; Lafrenz Samuels 2009). Based on the WHC and the Operational Guidelines (UNESCO 2017), ICOMOS and IUCN are responsible for providing advice on cultural and nature heritage nomination issues respectively, while ICCROM is responsible for advice concerning restoration techniques and training (UNESCO 2015; Turtinen 2000). These organisations have facilitated the globalisation of the UNESCO World Heritage Programme (Logan 2001; Askew 2010). As Logan (2001:52) comments:

> these organizations continue to play a powerful role on the global scene, laying down international standards for professional practice – 'world's best practice' […] In these respects UNESCO and its associated bodies may be said to be attempting to impose a common stamp on cultures across the world and their policies creating a logic of global cultural uniformity.

Although the World Heritage programme has proven to be both popular and influential around the world, the Convention's approach to OUV, and the related concept of authenticity, has not gone uncontested. With the concepts of OUV and of authenticity (as well as integrity) being widely used in the process of World Heritage nomination and management, limitations in their application have been increasingly discussed (Labadi 2007, 2013). Heritage, as defined by

UNESCO in the Operational Guidelines (2017: II.A 49), is the inheritance from our ancestors which possesses OUV, and which we convey to future generations. UNESCO points out that World Heritage sites represent collective constructs of humanity, and whose values extend beyond the countries in which they exist. Such sites are selected for nomination to the World Heritage List based on their OUV for listing as cultural, natural or 'mixed' heritage properties. UNESCO (2017: II.A 49) defines OUV as:

> Outstanding Universal Value means cultural and/or natural significance which is so exceptional as to transcend national boundaries and to be of common importance for present and future generations of all humanity. As such, the permanent protection of this heritage is of the highest importance to the international community as a whole.

There are ten criteria for the inscription of properties to the WHL, six for cultural heritage and four for natural properties (see UNESCO 2017: II.D 77). Application of the concept of OUV requires selection and evaluation on the basis that some heritage values are demonstrably more important than others. The international experts who possess specific expertise recognised by UNESCO and its associated organisations have power to decide the hierarchy of heritage values, and actively shape understandings of particular sites through the World Heritage listing process (Turtinen 2000; Logan 2001). Over the past decade, many scholars, such as Logan (2001), Musitelli (2002), Taylor (2004, 2010), Smith (2006), Labadi (2007, 2013), Waterton (2010) and Zhang and Taylor (2019) have criticised the establishing of these ten universal criteria designed to elicit OUV. Labadi (2007) argues that the current criteria used to demonstrate OUV, as well as the statements of authenticity, are focussed on the material dimensions of heritage sites. The establishment of the WHC was originally intended to protect and safeguard the World Heritage properties as well as represent the cultural or natural patrimony of the world. OUV is regarded in the WHC as the touchstone for all World Heritage properties. UNESCO (2017) points out that the properties have to meet at least one of the ten criteria, which reflect UNESCO, ICOMOS and IUCN's assumption of authority 'reinforced by the discourse of apolitical universalism.' Byrne (1991) criticises the concept of universal significance and argues that despite the diversity of heritage in each country, non-Western countries are compelled to utilise forms of assessment and management ideologies that derive from a European viewpoint. Byrne's research, which demonstrates that an ideologically Western understanding of heritage has been imposed both in Thailand and on Indigenous peoples in Australia, illustrates how the World Heritage system can marginalise indigenous and non-Western approaches to heritage (see also Pocock 1997; Cleere 2001; Sullivan 2004; among others). This European influence has seen the WHL dominated by monumentally grand and aesthetically valued sites and places (Arizpe 2000: 36; Cleere 2001; Yoshida 2004: 109). Labadi (2007) supports Byrne's arguments, and illustrates how World Heritage themes and frameworks, as well as the criteria for assessing the OUV of the World Heritage Sites and their authenticity, are Eurocentric. She further identifies an imbalance in the WHL, noting that more than half of inscribed World Heritage sites are located within the European region. This, she argues, is as a result of UNESCO's Eurocentric perspective, based on her quantitative research of 106 world culture heritage sites' nomination dossiers (see also Cleere 2001; Meskell 2002; Long and Labadi 2010; for similar arguments). Recent research conducted by Frey, Pamini and Steiner (2013) and Reyes (2014) on the number of World Heritage sites per country also confirms, despite UNESCO's attempts since 1994 to create a more balanced, comprehensive and credible List that is geographically inclusive, that Western Europe's disproportionate representation in the list remains.

'Boundedness' of heritage

A material dominated construct of heritage has facilitated a set of boundaries in the UNESCO World Heritage system. The original meaning of the word 'heritage' was generally used to describe 'an inheritance that an individual received in the will of a deceased ancestor or bequeathed when dead to descendants' (Graham et al. 2000: 1). Because of the global anxieties about loss and rapid post-war social and physical changes since the Second World War, international authorities like UNESCO, ICOMOS and IUCN institutionalised a conservation ethic and the 'conserve as found' ethos that had developed since the nineteenth century (Smith 2006: 27; see also Graham 2001; Long and Reeves 2009). The *World Heritage Convention*, adopted in 1972, has been seen as a canonical text that spreads heritage consciousness and particular heritage practices within national and international settings. Ashworth and Tunbridge (1996: 2–3) observe that the formerly precise legal term of 'heritage' has started to dramatically expand its original boundaries, from its primary meaning concerning individual inheritances into a much broader concept, which refers to physical relics or sites surviving from the past, non-physical or intangible cultural practices and crafts, biodiverse and geodiverse features of the natural environment, as well as systematically selling products and services linked to the heritage industry. In this sense, the concept of heritage has become framed as a 'site,' 'object' or intangible form of culture defined by Western experts with identifiable boundaries, and that is able to be managed and controlled by the application of relevant expertise. For instance, the dichotomy in how 'nature' and 'culture' are conceptualised has influenced the way international authorities have framed 'cultural heritage' or 'natural heritage' in heritage practice. However, in recent decades, heritage designations, particularly in the Asian context, have begun to reflect the fact that nature and culture are starting to be seen as indivisible on many non-Western contexts (see Taylor 2009, 2012; Inaba 2012; Zhang and Taylor 2019). In addition, international debates have, since the 1990s, enlarged their understanding of heritage with the introduction of the concept of cultural landscape (see Fairclough et al. 1999; Grenville 1999; Cotter et al. 2001; Fairclough and Rippon 2002; Russell 2012; Taylor 2009, 2012).

In 1992, UNESCO also recognised three categories of cultural landscape, which reflected an attempt by UNESCO to move from the 'Western notion of separation of culture and nature' within the World Heritage programme (Taylor 2009:15). The official definition of cultural landscape within the process of assessing 'outstanding universal value' is that the property should represent the 'combined works of nature and of man' which illustrates 'evolution of human society and settlement over time, under the influence of the physical constraints and/or opportunities presented by their natural environment and of successive social, economic and cultural forces, both external and internal' (UNESCO 2017: II.A 47). As Fairclough (1999) argues, the concept of landscape as proposed by the international heritage authorities not only stresses the protection of physical 'sites' with boundaries but also considers the relationship between linear time-periods and sites.

However, the implications of this new concept have been shown to be problematic by many scholars (Han 2012; Lennon 2003; Lowenthal 2005; Taylor 2009, 2010, 2012). Firstly, as Taylor (2012) and Lennon (2012) observe, based on their research in the Asia-Pacific region, there is a dilemma facing The World Heritage Committee as it inscribes and manages cultural landscape sites. The dilemma is that, first, cultural landscape properties are multi-layered, which not only includes traditional cultural and natural elements but also people who have a deep attachment to their centuries-old practices and customs. Existing boundaries defined by the WHC have been deemed inadequate because many countries cannot categorise their heritage landscapes in ways that align with the ten World Heritage criteria that are based on the dichotomy between nature and culture (Araoz 2008; Rössler 2008). Therefore, as Taylor (2009) reflects, there has been a tendency in the eyes of Western approaches to cultural heritage to ignore, or misunderstand, Asian thinking of landscape which, in effect, serve to marginalise local communities and their traditional rights to landscape.

Secondly, as Taylor (2009) argues, Southeast and East Asian countries often confuse the meaning of the 'international' definition of cultural landscape.

'Landscape' in Western contexts has been linked to the concept of wilderness or wild nature since the Enlightenment, from which the philosophical dichotomy concerning the concepts of 'nature' and 'culture' emerged (Head 2000b). As Waterton (2005) observes, international authorities such as UNESCO had deemed 'landscape' as innately 'natural.' In this sense, Taylor (2009:11) indicates that 'people were not seen as part of nature, and landscape was not seen as a cultural construct.' The conjunction of the word 'cultural' with 'landscape' that gained traction from a post-late 1980s movement extends the idea of landscape as a cultural product, to landscape as cultural process (Taylor 2012: 2).

Feng Han (2006, 2012), based on her research in China, argues that Chinese academics and practitioners have encountered difficulties in understanding the Western interpretation of the term 'cultural landscape.' She identifies that the Chinese traditional sense of landscape is 'a result of the interaction between nature and humans relies on the human-nature relationship driven by views of nature' (Han 2012: 92). One of the significant philosophical Chinese ideologies within Confucianism and Daoism is that *nature lives with me in symbiosis, and everything is with me* 天地与我并生，万物与我为一 (Zhuangzi and Lin 1957). In other words, the holistic idea of people, nature and cultural interweaving with identities, memories and other personal spiritual senses have been considered as the traditional Chinese understanding of landscape (Han 2006, 2012). In this vein, many Chinese scholars have extensively discussed and disseminated the discourse of cultural landscape (Shan 2009a; Han 2010, 2012; Wu 2011). Han (2012:103) points out that UNESCO promulgated the concept of cultural landscape, which has moved Chinese scholars, including her, to rethink the 'Chinese traditional views of nature, the interactions between Chinese and nature.' She also identified that because of the cultural differences between China and the West, 'there have been much cross-cultural misconception about the term "cultural landscape" previously' (Han 2012: 103). However, there has been little consideration to date as to why many Chinese people have not been able to make sense of the term cultural landscape, which is widely used in the international literature. One of the tasks of this study is to address this issue (see Chapter 4). Nevertheless, Han (2012:103) wrote approvingly of UNESCO's conception of cultural landscape:

> World Heritage categories provide a platform to share landscape heritage values and widen our horizons based on cultural diversity. This also offers a great opportunity for China to contribute and to benefit.

However, the Chinese traditional sense of 'harmony of human with nature,' by contrast with the Western sentiment that culture was seen as hierarchically dominant to nature (Lowenthal 2005), instead 'emphasized immanence and unity' (Chinaculture.org 2014). Many Chinese scholars believe that the philosophical integration of the harmony of man with nature in China resulted in the most significant characteristics of Chinese culture, which distinguish it from Western dualistic philosophies, which had led to an opposition between humans and nature (Han 2006:186; see also Gao 1989; Wang 1990; Feng 1990; Gong 2001; Zhou 2003). However, many Western scholars have recently begun to discuss the intimate link between heritage, identity and memory-making (see Graham et al. 2000; Bagnall 2003; Cleere 2001; Smith 2006, 2011, 2012, 2017; Smith and Akagawa 2009; Gentry and Smith 2019). For instance, Graham et al. (2000: 32) argue that 'landscape interconnects with a series of interacting and constantly mutating aspects of identity,' which they note includes 'nationalism, gender, sexuality, "race", class, and colonialism/postcolonialism.' However, Cleere (2001), Macdonald (2003), Graham et al. (2005), Smith (2006) and Byrne (2009) criticise the on-the-ground heritage practices that still focus on how the material of heritage and the conservation of its fabric informs a sense of nationalism. Many scholars have discussed the use of material culture in establishing and sustaining national identities (see for instance Trigger 1989; Hobsbawm 1992; Diaz-Andreu and Champion 1996; Spillman 1997; Boswell 1999; Carrier 2005; Hancock 2008; Winter 2015). Harvey (2001: 320) criticises contemporary heritage practices for focussing on specific technical issues around conserving and managing material culture for the purpose of bolstering national identity, which ignores other non-nationalistic uses of heritage, and its recruitment in the production of identity, power and authority. The marginalisation of non-nationalising uses of heritage and the associated sense of identities are attributed to what Smith (2006) has labelled the 'authorized heritage discourse' (AHD). The next section will analyse the concept and the consequence of the AHD.

The authorised heritage discourse

The criticism of World Heritage and its global authorising agents (UNESCO in particular) has been linked to the AHD. Smith (2006) argues that the AHD 'privileges monumentality and grand scale, innate artefact/site significance tied to time depth, scientific/aesthetic expert judgement, social consensus and nation building' (Smith 2006:11), and that the use of this concept is a useful heuristic device with which to analyse heritage policy and practice. The AHD is a professional discourse that frames policy and practice at national and international levels. There is not a single AHD, but there is a dominant Eurocentric one that influences many Western countries, and influential organisations such as UNESCO and ICOMOS, though its expression can vary between countries and organisations. For instance, Yan (2015: 65) puts forward the concept of 'the Chinese harmony discourse,' which he notes 'is as hegemonic as the Western authorised heritage discourse' in practice, which '[p]rivileges expert knowledge over local voices, while it empowers government by ignoring local residents' capability within heritage conservation.'

Waterton (2010) supports Smith's account of the AHD, and questions UNESCO's Eurocentric understanding of heritage as deriving from Western intellectuals and professionals such as archaeologists, historians and architects, who have held the authority to define and interpret what heritage is. These intellectuals are not only placed at the centre of understanding and defining the heritage values attached to the ten criteria of OUV, but they also dominate the management process in order to safeguard heritage for future generations. Smith (2006, 2011) based her research in Britain and Australia, and argued that the AHD determines the practices of defining what is or is not legitimate heritage. As she argued, some community groups (i.e. heritage professionals) have the power to make decisions about the hierarchy of heritage values based on their own preferences, while other subordinate communities or groups (i.e. local communities and tourists) can be excluded (see also Smith and Waterton 2009a; Waterton and Smith 2010). The AHD simplifies the complexity of the understanding of communities, which as Burkett (2001: 24) had previously noted, 'flips into homogeneity, a denial of difference, and an assimilation of the other.' I will further elaborate on the concept of community and its role in heritage below.

Many commentators have addressed how dominant communities or authorities use material culture to bolster nationalism (see for example Trigger 1989; Carrier 2005; Diaz-Andreu 2015). Heritage studies and practices focus on the conservation and management of treasured material cultural, while 'any real engagement with debates about how heritage is involved in the production of identity, power and authority are obscured,' a process through which national identity becomes naturalised (Smith 2006:17; see also Harvey 2001: 320). Both Harvey (2001) and Smith (2006) have noted that the historical origin of heritage management developed in the context of nineteenth-century nationalism and liberal modernity, which meant that Western values were emphasised. The obsessive focus on material culture has fostered what Smith (2006) has termed the 'authorised heritage discourse,' which stresses the innate value of material heritage. As Smith (2006: 21) argues the authorised heritage discourse has materialised contemporary heritage practices, which become hegemonic, so that 'the "preservation ethic" is imposed on non-Western nations.' The UNESCO World Heritage Programme can thus be seen as a result of this discursive influence and even 'further institutionalised the nineteenth-century preservation ethic' (Smith 2006: 27), and 'unintentionally identifies a hierarchy of monuments' (Smith 2006: 96).

International debate on heritage and tourism   29

The operation of the AHD is based on national and international heritage protection and management policies influenced by a European point of view (Smith 2006; Waterton 2010). This AHD relies on 'power/knowledge claims of technical and aesthetic experts,' which consist of archaeologists, historians, architects, planners and landscape architects (Smith 2006: 26). The politicians from international authorities and state parties also use the AHD as a tool for their own political and national purposes, which is evident in the competition and tensions between state parties in the World Heritage Committee, in terms of either the legitimacy or ownership of the nominated sites seen within political rationales (Beazley 2010; Meskell 2014). From the perspectives of many experts and politicians heritage is seen as material objects, sites, places and/or landscapes that are non-renewable, which are assessed by aesthetic, historical, scientific educational and political values. In this sense, the recognition of aesthetic, historical, educational and political values of a site only can be achieved by the guidance of experts. Experts from international authorities or state parties who dominate the politics of heritage lay down the global standards for 'world's best practice' in the heritage field in order to conserve and safeguard the material places or objects that represent important past nations, events, places and people 'for future generations' (Logan 2001; Smith 2006; Waterton 2010).

As Smith (2006) argues, the AHD is embedded in UNESCO's and ICOMOS's practices and policies. At a national level, different state parties also have dominant discourses or discourses that national bodies want to put forward as legitimate and that they then authorise. In terms of China, Yan (2015) argues that there is a Chinese version of the AHD – a harmony discourse that is the equivalent of, or even more hegemonic than, the Western AHD, which he called the 'Chinese harmony discourse,' based on his research on Fujian Tulou. He argues that this discourse ostensibly emphasises the harmony between human habitats and nature; however, 'supposedly aiming at maintaining a harmonious society, has created profound dissonance among the inhabitants' (Yan 2015: 65). Yan (2015) notes that he used the term 'Chinese harmony discourse' as it arises from the discourse of 'harmonious relationship between humans and nature,' which is a Chinese version of the AHD. There are two meanings embodied in the harmony discourse. On the one hand, the concept of 'harmony between nature and man' has been part of Chinese people's original cosmology and cultural characteristics, which date back to ancient China and the time of Confucius (Zhang 1986; Wang 1990; Xu 1996; M. Zhou 1999; Han 2006). Compared with the Western aesthetic theory of empathy and Western philosophy's subject–object dichotomy, the Chinese approach to aesthetic appreciation places more stress on the spirit of empathy as 'harmony between man and nature' (M. Zhou 1999; Han 2006). In this sense, many Chinese World

Heritage nomination files have used this meaning of harmony when describing the OUV of the properties under consideration (see Yan 2015's example of Fujian Tulou; Zhang 2017, Zhang and Taylor 2019's example of West Lake).

On the other hand, the word 'harmony' also entails another meaning, representing the coherent social fabric of society (Hevia 2001; Yan 2015). As Yan (2015: 70) argues, the harmony discourse in heritage practices is to some extent similar to the AHD, as it is still 'a top-down imposition with a universal framework,' rather than considering multiple narratives from non-dominant communities. In addition, the harmony discourse is tied to the national party's guiding ideology in China, the *'Harmonious Society'* (Yan 2015), which is the key feature of President Hu Jintao's signature ideology of the *Scientific Outlook on Development* 科学发展观[1] promoted since the mid-2000s (Zhong 2006). The initiative of the 'Harmonious Society' aimed to shift China's governing philosophy from being focussed 'around economic growth to overall societal balance and harmony' (The Washington Post 2006). Yan's (2015: 78) research on Fujian Tulous demonstrates that in order to maintain a 'Harmonious Society,' the dominant authorities 'tends to provide a single narrative for the site's value and privileges expert knowledge over local voices, while it empowers government by ignoring local residents' capability within heritage conservation.'

The politicians and diplomats who represent State Parties on the World Heritage Committee typically use their own form of AHD, usually for nationalistic purposes (Tunbridge and Ashworth 1996). For example, World Heritage nomination issues and the number of sites listed in China have become a signifier of the nation's image, and are therefore now playing a part in nationalist discourse. As Meyer (2008: 179) argues, 'China wants UNESCO World Heritage sites the same way actors want Oscars, for the recognition' (see also Turtinen 2000). The number of inscribed properties also offers a form of 'soft-power' that aims to place China, at least in the view of the Chinese, at the centre of the international stage. As Lowenthal (1998: 239) argued, the European domination of the WHL was a statement that the world's heritage was inevitably 'European.' China's extensive programme of WH listing is a similar statement about the role and standing of China in past and present international history, and how that standing can promote contemporary political and economic influence. Luo Zhewen, who is a pioneer architect and archaeologist with significant influence in the heritage field in China, states that Chinese World Cultural Heritage sites represent the nation's 'ancient history, unique land of charm and splendid scenery […] for thousands and even hundreds of thousands of years, the cultural tradition of the Chinese nation has all along continued without interruption, which is rarely seen among the ancient civilized states' (Luo 2008: 20–1).

Evolving of UNESCO World Heritage Programme

As a consultant with UNESCO for a long time, William S. Logan (2001) admitted that UNESCO and its associated bodies have imposed so-called 'world's best practice' on state parties in the cultural heritage field by improving international practice (such as the promulgation of international documents like the *World Heritage Convention*, and laying down common conservation methodologies and management plan requirements), promoting particular sets of heritage values and conservation practices, and establishing common management practices at World Heritage sites (see also Askew 2010: 27; Labadi 2013). However, Logan (2001) is unconvinced that the homogenisation of universal standards and management practises has mainly derived from international authorities, and he believes that the policies and criteria of the World Heritage Programme have progressively assimilated new concepts in order to incorporate wider communities' concerns. Askew (2010) notes that the UNESCO World Heritage Centre has been widening the number of listed sites and the diversity of heritage types in order to make the list more representative of the different cultural backgrounds of the member states since the late 1980s. The adoption of the 1994 'Global Strategy' has widened the diversity of the World Heritage categories. Since then, UNESCO has incorporated new categories including cultural landscapes, heritage routes, heritage canals, industrial sites, modern architecture, historic towns and historic city centres (UNESCO 2017), in order to accommodate diverse and complex sites from different cultural contexts. The key concept of 'outstanding universal value' has evolved 'from listing "the best of the best" ("iconic" or unique sites) to listing "representative of the best", the latter being a reflection of the necessity for comparison due to the surge in the number of nominated sites of similar character' (Askew 2010: 30; see also Cameron 2005).

The promulgation of *The Nara Document on Authenticity* in 1994, issued under the names of both UNESCO and ICOMOS, outlines how variant conservation practices should be interpreted, and underscores the importance of the cultural context for heritage. Since then, the term authenticity has been adopted as a central 'condition' for new World Heritage nominations by UNESCO. Starn (2002) points out that a concept of authenticity that focusses on preserving the material and inherent value of heritage was driven by anxiety about the destruction of cityscapes during the Second World War, as well as rapid urban development since the 1960s. As Winter and Daly (2012: 8) have noted, there have been dramatic physical changes in Asia since the 1990s, which disconnect people from their sense of place. The United Nations (2008:21) notes that nearly 80% (111 of 140) of new big cities emerging in the world after the 1990s are in Asia. For instance, as Campanella (2008: 286) indicates, 'China has built more housing in the last twenty-five years than any nation in history.' Cities in Southeast and East Asia such as Shanghai, Beijing, Tokyo, Singapore, Bangalore and Bangkok can hardly be recognised when compared to photographs taken in the 1970s, and in some cases even the 1990s. Due to anxiety over losing authenticity and tradition, international authorities adopted the concept of authenticity as a condition to measure the physically innate value of heritage from rapid changes in cities.

There are two critiques of the implications of authenticity. From a practical perspective, the concept of authenticity has been used as a condition for World Heritage nomination and management for more than two decades, yet many scholars maintain that it is still very hard to test authenticity, particularly in South-Asian nations (see Taylor 2009; Winter and Daly 2012). As Labadi (2010) argues, it is not compulsory to test for authenticity associated with intangible meaning in specific cultural contexts for World Heritage listing: 'the four degrees of authenticity relating to the "original" – material, workmanship, design and setting of the site – have been used predominantly by States Parties in the nomination dossiers' (Labadi 2010: 76). From an academic perspective, Smith (2006) argues that authenticity is still a part of the AHD that was formulated by experts, and essentially rests on an exaggerated appreciation of materiality. According to research by Chinese scholars such as Zhou et al. (2006), Zhang (2007), Ruan and Li (2008) and Zhang (2010), efforts have been made to translate the Western meaning of authenticity into the Chinese context, and to understand how to accurately include authenticity in Chinese heritage practices. Therefore, the 'official' concept of authenticity still serves within the Western conservation ethic, and is conducted by experts. The discussions of authenticity in heritage and tourism debates are much more complex than the focus on its physical manifestation suggests, however, and is being increasingly linked to people's emotions and feelings (see for instance, Wang 1999; Smith 2006, 2012; Zhu 2012; Smith and Campbell 2015; Zhang and Smith 2019). I will discuss this issue further below.

Scholars such as Logan (2001) and Askew (2010) note that the adoption of the 2003 *Convention for the Safeguarding of the Intangible Cultural Heritage* (ICHC) was another example where UNESCO accommodated alternative heritage forms. UNESCO states that the ICHC moved beyond the *World Heritage Convention* of 1972, which focussed on tangible properties and requirements to represent OUV and authenticity, to a wider discipline relating to cultural identity, diversity and continuity (UNESCO 2003).

The ICHC has been considered a counterpoint to the WHC, and its promulgation derived from both academic criticism of the Eurocentric understanding of heritage (see Byrne 1991; Cleere 2001; Sullivan 2004; Labadi 2007; among others), but also the practices from a range of non-Western countries (see

Aikawa 2004). Scholars such as Aikawa (2009), Blake (2009), Skounti (2009) and Hafstein (2009) acknowledge that it was a long and complex process for State Parties to draft the ICHC, which brought in non-Western understandings and practices of heritage. As Aikawa (2009) notes, non-Western countries, particularly Japan, have made great efforts to promote the inclusion of the concept of intangible heritage in the UNESCO World Heritage Programme, and finally intervened to influence the development of the ICHC. However, Smith and Waterton (2009a) argue that Western countries such as Australia, Canada, the UK, Switzerland and the USA abstained from ratifying the ICHC because they did not want indigenous groups taking governments to the high court for failure to comply with the ICIH (see also Kurin 2004). From a practical perspective, UNESCO has created an Intangible Cultural Heritage list that is separate from the World Heritage list. Therefore, scholars such as Kirshenblatt-Gimblett (2004), Smith and Waterton (2009a) and Hafstein (2009) question the implications of the ICHC in practice within nations of different cultural backgrounds. From a theoretical perspective, however, they acknowledge that the creation of ICHC was a milestone meaning making performance because it addressed intangible values rather than the object related 'criteria' of WHC. However, the values and meaning of intangible or tangible heritage were predefined by powerful international or national authorities such as UNESCO. Therefore, Kreps (2009:204) expresses concern that the ICHC 'can lead to the standardization and homogenization of practices that are inherently varied, and governed by specific cultural protocol.'

As Smith (2006: 111) argues, the World Heritage Programme is a cultural practice that was legitimised by UNESCO with its own recognition and 'validates certain cultural expressions as "heritage".' Therefore, Smith and Akagawa (2009: 4) are concerned with how successful UNESCO's definition of ICHC is in challenging the Eurocentric understanding of heritage, which has been determined by 'how that is done and by whom, and under what framing criteria and philosophies.' As Smith (2006, 2011, 2012) argues, one of the consequences of the AHD is that it legitimates 'experts,' who have the ability or authority to define what is heritage and is also reliant on institutionalised international and national cultural agencies, points also made by Byrne (1991) and Harvey (2001). Smith (2006) points out the AHD is a self-referential discourse that identifies 'heritage' as old, monumental and grand sites, buildings, monuments and places with aesthetic, scientific values which must be protected for future generations. The AHD defines a set of boundaries of heritage practices that privileges 'monumentality and grand scale, innate artefact/site significance tied to time depth, scientific/aesthetic expert judgement, social consensus and nation building;' however, at the same time it obscures or devalues the multi-vocality of sub-national cultural and social experiences and heritage understandings (Smith 2006: 11). The subordinate groups, such as local communities and tourists, do not have a chance to speak, and they are unlikely to escape from peripheral status in processes which privilege power and knowledge and are dominated by experts, diplomats and politicians.

Therefore, it is necessary to explore the process of how the dominant authorities translate the concept of World Heritage and apply it to subordinate groups. It is also necessary to document the reactions of those marginalised people and communities to dominant discourses, such as the AHD and the 'harmony discourse.' This book addresses these two issues within a Chinese context. In the next section, I discuss other forms of understanding of heritage, arising from discourses of subordinate groups rather than the 'official' meaning based on the AHD and the 'harmony discourse.'

Community and heritage

As Harvey (2001) argues, the dominant ideas of 'heritage' have centred on specific technical issues of conservation and management practices since the late nineteenth century, and have established a 'universalising' discourse since the advent of the *World Heritage Convention*. However, the dominant heritage discourse highlights the upper and middle classes' sense of identity, and that of dominant ethnic groups, while other wider social and cultural identities have been marginalised (Smith 2006). For instance, some researchers have criticised that what we may now define as the AHD worked to obscure the social and cultural work done by women (Smith 1993, 2008; Dubrow 2003), indigenous communities (Watkins 2003; Byrne 2009), ethnic and other community groups (Shackel 2001; Yan 2012; Ashworth et al. 2007) and the working class (Dicks 1997, 2000; Smith et al. 2011). My task in this section is to draw on the wider sense of what heritage is, which incorporates non-experts and sub-dominant identities.

As Graham et al. (2000), Smith (2006, 2012) and Waterton (2010) observe, the understanding of heritage that stresses the primacy of material culture tends to serve the dominant ideological discourse, but there is also a more self-referential understanding of heritage from non-expert and non-government users. There are two dissenting heritage discourses that have been widely discussed in the literature that stands outside the AHD. The first type of dissenting heritage discourse arises from local communities. The importance of community participation in heritage management, interpretation and conservation work has been extensively stressed in the heritage literature (see for example Hayden 1997; Newman and McLean 1998; Hodges and Watson 2000; Byrne et al. 2001; Smardz Frost 2004; Smith 2006; Smith and Waterton 2009a; Waterton and Watson 2010; among others). International heritage institutions such as UNESCO and ICOMOS stress that the discourse of community participation is as equally significant as the discourse of experts and policy makers. For instance, UNESCO published several official documents and papers to stress the importance of incorporating the concerns of local communities into the AHD and engage them in the stewardship of heritage conservation and management (see UNESCO 2012a, 2014; Brown et al. 2014). In this sense, the concept of community participation is only a 'subaltern' discourse that stands outside the AHD. As Smith (2006: 37) demonstrates, international authorities often 'tend to be assimilationist and top-down in nature rather than bottom-up substantive challenges to the AHD.' This has been demonstrated within the Asian context; studies on Cambodia (Winter 2007), China (du Cros and Lee 2007) and Southeast Asia (Dove et al. 2011) confirm that institutionalised practices dominated by Western discipline-specific knowledge and methodologies neglected localised, non-expert values and ideas.

In addition, this chapter accepts the concept of community put forward by Laurajane Smith and Emma Waterton which shows that communities are not fixed entities and concepts, but are rather unstable and uncertain 'social creations and experiences that are continuously in motion' (Waterton and Smith 2010: 8; see also Smith and Waterton 2009a). They went on to argue that heritage theory and practice are dominated by an authorised notion of community that 'works to reinforce presumed differences between the white, middle classes and "the rest", as well as the full range of heritage experts and "everybody else"' (Waterton and Smith 2010: 5; see also Smith and Waterton 2009a). This notion of communities within heritage study is framed by the AHD, which dominated communities via expert help by policymakers, professionals, and scholars who are 'in a position that regulates and assesses the relative worth of other communities of interest both in terms of their aspirations and their identities' (Waterton and Smith 2010: 11).

Issue of heritage tourism

The second type of dissenting heritage discourse arises from tourists. Via acts of heritage visiting, alternative and sometimes dissenting heritage discourses can be constructed. However, Smith (2006) points out the AHD incorporates local communities' discourses as subaltern discourses, and has not considered heritage tourist as part of any discourse. Indeed, the AHD attempts to construct heritage as a passive object that heritage visitors are led to rather than as an active process (Smith 2006, 2012, 2016). In this sense, the role of global institutions draws on the authorised heritage to manage perceptions:

the AHD establishes and sanctions a top-down relationship between expert, heritage site and 'visitor', in which the expert 'translates', using Bauman's (1987) sense of the word, the site and its meanings to the visitor.

(Smith 2006: 34)

Much of the work on the interaction between heritage and tourism describes this relationship as 'conflict and conflict' (see Nuryanti 1996; Robinson and Boniface 1999). Ashworth (2009) has observed that the mainstream literature considers that heritage visiting 'destroyed' fragile heritage, and that tourists were 'destroyers.' Firstly, he indicates that much of the heritage literature condemns tourists as shallow, superficial and inauthentic (see also McCrone et al. 1995; Brett 1996; Nuryanti 1996; Choay 2001; Burton 2003; also Graburn and Barthel-Bouchier 2001, who make similar points). Mason (2004, 2005) also defines the tourist as a passive consumer of received heritage messages. Therefore, the important responsibilities of a heritage manager are to mitigate potentially destructive tourist behaviour, and educate tourists to appreciate the historical, cultural and aesthetic values of the site (Pedersen 2002). Both the international and national authorities have developed educational strategies and policies to educate heritage visitors to appreciate heritage value from within the dominant discourse. An example is ICOMOS's promulgation of the *Seoul Declaration on Tourism in Asia's Historic Towns and Areas* in 2005, which states that heritage is considered as a non-renewable resource, and tourists should be educated to appreciate and conserve this resource to achieve sustainable tourism without exhausting heritage (ICOMOS 2005). This shows that ICOMOS's concern is about the 'importance of accurate and aesthetic interpretation and presentation of heritage places for tourism' (Ashworth 2009: 80).

The second problem, as Ashworth (2009) argues, is that much of the heritage literature has characterised tourists and heritage visiting as causing pollution and physical damage to heritage sites, and obscuring or eroding other values of heritage, particularly the aesthetic and visual value of sites. Therefore, the mainstream of heritage literature has primarily been concerned with visitor management, heritage resource conservation and mitigating negative physical impacts of tourist visitation (see for example, Harrison 1994, Swarbrooke 1995; Hall and McArthur 1998; Leask and Yeoman 1999; McKercher and du Cros 2002; Pedersen 2002 among others). However, since the 1960s and 1970s, mass consumption of heritage tourism has become an important global economic and cultural issue (Lowenthal 1998). The dramatic improvement of transport systems inherently challenges contemporary tourism (Prentice 1993). Mass tourism has become an important global economic and cultural issue, which has attracted considerable attention from a number of disciplines, including economics, history and social and cultural studies. Economic commodification and the 'Disneyfication' of mass heritage tourism are among the key problems in heritage research (Handler and Saxton 1988; McCrone et al. 1995; Choay 2001; Franklin and Crang 2001; McKercher and Du Cros 2002; Handler and Gable 1997; Winter 2007 and Su and Teo 2009). Patrick Wright (1985) and Robert Hewison (1981, 1987) in particular despairingly argued that Britain had become a heritage theme park because of the development of the 'heritage industry,' which they consider to be stifling cultural innovation and development in Britain. Ashworth and Tunbridge (1990: 54) also noted that 'Nottingham becomes the city of Robin Hood and Heidelberg the city of the student prince.' Handler and Gable (1997), in the United States, pointed out that Colonial Williamsburg becomes a city primarily associated with a sense of patriotism and nationalism. All those critiques show that the 'Disneyfication' of mass tourism simplifies and sanitises the past, stifling cultural nuance and creativity.

The third problem, as Ashworth (2009) has argued, is that it is a dilemma that tourism brings economic development and supports the maintenance of heritage sites, and the presence of tourists alters the so-called cultural authenticity of heritage. Extensive tourism and heritage literature inspired by MacCannell (1973, 1999) argues that tourists are motivated to visit a site by a quest for authenticity. Cohen (1988, 373) explains that authenticity is an 'eminently modern value' and 'prominent motif of modern tourism.' From MacCannell's perspective tourists are a kind of contemporary pilgrim, seeking authenticity in other 'times' and 'other place[s] away from that person's everyday life' (Urry 2002:10). However, MacCannell (1973, 1999) considers tourism as a prime example of a 'pseudo-event' (see also Cohen 1988; Coleman and Crang 2002). He argues that the advent of mass tourism obliterates cultural authenticity and ensures the 'Disneyfication' of heritage sites. As a result, Dicks (2003) has argued that the emergence of mass heritage tourism has transformed heritage resources into products for consumption via tourism marketing. As Smith (2006: 81) argues, this concern is engendered by the AHD, so that:

> This process, in which the past is seen (even if it is not) to become divergent from the direct objective and pastoral care and control of 'history', renders any interpretation subject to observations and criticisms of 'sanitization', 'trivialization', lack of authenticity and so forth.

In this sense, tourists and heritage tourism are simply connected to economic consumption, while heritage is only a product that is passively consumed by 'inauthentic' tourists. Because of the criticism of negative effects that tourists bring to heritage sites, the AHD constructs a hierarchy and passive meaning-making process to educate innately 'uncultured' and 'inauthentic' tourists to appreciate particular hierarchies of cultural expertise and experts' understanding of heritage (Smith 2006, 2012).

McKercher et al. (2005) identified five mitigation conditions affecting the relationship between heritage and tourism: (1) the independent evolution of cultural heritage management and tourism; (2) the politically imposed power balance among stakeholders; (3) the stakeholders with different levels of knowledge; (4) consideration of the diversity of heritage; and (5) different ways of asset consumption (see also Zhang et al. 2018). However, those conditions are still based on the assumption that tourists are passive message receivers in an up-down policy-making process. In the following section, I will explore the meaning of tourists beyond their construction as passive and incapable of meaning-making within the AHD. Before that I will address the issues of China's heritage tourism from Chinese scholars' perspective.

China's heritage tourism

Since the 1980s, tourism research in World Heritage sites has gradually moved from the edge to the core and has become one of the important topics in international tourism research (Rakic and Chambers 2008; Zhang et al. 2018). Chinese scholars' research on heritage tourism began in the 1990s. The research at that time was characterised by the analysis of specific cases of World Heritage sites and the development of heritage tourism strategies from a macro perspective (Leng and Zhang 2009). For example, Quan (1994) and Tang (1994) analysed the impact of Wulingyuan Scenic and Historic Interest Area's tourism on local development, and proposed how to optimise the development strategy. Liu (1994) used Mount Huangshan as an example to analyse the contradiction between the protection of heritage resources and tourism development, and proposed a macro development strategy. Gao (1998) takes the Mountain Resort and its Outlying Temples, Chengde World Cultural Heritage, as an example to explore how to promote local economic development on the premise of protection. These studies focus on tourism development, heritage value research and initial attention to heritage conservation and heritage monitoring. From the perspective of research methods, the research on quantitative analysis has gradually increased, emphasising tourism development and environmental science value research (Zhang and Li 2016).

By the beginning of the twenty-first century, with the rapid development of the economy and the popularisation of mass tourism, the contradiction and conflicts between the protection of China's heritage resources and the demand for commercial and economic development opportunities in the region have become increasingly prominent (Wang and Bramwell 2011). Many Chinese scholars have extensively addressed the conflicts between tourism and heritage protection, including: the destruction of natural resources caused by the construction of cable cars in Mount Tai (Fang and Dong 2001); the drilling of elevators on natural mountains in the Wulingyuan Scenic and Historic Interest Area (R. Li 2011); the national controversy triggered by the introduction of Starbucks in the Forbidden City (Hu and Lu 2007; Yan 2012); and the high number of tickets in multiple sites (Wang and Fan 2005). Chinese scholars also discuss the reasons for the contradiction and conflicts between heritage and tourism, including: local economic development as the main goal while heritage protection lack of financial support (Li et al. 2008; R. Li 2011); local governments attaching great importance to the construction of tourist facilities, ignoring the explore the natural meaning of heritage (R. Li 2011); a large number of vertical and horizontal management institutions from the state to the local, making the heritage management function unclear (Su and Wall 2011); and the lack of community participation (Su and Li 2012) among others. At this stage, compared with the 1990s, the research content included tourism development, sustainability, operation and management, heritage protection and other aspects. In addition, there were more problem-oriented empirical studies on research methods and more studies using quantitative and qualitative analysis (Zhang and Li 2016).

In recent years, the research objects of Chinese heritage tourism tend to be deepened and diversified. Chinese heritage scholars pay attention to the international development of heritage practices, by which cultural landscape, rural heritage, industrial heritage, cultural routes and other subdivided heritage types have gradually gained attention. In terms of research methods, the research using empirical research methods has increased significantly, but the research topics are still dominated by five major contents: value attribute of heritage, tourism development, industrial economy, relations of tourists and communities for management perspective and specific methods of protection management Zhang and Li (2016). Bao et al. (2014) summed up the Chinese tourism research and argued that the majority of tourism studies determine a macro structure, then tend to adopt top-down and government-policy oriented research. There has always been an imbalance in the types of tourism research (including heritage tourism research) in China. Most studies reflect applied research focussed on economic phenomena and conflicts of heritage protection and tourism development, while emphases on theoretical development, tourism sociology and tourism anthropology are absent (Bao et al. 2014). This does not mean that the application work is not important; rather it is an advantage of Chinese tourism research, in which the practice-oriented research and social services have unique values in the context of China's special social, economic and cultural context (Chen and Bao 2011). However, the lack of a theoretical system reflects the status quo of tourism research in the field of social science in China (Sharpley 2011; Tribe and Xiao 2011). This book will address

Bao et al.'s (2014) concern and contribute to a certain phenomenon and microlevel research by exploring individual tourists' emotional responses and feelings and what this means for the heritage meaning-making process.

The active sense of tourists

As noted above, the AHD has constructed a powerful intellectual framework which pre-judges tourism or tourists and what the consequence of tourism or tourists are. For instance, the official definition of tourist from the World Tourism Organization (WTO) (2009) is that it is the act of people travelling away from their usual environments, and/or their daily life for 'for not more than one consecutive year for leisure, business and other purposes' (WTO 1995, revised in 2009). In terms of heritage tourists, as McKercher (1993) and McKercher and du Cros (2002, 2003) argue, it is about tourists pursuing educational and recreational goals in a heritage setting.

Smith (2006, 2012) argues that those so-called 'official' definitions of tourists have simplified the complexity of tourists' engagement with heritage sites. The definition of tourists within the AHD assumes that tourists are geographically located, while tourists' activities are simply visiting 'other' cultures for a short time away from their everyday life. In this sense, as Smith (2012: 212) points out, the traditional definition of tourists 'ignores the possibility that those not living in a particular locality may nonetheless have close historical, cultural or emotional links to a place.' The vulgarity of destruction and commodification associated with heritage tourism is based on characterising tourists as passive, cultural outsiders, and tourists' activities as a largely passive process. It is necessary to understand how tourists can be active in constructing and consuming heritage sites.

One of the active things that tourists bring to heritage sites is the economic value supporting the maintenance of those sites. As Kirshenblatt-Gimblett (1998) argues, during the process of commodification of heritage sites, mass tourists not only have negative effects, they also work to create new cultural productions. For instance, the research of scholars such as Oakes (1993), Winter (2007), Taylor (2009, 2012), Byrne (2009), Su and Teo (2009) and Winter and Daly (2012) in Asian contexts shows that mass tourism has brought about positive social and cultural changes in Asia, particularly in some poverty-stricken areas. Oakes (1993) based his research in the Miao ethnic heritage sites in southeast Guizhou province in China. He identified commodification of local everyday life, and noted that this 'empowers the locals to "effectively maintain a sense of autonomy" by integrating them into the tourism system and reviving local tradition' (cited in Su and Teo 2009: 34). Su and Teo (2009: 9) further emphasise that tourism provides opportunities for local residents 'to modulate transnational cultures and global capital in their everyday lives.' These examples show that mass tourism in an Asian context has at least in some cases facilitated cultural creativity and site regeneration.

Smith (2006, 2012) and Sather-Wagstaff (2011) critically argue that the heritage sector has a tendency to passively concentrate on heritage tourists' economic or physical impact on heritage sites, while few studies seek to understand what it is that tourists do, think or actively feel in such sites (see also Bærenholdt et al. 2004; Biran et al. 2010). There are two levels of interrelation between heritage and tourism. On the one hand, it is within the AHD, which 'reside in the macro or institutional scale with the interchange between the creation of economic resources and marketable cultural meanings' (Smith 2012: 213). On the other hand, scholars such as Bagnall (2003), Poria et al. (2003), Palmer (2005), Smith (2006, 2012, 2015) and Waterton and Watson (2012), based on their research in Western contexts, argue that the individual visitor performance also constitutes the meaning of heritage. They argue that tourists at heritage sites do not necessarily passively accept the AHD, but exercise agency and engage in culturally sophisticated activities. Those activities and performances are embodied acts of remembering and commemoration that intimately link tourists' personal sense of identity, feelings and nostalgia, by constructing or reconstructing their sense of identity, place and belonging. In the last section, I will discuss how the individuals' sense of identity, place and belonging constructs or reconstructs the contemporary meaning of heritage.

Heritage as a cultural process

Extensive Western literature has been critical of mass tourism, believing that the meaning of heritage has been eroded by commodification, as well as the sanitisation of history and culture to amuse 'inauthentic' tourists for tourism income (McCrone et al. 1995; Schouten 1995; Brett 1996; Lowenthal 1998; Choay 2001; Gable and Handler 2003). Ashworth (2009), Hall (2009) and Smith (2006, 2012) point out that mainstream tourism literature has simplified tourism activity, focussing on marketing and consumption. As Smith (2006: 44) has indicated, these criticisms of commodification and uncultured tourists from the international literature 'share too much space with the authorised discourse,' and to some extent facilitate the AHD (see also Harvey 2001). Consequently, it is necessary to discuss the alternative discourses and understandings of heritage beyond the AHD.

Harvey (2001: 327) argues that heritage does not only speak to the past, but is a contemporary phenomenon that relates to human action, experience and agency. These phenomena are not only embodied in economic practices, but are rather a wider complex process with national and other cultural identities.

Scholars such as Harvey (2001) and Dicks (2000) have identified that heritage consists of social and cultural experiences and practices. However, they failed to identify what social and cultural work people 'do' or how people 'act' at heritage sites. Therefore, Bagnall (2003), Poria et al. (2003), Selby (2004), Palmer (2005), Smith (2006, 2012, 2015), Byrne (2009), Cameron and Gatewood (2012) and Waterton and Watson (2012) have started to fill this blank in the Western context, and argue against the traditional heritage tourism literature, which obscures the legitimacy of tourists' activities in heritage sites. They argue that people have agency, and heritage visiting is an embodied experience replete with emotional experiences. For instance, Poria et al. (2003) identified that visitors' sense of places links to their personal feelings, and further influences their behaviours at heritage sites. They argue that when tourists feel that the site is tied to their family or ethnic connections, a strong sense of feeling emerged. Smith (2006, 2012) observed that visitors often experienced strong emotional engagements, based on her research within Australia, England and the US. She argued that each visitation constructs heritage meaning:

> Heritage sites are not simply 'found', nor do they simply 'exist', but rather they are constituted at one level by the management and conservation processes that occur at and around them and, at another level, by the acts of visiting and engagement that people perform at them.
>
> (Smith 2012: 213)

Crouch (2010), Smith (2012) and Waterton and Watson (2012) have identified the linkage between heritage and tourism that they labelled 'cultural moments,' during which the performances and actions of tourists ultimately give an active sense of meaning to heritage sites in the contemporary world. They criticised the traditional ethic that considered heritage as being frozen in time and space, displayed behind glass, to be gazed upon, but is not something with which to be engaged. They argue that heritage is a verb, that it is about an active sense that people are 'doing,' performance and experiencing an encounter with heritage sites.

The idea of the tourist gaze put forward by John Urry (1990) criticises the tendency of heritage authorities to normalise touristic activities and experiences. Crouch (2010, 2012) developed Urry's arguments and indicates that the tourist gaze is not only about consuming and doing visual and detached activity; rather they are doing cultural work embodied in the engagement of remembering, commemorating, being emotional and affected and making sense of their identity. These individual processes of performance construct and reconstruct their sense of identity, place, nostalgia and belonging, which create a series of 'cultural moments.' In these cultural moments, people remember, forget, reminisce and make sense of place and their identity in the present. Therefore, tourists and the act of heritage visiting create the contemporary meaning of heritage.

Scholars such as Urry (1996), Misztal (2003) and Smith (2006, 2012) have identified that the association between heritage sites and the engagement of remembering and reminiscing is significant for the study of heritage. Although traditional heritage literature has acknowledged that memory is linked to identity, it has seen memory as a subaltern and insignificant nationalising discourse (Hall 2001). Within the context of the AHD, experts and heritage authorities use their expertise to construct memories, which inevitably link to a sense of nationalism or cultural pride in identity. However, memory is often subjective, and it is not the same as the AHD, and can even be oppositional. As Smith (2006: 58) argues:

> Thus, while heritage sites may help societies to remember, it is the legitimacy or facts of that remembrance or commemoration that is privileged and given critical attention, and not the emotional or subjective activity itself that is acknowledged, nor the possibility of meanings that this activity may have outside of the AHD.

Memory is not an object but rather a process; as Crouch and Parker (2003: 396) argue memory is recalled by 'doing.' Misztal (2003) defines memory as our ability to conceive and understand the world, and it is an active process of remembering and forgetting. Wertsch (2002) argues that remembering is an active process in which links to contemporary requirements of collective or individual memory from the past are involved in the construction of new subjective meanings. When tourists visit a heritage site, physically being at the site helps them to elicit memories. Those memories further reflect tourists' sense of place, belonging and identity. In this sense, heritage becomes a cultural tool that facilitates tourists' remembering (Wertsch and Billingsley 2011). Therefore, as Smith (2012: 214) argues, the 'cultural moment' builds a linkage between tourism and heritage; therefore:

> heritage, tourism and remembering interplay with each other to create meanings and understandings of the past that speak to and help people make sense of their sense of place, their own 'identity' or that of those 'others' being visited and explored.

Poria et al. (2003) pointed out that emotion plays an important role in building a sense of identity for visitors. This book draws on the pragmatic approach proposed by Wetherell (2012), emphasising that emotions can promote and coordinate people's perception of society or specific things or phenomena. As described by Williams (1977), there are 'structures of feelings' or emotional rules that have a coordinating and influential influence on history or social cognition. Wetherell (2012) also points out that emotions are controlled by individuals, and emotional responses are not only part of personal cognition, but also part of the individual's evaluation of specific issues or phenomena. Morton (2013) suggests that the meaning of an individual's emotional response is crucial to building an individual's perception of a particular thing. Bagnall (2003) associates the personal feelings of tourists with museums and heritage sites in a study of the Manchester Museum of Science and Industry in the United Kingdom, proposing that human–local interactions lead to 'emotional authenticity' and decisions. The 'emotional authenticity' of a visitor is the process of visiting a heritage site or museum that produces an understanding of the property and value of the site (i.e. 'sense of place') and interacts with the visitor's own culture, social context and memory. Inspired by Bagnall, Smith (2006) believes that during the visit to the site or museum, the 'emotional authenticity' of the visitors can be self-coordinated, and the 'sense of place' and 'sense of identity' determine the 'emotional authenticity' of the visitor.

The concept of authenticity is essential to understand the interrelation between heritage and tourism. Authenticity here refers neither to inherent material qualities within the heritage authorised management ethic nor to the traditional idea of the commodification of touristic experience. It is about emotional authenticity and the idea that how people feel, and the intensity of that feeling, helps people to remember and underpins that remembering with a sense of legitimacy and accuracy (Prentice 1998, 2001; Bagnall 2003; Smith 2006, 2012; Zhu 2012; Smith and Campbell 2015). The characteristic of emotional authenticity challenges the traditional understanding of authenticity, which assumes that heritage tourists are inherently passive, rather than acknowledging that authenticity is about an in-depth emotional engagement with experiences (Bagnall 2003; Belhassen et al. 2008). These arguments are based on acknowledging tourists have agency and engage in various activities activity rather than passively receive authorised messages (Bagnall 2003). As Zhu argues (2012: 1150), based on his work in Lijiang in China, authenticity is performative, and is 'embodied in the dialogue between practice and individual engagement and understanding.' Therefore, heritage visiting is not only physical experiences but also provides tourists with a sense that 'measure the legitimacy of their own social and cultural experiences outside of the heritage sites' (Smith 2006: 71).

In this book, my analysis will develop critiques base on the meaning of heritage put forward by Laurajane Smith (2006). She considers heritage is not reducible to sites, places, buildings or the other material objects, nor can it be simply be viewed as an educational resource; rather it is a 'cultural process engaged with acts of remembering that work to create ways to understand and engage with the present, and the sites themselves are cultural tools that can facilitate, but are not necessarily vital for, this process' (Smith 2006: 44). This idea builds on the idea of heritage developed by Kirshenblatt-Gimblet (1998), who argues that heritage is part of an ongoing process of cultural production, Dicks's (2000) idea of heritage as a communicative act, and Harvey's (2001) argument that heritage is a 'verb.' For Smith (2006) and Gentry and Smith (2019), heritage is an affective and emotional practice of meaning-making in which cultural values and the historical narratives and meanings they underpin are continually made and remade through the interaction with not only things and places labelled heritage, but also intangible qualities. Those things and events, often defined as 'heritage,' are the cultural tools that individuals, governments, communities and international agencies like UNESCO use to help them define and legitimise individual and collective remembering and the meanings that this makes (Smith 2006: 65; see also Smith 2012, 2016, 2017; Gentry and Smith 2019). This idea as heritage as an emotional and cultural process of meaning-making is adopted in this book.

Conclusion

This chapter, in outlining the core conceptual issues in the tensions between heritage and tourism, situates the research within the overall framework offered by critical heritage studies. I develop my critiques based on Smith's (2006) conceptualisation of the authorised heritage discourse (AHD) and Yan's (2015) identification of the Chinese harmony discourse throughout this book. This framework will be used to identify how the Chinese heritage authorities used AHD to shape the national heritage management system in Chapter 2.

The concepts and issues that will be used to frame the analysis in the book are based on ideas and concepts that privilege the active agency of heritage stakeholders. In addition to the AHD, I also discuss heritage as a process and performance, and stress the importance of emotions (Byrne 2013b; Smith and Campbell 2015), the idea of 'cultural moments' (Smith 2012; Waterton and Watson 2012; Cameron and Gatewood 2012) and the agency of tourists (Bagnall 2003; Poria et al. 2003; Selby 2004; Palmer 2005; Smith 2006, 2012, 2015; Byrne 2009); I use these insights to fame my analysis of tourists in Chapters 3–7. In addition, a key issue in much of the heritage tourism literature is the identification of actual and potential tensions between local residents and tourists; but what happens to our understanding of those tensions if we assume tourists and locals are active agents in the way they interact with both heritage and each other? These are issues that will be explored and expanded upon in the following chapters.

Note

1 Mr Hu Jintao was China's President between 2003 and 2012.

Chapter 2

Heritage and tourism in China

The purpose of this chapter is to provide relevant Chinese background for later chapters. First of all, this chapter briefly reviews China's historical and traditional philosophical concepts. These ancient philosophical views, especially the theory of the 'harmony of man and nature,' are very important for the Chinese tourists' emotional experience of the West Lake Cultural Landscape that I will discuss in Chapters 3 and 4. Second, this chapter discusses the history of China's tourism development, including the influence of ancient Chinese culture on tourism attitudes influenced by traditional philosophical concepts, the four critical stages of China's tourism development after the 1970s and the hot topic of contemporary Chinese tourism. Third, this chapter focusses on the three stages of China's heritage management development since the signing of the *World Heritage Convention* in 1985, and the issue of the institutional development of Chinese heritage management.

A context: China's history and its traditional philosophies

China has a land area of 9.6 million square kilometres (the third largest in the world), a coastline of more than 18,000 kilometres, and more than 4.7 million square kilometres of inland and coastal seas (National Bureau of Statistics of China, 2016). The provincial–level administrative regions are divided into 23 provinces, five autonomous regions, four municipalities directly under the central government and two special administrative territories (Gov.cn 2019). China has a long history as a nation; its culture can be traced back more than 5000 years and it leads the world in the number of World Heritage sites (SACH 2019b).

China has been a one-party state since the Communist Party came to power in 1949. The Chinese Communist Party's (CCP) ideas and policies are derived from so-called democratic centralism (China Today 2018). China's political system mainly includes the socialist system, the people's congress system, the system of regional ethnic autonomy, the system of community-level autonomy, and the multi-party cooperation and political consultation system under the leadership of the CCP (Xnhuanet.com 2018). Marxism–Leninism–Maoism is the ideology officially established after the Communist Party of China assumed power in 1949 (Heywood 2003). However, traditional Chinese philosophies such as Confucianism and Taoism still have a profound influence on the Chinese people.

For more than 5000 years, the Chinese people have created diverse cultural heritages and have a unique understanding of cultural and natural concepts which are an essential part of Chinese traditional culture (Shan 2010a). Research on physical geography and human landscape has a long history. The *Zhouyi* (周易) of the Shang (c. 1600–c. 1046 BC) and Zhou (c. 1046–c. 771 BC) Dynasties once put forward the viewpoints of 'depending on astronomy, observing time-changing; observing humanities, turning into the world' and 'seeing the heavens in the sky and leaning on the geography.' *Shang Shu·Yong Gong* (《尚书·禹贡》), which was written in the Warring States Period (475–221 BC), is the first regional geography work in China with the prototype of the Chronicles (Shan 2010a). According to the internal relations and differences of various elements of the geographical environment, the country is divided into *Jiuzhou* (九州),[1] establishing a regional vision centred on China, expressing the ancient local concept (Shan 2010a).

In Chinese history, from the Warring States Period to the end of the Qing Dynasty (1644–1911 AD) China's public philosophy was deeply influenced by the essential characteristics of public philosophy during the feudal period (475 BC–1911 AD) (Ye 2004). Confucian ethics and family values still dominate the grassroots of contemporary China. Many scholars believe that China is still culturally and socially conservative. From ancient times to modern times, the political system has basically not changed (Zhou 2003). China completed the transition from a slave society to a feudal society during the Warring States Period. Economic development during the feudal period led to changes in production relations and production methods, which led to the emergence of traditional Chinese philosophical concepts (Zhou 2003). Famous Chinese classical philosophers such as Confucius, Laozi, Zhuangzi and Mencius appeared in this period. They believe that human beings are natural products with natural attributes, and all human behaviours, ideas and morals must respect nature (M. Zhou 1999). As Laozi said in Chapter 25 of the *Tao Te Ching*,

> There is a kind of thing that has been created before it has existed in heaven and earth. It is silent and broad and invisible. It persists forever and never fails, and it is repeated. The earth runs in a loop and never stops. It can be used as the foundation of everything in the heavens and the earth.

I call it the 'Tao'.[2] It is endless and runs endlessly, runs continuously and stretches far away, and stretches far away to return to the original. So the Tao is great, heaven is great, earth is great, man is great. There are these four great places in heaven and earth, and man is just one of them. Among these four, people rely on the land to live and work, and prosper; the earth depends on the heaven to cultivates everything; heaven operates according to the big Dao and arrange the time series; the big Dao is natural according to its natural characteristics.[3]

In this sense, heaven, earth and people are inseparable. People come from nature and depend on nature to survive. People must follow the laws of nature in order to achieve sustainable development. Taoism opposes humanity as the centre and believes that man and nature are equal and dependent. A development model that excessively pursues material wealth and disregards the natural environment cannot be sustained (Shan 2008).

After the Warring States Period, the Qin Dynasty (221–206 BC) unified China and established a feudal state with authoritarian centralisation. This system of authoritarian centralisation has been sustained for more than two thousand years since the Qin Dynasty and has had a profound impact on China's history. After the Qin Dynasty, the Han Dynasty (206 BC–220 AD) identified Confucianism as a 'state religion' in 136 BC, which ensured the expansion of Confucianism and the rule of other philosophical schools (Tan 1971; Yan 2017). Confucian development has gone through four stages. They are: the pre-Qin Confucianism initiated by Confucius; the Confucianism of the Han Dynasty represented by Dong Zhongshu (179–104 BC); the Confucianism of the Song and Ming Dynasties marked by Cheng and Zhu Lixue (程朱理学, initiated by Chen Yi [1033–1107 AD] and Zhu Xi [1130–1200 AD]) and Lu and Wang Xinxue (陆王心学, initiated by Lu Jiuyuan [1139–1193 AD] and Wang Shouren [1472–1529 AD]); and the four stages of modern Confucianism under the influence of Western learning.

Chinese traditional Confucianism has a rich humanistic spirit. This has similarities and many differences with the Western 'human-centred' humanism. In essence, Confucian humanism is both human-centred and personal. Dignity is bounded by the ethical framework of the principle of feudal moral conduct, which is quite different from the Western humanistic tradition (C. Li 2011). In the Western Han Dynasty (202 BC–8 AD), the feudal state was powerful. In order to maintain the situation of China's reunification, it was necessary to establish an ideology that was compatible with it (Zhou 2003). Dong Zhongshu absorbed the elements of Taoism and Legalism, which were conducive to the rule of the monarchy. He reformed Confucianism and added the idea of the monarchical authority and the unification of China (Zhou 2003), which favoured the strengthening of feudal centralisation and social stability. Confucianism was consolidating and gradually became the orthodox philosophy of feudal society (Yan 2017).

This is because of its core principles, that is, the philosophical concept of heaven and man, the ethical '三纲五常 (Three Cardinal Guides and Five Constant Virtues)'[4] with the core of '仁 (benevolence),' and political unification (Tang 1991; Yao 2000). Fundamentally, these are ideas that adapted to the needs of the feudal autocracy. As Francis (1995) comments, Confucianism is not top-down, but bottom-up; the moral obligation to emphasise family life is the fundamental cornerstone of society. Confucian principles and rules are seen as the essence of life and the bond of community. In this way, Confucianism extends the boundaries of ethics from personal affairs to social and political spheres, providing not only ideology for the state but also a standard for judging behaviour and thought (Yao 2000). As Yan (2017: 31) comments, 'Confucianism's social utopia is the harmony of the individual, the group and the country.'

Confucianism is not only a set of historical norms but also a moral and ethical system that has had a profound impact on the Chinese people's ideology (Yan 2017). One of the significant concepts, that of 'harmony between human and culture' (or 'oneness with nature'), has widely influenced Chinese people's sense of place (Xu 1996; Han 2006; 2012). Confucianism believes that nature has all the characteristics of human beings and is the guiding principle of human beings; human beings are members of nature, they actively participate in the creation of life in nature, and realise the 'intrinsic value' of nature through their spiritual creation and practical activities (Yao 2000). In Confucius's *Analects* (论语), he argues that '[t]he wise man delights in water, the good man enjoys in mountains' (仁者乐山，智者乐水) (*The Analects*, Book Six, 21). In this sense, people are delighted by mountains and rivers, mainly because they have lofty and noble attributes, and not just from an aesthetic point of view. This thinking about nature from the perspective of morality has had a profound impact on China, especially for scholars. This was the first time that nature has given humanity an additional symbolic meaning in Chinese history, laying the foundation for the cultural symbolic sense of the landscape/place (Han 2006: 65).

Confucianism assumes political and ethical responsibility for the country in its social evolution, and positive and moral education, while Taoism is dominated by its negative outlook on life and romanticism (Han 2006). Taoism is another important local Chinese philosophy. It is generally believed to be derived from the philosophical thoughts of Laozi and Zhuangzi. The Taoist ideology has an essential influence on the entire East Asian culture and society. Tao is the core concept of Lao Zhuang's philosophy (Yan 2017). One of the critical concepts of Taoism is 无为 *Wuwei*, which literally means 'no action.' It is considered to be 'no artificial behaviour' rather than 'no action' (*Tao Te Ching,* chapter 25). In the eyes of Taoism, people created civilisation but lost morality. In order to avoid evil, one must be willing 'either to flee from civilised society or to destroy it' (Rubin 1976, quoted in Yan 2017: 32). Therefore, the concept of 无为 *Wuwei* advocated by Taoism did not please the Chinese ruling class during the feudal period. As Lin Yutang (2002: 54) comments:

> Taoism, in theory and practice, means a certain roguish nonchalance, a confounded and devastating scepticism, a mocking laughter at the futility of all human interference and marriage, and a certain disbelief in idealism, not so much because of lack of energy as because of a lack of faith.

However, the philosophical thinking of Taoism reflects the broad perspective of Chinese culture, especially in the interrelation between human and nature. It is encountered in the form of philosophy, medicine, martial arts (Taiji) and music (Yan 2017).

Taoism advocates the law of nature, non-interference and harmony with nature, and maintains that the natural world is in a fundamentally harmonious dynamic balance because it is composed of interdependent relationships, so there is no conflict (Jenkins 1998). The highest pursuit of Taoism is to use life to pursue the unity of the natural spirit, and finally to surpass the life of limited practical functions and realise a spiritual unity with nature (Han 2006). Lin (2002: 116) states that

> Taoism has always been associated with the recluse, retirement to the mountain, the worship of rural life, the cultivation of the spirit and the prolongation of man's life, and the banishment of all worldly cares and worries. From this we derive the most characteristic charm of Chinese culture, the rural ideal of life, art and literature.

In summary, both Confucianism and Taoism have taken the harmony between human and nature as an important concept, which has had a profound impact on the Chinese sense of place for over 2000 years. Chapters 3 and 4 will take West Lake as an example to discuss the emotions and feelings of tourists deeply influenced by the idea of harmony between human and nature.

China's tourism development

From ancient times to the present, the Chinese sense of nature is characterised by the unity of nature and humanity, and is reflected through *Lvyou* (meaning 'tourism'). In Chinese, two Chinese characters 'Lv' and 'You' form the word 'tourism.' 'Lv' is a journey of travelling from a place to another place in order to achieve a particular purpose; 'You' is a trip to go out for sightseeing and entertainment. The two words formed tourism (Gong 2001). Therefore, the new word tourism not only has the meaning of travelling from place to place but also has the meaning of sightseeing and entertainment. In ancient times, as Gong (2001) argues, there are three levels of meaning given to ancient Chinese tourism. First, it presents a simple lifestyle. Ancient nobles or scholars lived a comfortable life. They had a lot of free time, so they wandered around. The second is to eliminate annoyance, which is described in the *Book of Songs*. The third is the pursuit of the value of life, which is a way of life. Here, it mainly advocates the Taoist concept of finding the Tao in the natural environment (Gong 2001; also see Han 2006). Under the influence of Confucianism and Taoism, the Chinese know how to seek the comfort of life and the value of life in nature. That is why even in the most turbulent and dark times of the feudal era, there were still many people seeking enjoyment and entertainment in nature (Han 2006).

The introduction of modern tourism into China has experienced different stages since the establishment of the People's Republic of China (PRC). China's tourism development was politically oriented from the 1950s to the 1970s. In 1964, China established the Bureau for Travel and Tourism[5] under the supervision of the Foreign Ministry. Although it determined the task of absorbing free foreign exchange for the country, the country's policy of developing tourism mainly promoted the achievements of China's socialist reconstruction, expanded the political influence of foreign countries, and enhanced the Chinese people and the nations of the world (Zeng 2018). It was also meant to promote the mutual understanding and friendship of the people. In 1965, the central government and the state council pointed out in the *Report on the First Tourism Work Conference of China Tourism* that 'politics should take the lead, steady progress and gradual development' (Zeng 2018). At this time tourism served mainly political purposes.

The tourism industry began to develop after the launch of the 'Economic Reform and Open Door' policies in the late 1970s. Over the past 40 years, China's tourism industry has followed the national strategy, been continuously embedded in the process of reform and opening up alongside economic and social development and constantly adjusted and improved the positioning of tourism, which has been promoted roughly once every ten years (Du 2018). Du (2018) points out that China's tourism industry has undergone four significant stages since its reform and opening up in 1978.

In the first stage, the report on the work of the government, adopted by the fifth National People's Congress in 1978, explicitly stated that 'we should vigorously develop tourism' (Zeng 2018). When Deng Xiaoping inspected

Huangshan in 1979, he indicated that it was necessary to develop tourism there, which was the first time a national leader indicated the significance of tourism development at a provincial inspection (Fan and Hu 2003). In fact, between October 1978 and July 1979, Deng Xiaoping published five crucial talks on the development of tourism, which reflected an economic orientation towards tourism. For example, he said that 'there is much more to be done in the tourism industry, it must be prominently carried out, and it should be accelerated. Tourism makes more money, it comes faster, there is no problem of not being able to afford foreign debts' (Zeng 2018). At the same time, with the economic development of the *Third Plenary Session of the Eleventh Central Committee* as the focus of the party's work, the development of tourism began to be economically oriented (Zeng 2018).

In 1981, the State Council promulgated the country's first strategic document on tourism development – *Decision of the State Council on Strengthening Tourism Work* (State Council Document No. 80 [1981]). On the one hand, the document emphasises that 'tourism is both an economic undertaking and a part of foreign affairs in the PRC. The development of tourism must go beyond the path of the PRC's socialist national conditions and achieve political and economic win–win' (Du 2018, in *China Youth Daily*, 2 Aug. 2018). On the other hand, the document also clearly pointed out that the development of tourism is related to the national economy and people's livelihood and is an important part of China's national economy (Du 2018). This is the first time Chinese policy documents had identified tourism as an economic priority. After that, in December 1985, the State Council executive meeting decided to include the tourism development plan in the national 'seventh five-year plan.' The economic orientation of tourism had become the essential positioning of tourism development (Zeng 2018).

In the second stage, the China National Tourism Administration (CNTA) was established in the 1980s and was the central national tourism agency directly under the State Council. CNTA formed a leading group in 1988, for the preparation of the *Outline of China's Tourism Development Plan during the Eighth Five-Year Plan*, which was completed and adopted in 1991, entitled *Ten-year Plan for China's Tourism Development* (Fan and Hu 2003). This plan was China's first systematic tourism industry development plan after the reform and opening up. In February 1996, the National Tourism Administration compiled and adopted the *Ninth Five-Year Plan for China's Tourism Development and the Outline of the 2010 Vision*. Fan and Hu (2003) indicate that this tourism development plan attached great importance to domestic tourism and international tourism. It highlighted the forecasting of the tourism market and proposed tourism product development. Du (2018) states that the period from the end of the 1980s to the 1990s was the decade when tourism started its industrialisation and marketisation.

In the third stage, mass tourism had become the base of the tourism market (Du 2018). In 2001, the State Council convened a national tourism development work conference and issued the *Notice of the State Council on Further Accelerating Tourism Development*. Since then, the positioning of the tourism industry in the country's economic development has been continuously strengthened, and the importance attached to the development of tourism throughout the country has also increased significantly (Zeng 2018). In 2009, the promulgation of Document No. 41 (*Opinions of the State Council on Accelerating the Development of Tourism Industry*; No. 41 [2009]), clearly proposed to 'develop tourism into a strategic pillar industry of the national economy and a modern service industry that the people are more satisfied with.' Therefore, tourism was identified by the state council as one of China's pillar industries at this stage (Bao et al. 2014). Du (2018) argues that the promulgation of the *Law of the People's Republic of China* and the first *National Leisure Programme* in 2013 jointly reflected the increasingly significant of the role of the tourism industry in the national economy and people's lives.

In the fourth stage, according to the *National Opinions on Promoting the Reform and Development of Tourism* (Development Research Centre of the State Council [2014] No. 31), the tourism industry took the initiative to integrate with new industrialisation, information sources, urbanisation and agricultural modernisation. The industry was expected to meet the national strategic system's emphasis on the spirit of reform of economic, social, cultural and ecological synergy (Du 2018). In 2016, the *Thirteenth Five-Year Plan for Tourism Development* was first released as an essential plan of the State Council. The economic orientation of tourism had now become more comprehensive, and the overall development of tourism and the national economy was linked more closely (Zeng 2018).

In the 2017 government work report, Premier Li Keqiang mentioned the important concept of 'all-for-one tourism' (Li 2017). The report pointed out that it is necessary to improve tourism facilities and services and vigorously develop rural, leisure and all-for-one tourism. This was the first time that 'all-for-one tourism' has been written into the government work report, and aroused widespread public concern. President Xi Jinping also pointed out that 'to develop all-for-one tourism is the right path and we must stick to it' (China.com 2018). The concept of all-for-one tourism is a holistic idea of tourism development involving 'overall planning and cooperative mechanisms' (Jiang et al. 2018:1). Li Jinzao, the Deputy Minister of Culture and Tourism, clarifies that all-for-one tourism refers to the construction and operation of a region as a tourist destination, realising the organic integration of regional resources, industrial integration and development, social co-construction and sharing, and the promotion of coordinated economic and social development by tourism (Li 2016). In March 2018, the General Office of the State Council issued the *Guiding Opinions on Promoting the Development of 'all-for-one tourism'* (State Council [2018] No. 15), which clarified the guiding ideology and specific objectives of global tourism. According to this document, the key to achieving 'all-for-one tourism' is to involve the participation of the whole society.

In the fourth stage, another important change in China's tourism development is the Institutional Reform Plan of the State Council in 2018. According to the plan, the CNTA merged with the Ministry of Culture to form the Ministry of Culture and Tourism as a new component of the State Council. In the past 30 years of tourism development, tourism has been used more as a political and economic resource. The establishment of the Ministry of Culture and Tourism demonstrates the integration of tourism and culture. As stated in the *Guiding Opinions on Promoting the Combination of Culture and Tourism*, 'culture is the soul of tourism, and tourism is an important carrier of culture' (Gov.cn 2009). Li Jinzao delivered a speech entitled 'Promoting the integration of the arts and tourism and developing the whole world tourism to create a better life' in the *China Tourism Day* event in 2018, and stated that:

> Culture is the spirit and soul of a nation and a powerful driving force for national development and national rejuvenation. Tourism is a bridge for spreading civilization, exchanging culture and enhancing friendship. Culture and tourism have a natural affinity and strong integration. From an economic and industrial perspective, culture is the best resource for tourism, and tourism is the largest market for culture.
>
> (Li 2018)

In the context of the establishment of the Ministry of Culture and Tourism and the development of all-for-one tourism, there are three types of tourism that the country strongly values, including red tourism, rural tourism and heritage tourism.[6]

Red tourism

Red tourism is a new type of themed tourism that is based on revolutionary narratives of memorials and places, using the tourism industry to teach the history of Chinese people associated with the birth of the CCP, the anti-Japanese war, the civil war and the founding of the new China (Gu, Ryan and Zhang 2007; Zhao and Timothy 2017). Gao and Guo (2017: 252) point out that the politics of China's red tourism consists of two dimensions. First, it serves as a hegemonic tool for the state to be incorporated into and affiliated with a particular Chinese middle class. Second, it has the potential to actively shape Chinese politics by articulating socialist ideals in the public domain, which reinforces the legitimacy of the leadership of the CCP, addresses the current narratives of China's moral decline and narrows the regional development gap (see also Zhao and Timothy 2017). In December 2004, the Office of the Central Committee of the Communist Party of China and the General Office of the State Council issued the *2004–2010 Red Tourism Development Planning Outline*. Red tourism has developed rapidly in China. In 2018, the People's Daily Public Opinion Monitoring Office released the *2017 Red Tourism Impact Report*, which pointed out that in 2015–2017, China's red tourism received a total of 3.478 billion tourist visits, generating an income of 929.5 billion RMB (People.com 2018).

In recent years, China's red tourism is a hot spot in academic research. However, the two case studies in this book are not in the category of red tourism, so there will be no more discussion of red tourism in this book.

Rural tourism

The characteristic of rural tourism is that it has natural and rural objects as tourist attractions, relying on the landscape, natural environment, architecture and cultural resources of rural areas, combining traditional rural leisure and agricultural experience tours, and emerging tourism types (i.e. development of conference services, leisure and entertainment) (Zheng 2017). In 2015, the No. 1 Document of the Central Committee of the CCP proposed to 'actively develop various functions of agriculture and explore the value of rural ecological leisure, tourism, and cultural education' (CCP 2015). In December 2018, 13 departments including the National Development and Reform Commission (NDRC) jointly issued the *Action Plan for Promoting the Upgrade of Rural Tourism Development* (2018–2020) and proposed to encourage and guide the participation of social capital in the development of rural tourism and increase supporting policies for rural tourism development (NDRC 2018).

The development of rural tourism is an important strategic goal of CCP in recent years. Chapters 5 and 6 will analyse the process of rural tourism development, the role of tourists in rural tourism and the emotional expression of tourists as individuals in the Ancient Villages in Southern Anhui – Xidi and Hongcun, which are both World Heritage sites and important rural tourist destinations.

China's heritage development

In 2019, China marked its 34th anniversary as a signatory of the *World Heritage Convention*. The 43rd session of the UNESCO World Heritage Committee in Baku, Azerbaijan inscribed the Archaeological Ruins of Liangzhu City <https://whc.unesco.org/en/list/1592> and the Migratory Bird Sanctuaries along the Coast of Yellow Sea-Bohai Gulf of China (Phase I) <https://whc.unesco.org/en/list/1606> to the WHL. To date, the total number of World Heritage sites in China has reached 55, the same number as Italy, making them the nations with the highest number of WH sites. During this period China's engagement with the World Heritage system developed in three stages. The first stage, from 1985 to 2000, saw a process in which China accepted the international authorised heritage discourse, and explored its meaning. A significant Chinese architect and heritage expert, Zhewen Luo, who was also an initiator of China's ratification of the *World Heritage Convention*, said that:

> As a responsible state party of the World Heritage Program, we must ensure the safeguarding and protection of our World Heritage sites. It is a difficult but glorious task for our ancestors and future generations.
>
> (Luo 1999: Issue 36)

Another influential heritage expert, Professor Zhou Lv noted:

> The UNESCO World Heritage Program provided an international framework for the Chinese domestic cultural relic system and reinforced that system. However, without China's participation, the integrity and representativeness of the World Heritage Program are incomplete.
>
> (Lv 2008: 2)

Their statements reflect the strong sense of nationalism and patriotism underlying China's ratification of the WHC. This sense of nationalism emerged in the 1990s and was valued as a significant phenomenon in contemporary China (Zhao 2002; Su and Teo 2009; Yan 2018). As Su and Teo (2009: 56) point out, 'today's nationalism aims to build a strong sense of belonging among the Chinese people so as to foster a political ideology that would facilitate social control in the country.' Although most Chinese knew little about World Heritage in the late 1980s and 1990s, it provided an international platform for expressing Chinese nationalism and soft power. From 1985 to 2000, 23 sites were inscribed on the WHL. While the Chinese governments were exploring the rules of the World Heritage Programme, they found that they could gain substantial benefits from it. Two benefits are obvious. Firstly, the successful listing of a site fostered a sense of nationalism (see Luo 1999, 2008; Su and Teo 2009). Based on his research on the Mountain Resort and its Outlying Temples in Chengde (listed on the WHL in 1995), which contains a miniature replica of the Potala Palace of Lhasa, Hevia (2001) argues that the Chinese government utilised the World Heritage listing process to 'harmonise' the Tibetan minority into Han Chinese majority culture (see also Askew 2010). Yan (2012, 2015,

2018) further argues that China has actively incorporated a domestic narrative with a strong sense of nationalism in the process of World Heritage nomination, which he labelled 'the harmony discourse.' For instance, he observed that The Great Wall's[7] original meaning as 'the great military defence project of successive Chinese Empires' (UNESCO 1987) incorporated a domestic narrative that 'not only represent[s] the Chinese fine culture ... but it also constitutes an important part of the cultural heritage of all human beings' (Yan 2018: 34; quote from SACH 2009[2003]c:477). Secondly, the Chinese government also found that the 'World Heritage Brand' serves as a catalyst for attracting tourists, which has significant utility for economic development, particularly for remote areas. At the Chinese World Heritage site Pingyao ancient city, the annual ticket income grew dramatically from 180,000 RMB in 1998 to 5,000,000 RMB in 1999, an almost 18 fold increase, after its inscription as a WHS in 1997 (Wu et al. 2002; see also Su and Wall 2011). Many other Chinese World Heritage sites, such as the Wulingyuan Scenic and Historic Interest Area and Wuyi Mountain, have experienced similar increases in tourism revenue after being inscribed on the WHL (Leng and Zhang 2009). Therefore, Chinese governments at national, provincial and local levels have been preoccupied with World Heritage applications since the 1990s. At this stage, the ideas and rules of heritage preservation based on the protection of material were initially formed, while China's tourism industry was in the early stage of development. Conflicts between tourism development and heritage protection occur frequently, and tourism is often considered to be the 'destroyer' (Zhang 2018a).

The second stage, from 2000 to 2011, was a process in which China gradually came to understand the international AHD, and made adjustments to its original national management systems and heritage policies based on international principles and policies. In 2000, the 24th session of the World Heritage Committee adopted the *Cairns Decision,* which aimed to restrain the number of sites nominated by state parties. The first version of the *Cairns Decision* only allowed for one site to be proposed to the World Heritage list by each State Party per year (UNESCO 2000a). This new international policy caused dramatic changes in the Chinese heritage management systems at national, provincial and local levels, as well as its administrative policies (this will be elaborated in the next section). In the meantime, the official national terminology of *Cultural Relics* was replaced by *Cultural Heritage,* and gradually accepted by most Chinese (Shan 2008; Yan 2018).

In this stage, an international landmark event was the 28th World Heritage Committee held in Suzhou in 2004. The conference made two contributions to international heritage practice (Lv 2019). First, based on the World Heritage Global Strategy, the amended version (issued in 2004) allowed each State Party to put forward two sites, with at least one being a natural heritage or mixed heritage site (UNESCO 2004). Another contribution was to establish a World Heritage Institute of Training and Research for the Asia and the Pacific Region (WHITR-AP).[8] This centre (founded in 2006) has become an important training institution in the World Heritage field (Lv 2019). Lv (2019) states that the Suzhou World Heritage Committee 'sparked Chinese society's attention to World Heritage and promoted the study of World Heritage by Chinese heritage protection and academia.' Since then, Chinese government agencies such as SACH and MHURD have organised conferences and seminars to discuss World Heritage development such as new heritage categories (industrial heritage, rural heritage, cultural landscape and cultural routes etc.).

In terms of heritage tourism development, the idea of 'reasonable use' and 'sustainable use' has been continuously strengthened in the protection of Chinese heritage sites (Zhang 2018a). China's tourism development has also consistently improved its quality, 'from development and construction to environmental and order governance' (Zhang 2018a). However, due to the rapid development of the Chinese economy, tourism has become an excuse for large-scale construction of real estates, which has had negative impacts on the protection of heritage sites (Zhang 2018a). Zhang (2018a) further comments that the relationship between heritage protection and tourism development at this stage was gradually 'moving towards multidimensional development, consensus and contradictions are constantly intertwined.'

The third stage is from 2011 to the present. In 2011, the 35th session of the World Heritage Committee inscribed the West Lake Cultural Landscape of Hangzhou on the World Heritage List. It was the first time that China attempted to nominate a cultural property in the cultural landscape[9] category. The successful listing of West Lake under this designation has given Chinese governments greater confidence to nominate new types of World Heritage sites. In 2013, another cultural landscape site, the Cultural Landscape of Honghe Hani Rice Terraces, was successfully inscribed on the World Heritage List. Lv (2019) states that the successful inscription of the Hani Rice Terraces marks the cultural landscape as an important part of the new category of heritage in China, 'representing the re-recognition of the value of the human living environment and the practice of incorporating it into the Chinese protection system.'

In 2014, the Chinese government nominated two properties categorised as 'cultural routes,' The Grand Canal <https://whc.unesco.org/en/list/1443> and Silk Roads: the Routes Network of Chang'an-Tian-shan Corridor <https://whc.unesco.org/en/list/1442>. Eventfully, those two sites were successfully designated on the 37th session of the World Heritage Committee. As Lv (2019) points out the inscription of these sites as cultural routes encouraged the public to view the value of historical transportation routes (such as Ancient Shu Road, Tea-horse Ancient Road, Tea Road and Long March Route) and similar heritages from the perspective of cultural exchange and communication. The success of these new cultural properties illustrated that China had become quite familiar with the international AHD. The two properties inscribed in 2014 further demonstrate that the Chinese government is capable of manipulating the World Heritage Programme for its own aims.

Meskell et al. (2015) note that China was the most successful country in terms of the continual listing of World Heritage sites in recent years, and stressed that 17 sites were proposed from 2002 to 2013, while 16 were inscribed. As noted above, a state party can only nominate one cultural site each year in line with the *Cairns Decision*. Therefore, it was the first time China nominated a joint cultural site, Silk Roads: the Routes Network of Chang'an-Tianshan Corridor with Kazakhstan and Kyrgyzstan, which used Kyrgyzstan's nomination for World Heritage status. Since 1988, UNESCO has conducted Silk Roads research, and China has been actively involved in the research and dominated the World Heritage application process.[10] The sites located in China's territory account for 22 of 33 sites of the Silk Roads property, and the nomination dossier was written by a Chinese agency, the Institute of Architectural History[11] (Shan 2009a; Gao 2014; Zhang and Taylor 2019). The aims of the Silk Roads World Heritage application were not only to boost nationalism and tourism development, but also to support the Chinese international economic policy '*One Belt, One Road*'.[12] In late 2013, the President of the People's Republic of China, Xi Jinping, proposed an international strategy called '*One Belt, One Road*' (or the Belt and Road Initiative), which has been seen as 'the most significant and far-reaching initiative that China has ever put forward' (Wu 2015). The strategy underlines China's push to take a more significant role in global affairs, and consists of two components, the land-based '*Silk Road Economic Belt*' and oceangoing '*21st Century Maritime Silk Road*'. The success of the Silk Roads World Heritage nomination has provided substantial cultural and historical support for the '*Silk Road Economic Belt*' project, which aims to build a link between China and Europe through Central and Western Asia and make it a cohesive economic area.[6] Feng Jing, the Director of Asia and the Pacific Unit of the UNESCO World Heritage Centre states: 'the "*One Belt, One Road*" gives the Silk Road World Heritage projects a practical meaning' (Jing 2019). He further states in the People's Daily (2019) that:

> the success of the World Heritage nomination [Silk Roads] is an important achievement in the cultural field of the '*One Belt, One Road*' initiative, which makes the project no longer limited to the scope of heritage

protection, but also an important platform for regional development and cultural exchange.

On 2 February 2019, SACH proclaimed a decision that the Historic Monuments and Sites of Ancient Quanzhou (Zayton) will represent China in the World Heritage bid in 2020 (SACH 2019a). The site has been seen as a significant part of the Maritime Silk Road, representing 'Historical relics of navigation and trade,' 'historical relics of multi-culture' and 'historical relics of urban construction and land transportation' (UNESCO 2016: 69–72). In addition to Quanzhou, SACH also conducted a comprehensive survey and selected 31 representative historical sites related to marine activities in nine cities (including Guangzhou, Jiangmen, Quanzhou, Zhangzhou, Putian, Ningbo, Longquan and Nanjing), which were already on the tentative list[13] (Shen and Yan 2018). The above two Maritime Silk Road projects have also been seen as a cultural asset for the '*21st Century Maritime Silk Road*' that aimed at investing in and fostering collaboration in Southeast Asia, Oceania and North Africa, through several contiguous bodies of water – the South China Sea, the South Pacific Ocean, and the wider Indian Ocean area.[14] Therefore, from the Chinese government's perspective, the concept of Silk Roads heritage is not only about the past, rather it is a development concept that serves political and economic strategies in the present.

In 2018, the establishment of the Ministry of Culture and Tourism marks the transformation of the function and mission orientation of tourism (Zhang 2018a). Instead of pursuing GDP and foreign currency exchange, the focus is on the quality of life of the people (Zhang 2018a). As Zhang (2018a) indicates the mission of integrating tourism and culture is to inherit Chinese civilisation and the revolutionary spirit, so that the relationship between heritage protection and tourism utilisation has therefore entered a new stage. He further argues that the individual tourists and national collective search for cultural identity are the origins of tourism and cultural relations (Zhang 2018b). The following chapters will explore the emotional expressions and value understanding caused by the difference in individual tourists, which is the key to the integration of culture and tourism.

After the above three stages of heritage development, China's participation in international exchanges and cooperation on World Heritage protection has been on the increase (*People's Daily* 2019). For instance, China has established close cooperative relations with international organisations such as UNESCO, ICOMOS, International Union for the Conservation of Nature (IUCN) and International Centre for the Study of the Preservation and Restoration of Cultural Property (ICCORM) (*People's Daily* 2019), and actively participates in international projects such as the Angkor Wat conservation project in

Cambodia, the Silk Road projects and the Safeguarding African Natural and Cultural Heritage Projects (Du and Zhou 2019). As the Director of SACH, Yuzhu Liu declares that:

> The further consolidation of the status of a world heritage power means that China has to bear more international responsibilities and obligations in heritage fields […] China will continue act as a responsible big country on heritage platforms, further promote the concept of world heritage protection, and share the Chinese experience and Chinese ideas accumulated in the protection of world cultural heritage with the world peers in various forms.
>
> (SACH 2019b)

The three stages of China's heritage development demonstrated, as Yan (2012, 2015, 2018) has argued, that the Chinese government utilised the iconic status of World Heritage, and its relevant international policies, to reshape the national heritage management system, legitimate national heritage policies and practices and strive for the right to speak internationally. His research identified the discursive influences and policy changes in one of the key national heritage authorities – the State Administration of Cultural Heritage (SACH). He argued that there is an authorised discourse, which he calls the 'harmony discourse,' that frames 'non-heritage practices such as public health and moral norms, to legitimise the governmental power,' and privileges experts' or governments' narratives over local discourse (Yan 2015: 65). Chinese national heritage management is multilayered: the National Commission of UNESCO under the supervision of the Ministry of Education is the department responsible for communicating with the UNESCO World Heritage Centre; the State Forestry and Grassland Administration (SFGA) is responsible for the management of natural heritage sites (the Ministry of Housing and Urban-Rural Development [MHURD] used to have charge of natural heritage sites);[15] whereas the SACH takes responsibility for cultural heritage. They are both in charge of mixed sites and cultural landscape management. Su and Wall (2011) note that there is a second layer of governmental management which includes the department of forestry, water resources, environmental protection, religion, ethnic affairs and tourism, all of which are potentially involved in management, depending on the specific natural, cultural and social characteristics of a heritage site. The third level includes local government, site management officers, visitors, local communities and tourism entrepreneurs. The specific management affairs of heritage sites are implemented by local governments, which are authorised by the SFGA or the SACH. This multi-department and multilevel management structure mean that profits and responsibilities overlap, which creates coordination problems for the management of World Heritage applications. One of the tasks of this chapter is to further elaborate China's heritage management system and its relevant policies and analyse the interactions between China's heritage management system and UNESCO's World Heritage Programme.

China's heritage management systems

From 1985 to 2019, 55 Chinese properties (37 cultural, 14 natural and 4 mixed) were inscribed on the World Heritage List. Along with Italy, China is now ranked equal first in the world for the total number of listed World Heritage Sites (UNESCO 2019). There are also 41 intangible cultural heritage practices listed as of 2018, meaning China has the most listings in the World Intangible Cultural Heritage List (UNESCO 2018a). In addition, 60 sites are on the tentative list, and many more may be put forward in due course (UNESCO 2018b). UNESCO requires that State Parties have the responsibility of ensuring the conservation and management of World Heritage sites within their territory. China has a complex heritage management system at the national level. In 1978, the Chinese government decided to embark on an economic reform programme, and in the last two decades, China's tourism industry has become a new source of growth for the national economy (Han 2006). The Chinese government realised the need to develop management systems to ensure the protection of heritage resources. There are two different heritage management systems that underpin MHURD and SACH. The MHURD established the '*Scenic and Historic Interest Areas*' system in 1981, defining these sites as 'areas with outstanding aesthetic, scientific, cultural and natural value, open for scientific research and tourism activities' (State Council 2006a). The promulgation of the '*Scenic and Historic Interest Areas Ordinance*' by the State Council of the People's Republic of China in 2006 legitimated the MHURD power to plan and manage these sites. This system is inspired by a designated national park system defined by the IUCN (Han 2006). The IUCN national park system only represents natural protected areas; however, the Chinese version includes both cultural and natural properties. As Han (2006: 7) observes, 'they are predominantly nature-dominated, while the natural beauty and cultural elements are considered to be at "perfect oneness".' As of 2017, there were 244 Scenic and Historic Interest Areas designated at the national level (State Council 2017). On the World Heritage list of China, 29 of China's 55 World Heritage sites are Scenic and Historic Interest Areas or are located in these areas. These 29 World Heritage sites include 12 natural and 4 mixed sites as well as 13 cultural sites which represent, from a Chinese viewpoint, the combination of cultural and natural elements. Scenic and Historic Interest Areas are also significant components of the World Heritage tentative list for China.

On 21 March 2018, the CCP released the Plan on Deepening Reform of Party and State Institutions, which will have a considerable impact on the management of Scenic and Historic Interest Areas and natural heritage sites. According to this plan, the CCP established the Ministry of Natural Resources (MNR) to undertake the overall protection, system restoration and comprehensive management of lakes and grasses in landscapes (Su 2018). The State Forestry and Grassland Administration (SFGA) will be created under the supervision of MNR, which will be responsible for the management of natural heritage and scenic and historic interest areas instead of MHURD (scio.gov.cn, 2018). Su (2018: 47) shows that natural heritage and scenic and historic interest areas belong to the protected areas of forbidden development zones, irrespective of national laws and regulations, though in past practice they were more kinds of tourism resources. In this institutional reform, the management of resource-based sites such as natural heritage sites and scenic and historic interest areas aim to adopt the national park system from Western countries, focussing on resource protection and social welfare (Su 2018: 48). In this sense, tourism still has been seen as a 'problem,' which may contaminate the natural resources such as those at natural heritage and scenic and historic interest areas. At the time of writing, the institutional reform had limited influence, and areas of natural, heritage, scenic and historic interest are still managed by MHURD. Therefore, my analysis throughout this book is based on the MHURD management system.

In regards to the heritage management systems of SACH, the National People's Congress of the People's Republic of China promulgated the *Law of the People's Republic of China on Protection of Cultural Relics* (National People's Congress Standing Committee 2002), which was led by the needs of conservation and the desire to promote tourism at cultural properties, including imperial palaces, temples, historical buildings, monuments as well as some traditional villages with buildings and gardens (Gao and Woudstra 2011). SACH takes charge of 'National Cultural Heritage' listed under this Act. In 2001, the SACH, assisted by ICOMOS Australia and the Getty Conservation Institute from the USA, developed the *Principles for the Conservation of Heritage Sites China (China Principle)* (ICOMOS China 2002), which is the first set of conservation regulations following international standards implemented as national guidelines for cultural heritage conservation and management. In 2005, the State Council of the People's Republic of China issued *State Council Circular Concerning the Strengthening of Cultural Heritage Conservation* (State Council of PRC 2009[2005]), which means that the official use of the term 'Cultural Heritage' replaced cultural relics as the primary term in the national heritage protection and management system (Shan 2008; Yan 2018). In 2006, the State Council (2006b) reported that there were 2351 National Cultural Heritage sites in China as of that year. On the World Heritage list of China, 31 World Heritage properties were designated by SACH as 'National Cultural Heritage' before they were inscribed on the WHL as of 2009. In 2015, SACH re-enacted the revised edition of the *China Principle*, the significant changes being the addition of cultural and social values, which indicates that the protection of Chinese cultural heritage has changed from being 'material-centred' to 'people-centred.' It emphasises the protection of living cultural heritage and pays attention to the new heritage categories such as cultural landscape, cultural route, industrial heritage and scientific and technological heritage (Lv 2014). The latest version of the *China Principle* also addressed the need for authenticity to be regarded as a critical protection principle particularly considering tangible and intangible cultural heritage as a whole.

As noted above, the *Scenic and Historic Interest Areas* and the *National Cultural Heritage* are the two central heritage management systems in the current Chinese administrative setup. The former focusses on 'integrated sites' with cultural and natural values, while the latter aims to manage iconic cultural objects rather than 'sites.' Since China signed the *World Heritage Convention* in 1985, all the inscribed World Heritage sites, as well as properties on the Tentative List, were selected from these two systems. The Operational Guidelines (2011) mentioned that State Parties to the WHC have the responsibility to develop management policies and services to ensure the protection, conservation and presentation of the heritage sites. Therefore, the Chinese government has replicated the existing management policies and systems from those developed by *Scenic and Historic Interest Areas* and *National Cultural Heritage*, and used these for the World Heritage sites.

Influence of the Cairns Decision

In 2000, the promulgation of the *Cairns Decision* had a significant impact on the management of World Heritage in China. Before the *Cairns Decision*, UNESCO did not limit the numbers of sites nominated by each country. The provincial governments of China had the right to provide their suggestions of local heritage sites for World Heritage nomination. The MHURD and the SACH would make final decisions to nominate more than two qualified sites based on the Chinese national heritage management systems. For example, there were four cultural properties inscribed on the World Heritage List in 2000, which were the Ancient Villages in Southern Anhui – Xidi and Hongcun, Mount Qincheng and the Dujiangyan Irrigation System, Imperial Tombs of the Ming and Qing Dynasties and Longmen Grottoes (UNESCO 2000d). However, the diffusion of international policies and regulations such as the *Cairns Decision* has changed the power relations within the original national management practices. The

MHURD has gradually lost influence, which has been assumed by the SACH, because of the promulgation of the new category Cultural Landscape and the implications of the *Cairns Decision*. The MHURD used to be in charge of the majority of cultural landscape management, based on the Chinese original national heritage management systems, which have different categories and standards than the UNESCO models. In order to introduce the UNESCO model, the central government of China reshaped the power relations in the management system so that the MHURD took charge of natural heritage and the SACH was placed in charge of cultural heritage. However, based on UNESCO's model, cultural landscape belongs to cultural heritage for the WH listing. Therefore, the changes in power relations have caused conflict within the Chinese management system (Han 2006).

The MHURD lost power over cultural landscape sites' nomination on the WH listing, but they still have responsibility for the management of those sites selected from the scenic and historic interest areas. The other reason that the MHURD complained was that inscribing a natural property is much more difficult than a cultural site. This is evidenced by there being only 213 natural properties on the World Heritage list compared to 869 cultural sites (UNESCO 2019). Many scholars made strong complaints about the implementation of the *Cairns Decision* (see X.K. Li 2005; Li et al. 2006; Li 2007b). Li Xiankui, the Director of the Department of Foreign Affairs of MHURD, in his article 'Breaking Through "Keynes" [Cairns], Promoting the World Heritage to Develop in Harmony,' states that the limitation of the *Cairns Decision* is that it is obviously unfavourable to China as a big legacy county [sic]. 'We prepared a list of more than 100 items of declaring world legacy, and if only one quota is allowed to declare in one year, it will take 100 years to realise the full declaration' (X.K. Li 2005: 27).

He pointed out that one of the significant tasks for holding the 28th Session of the World Heritage Committee in Suzhou was to break through the 'one country, one quota' limit (X.K. Li 2005: 27). His article elaborated on the difficult process that the Chinese experts are now engaged in as they fight to amend the *Cairns Decision*. Finally, he indicated that the World Heritage Committee had adopted the 'Suzhou Decision' and 'Suzhou Declaration,' which means that the World Heritage Committee will consider requests for the inscription of 45 nominations each year instead of the 30 new ones set by the *Cairns Decision* (China.org.cn 2004). The Committee also agreed to revise the *Cairns Decision* and published *Global Strategy: Evaluation of the Cairns-Suzhou Decision* that allowed each State Party to put forward two sites, with at least one being a natural heritage site (UNESCO 2007).

On the other hand, the SACH actively accepted the *Cairns Decision* and a series of actions and policies were developed. In 2000, they developed the *Principles for the Conservation of Heritage Sites in China* (ICOMOS China 2002), which was seen as the Chinese version of the Burra Charter. In December 2005, the State Council issued the *State Council Circular Concerning the Strengthening of Cultural Heritage Conservation* (2009[2005]). It represents a milestone of Chinese heritage development as China officially used the term 'cultural heritage' to replace 'cultural relics' (Shan 2008; Yan 2018). Since then, government authorities and research institutes, as well as official government documents, have been using the term 'cultural heritage' to replace the old term 'cultural relics.' In addition, the *State Council Circular Concerning the Strengthening of Cultural Heritage Conservation* proclaimed that the second Saturday of June was designated as China's Cultural Heritage Day. In 2017, the State Council agreed to the request of the MHURD to adjust the 'Cultural Heritage Day,' and re-brand it as the 'Cultural and Natural Heritage Day' from 2017 (State Council 2016). As Yan (2018: 56) indicated, the designation of China's Cultural Heritage Day 'has drawn remarkable public recognition and appreciation as well as bear witness to the development and solidification of China's cultural preservation in its "cultural heritage phase".' In addition, when the international authorities issued new documents relating to new types of cultural properties, the SACH and ICOMOS China have correspondingly developed Chinese domestic versions (see Table 2.1).

Table 2.1 Comparison of the original international documents with the Chinese version

Name of documents (original)	Name of documents (Chinese version)	Comments
The Burra Charter (1999)	The Principles for the Conservation of Heritage Sites in China (2000, 2004, 2015)	
The Convention for the Safeguarding of Intangible Cultural Heritage (2003)	State Council Circular Concerning the Strengthening of Cultural Heritage Conservation (launched in 2005) Law on the Protection of Intangible Cultural Heritage (2011)	Intangible cultural heritage
Nizhny Tagil Charter for the Industrial Heritage (launched in 2003)	Wuxi Recommendation on Protecting Industrial Heritage during Fast Economic Development (launched in 2006)	Industrial heritage
ICOMOS Charter on the Built Vernacular Heritage (launched in 1999)	Circular on Strengthening the Protection of Vernacular Architecture (launched in 2007)	Vernacular heritage
One-year Montreal Action Plan focussing on 20th Century Heritage (launched in 2001)	Circular on Strengthening the Protection of 20th Century Heritage ((launched in 2008)	
Routes as Part of Our Cultural Heritage (launched in 1994) Charter on Cultural Routes (launched in 2008)	Wuxi Recommendations on the Protection of Cultural Routes Heritage (launched in 2009)	Cultural routes

The actions and policies listed in Table 2.1 demonstrate that SACH has actively accepted the international AHD by creating Chinese versions of principles and policies underpinned by original documents from UNESCO and ICOMOS, reconstructing its bureaucratic system (see Yan 2012). Waterton (2010) criticises the original version of *China Principles* (issued in 2000) because, despite having a unique history and different ideology to Western nations, the *China Principles* were not created based on Chinese culture and understandings of cultural heritage. Qian (2007) argues that the promulgation of the *China Principles* reflects the Chinese government's endeavour to develop their own national terminology drawing on international heritage discourse. The development of internal documents and the designation of China Natural and Cultural Heritage Day demonstrates that China actively endeavours to participate in the UNESCO World Heritage Programme. It aims to play a leading role in heritage preservation and narratives in Asia, and even the world. It also aims to reframe 'itself to be an integral part of the world culture' (Yan 2012: 101). In this sense, the Chinese government has developed a preoccupation with accumulating both numbers and diversity of World Heritage sites. From the Chinese government's perspective, the increasing numbers of Chinese World Heritage sites, with diverse types of cultural properties, can reflect China's abundant and varied cultural status (Li 2007b; Yan 2012).

Discussion

As has now been extensively discussed in the international literature, the globalisation of the World Heritage Programme can be identified as a hegemonic process, with the so-called 'universal' standard largely deriving from Western countries (Byrne 1991; Harvey 2001; Smith 2006; Labadi 2007, 2013) One of the key concepts of the UNESCO World Heritage Programme is the idea of 'outstanding universal value,' which requires the selection and evaluation of sites on the basis that some heritage values are not only more important than others but will be so in all circumstances. UNESCO identifies international experts as having specific expertise, and its associated organisations have the power to decide the hierarchy of heritage values, thus actively shaping the discourses of particular sites through the World Heritage listing process (Turtinen 2000; Logan 2001). Although Meskell et al. (2015) argue that a shift is taking place in the dominance of Western states in the decision-making processes of the World Heritage Committee, the authority of particular framing discourses about the value of heritage remain enshrined in the OUV criteria. Since 1985, when China ratified the WHC, the Chinese government has been engaged in a long process that has gradually accepted, understood and negotiated the concept of 'World Heritage.' Over the last 34 years, the Chinese government realised that 'World Heritage' is not only entangled with practical issues of cultural, environmental or historic preservation but also influences the discursive structure of identity, power and authority. The World Heritage nomination process has become an excellent opportunity to display China's national image and project 'soft' power, and has facilitated the construction of a stable and harmonious national discourse (Yan 2015, 2018). Thus, the Chinese government's responses to the WHC and its relevant policies are actively, even obsessively, concerned with inscribing sites on the World Heritage list (Meyer 2008; Yan 2018).

As Lowenthal (1994), Smith (2006) and Labadi (2007) argue, the Western understanding of heritage is intrinsically interwoven with senses of nationalism and the material past. From the Chinese heritage authorities' perspective, the introduced concept of 'World Heritage' has been helping to build Chinese national and cultural identity. Winter and Daly (2012: 3) argue that Asian countries, in particular, China, use 'World Heritage' designation to demonstrate national power and confidence, so that 'the past is embraced as part of the future.' The most significant task for national heritage authorities is to ensure the increasing numbers and types of properties presented for World Heritage nomination. Ostensibly, the Chinese government seems uncritically accepting of the received authorised heritage discourse which frames international heritage practice. Essentially, they are quite mindful, even cynical (Zhang 2017). As Zhang (2017) identifies that both national and local governments clearly show that they could not convert Chinese values to fit the OUV and that they frequently used the word 'game' to describe the World Heritage listing process. In their sense, World Heritage is an imitation process of UNESCO and other international authorities' regulations and policies (Yan 2012; Meyer 2009). This chapter identified that the State Administration of Cultural Heritage (SACH) actively imitated documents from international authorities when framing national documents or policies. My research reveals that the Chinese governments at both national and local level have been cynical and pragmatic during this replication process, as they have intended to use the *World Heritage Convention* as a cultural script for implementing Chinese political, economic and cultural strategies in the domestic and international arenas.

At the national level, the World Heritage Programme and its relevant policies have inspired changes leading to the reshaping and reformulation the national heritage system by Chinese governments. National and local discourses and visions of China's historical continuity and cultural diversity have been promulgated, in line with the Chinese Communist Party's position. The adoption of the *Venice Charter* of 1964 and the *World Heritage Convention* of 1972 are significant milestones in established Eurocentric heritage discourse and international heritage practice. Since then, there have been extensive debates about the significance of developing 'best practice' for heritage conservation and management worldwide (for instance, McGimsey 1972; Lipe 1977; Fung and Allen 1984; Sullivan and Bowdler 1984; Johnston 1992; Clark 1999, 2005; Pearson and Sullivan 1995; Byrne et al. 2001). Smith (2004, 2006) pointed out that the governments of Australia and the United States in the 1970s adopted international Charters and Conventions for protecting their natural and cultural resources. The two countries also adapted the Eurocentric heritage discourse from international documents and further developed their heritage practices[16] to suit local issues and aspirations (Smith 2006).

In China, since the reform and opening policy in the late 1970s, the People's Republic of China has established nation-wide systems of cultural and natural conservation. Just like Australia and the United States, the Chinese government introduced the Western concept of World Heritage and the relevant international charters and conventions. However, the process that the Chinese government used to incorporate the international regulations and policies into the existing national policies and bureaucratic systems are complicated. Based on the *World Heritage Convention*, the Chinese government has institutionalised and modified China's heritage management system since the early 1980s (Han 2006; Luo 2008; Yan 2018). This chapter shows that the institutional reframing of China's existing policies and bureaucratic systems to take into account international policy has been an active process, in which the Chinese government actively accepted and incorporated the dominant Western understanding and discourse of heritage. Scholars such as Byrne (2008), based on his research in Thailand, show that European/World Heritage values have simply been accepted as 'right and correct,' often through the colonial process in Southeast Asia (see also Dewi 2016). However, Zhang (2017) argues that Chinese governments at both the national and local levels are critically aware of what they are doing. China is not influenced by a colonial or neo-colonial legacy; rather they clearly characterised the World Heritage listing process as a game they are playing for national and local political and economic purposes (Zhang 2017). The fomer director of the SACH, Shan Jixiang, metaphorically used a traditional old Chinese saying, 'a stone from other hills may serve to polish the jade of this one' to indicate Western heritage policy can be 'polished' to fit the Chinese situation (People.com 2011a; Yan 2012: 42). The Chinese government claims that it is important to both absorb the 'advanced and progressive' Western heritage policy and ensure the recognition of Chinese-oriented characteristics (Cao 2007; Li 2007; SACH 2009[2002]; Yan 2018). The diffusion of international policies at a national level has changed the existing bureaucratic systems and management policies.

At first, the Chinese government issued a series of principles and policies based on existing international policies. For example, in 2000, they developed the *China Principle* (ICOMOS China 2002), which has been characterised as the Chinese version of the *Burra Charter* of 1999 (Waterton 2010; Yan 2012). Those introduced and modified policies have provided practical tools for translating or shaping Chinese heritage values to conform to the UNESCO World Heritage standard. Second, the Chinese government has used the term 'cultural heritage' instead of the old term 'cultural relics,' as represented by the national document: *State Council Circular Concerning the Strengthening of Cultural Heritage Conservation* (2009[2005]). The Chinese government has also kept renewing and incorporating new heritage concepts such as intangible heritage, cultural landscape, cultural route and industrial heritage into national policies (Lv 2019). The discourse of heritage in China has been dramatically changed during the last two decades, and certainly since the adoption of the *China Principles*. Third, the Chinese government has reinforced the concept of 'heritage' in peoples' daily lives. For instance, the creation of Chinese National Cultural Heritage Day from 2006, the nation-wide debate critical of the Korean nominated Seowon, Korean Neo-Confucian Academies[17] in the World Heritage list in 2019, and the protests over the successful Japanese inscription of Sites of Japan's Meiji Industrial Revolution: Iron and Steel, Shipbuilding and Coal Mining on the WHL in 2015, have demonstrated that World Heritage serves as a political tool for nationalism. This was illustrated on 14 May 2005, with a Spokesperson of the Ministry of Foreign Affairs, Hua Chunying, claiming that: 'World Cultural Heritage nomination should be consistent with the United Nations' fundamental principles for the "culture of peace" … Chinese people are firmly against this nomination, which only nominated the "glory" side of the history, and ignored its cruel fact that using Chinese and Korean labourers and as a tool of Japanese militarism and colonialism' (*China Daily* 2015).

Therefore, I argue that the Chinese government has used the *World Heritage Convention* as a cultural script and has been an active participant in international heritage activities. It aims to establish a legitimised national discourse congruent with the Chinese Communist party line of 'Building a harmonious socialist society.' Yan (2018) has used the term 'Chinese harmony discourse' to interpret this process:

> On the one hand, it provides a set of scientific statements, which are disseminated among people via educational programs and mass media, and it asserts that the knowledge provided by the government on heritage preservation has solid scientific roots and represents advanced theories of preservation. On the other hand, it is enfolded within a nationalistic discourse that promotes the message that it is only a nation imbued with heritage that supplies its people security and position in world society. Therefore,

preserving and appreciating national heritage is emotionally powerful and evocative for the citizens.

(Yan 2018: 193)

The changed national policies and discourses have caused dissonance. China is a country of extraordinary levels of political, cultural, religious and ethnic diversity, and the Chinese central government had established a sophisticated heritage bureaucratic system before being influenced by the *World Heritage Convention*. The MHURD and the SACH are two national authorities that are responsible for Chinese heritage affairs. The UNESCO heritage categories, in particular, the definition of cultural landscape, are not compatible with the existing Chinese heritage system. This has caused conflicts between the two national authorities over World Heritage applications and management, as well as policy-making (Zhang 2006). Although policy changes have been made in recent decades, the problem is still unresolved. The new State Council's institutional reforms allocate natural heritage management to the SFGA, and the provinces will also establish management departments affiliated with SFGA. The changes to the management system suggest a period of adjustment and challenges to the management of China's heritage sites.

Conclusion

First, this chapter reviews China's history and traditional philosophical views that influence Chinese values. These values are the basis for China's more than 2000 years of feudal rule. Although it was replaced by the new ideology of the Chinese Communist Party in the past 100 years, especially after the founding of China in 1949, some philosophical concepts, such as the 'harmony between nature and man' advocated by both Confucianism and Taoism, are still regarded as a feature of Chinese culture that Chinese people are proud of, and has been communicated through culture and education. Such philosophical ideas affect the collective memory of each generation. Tourists may display emotional expressions and feelings characteristic of Chinese tourists in the process of visiting the sites of the heritage sites. Chapters 3 through 6 of this book will discuss this through two case studies.

Second, this chapter reviews the development of tourism after the founding of the PRC and discusses the policy documents that are crucial to the development of China's tourism at each stage. The policy of the CCP determines China's tourism development. Tourism was politically oriented from the 1950s to the 1970s, while the 1980s–2000s was economically oriented. Subsequently, there was an emphasis on the integration of tourism and culture, aiming to spread traditional Chinese culture and the ideology of the CCP through the forms of heritage tourism, red tourism and rural tourism.

Third, this chapter focusses on the analysis of the three stages of the development of Chinese heritage, as well as the Chinese heritage management system. The Chinese government has its own aims in participating in the World Heritage Programme. In the first stage of China's engagement with UNESCO and its World Heritage Programme, it aimed to express a sense of nationalism and the 'soft power' of China. The Chinese government had been concerned with increasing the quantity and diversity of types of Chinese World Heritage sites, which is seen as one of the most important missions of World Heritage applications. As Li (2007b: 38) states: 'We are undoubtedly a big heritage nation, in terms of both quantity and variety, however, as an ancient country that has plentiful natural and cultural heritage, the current quantity of our World Heritage Sites is still not matched with our actual resources' (quoted in Yan 2012: 82). In the second stage, the Chinese government is being cynical, when it accepted the concepts from the international AHD and translated them into the Chinese domestic heritage discourse in order to play an active role in international heritage affairs (see also Zhang 2017). The reframing of China's existing policies and bureaucratic systems to take into account international policy has been an active process, in which the Chinese government accepted and incorporated the dominant Western understanding and discourse of heritage. Scholars such as Byrne (2008), based on his research in Thailand, show that European/World Heritage values have simply been accepted as 'right and correct,' often through the colonial process in Southeast Asia. However, I argue in this chapter that the Chinese government at the national level are critically aware of what they are doing. China is not influenced by a colonial or neo-colonial legacy; rather they clearly characterised the World Heritage listing process as a game they are playing for national and local political and economic purposes. In the third stage, the Chinese government aims not only to claim domestic solidarity and sovereignty with the world sociality but also influence Asia and the world decision-making process regarding heritage issues. This has been particularly striking in the *Silk Road* and *Maritime Silk Road* programmes, where the Chinese government has used a World Heritage application as a tool to not only enhance its position in the UNESCO World Heritage Programme but also to legitimise cultural and social contexts which serve the Chinese international strategy 'One Belt, One Road'. In the next chapter, I will analyse my interview data with the Chinese national and local authorities to identify their understanding of the role of tourism in China's heritage affairs.

Notes

1 Kyushu, namely Ganzhou, Zhangzhou, Qingzhou, Xuzhou, Yangzhou, Jingzhou, Yuzhou, Liangzhou and Zhangzhou.
2 Tao is a term used by the Chinese nation to understand nature for itself. It means the way or way of all things, or the place where things change and move.
3 Translated by the author.
4 Three Cardinal Guides are 'the sovereign guides the ministers, the father guides the son, and the husband guides the wife' (Yao 2000); Five Constant Virtues are 'Ren (benevolence), Yi(righteousness), Li (propriety), Zhi (knowledge/wisdom) and Xin (sincerity)' (Tang 1991).
5 In August 1998, with the approval of the State Council, the Bureau for Travel and Tourism changed the name to National Tourism Administration.
6 Heritage tourism is the main type of tourism discussed in this book, and the details are covered in the first chapter.
7 The Great Wall was inscribed on World Heritage List on 1987.
8 WHITR-AP (based in Beijing, Shanghai and Suzhou) is the UNESCO Category 2 Centre and the first professional institution in the field of heritage protection established in developing countries. It serves the States Parties to the *World Heritage Convention* in the Asia-Pacific region and other UNESCO Member States and is committed to the protection and development of World Heritage in the Asia-Pacific region. (Source: www.whitr-ap.org.)
9 *Lushan National Park* (inscribed on the World Heritage list on 1996) was the first Chinese Cultural Landscape site defined by UNESCO. West Lake Cultural Landscape of Hangzhou was the first time Chinese governments used the cultural landscape concept to formulate a nomination dossier for an application to the World Heritage Committee.
10 In 1988, UNESCO initiated a study of the Silk Road to promote understanding of cultural diffusion across Eurasia and the protection of cultural heritage. In August 2006, UNESCO and the State Administration of Cultural Heritage of the People's Republic of China co-sponsored a conference in Turpan, Xinjiang on the coordination of applications for the Silk Road's designation as a World Heritage Site. At this conference, China and five Central Asia republics, Kazakhstan, Kyrgyzstan, Tajikistan, Uzbekistan and Turkmenistan agreed to make a joint application in 2010. The six countries formed a coordinating committee in 2009 to prepare for the joint application. (Source: https://en.wikipedia.org/wiki/Silk_Road_UNESCO_World_Heritage_Sites.)
11 Under supervision of the *China Architecture Design and Research Group*.
12 On 7 Sep. 2013, during his state visit to Kazakhstan, Mr Xi Jinping, President of the People's Republic of China, proposed in his speech at Nazarbayev University that China and the Central Asian countries build an 'economic belt along the Silk Road,' a trans-Eurasian project spanning the Pacific Ocean to the Baltic Sea. On 3 Oct. 2013, Xi Jinping proposed a new maritime Silk Road in his speech at the Indonesian Parliament during his state visit to Indonesia. (Source: www.chinausfocus.com/finance-economy/one-belt-and-one-road-far-reaching-initiative/.)
13 Chinese Section of the Silk Road: Sea Routes in Ningbo City, Zhejiang Province and Quanzhou City, Fujian Province – from Western-Han Dynasty to Qing Dynasty (UNESCO 2019).

14 Source: https://en.wikipedia.org/wiki/One_Belt,_One_Road.
15 On 21 March 2018, The Communist Party of China (CCP) releases *Plan on Deepening Reform of Party and State Institutions*. According to this plan, State Forestry and Grassland Administration will take charge the natural heritage management from MHURD. (Source: scio.gov.cn, 2018.)
16 For instance, Australian ICOMOS issued *the Burra Charter* (1979, 1999, 2013) which incorporates significance and assessment processes for cultural heritage properties. Many European countries, in particular the UK, have actively included the *Burra Charter* in their heritage practice.
17 The site was inscribed as a cultural property at the 43rd session of the UNESCO World Heritage committee in Baku. Chinese social media widely reported the news that the Seowon, Korean Neo-Confucian Academies originated from the Chinese academy. The Korean government 'stole' the Chinese concept.

Chapter 3

The Chinese sense of heritage
The nature–culture journey

UNESCO's 1992 introduction of three categories of cultural landscape for World Heritage purposes 'extended existing emerging concepts and international cultural heritage conservation thinking and practice which embraced associative values rather than a sole focus on tangible, physical fabric' (Taylor 2017: 7). It was part of the shift away from the 1960s and 1970s Western view of heritage as residing in the physical fabric of famous monuments and sites. Interest in the cultural landscape concept has therefore been an essential part of a broadening critical scholarly discourse on heritage and what it means, leading to what has essentially been a rethink of the process of heritagisation grounded in an understanding of the link between culture and heritage (Taylor 2017: 9). Integral to this is the notion of landscape as process not product, succinctly expressed by Mitchell (1994: 1) as 'not as object to be seen or a text to be read, but as a process by which identities are formed.' It is a line of thinking parallel with critical inquiry into the concept of heritage as process, not a product (Harvey 2001; Howard 2003). Covering far more than simply buildings, structures and sites, such processes embrace concepts of living history and living heritage to encompass the full spectrum of people's sense of place, traditional knowledge and its transmission, cultural production including equity and access, and creativity and innovation (Taylor 2017: 9).

Although, as Taylor (2009) observed, the definition of cultural landscape has been confused within the Southeast and East Asia context, Chinese scholars have extensively discussed and disseminated the international discourse of cultural landscape since the late 2000s (Shan 2009a; Han 2010; Wu 2011). These scholars believe that the concept of cultural landscape has some synergy with the traditional Chinese value of harmony between culture and nature, and provided a useful tool both theoretically and practically to fill the gap between nature and culture in China (Han 2010). Wu (2011) suggested that the Western concept of cultural landscape provides an opportunity for the Chinese government to enlarge China's stable of World Heritage sites. Indeed, in the last six years, the Chinese government has successfully nominated three Cultural Landscape sites (including West Lake Cultural Landscape of Hangzhou (inscribed in 2011) Cultural Landscape of Honghe Hani Rice Terraces (inscribed in 2013) and Zuojiang Huashan Rock Art Cultural Landscape (inscribed in 2016) on the World Heritage list.

In 2013 and 2014, I undertook field research relating to West Lake Cultural Landscape of Hangzhou following its listing as a World Heritage property in 2011. The purpose was to examine how World Heritage listing may be seen to influence the ways West Lake is given meaning by a range of stakeholder groups, including government officials, residents and tourists. Based on research at West Lake, Zhang (2017: 2) identified that both the Chinese national and local governments considered World Heritage listing as a political game. It also suggested that the listing process was made to fit what Smith (2006) calls the AHD. The AHD is claimed to be a dominant discourse based on the hegemony of the notion of universality in the *World Heritage Convention* (1972) which is determined by adherence to a Western Eurocentric ethic which defines heritage in narrow and specific ways (Harrison 2013).

During the listing process, the Chinese local government personnel and experts who wrote the nomination dossier nicely incorporated through the wording of the text what are regarded as quintessential Chinese feelings and values into UNESCO criteria. As I reviewed the *West Lake Nomination Dossier*, the Chinese government personnel and experts initially thought to incorporate those Chinese feelings and values into criterion (iii), (iv), (v) and (vi) for the assessment of OUV as specified in Paragraph 77 of the *Operational Guidelines for the Implementation of the World Heritage Convention* (SACH 2011: 19–20). However, the ICOMOS (2011: 146–148) report for the World Heritage Committee suggested that besides criteria (iii) and (iv), the West Lake nomination should also incorporate criterion (ii), but exclude criterion (v) and (vi). The 35th World Heritage Committee eventually accepted the ICOMOS report and nominated West Lake as a cultural landscape site based on criteria (ii), (iii) and (iv). Zhang (2017) illustrates that the Chinese government personnel and experts perceived themselves to be playing a game in which they tried their best to translate Chinese values into OUV yet frame them within international policy and expertise. Despite their best efforts, they still were not fully understood by international experts. Zhang (2017) and Zhang and Taylor (2019) further indicate that the Western advisor from ICOMOS did not make sense of the Chinese values, and this was replicated in ICOMOS's recommendations particularly not to include the tea plantation which was considered by Chinese officials and experts as a key element representing the Chinese sense of cultural landscape within the listing at West Lake. They also identify that the two key stakeholders, tourists and local people, were marginalised during the listing process. Local people did not participate at any stage in the decision-making process about WH listing, and tourists were considered as a 'problem' to be 'managed' or 'educated' (Zhang 2017; Zhang and Taylor 2019).

Chapters 3 and 4 outline the results of interviews with 133 residents and tourists at West Lake in November 2013 and February 2014. This is the first of two chapters that analyse interviews from West Lake, and it focusses on the meanings of World Heritage as a concept and the essential value of West Lake for local people and tourists. It then compares their views with those of international and Chinese experts, while the next chapter considers what tourists do and feel at West Lake, as well as local people's responses to mass tourists after the World Heritage listing. This chapter argues that the majority of those interviewed, whether tourists or local people, did not passively accept the authorised discourse from national and local heritage authorities that had framed the management and interpretation of West Lake. This interpretation stressed a dichotomy between the natural and cultural heritage embedded in the UNESCO/ICOMOS concept of cultural landscape. Interviewees instead expressed an active sense of an aesthetic or poetic idea of the heritage site which is firmly linked to traditional Chinese philosophy of 'harmony with nature,' as Lin (1935); Zhang (1986); Wang (1990); Xu (1996) and Han (2006) have illustrated.

Case study background

West Lake Cultural Landscape (Figure 3.1) is located west of the urban centre of Hangzhou, which is the capital city of Zhejiang province. The history of West Lake can be traced back 2000 years to when it was a part of the Qiantang River. Due to soil sedimentation, a lagoon that was the old West Lake emerged to the west of Hangzhou, at the feet of Wu Mountain and the Baoshi Mountains. In the ninth century, West Lake Landscape as it is known today began to develop. The layout of West Lake Landscape matured in the thirteenth century and was characterised as 'Cloud-capped hills on three sides of the Lake and the City on the fourth' (UNESCO 2011a West Lake Cultural Landscape: 47). The lake was divided by the 'two causeways and three isles,' which is considered to be one of the significant traditional landscape designs in China.[1] The two causeways are the Su and Bai Causeways, which were built by Bai Juyi[2] and Su Dongpo[3] respectively during the Tang (618–907 AD) and Song Dynasties (960–1279 AD). This landscape design at West Lake not only represents a typical traditional Chinese landscape design but has also influenced landscape design in East Asia, in particular, Japan and Korea (UNESCO 2011a).

Since the Southern Song Dynasty (thirteenth century), Poetically Named Scenic Places[4] emerged, which are called the '西湖十景 Ten Poetically Named Scenic Places of West Lake' in the present. The series of ten scenic

Figure 3.1 The view of West Lake (photo by Rouran Zhang)

places were contributed to by many scholars and artists from the thirteenth to eighteenth centuries and include: 苏堤春晓 Su Causeway in the Morning of Spring, 曲院风荷 Breeze-ruffled Lotus at Winding Garden, 平湖秋月 Autumn Moon over the Calm Lake, 断桥残雪 Lingering Snow on Broken Bridge, 花港观鱼 Viewing Fish at Flowery Pond, 柳浪闻莺 Orioles Singing in the Willows, 三潭印月 Three Pools Mirroring the Moon, 双峰插云 Twin Peaks Piercing the Clouds, 雷峰夕照 Leifeng Pagoda in the Evening Glow and 南屏晚钟 Evening Bell Ringing at Nanping Hill. Each of them has its poetic meaning consisting of five essential elements, as defined in the nomination documents:

1 viewing places (points) and scopes of sights chosen by painters for over ten centuries;
2 a stele with the name of the place inscribed on it following the emperors' calligraphy of the eighteenth century and sheltered by a pavilion, serving as the mark of the place;
3 a four-character poetic name given by poets to the place which has passed down for over ten centuries;
4 historic sites, cultural relics, characteristic plants and natural views within the specific scopes of the place that are directly associated with the name of the place;

5   famous literature, historic and artistic works, stories of associated historical figures, as inspired by the place, as well as the spiritual and emotional bonds of traditional Chinese culture these works and stories represent.

(SACH 2011: 68)

The nomination dossier of West Lake documents that those sites have 'embodied exceptional wealthy and diverse cultures and traditions, and are supporting component of the nominated property as a "lake with cultural meanings"' (SACH 2011: 15).

On 24 June 2011, UNESCO inscribed West Lake Cultural Landscape of Hangzhou on the World Heritage List, with a property area of 4235.76 hectares, claiming that it 'bears an exceptional testimony to the cultural tradition of improving landscapes to create a series of vistas reflecting an idealized fusion between humans and nature' (UNESCO 2011b) based on criterion (ii), (iii) and (vi).

> Criterion (ii): The improved landscape of West Lake can be seen to reflect Buddhist ideals imported into China from India such as 'Buddhist peacefulness' and 'nature as paintings,' and in turn it had a major influence on landscape design in East Asia. Its causeways, islands, bridges, temples, pagodas and well defined views, were widely copied over China, notably in the Summer Palace at Beijing and in Japan. The notion of ten poetically named scenic places persisted for seven centuries all over China and also spread to the Korean peninsula after the 16th century, when Korean intellectuals made visits to the West Lake.
>
> Criterion (iii): The West Lake landscape is an exceptional testimony to the very specific cultural tradition of improving landscapes to create a series of 'pictures' that reflect what was seen as a perfect fusion between people and nature, a tradition that evolved in the Tang and Song Dynasties and has continued its relevance to the present day. The 'improved' West Lake, with its exceptional array of man-made causeways, islands, bridges, gardens, pagodas and temples, against a backdrop of the wooded hills, can be seen as an entity that manifests this tradition in an outstanding way.
>
> Criterion (vi): The Tang and Song culture of demonstrating harmony between man and nature by improving the landscape to create pictures of great beauty, captured by artists and given names by poets, is highly visible in the West Lake Landscape, with its islands, causeways, temples, pagodas and ornamental planting. The value of that tradition has persisted for seven centuries in West Lake and has spread across China and into Japan and Korea, turning it into a tradition of outstanding significance.

(UNESCO 2011b)

The authorised heritage discourse and harmony discourse of West Lake

After the successful designation of the World Heritage site, millions of Chinese people used weibo.com (the equivalent of Twitter) to circulate the news. The Hangzhou government put considerable effort into the World Heritage listing. For instance, the local government has invested more than ten billion RMB for the 西湖综合保护工程 West Lake Protection Project since 2001, and one of the main aims of the project was to ensure the success of the World Heritage Listing (The Hangzhou Government 2002). In July 2011, one month after West Lake was successfully inscribed on the World Heritage list, the Cultural Heritage Monitoring and Management Centre of West Lake was established to ensure the management and sustainable development of the West Lake Cultural Landscape. The central government of Hangzhou also established the West Lake Research Institute and International Urban Research Centre of Hangzhou, which has published over 31 million words, including the *West Lake Literature Integration* 西湖文献集成, *Stories of West Lake* 西湖全书, *General History of West Lake* 西湖通史, *Lexicon of West Lake* 西湖辞典, and *Research Report of West Lake* 西湖研究报告 during the ten years of the World Heritage listing process (The Cultural Heritage Monitoring and Management Centre of West Lake 2012). These research reports have either documented the cultural history of the past or recorded the achievements of the present. Along with the *West Lake Nomination Dossier* (SACH 2011), this research, funded by the central government of Hangzhou, incorporated a Chinese version of the authorised heritage discourse, which Yan (2015) called 'the harmony discourse.'

Yan (2015) argues that in China the harmony discourse is the equivalent of, if not more hegemonic than, the Western AHD. The definition and characteristic of the harmony discourse have been analysed in Chapter 1. My research reveals that, during the World Heritage listing process at West Lake, the harmony discourse has been incorporated into the nomination dossier, local research reports and other local management policies, in a similar way as Yan (2015) demonstrated based on his research on Fujian Tulou. According to the *West Lake Nomination Dossier* (SACH 2011), the words 'harmony' and 'harmonious' are used 55 times and 46 times respectively. For instance, according to UNESCO's official description (UNESCO 2011b), West Lake Cultural Landscape of Hangzhou represents '[t]he Tang and Song culture of demonstrating harmony between man and nature by improving the landscape to create pictures of great beauty, captured by artists and given names by poets, is highly visible in West Lake, with its islands, causeways, temples, pagodas and ornamental planting.' The concept of 'harmony between man and nature' used here was imported directly from the *West Lake Nomination*

Dossier. Ostensibly, the harmony discourse stresses the inclusion of people, and emphasises the 'fusion between man and object' that is antithetical to the AHD, which focusses on the materiality of heritage and privileges the heritage expertise of experts and politicians. However, as I found when I interviewed the government officials and site managers who are in charge of the World Heritage nomination process for West Lake, the interviewees mentioned that the local communities did not participate in any part of the decision-making process for the World Heritage Listing (see also Zhang 2017). The AHD was the key factor that facilitated Chinese policymakers and managers ignoring local communities and their values, rather than the national harmony discourse. Although, as I reviewed the *West Lake Nomination Dossier* (SACH 2011), the harmony discourse was not only included in the OUV descriptions but also discursively influenced the West Lake local management principles and policies. The AHD still seemed to be the primary concern of the Chinese government officials and experts, at least during the World Heritage listing process at West Lake (see also Zhang 2017).

Many other materials support my observations. I reviewed the academic attention that has been paid to the World Heritage listing process, for example, Yang (2007), who focusses on the protection, management and development issues, while Shi (2012) discusses how West Lake meets the criterion of UNESCO, and the connection between material heritage and its spiritual meaning has been considered by Ni and Xu (2012). Those authors either discussed the technical issues that ensured the aesthetic or spiritual values were recognised by the international experts or introduced ways to appreciate the cultural or spiritual meaning of West Lake. As I reviewed the relevant local newspapers, including the *Hangzhou Daily, Zhejiang Daily, China Tourism News* and *Xinhua Daily Telegraph*, from 2004 to 2013, the majority of articles stressed the management strategies needed to meet the international criterion provided by local or national experts (*China Tourism News* 2008). They also discussed the great sense of pride the WH listing brought to Hangzhou citizens (see *Daily Business 2011*), reemphasised the difficulty of the local governments' great efforts to help Western experts 'understand' West Lake (*China Tourism News* 2009; *Zhejiang Daily* 2010; *Daily Business 2011*), and introduced the so-called 'international concepts' such as Cultural Landscape, as well as discussing how those concepts can be used to fit the Chinese World Heritage strategies (*China Business Herald* 2011).

Many reports in the tourism literature and newspapers emerged during the WH listing process. For instance, reports: discussed how to use the WH listing as a resource to develop so-called 'international tourism,' and disseminated the term the 'International Tourism City Hangzhou' (Fu 2004; Lu 2010; Li 2012; Wei 2012; Zhang 2012); discussed the changes of government policies, city planning strategies and tourism strategies that World Heritage listing has brought to the site (see Lv 2006; Wang 2008; Zheng 2008); and characterised the touristic types of Hangzhou (S.X. Li 2005; Li 2007; Hu 2005). Some newspapers wrote about interview reports of local people's reactions to the increased tourism issues after WH listing (see *Zhejiang Daily* 2011, 2013), which simply complimented the government's management, such as free entrance fees and improved infrastructure for Hangzhou city. There are also some non-academic surveys conducted with tourists, including a survey of tourists' satisfaction with their visiting experiences using framed research questionnaires (see *Zhejiang Daily* 2013). The purpose of those surveys was to provide statistical data on tourists for tourism development. Few studies focussed their research on tourists' sense of West Lake or what they feel at the site. There are also few in-depth examples of research on communities' reactions to the presence of mass tourism and the interaction between local people and tourists. I will further discuss this in Chapter 4.

In addition, the arguments of those academic and non-academic researchers of heritage and tourism during the WH listing process of West Lake are congruent with top-down experts' perspectives or government policies and described their achievements. Little work has been done from a sociological and anthropological perspective to compare the cultural landscape value of West Lake. This chapter aims to compare the understanding of the meaning of cultural landscape among tourists, residents, Chinese heritage experts, Chinese government officials and international heritage authorities (such as UNESCO and ICOMOS) with regard to West Lake. The chapter argues that the meaning of cultural landscape is multi-layered in the Chinese context and is difficult for Western experts to fully appreciate, while Chinese heritage users such as residents and tourists exercised agency and engaged in culturally sophisticated activities entangled with the meaning of cultural landscape.

Fieldwork

This chapter and Chapter 4 draw on data derived from research which adopted the following research methods.

Analysis of documentary sources

Chapters 3 and 4 review the text of the *ICOMOS Report for West Lake Cultural Landscape* (ICOMOS 2011) and UNESCO's official justification of West Lake, which is itself based on the Chinese nomination dossier (SACH, 2011). I also reviewed the relevant local newspapers and internet resources, including *Hangzhou Daily, Zhejiang Daily, Xinhua Daily Telegraph, China.com* and *ChinaDaily.com*. These chapters aim to compare the tensions between the Chinese national discourse of West Lake and those of ICOMOS and UNESCO.

It also critically reviews the text of those documentary sources and compares their language with the discourse of tourists.

Qualitative interviews with Chinese government officials at both national and local levels, and with experts

Semi-structured interviews were undertaken to determine how Chinese government officials and experts (both intentional and Chinese experts) define the concept of cultural landscape and their responses to tourism in WH listing and management processes. The data was recorded by audiotaping and note-taking. Interviews were undertaken with three groups:

(a) Interviews with key officials from national governments

Interviews were conducted with two directors from the Ministry of Housing and Urban-Rural Development (MHURD hereafter) and the State Administration of Cultural Heritage (SACH hereafter) who are in charge of the World Heritage application and management issues, on 2 December and 4 December 2013 respectively (they are hereafter referred to as GO001 and GO002 respectively). Interviews were also conducted with an official (GO003) from the China National Commission for UNESCO (under supervision of the Ministry of Education) who is responsible for communicating with the UNESCO World Heritage Centre, on 9 December 2013. The official (GO001) from MHURD did not want to be recorded, so I took notes.

(b) Interviews with key officials from the local government of Hangzhou

Interview with a director (WL140) and a vice-director (coded WL141) of the Cultural Heritage Monitoring and Management Centre of West Lake, who was in charge of the World Heritage application and management issues, was conducted on 13 November 2013.

(c) Interviews with experts

Interviews were conducted with a UNESCO expert (a vice-director) (GO005) from the World Heritage Institute of Training and Research for Asia and the Pacific on 20 November 2013 in Shanghai. I also interviewed a director (WL144) and two vice-directors (WL142 and WL143) from the Institute of Architectural History on 26 December 2017 and 4 December 2013 in Beijing, who are responsible for the preparation of the *West Lake Nomination Dossier*. Interviews were also conducted with a researcher (GO004) from the China Tourism Academy, which is under the supervision of the Ministry of Cultural and Tourism of the PRC.

Qualitative interviews with Chinese domestic tourists and residents of Hangzhou

Interviews on site with domestic tourists and residents were conducted during November 2013 and February 2014. Of the 64 domestic tourists interviewed 51.6% (33) were male and 48.4% (31) were female. Those aged 25–34 were the most frequent (50%) age group encountered, followed by those aged 18–24 (23.4%). The educational attainment of most visitors was high, with 68.3% of visitors having some level of university education. Of 36 (56.3%) domestic tourists this was their first visit to West Lake, while 29 (43.7%) were return visitors. The majority of tourists (44, 68.8%) had travelled from a home address; followed by 20.3% from a holiday address. The majority (81%) of visitors had planned to visit Hangzhou for less than three days. Only six (9.5) % tourists had planned a longer visit of more than a week.

Of those 69 residents interviewed at West Lake, over half of those surveyed were male (56.5% to 43.5% female). Those aged 18–34 were the most frequent (52.2%) age group encountered, followed by people over 65 (21.7%). The majority of local people (71%) frequently spend time at West Lake, while 29% did not come to the site very often. More than half (52.2%) of local people who had lived in Hangzhou for less than five years defined themselves as 'new Hangzhou citizens,' while 33 (47.8%) local people had lived in Hangzhou for more than five years. The majority of local people (71%) frequently spend time at West Lake, while 29% did not come to the site very often. Nearly half (46.4%) of the local people interviewed use West Lake as their 'city park,' a place for recreation or enjoying nature. The next section of the chapter will first examine tourists and local people's understanding of the meaning of World Heritage and the term of cultural landscape.

Tourists' and local people's discourses of World Heritage and cultural landscape

Three questions were asked for both tourists and residents about their understanding of 'World Heritage' and 'cultural landscape' (Table 3.1). Nearly a quarter of tourists (19.5%) and 16.1% of local people did not know about the UNESCO programme or they had no idea about World Heritage. The result is not surprising, as the concept of 'World Heritage' originated in the West and was not officially introduced in China until China signed the *World Heritage Convention* in 1985 (Yan 2018). However, nearly half of the interviewees'(41% tourist and 46.8% local people) understanding of the concept of heritage sites drew on the official versions of what World Heritage is considered to be. This included considering World Heritage to be related to culture and history, 13 of these respondents were tourists and 16 were local people. For example:

Table 3.1 What does World Heritage mean to you? (N=118, 56 tourists, 62 residents)

	Tourists (%)	Local people (%)
Within the official discourses of what World Heritage is considered to be	41.0	46.8
Don't know	23.2	16.1
Advertise / regional business card / local business card / famous Touristic brand (positive)	5.4	11.3
Identity/memory work	8.9	6.5
Patriotism, nationalism	7.2	4.7
Natural landscape/ aesthetic	3.6	3.2
Others	10.7	11.4
Total	100.0	100.0

> World Heritage represents a specific culture that has been developed over a long time. Our ancestors and people have made a significant contribution during this process.
>
> (WL062, male, 25–34, tourist)

> I think World Heritage refers to valuable sites or things that need to be passing to future generations.
>
> (WL020, male, 25–34, tourist)

> Urr, I think World Heritage is something that culture and history has bequeathed to us.
>
> (WL042, female, 25–34, tourist)

> World Heritage is a precious gift from God or from our ancestors. It belongs to the whole world. Everyone has a right to visit.
>
> (WL078, female, 18–24, tourist)

Those examples represent the traditional AHD, which defines heritage as non-renewable sites, objects or culture we inherited from our ancestors, and we have a responsibility to protect and pass it on to the future. Twelve interviewees nominated preservation or doing preservation; eleven nominated that natural and cultural heritage were from different categories, for example:

> I think World Heritage is a comprehensive concept, which includes landscape sites, scenic and Historic Areas. It also relates to things with historical and cultural meanings. Therefore, the inscription on the World Heritage list of West Lake is qualified.
>
> (WL027, male, 25–34, tourist)

Those examples reflect that a large number of tourists and local people accepted the Western discourse of 'World Heritage.' In this sense, the 'official discourse' seems to have been successfully disseminated to local people and tourists via the government's interpretations. However, my interview also documented that there were some tourists and local people who considered the meaning of 'World Heritage' beyond the AHD. For instance, nine interviewees considered World Heritage had links to identity and/or memory, such as:

> World Heritage represents a kind of precious memory by each person of their visiting.
>
> (WL083, female, 25–34, tourist)

> World Heritage represents places or things that can be elicited from our old memories or even a sense of traversing. For example, compared to Shanghai, Hangzhou city has a different history, environment and feeling. Being in Hangzhou, you can feel that the atmosphere from when it used to be the capital city and economic centre of the Southern Song Dynasty.
>
> (WL096, male, 18–24 tourist)

> I do not care if West Lake is heritage or not, even the meaning of heritage is not important. How local people and visitors use West Lake is much more significant. If you insist on an answer, I think heritage is a place for local people and visitors. If both of them satisfied they have been in a heritage, the World Heritage programme is successful.
>
> (W120, male, 45–54, tourist)

> I do not know whether my opinion will fit your question or not. I think World Heritage is the stories behind a site or places. If the stories do not exist, the site is meaningless.
>
> (WL115, male, 25–34, local)

WL115 considered that stories and intangible things are more important than material heritage. WL083 pointed out the linkage between heritage and tourism, which memory brings together. WL096 further considered that tourists' memories and sense of place can be elicited by visiting heritage sites which reflect their personal or collective identities. The sense of feeling WL096 mentioned is a significant concept in this book. WL096 explicitly knew that being in the place had invoked his sense of feeling as he empathetically experienced the 'atmosphere' of West Lake in the Southern Song Dynasty. His sense of feeling was about communication between the past and the present. In addition, from WL083 and WL096's perspective, heritage, tourism and

88 The Chinese sense of heritage

Table 3.2 Do you understand the meaning of cultural landscape? (N=37, 14 tourists, 23 local residents)

	Tourists (%)	Local people(%)
Do not understand literally, but can describe	0.0	47.8
Confusion, but still answered base on their own experiences	57.1	8.7
No	28.6	17.4
Talking about the new development of West Lake – positive	14.3	17.4
Yes	0.0	8.7
Total	100.0	100.0

memories have an interplay with each other and reflect people's identities. WL120 indicated that local people and tourists have the right to define what heritage is and how to use heritage. This group of interviewees reflect that the meaning of World Heritage is not only about the AHD, but a far more complicated link to people's memories (WL083), their sense of place (WL096, WL115), their sense of feeling (WL096) and the interactions between tourists themselves (WL083) or between tourists and local people (WL120).

In terms of the question asked of both local people and tourists 'what do you understand by the meaning of cultural landscape?', only 14 tourists answered. Four of them didn't understand the meaning (Table 3.2), while two tourists nominated the new development of West Lake. Eight tourists were confused but still answered based on their own experiences. Below are two examples:

> I think landscape is a dominant element of West Lake. People are also very important to the sites, and I think local people's daily lives are perfectly merged with tourism development which is better than other places.
> (WL078, female, 18–24, tourist)

> I think West Lake represents a city merged with its landscape, a modern city and historical setting. It is fascinating.
> (WL102, male, 25–34, tourist)

As for local people, four local people nominated the positive development of West Lake over the previous ten years. Eleven (47.8%) did not understand the term cultural landscape explicitly, but can describe it. For instance:

> I think, compared to the landscape in Suzhou, West Lake is changing in a different period. The new Xixi National Wetland Park is a recent

development of West Lake. In general, West Lake is a combination of culture and nature, and culture dominates nature.

(WL030, female, 45–54, local)

The interview result shows that the majority of tourists and local people did not know how to answer or were confused by the concept of cultural landscape. Only some local people had a relatively clear answer to this question. One of the significant reasons for this is, as Zhang (2017) reveals, that both local people and tourists did not participate in the World Heritage listing process. The Hangzhou government only used the Western AHD, including the definition of cultural landscape, as a guide on how to treat local people and tourists, and disseminated this concept through the internet, newspapers and TV broadcasts (Xinhuanet.com 2011; People.com 2011a). Therefore, to some extent, the percentage of local people who can describe some characteristics of the cultural landscape was higher than tourists.

The interview results also reveal that many local people and tourists were constructing their ideas of heritage and the meanings of the sites without necessarily referencing the authorised discourse. For instance, a question was asked about 'what categories of World Heritage do you think make up West Lake?' (Table 3.3). The majority (81.8%) response was shared by both local people (77.4%) and tourists (87%): that West Lake is predominantly a site which displays a combination of both culture and nature. Examples of these include:

> West Lake possesses both nature and culture. As I said, many sites have a similar lake including, for instance, South Lake in Jiaxing city and East Lake in Shaoxing city. They all look beautiful, but without cultural accumulation. When you are visiting West Lake, you can find every architecture, temple, street and even tree have a long history or an interesting story. These are the reasons why West Lake is outstanding and unique.
>
> (WL006, male, 18–24, local)

Table 3.3 What categories of World Heritage do you think make up West Lake? (N=99, 46 tourists, 53 residents)

	Tourists (%)	Local people (%)
Combination by both nature and culture	87.0	77.4
Natural	4.3	15.1
Cultural	8.7	0.0
Cultural landscape (similar define with UNESCO)	0.0	7.5
Total	100.0	100.0

West Lake is dominated by nature. There are more than 1500 years of a long history. Hundreds and thousands of paintings, poems and stories were being created to compliment the natural beauty of West Lake. Without the natural elements, the cultural parts were meaningless [...] In my mind, West Lake accounts 70% for nature. The Summer Palace that is located in Beijing, I would say 90% accounts for culture. Because the Summer Palace serves the imperial family, although it is affected by the design of West Lake.

(WL033, female, 24–34, local)

West Lake is like a masterpiece of traditional Chinese landscape paintings. The distance and size between the lake and the distant mountains cannot be copied. Together with the intangible cultural heritage of the White Snake and the spiritual sustenance of the literati of the past dynasties, it perfectly reflects What is the fusion of culture and nature.

(WL043, male, 25–34, tourist)

I think West Lake is dominated by cultural, which could account for 70% of it. In my opinion, the most important [aspect] of a World Heritage [site] is the historical value, which provides meaning to the site. West Lake used to be a capital city of the Southern Song Dynasty, and the traditional literature and poems were written to describe the beauty of the Lake. Nature is [also] a key element.

(WL075, male, 25–34, postgraduate, tourists)

The majority of interviewees saw the interrelationship between culture and nature as critical to the character of West Lake. However, their sense of place was different: some of them considered that culture and nature are equally significant (WL006 and WL043); some of them considered that culture carries more weight than nature (WL075); while some of them nominated nature to be more important than culture (WL033). Nevertheless, the answers they provided are very sophisticated, which reflects that they had been engaged in a deep thought process during their visit rather than receiving the authorised discourse. The above four examples show that both local people and tourists clearly understand the cultural significance or OUV of West Lake nominated by the local government. WL006 compared West Lake to South Lake in Jiaxing and East Lake in Shaoxing, which was linked to his personal memories or experiences. WL033 nominated histories and culture based on their personal interest in answering the question. WL033 compared West Lake to the Summer Palace in Beijing to explain his sense of culture and nature. The interview results reveal that nature and culture are seen as indivisible by the majority of interviewees.

Gong (2001) and Han (2006) argue that a key difference between Chinese and Western culture is the Chinese sense of nature. Confucianism and Daoism are the two most significant Chinese philosophies and are considered to be the roots of Chinese ideology. They have been influenced by Chinese theories and practices for more than 3000 years (Zhang 1992; Wang 1998; Han 2006, 2012). Both of these philosophies have pointed out that the link between culture, nature and people is that of 'Oneness with nature where nature and people form a cosmological whole' (Han 2012: 93). This discourse of harmony is ubiquitous in Chinese school textbooks, paintings, stories and poetry, and has influenced local people's and tourists' sense of West Lake. The poems in textbooks all Chinese students use at primary school and high school give them an empathetic sense of the ancient scholars visiting a pretty landscape with mountains and water features, drinking wine, composing poems and enjoying themselves. It represents how the Chinese people have been influenced by the sense of 'harmony between human and nature' from childhood, which explains why WL043 when interviewed explicitly described his aesthetic and poetic sense of feeling about the 'landscape painting' at West Lake. Many other examples of tourists and local people's sense of feeling will be discussed in Chapter 4.

This section shows that tourists were asked about official terms such as 'World Heritage' and 'cultural landscape'. The majority of visitors' responses are still influenced by the AHD and tended to provide passive messages. However, when asked whether West Lake is a natural or cultural heritage, the answers from tourists and residents have become more active. The key reason is that their collective memory is influenced by traditional Chinese philosophy, so they can better understand the natural and cultural integration value of West Lake. In the following sections, I will illustrate that both tourists and local people can provide more sophisticated understandings of West Lake than UNESCO and ICOMOS experts from Western countries with expertise in heritage assessment. I will unpack their responses based on three essential themes that are critical to West Lake World Heritage bidding: 'The cultural diversity and integrity of West Lake,' 'West Lake is a changing landscape' and 'Emotional feeling associated with the notion of ten poetically named scenic places.'

West Lake: cultural diversity and integrity

In the *West Lake Nomination Dossier*, Chinese officials and experts believe that West Lake's Confucianism, Buddhism, Taoism, loyalty and filial piety, hermit life, collections of books, Tea-Zen and Sphragistics are witness to China's longstanding cultural diversity and reflect outstanding universal values (SCAH 2011). However, the *ICOMOS Report* points out that West Lake values such as Confucianism, Buddhism, and Taoism cannot be used as proof of the OUV of West Lake. On the one hand, those cultural elements are separate and cannot express the cultural value of West Lake as a whole, so they do not have OUV. On the other hand, there are more extensive and important proofs in other domestic and international heritage sites. ICOMOS also believes that the reason why West Lake has OUV in loyalty and filial piety, hermit culture, collection of books, tea meditation and seal carving is not sufficient (ICOMOS 2011:145). Interviews with Chinese officials and experts showed that they were not convinced by the *ICOMOS Report*, as one expert states:

> I doubt ICOMOS judgement because they did not mention any example in the ICOMOS report. Obviously, Western people did not understand the importance of cultural diversity of West Lake.
> (WL142, vice-director from the Institute of Architectural History)

In terms of the issue of integrity, there is still a significant disjuncture between Chinese experts and ICOMOS recognition, such as ICOMOS's rejection of the Longjing Tea Plantation Garden's inclusion in the boundary of the nominated area. The *ICOMOS report* points out that:

> The one area of the landscape that ICOMOS did not consider fully exemplified the ideals of landscape aesthetics were the extensive area of tea gardens to the west of the lake. Although the mountains that rise above the tea gardens form part of the backdrop of the lake the tea plantations are a 'farmed' landscape that do not contribute to the designed landscape.
> (ICOMOS 2011: 145)

> ICOMOS considers that the tea plantations should be considered as a separate unit and not included within the nominated area. Tea growing is of fundamental importance to Chinese society and perhaps consideration could be given to including Longjing with other properties in a nomination that reflects aspects of tea culture.
> (ibid., 2011:152)

Interviews with Chinese experts and officials (GO002, WL142 and WL143) revealed that the Longjing Tea Plantation area is inseparable from West Lake, which 'bears an important value of Chinese Tea-Zen cultural tradition,' and contributes to the integration of West Lake's value (SCAH 2011:16). Therefore, they were still confused about why ICOMOS experts made such a decision, as one expert commented:

> We have no choice but to remove Longjing Tea Garden from the core area of West Lake as a World Heritage site. There has been a tradition of 'drinking Longjing tea and taking a boat to West Lake' since ancient times in China, and the water of West Lake is connected with the mountains of Longjing Tea Garden. To the Chinese, mountains and water symbolise the

universe or everything in nature. It is not the western understanding that mountains and water are viewed independently. Therefore, we consider Longjing Tea Garden and West Lake as a whole. But ICOMOS experts don't understand the connection. They think the tea garden is an agricultural landscape and has nothing to do with the cultural connotations expressed by West Lake. We went on to find a lot of classic books that proved the importance of Longjing Tea Garden from the perspective of historical value, but ICOMOS experts still don't agree.

(WL144, director from the Institute of Architectural History)

As I interviewed residents at the Longjing Tea Plantation area (Figure 3.2), local people were shocked that the international authorities excluded the area and any Longjing Tea element as a part of OUV. Some local people were convinced I had made a mistake, as the UNESCO experts would find it impossible to reject such a unique tea cultural site given their 'international vision.' For example:

> I think one of the key reasons that West Lake inscribed on the World Heritage list is international experts who have tasted our Longjing tea[smile].
>
> (WL094, male, over 65, local)

Figure 3.2 Longjing tea plantations (gardens) to the west of the lake (photo by Rouran Zhang)

> West Lake without Longjing Tea Garden is like a beautiful woman losing her unique characteristic and becoming mediocre.
>
> (WL095, male, 25–34, local)

> Lu Yu's *The Book of Tea* [published around 758] recorded the Longjing tea as the earliest tea monograph in the world, and Longjing tea culture has been constantly developed in each Chinese dynasty. [...] It is significant to the cultural integrity of West Lake, and enable West Lake inscribed on the World Heritage list.
>
> (WL097, female, 25–34, local)

Interviews with domestic tourists also reflected the cultural diversity and integrity of West Lake. Many tourists to West Lake were not there for recreation or education, but rather they expressed an active sense of their feeling for heritage, and engaged with multiple cultures either in their material forms or intangible elements (for further discussion see Chapter 4). Typical of their responses against the *ICOMOS Report* that trivialises values such as Tea-Zen culture, loyalty and filial piety are:

> (1) Loyalty and filial piety
> Yue Fei is my idol. [...] I thought it was a shame that the King in the Southern Song Dynasty killed such a hero, a good person [Yue Fei]. Why did such a glorious Kingdom [Southern Song Dynasty] decay? I think the leader of a country is significant for the past and present.
>
> (WL064, male, 35–44, tourist)

> (2) Buddhism and Taoism
> Buddhism and Taoism have the concept of harmony between human and nature. If you look closely and feel West Lake, its all-embracing combination of mountains, water, culture, history and spirit, which is a testament to Buddhist and Taoist thought.
>
> (WL125, male, 25–34, tourist)

> (3) Tea-Zen culture
> Sit on the edge of the lake and taste Longjing Tea, then I can feel the beauty of West Lake.
>
> (WL090, female, 35–44, tourist)

Some tourists understand that the integration of cultural and natural values is the essence of the value of West Lake. A typical example is:

The Chinese sense of heritage 95

> I think nature and culture have merged for a long time [at West Lake]. Take Leifeng Pagoda as an example, it has a long and profound history. The origin of this pagoda is that it was built in 977 AD during the Wuyue Kingdom. It was a Buddhist pagoda, and built for Buddhist reasons or maybe built for one of the imperial concubines. Leifeng Pagoda is located in the middle of the bridge of Xizhao Hill, face to the lake, and absolutely beautiful scenes. The design of the pagoda and its location reflect the Chinese traditional '风水 Fengshui' concept. The pagoda has been changed during different periods with profound stories and culture. You can find many poems and stories written for the pagoda.
>
> (WL027, male, 25–34, tourist)

West Lake: a continually changing landscape

As I reviewed the *West Lake Nomination Dossier*, the Chinese government officials and experts considered that West Lake is a typical case in which people effectively used water resources for thousands of years (from the Tang Dynasty to the present), and considered incorporating those Chinese values into criterion (v):

> West Lake Landscape is an outstanding example of using an ancient lagoon to create beautiful scenery, which have significantly improved the living environment. It has retained its spatial feature of 'cloud-capped hills on three sides of the Lake and the City on the fourth', and witnessed how people organically transformed the ancient lagoon into this world-famous lake with beautiful scenery and cultural meanings, through active efforts against its natural process of swamping. […] It has been serving the ecological, cultural and tourism functions for the city of Hangzhou in the face of rapid process of urbanization. Boasting the history of over a millennium and world-acclaimed scenic area it remains in use today.
>
> (SACH 2011: 20)

However, ICOMOS were not convinced by Chinese experts that West Lake is an evolving landscape, which cannot be nominated based on criterion (v) (ICOMOS 2011: 145). International experts considered the OUV of West Lake is closely related to the classical literature, culture and creativity of the Chinese feudal empire, spanning thousands of years from the Tang to the Qing Dynasty. However, ICOMOS believed that the development and changes from the Republican period to the present-day were not associated with OUV (ibid., 2011: 145). In this understanding, ICOMOS and the World Heritage Committee disregarded the position put forward by Chinese experts, and considered the value of West Lake in the present day is not relevant to OUV.

Interviews with the residents of Hangzhou showed their support for the Chinese experts' argument that West Lake is constantly evolving from the Tang Dynasty to the present day. International experts excluded the value from the Republic period to the present-day from the OUV, while many local people's understandings reflect their belief that the 100-year history of West Lake to the present day is as important as the history of ancient times. The following examples show that local people were concerned about how the new development in the present had become part of the site.

> I think cultural heritage does not just reflect the past, you know, West Lake was a natural lagoon, it has been changed to be such a meaningful place because for more than a thousand years it has been worked on by people. West Lake is still changing now.
>
> (WL007, female, over 65, local)

> WL032: Well, I think West Lake is an integrated natural and cultural site.
>
> WL033: You know, without Bai Juyi, Sun Dongpo, Yang Gong, and other people who were in charge of the management of West Lake, there would be no such beautiful place today. Every generation has contributed to the development of West Lake. We are also making our contribution. In recent decades, there is a project that has used the sludge dug from West Lake to create a new wetland Park, Jiang Yangfan Park.
>
> WL034: Well, this is a part of West Lake Protection and Management Project. It is still unfinished and with minimal tourists.
>
> WL032: I think this is a new development of West Lake, with contemporary technology and modern design.
>
> WL033: I agree, in addition, West Lake has become larger than before, in particular, the Mao Jiabu area because of the protection project. In different times people would do something for West Lake.
>
> (WL032, WL033 and WL034, female, 24–34, locals)

> … the natural landscape is just one aspect of West Lake, more important are the stories in different places of the Lake. For example, every person in 南山路 Nanshan Road has their own stories, their stories construct the meaning of West Lake.
>
> (WL080, male, 35–44, local)

Interviews with domestic tourists also supported both residents' and Chinese experts' views that the critical characteristic of West Lake is that it is constantly evolving in both material and non-material form, spanning the history from the Tang Dynasty to the present over thousands of years.

> The most attractive characteristic of West Lake is that historic architecture has been perfectly merged into the modern elements. You hardly notice actually you are in the city centre of Hangzhou during your visit. The situation during the holiday season may be different. But now we are absolutely satisfied, just like being in a paradise.
>
> (WL038, female, 25–34, tourist)

> I love the music fountain of West Lake, where I can see the life of contemporary Hangzhou citizens. I talked to them and expressed the feeling that Hangzhou has developed over the years. This is a city with style.
>
> (WL067, male, 25–34, tourist)

> You see that there is a broken bridge and Leifeng Pagoda represent the ancient West Lake, and there are new buildings design by Wang Shu [the first Chinese citizen to win the Pritzker Prize] and other pioneer architects in modern times, such as Chinese Academy of Fine Arts. Each era has her [West Lake] charm.
>
> (WL075, male, 25–34, tourist)

For some tourists, the charm of West Lake lies in its changes. Visitors can experience both history and the beauty of contemporary West Lake. Many tourists have pointed out that the new buildings and lifestyles of West Lake in Nanshan Road are the most attractive to them. Ironically, these modern settlements are often characterised by national and international heritage experts as a threat to the integrity and authenticity of the designated heritage area. In recent decades, some returning visitors have witnessed the positive changes in West Lake and believe that these changes are distinctive features of the lake. For instance:

> I have been to Hangzhou many times. I come to visit not because of West Lake. I prefer the surroundings, that the modern merges into the historical settlements. […] For example, there are many modern hotels and restaurants located at the Nanshan road [on the east side of West Lake]. They are new buildings which represent the latest development of West Lake, and they have perfectly merged into the traditional setting.
>
> (WL072, male, 25–34, tourist)

> In my mind, West Lake is bigger and more beautiful than it was a decade ago. In addition to the *'Ten Poetically Named Scenic Places'*, 20 new poetic

attractions have been added because of new development of West Lake. I heard from local people, the local government use the sludge dug from West Lake to fill in some low-lying land, which created a new wetland park – 江洋畈公园 Jiang Yangfan Park in recent ten years.

(WL129, male, 25–34, tourist)

Some tourists believe that the history of the Republic of China was ignored by domestic and international public opinion. One tourist commented: 'I think the history of the Republic of China has been forgotten. All attractions are about ancient values or development in the last two decades.' One interviewee provided an emotional response, his grandparents having moved from mainland China to Taiwan in the Republic period because of the Chinese Civil War from 1945 to 1950. Therefore, he was not just visiting the site. Instead, he was looking for a lost family identity.

> I was born in Taiwan. However Hangzhou is my native place, and I had no relatives here because of the political situation in China 60 years ago. My grandparents very much miss their hometown and always told me stories of West Lake and Hangzhou. Unfortunately, they had no chance to come back before they passed away. This time I have joined a tour group to West Lake in order to fulfil their uncompleted wish. I am very impressed by the scenery, culture and history of West Lake, which is just like the stories that my grandparents have told me. I am very proud of my hometown with its new development.
>
> (WL064, male, 35–44, tourist)

The emotional feeling associated with the notion of *Ten Poetically Named Scenic Places*

The World Heritage Committee and ICOMOS experts believed that the quintessence of West Lake values are the physical and intangible components of West Lake, embodied in the notion of *Ten Poetically Named Scenic Places*, representing the traditional Chinese philosophy of 'harmony between man and nature' and 'project feelings onto the landscape' (UNESCO 2011b). As the director from the Institute of Architectural History said:

> West Lake can best prove China's concept of 'harmony between human and nature' and 'project feelings onto the landscape.' Zhou Mi, a famous lyricist of the Southern Song dynasty (1127 AD–1279 AD), came up with the concept of 'project feelings onto the landscape' by West Lake.
>
> (WL144, director from the Institute of Architectural History)

However, Chinese experts encountered difficulties in explaining the Oriental values to Western experts. The *China Daily* interviewed Zhang Jiangting, the vice mayor of Hangzhou after West Lake was successfully inscribed on the World Heritage list on 24 June 2011:

> …He remembered the first time West Lake made a bid several years ago and how a European world heritage expert had told him: 'There are thousands of lakes like that in my hometown.' […] That summed up the frustration he felt with so many Westerners who had yet to realize the true significance of the lake.
>
> China Daily (2011)

Interviews with Chinese experts and officials also reveal that the European expert from ICOMOS clearly did not understand Chinese values:

> I stood in the Su causeway with the UNESCO experts and explained to him what is Chinese 'poetic and artistic meaning.' Poetry originally intended to convey feelings by reading aloud, and paintings must also be viewed to understand what it means. But the Chinese philosophy is that man stands in nature, feeling 'the emotion of poetry and the meaning of painting' from the water beating on the shore, the wind blowing and the birds singing. I think I have explained it very clearly, but the UNESCO expert said, 'He doesn't feel anything.' 'That's the difference between eastern and western cultures,' we spoke at the same time.
>
> (WL144, director from the Institute of Architectural History)

> …断桥残雪 Lingering Snow on Broken Bridge has threefold meanings that were very hard to explain to Western experts. As for what kind of beauty or what Chinese ideology of the sites, they may not understand, unless they grow up in the Chinese southern cultural background. Nevertheless, UNESCO understood that West Lake represents the Chinese understanding of landscape and perspectives of beauty.
>
> (GO002, director of World Cultural Heritage from SACH; see also Zhang and Taylor 2019)

In contrast to international experts' problems with understanding Chinese sentiments, interviews with residents and domestic tourists demonstrated that emotional feeling is a significant theme for many of them. The examples here are of a local and a tourist who explicitly talked about seeking a sense of 'feeling':

…[T]he meaning of 断桥残雪 Lingering Snow on Broken Bridge reflects the scenery on a sunny day after heavy snow, the snow on the bridge melts and shows the brown floor, which gives people a feeling that the chain is broken.

(WL043, male, 25–34, tourist)

You need to take your time during your visit to West Lake. Otherwise, you won't be able to understand the in-depth meaning of the site. For example, if you visit 三潭印月 Three Pools Mirroring the Moon (Figure 3.3) in a rush, you might think they are just three normal sculptures. However, if you come to the site during the moonlit night, take your time to feel the place, you will suddenly understand how wise and romantic our ancestors were for naming it. Just like Longjing tea, if you drink it very quickly you never know how good the tea is.

(WL093, male, over 65, local)

My research reveals that Chinese people (both tourists and local people) who I interviewed seem to easily understand the poetic meaning of West Lake. More

Figure 3.3 The view of 三潭印月 *Three Pools Mirroring the Moon* (photo by Rouran Zhang)

than one-third of domestic tourists (23 of 64 tourists) and nearly a quarter of local people (16 of 69 local people) interviewed were overt in acknowledging that they were having or seeking feelings. Ironically, this was often at the *Ten Poetically Named Scenic Places* where government officials and experts tried to, but failed, to explain the poetic meaning of to the European expert from ICOMOS. The reason is that this poetic or aesthetic thought process was embodied in Chinese traditional culture, and represents and speaks to Chinese identity and is easily made sense of by Chinese people. While Westerners were not influenced in this way, even the European expert's expertise could not readily fill the gap of cultural differences. Chinese tourists' emotional expression and feeling will be further discussed in Chapter 4.

Conclusion

This chapter has identified local people's and tourists' responses to their understanding of the term 'World Heritage' and 'cultural landscape.' Local government and experts attempted to disseminate the AHD and harmony discourse to local people and tourists through social media (newspaper and internet). On the face of it, they seem to have been successful. In terms of the questions I asked interviewees about their understanding of the meaning of World Heritage, although nearly 20% of people I interviewed did not have a sense of what it is, the majority of local people and tourists have accepted the Western discourse of 'World Heritage.' However, many local people's and tourists' answers are active, and much more complicated when tied to their personal or collective identities. World Heritage, and being at the World Heritage site, saw many tourists offer active discussions of a sense of feeling (e.g. WL043, WL096) and belonging (e.g. WL035, WL076). Those personal senses further linked to interviewees' memories and reflected their personal or collective identities. Therefore, my interviews supported Smith's (2006: 83) contention that:

> Although heritage is something that is done at places, these places became places of heritage both because of the events of meaning-making and remembering that occur at them, but also because they lend a sense of occasion and reality to the activities occurring at them.

The interviews also reveal that both local people's and tourists' understanding of West Lake did not reproduce, nor was it based on, the dichotomy between nature and culture that underpins World Heritage practice, and they did not make easy sense of the concept of cultural landscape. This does not mean that local people and tourists do not understand the site, on the contrary, their understanding of West Lake is far more interesting, active and complicated than the AHD and the official harmony discourse allows. For many local people and tourists, their sense of nature and culture are linked together and tied to their sense of place and their sense of feeling. WL043 and WL096 (many other examples are analysed in Chapter 4) are explicit about seeking a sense of 'feeling,' which they express with extensive use of metaphor, and they clearly know what kind of feeling they were experiencing. In other national contexts, Poria et al. (2003) and Smith (2006, 2012) noted that feeling was important; however they use the term 'feeling' to describe a difficulty their interviewees had in putting their feelings into words or even acknowledging them (see also Cameron and Gatewood 2000, 2012). The reason Chinese interviewees are more aware and were clear in describing their sense of feeling may be because of the Chinese interlinked view of nature and culture. As W. Zhou (1999: 39) notes:

> Western culture is remarkably characterised by Natural Science that has its origins in Natural Philosophy; while Chinese culture is characterized by the study of humans, for which the core is morality and ethics.

Therefore, what the interviews reveal is that both local people's and tourists' sense of feeling was not only influenced by the aesthetic characteristics of nature and culture, rather they pursued their inner understanding of nature and culture which was tied to their personal memories and experiences. As Lin Yutang (1935: 291), one of the most influential Chinese writers and linguists, commented on Chinese painting:

> Chinese painting, the flower of Chinese culture, is distinguished by a spirit and an atmosphere all its own […] we decidedly feel that the artist has interfered with material reality and presented it to us only as it appears to him, without losing its essential likeness or intelligibility to others [and] it manages to achieve a decidedly subjective appearance of things without creating contortions.

A British artist David Hockney also commented that 'Chinese paintings do have perspective, but their perspective is memory' (quoted in Yang 2003). Local people and tourists being at the heritage site, experiencing the site, means that their sense of feeling constructed heritage from their 'personal inner world.' In this sense, as Smith (2006, 2012) argues, the meanings for heritage is not only constructed from the AHD, rather each individual who visits the site actively constitutes the meaning of heritage. In the next chapter, I will further analyse what tourists do and feel at West Lake, as well as local people's reaction to the presence of mass tourists.

Notes

1 It symbolises the scene of 'three hills in a pool' in the fairyland as described in legends since the Qin and Han dynasties. (Source: SACH 2011: 64.)
2 Bai Juyi (772–846) was a renowned Chinese poet and Tang Dynasty government official. (Source: http://en.wikipedia.org/wiki/Bai_Juyi.)
3 Su Dongpo (1037–1101), a Chinese writer-poet, painter, calligrapher, pharmacologist, gastronome and a statesman of the Song Dynasty. A major personality of the Song era, Su was an important figure in Song Dynasty politics. (Source: http://en.wikipedia.org/wiki/Su_Shi.)
4 Based on poets' 'aesthetic perception of natural landscape, especially famous scenic places, and on the ideas or feelings he intends to engender, a painter composes a work to capture an "enframed scenery" of specific conception; then a poet gives the "enframed scenery" a four-character poetic name according to the aesthetic features of the paintings. Hence a "scenic place with a 4-character poetic name" came into being; and finally viewers form a landscape unit out of the scenery represented by the painting.' (Source: SACH 2011: 48.)

Chapter 4

Feeling a sense of place

An old Chinese saying goes:

> 读万卷书，行万里路 Learn knowledge from thousands of books and accumulate experience by travelling thousands of miles.

This is from 董其昌 Dong Qichang, perhaps the most influential Chinese artist from the Ming Dynasty (1368–1644), who pointed out that travelling and learning are two important accomplishments. The modified popular version, in recent decades, goes:

> 读万卷书，不如行万里路 It is better to travel ten thousand miles than to read ten thousand books.

Many debate competitions and essay examinations have used this new version, even the then First Lady of the United States, Michelle LaVaughn Obama, used it as the topic at her public speech at Peking University in March 2014. Both versions point out the significance of the experiences a person can gain from travelling. The word 行 travel means to spend time in different places, which is the key concept I explore in this book.

This chapter has three tasks. Firstly, as discussed in Chapter 2, mainstream practitioners and researchers in heritage studies have tended to describe tourists as superficial, inauthentic, destructive and culturally ignorant (see Graburn and Barthel-Bouchier 2001; Ashworth 2009). Chapter 3 illustrated that tourists and residents are to some extent influenced by these dominant understandings, because when I interviewed them about their understanding of some official concepts, such as 'heritage' or 'cultural landscape,' most tourists either do not know about them, or their answers draw on the framework of the AHD. This chapter aims to explore how Chinese government officials at both national and local levels, UNESCO experts, and national experts concerned with tourism, and tourists' impacts based on their experiences of the World Heritage listing and management processes of West Lake.

Secondly, as I asked the question 'what categories of Word Heritage do you think make up West Lake?' in Chapter 3, both tourists' and local people's answers were more active and unaffected by the AHD, reflecting the traditional Chinese concept of 'harmony between human and nature.' Indeed, Chapter 3 identified that many visitors and local residents have a deep understanding of the value of the West Lake that ICOMOS experts don't appreciate. It also demonstrated that many tourists do not necessarily passively accept the received discourse; rather, many actively engaged in creating their own understanding of heritage. To extend our knowledge of the ways in which tourists engage, or do not engage, with heritage sites it is useful to explore these issues with the tourists themselves. To address this, a number of questions were asked that explored the reasons for their visit and the experiences tourists valued.

Thirdly, the mainstream heritage literature also tends to focus on the negative impacts of tourism on local communities (see Ap and Crompton 1993; Brunt and Courtney 1999). This chapter will also discuss residents' reactions to the presence of mass tourists, and what local people and visitors' understood about each other. The results of each question asked in the structured interviews are outlined below. Overall, the chapter argues that an active sense of emotional engagement is widely expressed in my interviews with domestic tourists at West Lake. There is a multi-dimensional sense of feeling that emerged, and many tourists talked about their feeling in a self-conscious way that is tied to their sense of connection with physical sites or with residents. Many local people I interviewed at West Lake also spoke in deep emotional registers tied to a sense of pride they feel when they connect with tourists.

Tourism as a problem: discourses from officials and experts

My analysis is based on interviews with three national government officials (GO001, GO002 and GO003), a local government official (WL140), a UNESCO expert (GO005) and three national experts (GO004, WL142, WL143 and WL144). Selective representation of the key open-ended questions will be analysed to explore how Chinese officials and experts understood the relationship between heritage and tourism. As I asked 'what is the role of tourism in the World Heritage listing process?', GO005, reflecting on his understanding of tourism's roles in World Heritage issues, responded that:

> I think tourists just come to a place for a few days, why would you be concerned with the values of the tourists? Well, the nomination file has a concern about tourists that is indeed an issue at the management level. The *Operational Guidelines* mentioned that. But you talk about value; it is all about local communities. What is good for local communities is good for tourists.

So, it is the only thing to say about tourists. Because you deal with local people, they are far more important to deal with than tourists. Heritage preservation and conservation is done for the betterment of local communities. It is not for tourists. Tourists are welcome to enjoy the site, and experience the site, and bring their money for local people. But it is all done for the local communities. This is the principal idea behind conservation from my view and also World Heritage conservation. Many national governments focus exclusively on tourism. It is their fault and it is their mistake. It is nothing to do with UNESCO. UNESCO has to deal with the side effects of WH listing. UNESCO deals with the management aspects of tourism.

(GO005, UNESCO expert)

He criticised many state parties who consider tourism before site protection. His argument represents international authorities' attitude towards tourists, i.e. that tourists should only be considered as a heritage management issue or problem (e.g. Ashworth 2009; Hall 2009). His argument is confirmed by the officials from the SACH, the China National Commission for UNESCO and the China Tourism Academy. As GO002, GO003 and GO004 note:

GO002: Tourism did not play any role in the World Heritage listing process.

GO003: Tourism? I do not think tourism has been considered during the WH listing process. It is important to discuss the tourism issues after World Heritage inscription, and experts would consider whether tourism influences the protection and the possess OUV of the sites. You know, World Heritage belongs to all human beings, and tourists have the right to appreciate this resource. However, international experts have been worried that mass tourists would cause negative effects on heritage protection. I think governments should carefully make tourism strategies in order to limit the number of tourists.

GO004: I do not think there is any relevance of tourism in the World Heritage listing process. According to the current criteria and standards of the World Heritage Programme, tourism has been seen as a negative effect on the application and management of heritage sites. For example, you know, Shilin Karst had already been a well-developed tourism destination. The local governments of Shilin Karst considered that tourism development might be undetermined by their World Heritage application. Therefore, they had made a decision that joined with Libo Karst, and Wulong Karst is applying as Joint World Natural Heritage sites and was inscribed on the World Heritage List in 2007. However, I think tourism plays an active role in heritage operating and management. One of the significant values that relate to tourism is education, so that tourists could learn something from the sites during their visiting.

(GO002, GO003, GO004, national government officials)

The narratives from the three respondents illustrate that there was no consideration of the relationship between tourism and heritage during the WH listing process. Indeed, in their view, tourists' activities at heritage sites need only to be considered as a management issue. These views are identical to those of UNESCO and are framed by the AHD (Smith 2006). During the process of World Heritage application, the government officials and heritage site managers attempted to avoid the tourism issues, rather than explore what tourists do or think when they visit heritage sites, and increased tourism was seen as a potential problem for the Shilin Karst nomination. In addition, GO004 also pointed out that the other relation between tourism and heritage is about education. Smith (2006) argues that education is one of the significant aspects of the AHD, in which the idea that educating tourists about the historic and aesthetic values of heritage sites is embedded in international heritage principles and policies. The possibility that tourists or other forms of visitors could have their own agency is simply not considered possible (Mason 2004; Smith 2006; Sather-Wagstaff 2011). GO002 also demonstrates this when he states that:

> In my opinion, tourists have played an important role in heritage issues, they are receivers of the discourse and display of World Heritage OUV and other values.
>
> (GO002, national government official)

Tourists are often characterised as passive message receivers, and incapable of meaning-making (Mason 2004). The international authorities through the AHD construct tourists as part of the hierarchy of the meaning-making system. As Smith (2012: 213) notes, 'the idea of the vulgarity of tourism is simply about ensuring the maintenance of certain cultural values and meanings, and the political and cultural hierarchies that they underpin.' The Chinese national authorities accepted the definition of tourism from the international AHD during the WH listing process. As I asked the two officials (GO001 and GO002) who are directly responsible for management of all Chinese heritage sites, 'What do you think the relationship between tourism and heritage is?' They answered that:

> GO001: The World Heritage Programme welcomes and absorbs new concepts or ideas. I think tourism can perfectly link to the World Heritage programme, and tourists could understand heritage value during their visiting. You know, if there are no tourists visiting heritage sites, how would they know the value of the sites, and who we protect those sites for? Tourism also promotes communication between tourists and local communities. However, China has a large population. With economic growth, most people have enough money to plan tours. There are dramatic increases in tourists at Chinese heritage sites in the last ten years,

however, mass tourists have created pressures for those sites. For many WHS, the tourism infrastructure cannot accommodate the number of tourists. This causes negative touristic experiences. It is our responsibility to improve tourism infrastructures, not only for the protection of heritage sites but also enhancing tourists' experiences. Site managers should keep in mind that conservation and protection are keys in disseminating heritage values to visitors. I think both national and local tourism departments should consider how to provide more in-depth information to visitors to simultaneously improve their tourist experiences. In my view, I think World Heritage and tourism are interlinked with each other. Tourist problems such as superficial mass tourists and a disordered tourism market are caused by immature Chinese tourism policies. However, the problems we have to deal with are more complex than other countries in the world. We should be patient.

GO002: The majority of people who use heritage site are tourists, not experts. World Heritage belongs to everyone in the world. One of the aims of the World Heritage Programme is to display the OUV of sites to the public. Therefore, tourists have very close relations with heritage issues. However, we have to pay attention to tourism management, particular the tourism environment bearing capacity, in order to develop sustainable tourism. It is important to plan a comprehensive tourism strategy in order to protect the sites, and simultaneously improve tourists' experiences. Heritage values could be delivered to tourists when they are satisfied with their touristic experiences during their journey. We still have management difficulty during the public holiday seasons.

(GO002, GO003, national government officials)

Although the two respondents mainly talked about the importance of tourism management to heritage sites, they also pointed out tourists are the key users of heritage sites, rather than experts. As GO001 stated, 'if there are no tourists visiting heritage sites, how would they know the values of the sites, and who we protect those sites for?' Both of the respondents illustrated that the act of visiting by tourists is creating the contemporary meaning of heritage, and the reason to develop systematic heritage protection systems is for tourists. As Smith (2006) argues the performances of heritage are constructed not only by the international or national heritage practices, such as the accumulation of World Heritage lists and the various management practices, but are also formulated by individual acts of visiting heritage places. However, the directors from the Chinese national authorities realised tourists and heritage are interlinked conceptually, yet they still uncritically accept the international AHD and consider tourists as a management issue in practice, and have not considered what it is tourists may be doing at the sites.

Interviews with officials shows that tourism has not been considered in the WH listing or associated decision-making processes. Although they nominated that tourism could be positive for heritage sites, they noted that this depended on well-designed management strategies or policies. In terms of tourists, GO004 considered the relationship between heritage and tourists is that tourists are passive receivers of the educational, historical and cultural values of heritage sites. However, respondents GO001 and GO002, from two key national heritage authorities, argued that tourists are the key stakeholders in contemporary uses of heritage. Although, as the directors of national heritage authorities, GO001 and GO002 realised the conceptual link between tourists and heritage, tourism or tourists have only been addressed as a heritage management issue. One of the key reasons that the Chinese government tends to disregard the conceptual relation between tourists and heritage is derived from the influences of the international AHD. Government officials and experts have the power to define heritage principles and policies at international, national and local levels. During the WH listing process, they also have the right to evaluate whether the sites possess OUV for World Heritage inscription, not tourists or local communities.

Interviews were also conducted with the director of the Cultural Heritage Monitoring and Management Centre of West Lake (WL140) and experts who wrote the *West Lake Nomination Dossier* (WL142 and WL143) to discuss their perspectives on tourism.

Author: What do you think of tourism?

WL140: I think tourism and the World Heritage application and inscription have no relevance. I think the key issues of World Heritage concern site protection and management and its relevant authenticity and integrity. But the successful WH listing, of course, brings more tourists to sites. In terms of West Lake, we have considered the tourism problems in the process of WH listing, in particular the tourists' pressure at popular touristic points during the public holiday. Therefore, we have made a great effort and developed strategies in order to mitigate negative effects from tourists. For example, we have developed other touristic places such as The Grand Canal [Listed on World Heritage list in 2014] and Xixi National Wetland Park in order to mitigate tourism pressure on West Lake, and also provide a comfortable touristic experience for mass tourists. In addition, you know, West Lake is famous for all Chinese people. Therefore, WH listing has brought stable increases of tourists, rather than dramatic changes as at other WHS. The listing actually attracted more international tourists.

Author: Do you think tourism is one of the key issues that led to West Lake applying for World Heritage inscription?

WL140: Absolutely not. As I said, the rules of the World Heritage game do not have any relevance for tourism. The *World Heritage Convention* and the *Operational Guidelines* do not mention anything about tourism. However, tourists, as one of the stakeholders, whether they support the World Heritage application or not, their involvement in the protection of the site by their visiting is important for us. But tourism and World Heritage are two different things.

Author: What is your perspective on tourists?

WL140: We have done some research relevant to stakeholders. My perspective is that tourists, of course, are one of the stakeholders. However, they are not key stakeholders, because they just come to visit for a short time. Local people are far more important than tourists.

(WL140, director)

Her response illustrates that tourism and heritage are two different issues as understood within the World Heritage listing and management. Although WL140 admitted that tourists are one of the stakeholders, but not a consequential stakeholder, because they just visited for a short time, she noted that, from her understanding of the World Heritage Programme, they had to be treated as irrelevant, or more particularly as a management 'problem.' However, her response also reflects that mass tourists have stimulated the development of other heritage sites, such as The Grand Canal and Xixi National Wetland Park. In addition, WL140 identified that she considered local communities to be important stakeholders, however, they were not involved in decision making during the WH listing process (Zhang 2017), as their presence outside of the designated area meant that, according to the rules of WH listing, they could not be included. As she notes this exclusion went against her own understanding of their role, indicating how the World Heritage 'rules' overwrote the values of local experts and policy-makers. I also asked WL142 and WL143 the questions related to tourism:

Author: What do you think the relationship is between tourism and heritage?

WL143: Tourism was not the main purpose of WH listing.

WL142: Yes. Firstly, West Lake was already very famous in China before WHL, and the tourists' numbers were in the top three of Chinese touristic destinations after the Forbidden City and the Mausoleum of the First Qin Emperor. Therefore, unlike Xidi and Hongcun, WH listing has not brought dramatic tourism increases to West Lake. During the listing process, we communicated with relevant local governments in order to develop management strategies limiting the number of tourists, as well as mitigating the negative effects of tourism such as destroying cultural relics.

WL143: I think tourism, from the perspective of protection, has been a threat to World Heritage sites, not least in China. However, tourism is important for local development at many heritage sites. At some heritage sites, local people and local governments have a great deal of enthusiasm to protect their places because of tourism. You know, tourism is significant for everyone, including me. I always prefer to have a tour in heritage sites. During my visit, I want to have a good touristic experience as most tourists wish, which requires a well-developed tourism infrastructure. You know, tourism is not all bad things. We are using such '展示 display and 传播 disseminated' linked with touristic activities in heritage issues, which means that we have tried to balance the role of tourism.

(WL142, WL143, experts)

WL142's discourse represents a mainstream practitioners' perspective on tourism and tourists, in which tourists are regarded as only a problem or threat to be dealt with in terms of their physical impact, and that their main value is economic. WL143 shares similar ideas with WL143, and considered that tourists need to be educated, and used the terms '展示 display and 传播 disseminated' to link tourists and heritage.

My interview with government officials and experts provides evidence that the meaning of World Heritage is constructed by governments and professional experts, while the perspectives from local communities and tourists have been marginalised or ignored. However, a problem emerged as I interviewed officials and experts; if, as they said, we need to display the sites for their OUV, what do tourists do and feel during their visits to WH sites? Do tourists simply take up the OUV, or are they doing something more organically Chinese, or are they assimilating the OUV? I will unpack these issues in the following sections.

Tourists' active sense of heritage

Sixty-four domestic tourists were interviewed at West Lake (for details see Chapter 3, p. 85). When I asked domestic tourists, 'what are your reasons for visiting West Lake?' (Table 4.1), nearly a quarter of visitors (21.9%) nominated intangible things including myth, stories, poetry, proverbs, or the White Snake TV show as the inspiration for their visit, rather than seeing material objects. For instance:

Table 4.1 What are your reasons for visiting West Lake? (N=64)

	Tourists (%)
Identity/memory	31.3
Myths/stories/poetries/proverbs/White snake TV show	21.9
Recreation/leisure/aesthetic	20.3
Enjoy modern city/modern city merge into historical settlements	10.9
Enjoying nature	9.4
Others	6.2
Total	100.0

Because of the reputation of West Lake, particularly the White Snake TV show, I am going to find my Xu Xian [The actor of the White Snake TV show, represented as husband] during this trip (laughs).

(WL011, female, 25–34, tourist)

[…] a saying goes, 'Heaven above, Suzhou and Hangzhou below.' When you come to Hangzhou, the image of West Lake will jump out of your mind, just like the Forbidden City represents Beijing.

(WL049, male, 25–34, tourist)

I read the ancient poems 'After rain comes fair sunshine' and 'The Lakeside Temple at Dawn.' I also know that ancient poets once visited West Lake. This is the reason why I came to West Lake.

(WL077, male, 25–34, tourist)

These three examples show that the reasons those visitors gave for coming to West Lake are linked to their personal understanding or imagination of the site. The reasons they were attracted to West Lake drew on their personal or collective memories. They wanted to reminisce and remember those memories during their journey. For instance, WL077 listed Yang Wanli and Su Dongpo's poetry which all Chinese students learned about in primary school. The poems that praise the West Lake culture and natural beauty are important chapters in the textbooks used in Chinese elementary and junior high schools. During the tour of West Lake, tourists encountered the scene and recalled the beauty of West Lake in their memory. Those collective memories facilitate a Chinese sense of feeling that each Chinese person has a personal image of West Lake. Therefore, tourists had their own understanding or imagination of West Lake before they came, while being at the site may facilitate or change their sense of place.

In the most frequent response 31.3% of respondents (22 tourists) referred to their identities or memories when they nominated the reasons they came to West Lake. Examples include:

Well, I come here because of the White Snake TV show. When I was a kid, I was attracted to this show. When I go across the Broken Bridge, I remembered the scene in that show.

(WL044, female, 25–34, tourist)

I came to visit West Lake because of Yue Fei, who was a famous general who fought against the Jurchen invaders in the early Southern Song Dynasty. I respect Yue Fei; he is my hero; I want to see the place where Yue Fei lived before. I spent a whole day in Yue Fei's Tomb, although I already know everything about him [...] It is a kind of feeling you can gain by visiting the site where Yue Fei had lived before.

(WL040, male, over 65, tourist)

I come from the city of Huizhou in Guangdong province. There is another West Lake in my city, to which Su Dongpo also made a great contribution. I would like to compare the similarity and differences between the two places.

(WL062, male, 25–34, tourist)

WL044 said that her memory of the White Snake TV show was the key reason that brought her to the site. Her sense of place was elicited by her memories. WL040 said that Yue Fei was his idol and had a significant influence on his life. He did not care about the aesthetic view of West Lake; instead, he commemorated his memories by visiting the site. WL040 considered that physically being at the Yue Fei Temple was important for him, noting that 'it is a kind of real feeling.' The 'real feeling,' the emotional authenticity of this feeling (Bagnall 2003), was linked to his sense of nationalism. As every Chinese person knows, Yue Fei is considered an ancient patriot who has had great symbolic meaning for Chinese nationalism for generations (James 1972). The origin of his sense of nationalism is linked back to collective memories and his personal identity. Heritage for WL040 is not only a physical place but also a process of spirituality-seeking. The responses from WL044 and WL040 support Smith's (2012: 214) argument that reminiscing and remembering are significant activities or reasons that tourists come to visit heritage sites. The responses from WL062 illustrate that visiting West Lake was linked to their personal identities and that they simply wanted to see or experience the cultural or natural differences between West Lake and where he came from.

In addition, seven visitors (10.9%) went to the site to enjoy the modern city or see how the modern city merged into historical settlements and landscapes. Examples have been used in Chapter 3 (p. 97, WL038, WL067, WL075, WL072) to support the argument that West Lake as a continuously changing landscape.

Tourists were also asked about their experiences during their visit to the different sites at West Lake and what those experiences meant to them (Table 4.2). Only 15% of tourists considered that they were having a recreational or touristic experience. The majority of respondents' experiences linked to their sense of place which include experiencing the culture and history of West Lake (28.3%), having positive social connections with local residents (16.7%), engaging empathetic feeling of specific history or with people in the past (11.7%), having spiritual or personal feeling (8.3%), or experiencing negative feeling because of commercialisation or urbanisation changes at West

Table 4.2 What experiences do you value on visiting this site? (N=60)

	Tourists (%)
Experience the culture or history of West Lake/Hangzhou	28.3
Social connection – positive	16.7
Touristic/recreational/happy day out of the site	15.0
Empathy specific history / with people in the past	11.7
Aesthetic	8.3
Spiritual or personal feeling	8.3
Disappointed commercialisation/ urbanisation/ too many visitors crowded-negative	6.6
Others	5.1
Total	100.0

Lake (6.6%). Their sense of place was elicited by visitors' personal (e.g. WL48, WL082, WL021), and/or collective memories (e.g. WL042, WL064, WL122). Examples include:

Personal memories

> I did my undergraduate in Luoyang city which is close to the capital city of the Northern Song Dynasty. I wanted to experience the cultural connection between the Northern and Southern Song Dynasty [Hanzhou was the capital city of the Southern Song Dynasty]. However, I was enjoying the history and trying to imagine [myself] in the Southern Song Dynasty, which is always interrupted by some noisy tour group or canteen that is trying to sell their items.
>
> (WL048, male, 25–34 tourist)

> I am very interested in the culture and history of the Song Dynasty. I did my undergraduate in Kaifeng city which is the capital city of the Northern Song Dynasty. Well, Hangzhou is the capital city of the Southern Song Dynasty. I am so curious [about] the differences between them. In my opinion, the architecture and landscape are very different, where I prefer Kaifeng city where I can feel the cultural atmosphere of the Song Dynasty.
>
> (WL082, male, 25–34, tourist)

> I came to West Lake ten years ago. At that time, I had a very deep impression of the old houses around West Lake and the beauty of the lake itself. I come back here because I want to search the old memories and enjoy the histories and natural beauty that I experienced before. However, I am disappointed. Many old houses had been demolished

around the lake and replaced by commercial facilities. It is no longer the West Lake of my memory any more.

(WL021, male, 25–34, tourists)

Collective memories

The story of "White Snake" is the first thing that comes to my mind. When I was at Broken Bridge and Leifeng Pagoda, I felt very romantic, because of Xu Xian and Bai Niangzi's story.

(WL042, female, 18–24, tourist)

Yue Fei is my idol. I just watched a TV show called '精忠岳飞 The Patriot Yue Fei,' and I watched several times, every time I dissolved in tears. I thought it was a shame that the King in the Southern Song Dynasty killed such a hero, a good person [Yue Fei]. Why did such a glorious Kingdom [Southern Song Dynasty] decay? I think the leader of a country is significant for the past and present.

(WL064, male, 35–44, tourist)

Well, the West Lake I used to know is very superficial. I have a deeper understanding of the site during my visit. For example, I thought Leifeng Pagoda was just architecture related to the White Snake story before my visit. Now I understand the more in-depth knowledge that Leifeng Pagoda is a Buddhist pagoda that had collapsed in 1924 during the Republic period and only the solid brick body remains. When I was standing in front of the remains of the old Leifeng Pagoda, I thought how much wisdom our ancestors had, with their pursuing a peaceful Buddhist philosophy, rather than superficial things that we require today such as desire and money. I will come to West Lake again to learn more I did not know before.

(WL078, female, 18–24, tourist)

I have been to the house of Yuqian[1] and Hu Xueyan,[2] I also went to the 'Xiling Seal Engravers Society.' When I was in my twenties, I had dreamed of these places, in particular, the 'Xiling Seal Engravers Society,' which represents the earliest Chinese national academic institution on the research of epigraphy, sphragistics and seal-engraving. I glad to see the development of this institute over the last ten years.

(WL122, male, 55–64, tourist)

WL048 and WL082 compared Hangzhou to the cities they were living or used to live in, which represents their sense of belonging invoked by visiting another place that has a similar or interlinked historical or cultural background. WL021 expressed his disappointment because of the economic changes of West Lake and offered nostalgic memories of a past that was 'better' than the present. The positive experiences when he first visited West Lake engendered a very pleasant memory. This memory influenced his visit at the time I interviewed him. However, the performance of his second visit also engendered a new memory. As Smith (2006: 154) pointed out, heritage is a 'theatre of memory' (Samuel 1994), 'in which the performance of remembering is not only about the past, but also specifically about the creation of new memories that may be returned to and remembered off-site.' Unfortunately, for WL021 these new memories were disappointing.

WL078 took away memories of his sense of wonder and humility generated by physically being at the site (standing in front of the remains of the old Leifeng Pagoda). WL122 reflects that he had a strong sense of belonging that was linked to his sense of national identity, which was tied to his collective memories. The response from WL064 reflects that he deeply empathises with Yue Fei's experience in the past which is linked to his recent memory. The interesting thing is that when I approached him to be interviewed I waited for a long time, as he was taking photos of Yue Fei's sculpture from different

Figure 4.1 Yue Fei's sculpture in West Lake Museum (photo by Rouran Zhang)

angles in the West Lake Museum (Figure 4.1). Physically being in the site elicited a deep emotion of sympathy. Indeed, as I interviewed him about his reasons for visiting West Lake, his initial reason was his sense of searching for a lost familial identity (see above questions). During the time he visited, his sense of place had been changed and linked to different personal memories, while new memories were created. His experience of heritage was about different memories overlapping, which created his sense of heritage. WL042 talked about the sense of feeling, and they explicitly knew what this feeling is. WL042's sense of feeling was also invoked by 'being in the Broken Bridge,' and she felt a particular romantic sense of his link to her collective memories of the 'White Snake' story.

The performativity of the visit to a heritage site was about remembering and reminiscing. It was about remembering the social and cultural values that constitute their social place in Chinese society. Some responses from interviewees, such as WL021 and WL064, reflected that their sense of place was not only about remembering the past but was also influenced by their experiences in the present. The sense of place entangled with their sense of feeling helps to create new memories during their visit. The new memories could be positive or negative. Nevertheless, it reinforced their sense of the place which could be remembered later. A heritage site is not only a physical place but is tied to the process of remembering and reminiscing.

The above responses show that these tourists' experiences at a heritage site are not necessarily passive, nor primarily linked to receiving educational or aesthetic information, as the AHD might expect. Significantly, no respondents nominated education as a key issue during their visit. They come to a heritage site not to be educated, but to explore their own identities in a range of different ways. Their performances at heritage sites confirm what Smith (2006, 2012) has argued can be summarised as 'embodied acts of remembrance and commemoration, which are about negotiating and constructing or reconstructing a sense of place, belonging and understanding in and of the present' (Smith 2012: 213). In the next section, I will discuss one of the key themes that emerged from this research – tourists' sense of feeling

Sense of feeling

Questions were asked of domestic tourists about the 'experience' they gain from their trip, 'messages' they take away from sites, and their perspectives on tourism. More than one third of domestic tourists interviewed on-site (23 of 64 tourists) were more overt in acknowledging that they were having or seeking feelings, and they explicitly expressed their feeling in a more self-conscious way than so far recorded in Western contexts (Cameron and Gatewood 2000,

2003; Poria et al. 2003; Smith 2006). Some of the tourists were clearly aware they were seeking a sense of 'feeling' through an encounter with the physical site. For example:

> [...] I had a kind of feeling about the lifestyle of the Ming and Qing dynasties from visiting Beijing. The reason I come to West Lake is that I want to feel or experience the culture and customs of the Song dynasty. When I walked on the Su crossway, my imagination automatically linked to the scene when Su Dongpo was walking on that Crossway as well. It is a very real feeling.
> (WL010, male, 18–24, tourist)

> If we hypothesise that West Lake is a man who has feelings, and someone came to West Lake just because of the reputation of the lake, West Lake would not welcome those visitors.
> (WL049, male, 25–34, tourist)

> [...] the natural beauty of a site can bring me a pleasant aesthetic feeling. However, cultures I gain knowledge of, or I felt from my journey, are more important. It is a spiritual sublimation. When I went to a heritage [site] related to famous people in history, I have been inspired by their story or their spirit.
> (WL027, male, 25–34, tourist)

> During my visit a new place, it is a kind of feeling like time-travel, just like I have been in a particular moment of the story or history.
> (WL042, female, 25–34, tourist)

> Well, each tourist visits West Lake with a different purpose. For example, most people come to Linying Temple to pray. Some of them pray for religious reasons, some may consider spiritual need. It is a form of traditional Chinese culture. People can gain a kind of feeling of religion, spirituality and culture in their journey.
> (WL104, male, 45–54, tourist)

> I have been to Linying Temple many times. I am a Buddhist. I feel very peaceful and quiet in my soul by visiting here.
> (WL099, male, 45–54, tourist)

> Well, I was here with my ex-boyfriend five years ago. At that time, West Lake was beautiful. Today, I come here in the same season [emotional].

However, I just climbed the Leifeng Pagoda, and was thinking about the happiness I had before…

(WL129, female, 25–34, tourist)

Tourists such as WL010 displayed a sense of feeling in trying to engage with the 'atmosphere' of ancient China. His sense of belonging was enhanced by visiting another place that has a similar or interlinked historical or cultural background. WL049's sense of feeling was expressed by the use of metaphor, when he imagined West Lake as a human being, and he engaged in an active empathetic process to imagine West Lake as a person who inspired people's understanding of her stories, rather than a place with a superficial reputation, shows a sensitivity to the emotional aspects of the site. WL027's sense of feeling engendered by his cultural or natural touristic journey meant he could gain 'spiritual sublimation' from celebrities. W042 described an interesting context that her sense of feeling was moving from the past to the present elicited by visiting new places. WL104's sense of feeling was linked to religion or spiritual seeking. WL099 was the only visitor I interviewed who spent more than one month in Hangzhou. He was not interested in the physical objects or sites; rather he was seeking a 'pilgrimage.' In his case, the sense of pilgrimage was underlined by not simply the length he spent at the site, but the degree of his spiritual need. WL129 reflects on her sense of feeling excited by visiting West Lake, tied to her personal memory, and recalling a better time associated with a previous visit.

The sense of feeling was also widely expressed by tourists by quoting the poetry from ancient scholars. For instance:

> I was attracted by Su Dongpo's poetry that '欲把西湖比西子淡妆浓抹总相宜 The West Lake looks like the fair lady at her best. Whether she is richly adorned or plainly dressed.'
>
> (WL083, female, 25–34, tourist)

WL083's sense of feeling was evoked by the poetry before she actually came to the site, and she quoted one of the most popular poems from Su Dongpo's '饮湖上初晴后雨 After rain comes fair sunshine.' Su Dongpo, in this poem, used metaphor comparing West Lake to Xizi, who is one of the renowned *Four Beauties* of ancient China. Some tourists came to West Lake expecting to experience the scene that the poetry described. Their sense of place was stimulated as they felt the metaphor and the meaning in the poetry become entangled with their personal or collective memories. Those memories further influence their emotional engagement and the way they understand the world. I nominated just one poem, but thousands of poems have been written to

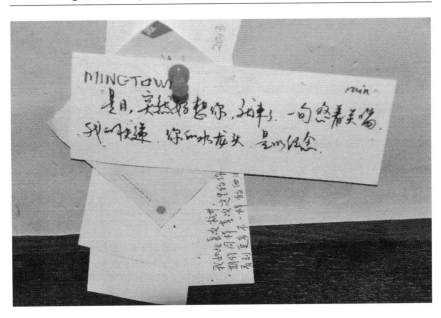

Figure 4.2 Tourists left poems and emotional messages on the message board (photo by Rouran Zhang)

describe the beauty and stories of West Lake by the ancient Chinese. The classical scholars, such as Su Dongpo, created the meaning of heritage in the past, and tourists in the present are creating the contemporary meaning of heritage. As WL115 comments:

> On the message board (Figure 4.2), many tourists had written poems, their emotional message and their stories linking to West Lake or Hangzhou City. Maybe one hundred years later, some of their writing will be famous and documented just like our ancestors before.
>
> (WL115, male 25–34, local)

The sense of feeling is also expressed by some of the tourists metaphorically, though they are explicitly aware that they are constructing their own meaning of heritage and utilising the past in the present. Some of those senses of feeling become entangled with the issue of authenticity. For instance:

> When visiting the Yue Fei Temple, I was thinking why was such a good person executed because of false charges. There is good or evil in the world; sometimes good may take advantage, sometimes not. History is the best teacher. What can we learn from Yue Fei's case today?
>
> (WL040, male, over 65, tourist)

WL040 was aware that being in the Yue Fei Temple allowed him to have an emphatic emotional engagement with Yue Fei's stories from the past, and further influenced his view of the world in the present. The physical authenticity of the Yue Fei Temple triggered his feeling that he was engaging in a dialogue between past and present. However, sometimes visitors' sense of feeling does not link to the physical authenticity of the site. For example:

> On the Broken Bridge and Leifeng Pagoda. I am thinking of the moment Su Dongpo and Baijuyi were writing poetry, and I am right there drinking [wine] with them (laugh).
>
> (WL089, female, 35–44, tourist)

WL089's sense of place drew on their romantic and poetic feelings about The White Snake story. Her feelings were moving between the past and the present, and from the spiritual to the mundane. In her case, being in the physical place allowed her to be spiritually linked to the past in a quite poetic way. This deep intellectual engagement was not evoked by the physical authenticity of the site but was rather influenced by her personal memories and the experiences of her journey.

There is a subtheme of a sense of 'freedom' that links to local people and tourists' sense of feeling. Poria et al. (2003: 248) identified that 'tourists who are motivated by heritage attributes of the sites and considered these attributes as part of their own heritage' have a deeper sense of emotional engagement to the site than those visitors who are motivated by recreation or entertainment. However, interviews with tourists at West Lake show that whether tourists' motivations for visiting the site were for in-depth cultural and historical engagement, or just for relaxation or recreation reasons, they had expressed deep emotional engagement when they felt a sense of freedom during the journey. For instance, some tourists' motivations for visiting West Lake were for recreation to relieve the pressures of work:

> I was sick to see my office and the skyscrapers in Shenzhen. Being in Hangzhou, I can have some fresh air and recharge myself … I can walk along the lake and the river. Walking is the best way to 'feel' West Lake. I do not know how to exactly to describe this feeling. It is a kind of freedom.
>
> (WL012, female, 25–34, tourist)

WL012 indicated that physically encountering the site and particular natural attributes made her feel a sense of 'freedom.' There is a Chinese tradition that many travellers in ancient time such as Bai Juyi and Su Dongpo pursued the

Figure 4.3 The view of 花港观鱼 *Viewing Fish at Flowery Pond* (photo by Rouran Zhang)

beauty of nature to forget reality. Han (2006: 90) used the term '*Shanshui Tour*' to argue that:

> In this travel, there was no bitterness at leaving home, no discontent with reality, no worries about life, and no burden of moral cultivation. The only thing it had was pure spiritual enjoyment obtained from beautiful destinations.

Thousands of poems describe the beauty of West Lake, which have been created by people who tried to engage themselves in nature and escaped from reality during their journey. Therefore, this study argues that some tourists visiting heritage sites are not pursuing something external; rather, they are searching for the feeling of 'freedom.' However, sometimes their sense of freedom is restrained by physical and invisible boundaries. The physical boundaries include 'walls,' 'fences' and 'entrance gates,' while the invisible boundaries are 'entrance fees' and 'government policies.' Some tourists' interviewed on-site showed that to some extent their sense of freedom was constrained by those boundaries. For instance, seven tourists and ten residents complimented the Hangzhou government for removing the entrance fee for the entire area around West Lake.

> I remembered the last time I was walking through the Su Causeway and enjoying the fantastic autumn feeling at the site. When I wanted to visit

花港观鱼 *Viewing Fish at Flowery Pond* (Figure 4.3) where it connects to the Su Causeway, I was blocked by the entrance gate and walls where I had to pay an entrance fee to get in. I suddenly lost my interest in visiting. I think the Hangzhou government did a good thing [to waive the entrance fee]. It is a fantastic journey this time to visit the whole site without seeing those annoying walls and paying entrance fees.

(WL089, female, 35–44, tourist)

I was here 15 years ago. Walls and gates separated West Lake. I had a terrible experience as I had to pay to get into different 'theme parks' around the lake. I did not worry about my money; rather I remembered that I felt West Lake was cut into several pieces by those walls and gates. The Hangzhou government did a good thing removing the walls and opening the gates for free.

(WL099, male, 45–54, tourist)

The greatest management change is that the local government open West Lake for free. Ten years ago, I would only visit West Lake if I had to take my friends for sight-seeing. I had to pay the entrance fee for visiting each park […] Now, I come to those parks around West Lake every week, just like visiting my own garden! It is a feeling of freedom.

(WL030, male, 45–54, local)

The three examples above illustrated that not only the physical boundaries of 'walls,' 'fences' and 'entrance gates,' but also the intangible boundary of 'entrance fees' had interfered with both local people's and tourists' sense of place. Both local people and visitors I interviewed complimented the local government allowing free entrance to West Lake. For the local people, the three examples above reflect a sense of pride the 'free' site had brought to them. It is necessary to stress that the sense of metaphor that tourists were using, and the sense of feelings tied to an in-depth empathetic process, were magnified when they felt they were 'free.' WL089 actively offered a romantic empathetic scene that she was drinking wine with Su Dongpu and Bai Juyi. However, as a return visitor, she also remembered her sense of feeling had been blocked by 'the entrance gate and walls' the last time she visited West Lake. For WL099, his sense of feeling 'was cut into several pieces by those walls and gates.' Therefore, the sense of 'freedom' was key for tourists to register deep emotional engagements when they connected to local people or connected to physical sites. Both the physical boundaries of 'walls,' 'fences' and 'entrance gates' and invisible boundaries such as 'high entrance fees' blocked both tourists and local people's sense of feeling.

Cameron and Gatewood (2003, 2012) argue that the sense of feeling represents something spiritual that is difficult to express, which they refer to as 'numinous.'

Poria et al. (2003) and Smith and Campbell (2015) argue that the sense of feeling is not necessarily spiritual, but is expressive of genuine emotions that facilitate and legitimate certain memories. However, those Western scholars had difficulty in putting interviewees' feelings into words (see also Smith 2012). In Chapter 3 as well as this chapter, I identified many Chinese tourists and local people who were more aware of their sense of feeling than I have found in the Western literature. One of the reasons is embodied in the traditional Chinese view of nature and culture, which has been reinforced in school textbooks, Chinese poetry, traditional Chinese paintings and TV shows so that it infuses both the personal and collective memories of Chinese people. However, tourism is the other significant reason that tourists identified and made sense of their feelings. I identified several types of sense of feelings as I concluded the interview results from West Lake. Firstly, some of the tourists noted that feelings were important. However, they use the term 'feeling' to describe something simply felt rather than clearly articulated, as Poria et al (2003) and Smith (2006, 2012) have identified in Western contexts. An example is WL104, whose sense of feeling was vague, perhaps what Cameron and Gatewood (2003, 2012) identified as 'numen-seeking.'

Secondly, some of the tourists were clearly aware they were seeking a sense of 'feeling,' for example, WL078 (see the following section), whose expression of feeling and genuine emotions linked his interaction with social issues. Another example is WL043 (see Chapter 3, p. 100), whose sense of feeling was expressed aesthetically, when he vividly described the scene of 断桥残雪 *Lingering Snow on Broken Bridge* that 'reflects the scenery that on a sunny day after a heavy snow, the snow on the bridge melts and shows the brown floor, which gives people a feeling that the chain is broken.' In contrast, the ICOMOS experts when evaluating the West Lake World Heritage nomination did not get the feeling of *Lingering Snow on Broken Bridge* at all (see Chapter 3, p. 99, also see Zhang 2017; Zhang & Taylor 2019).

The linkage between the sense of feeling and empathy were identified in many of my interviews. Tourists such as WL096 (see Chapter 3, p. 87), WL027 and WL082 (in this chapter) both displayed a sense of feeling that tried to empathetically engage with the 'atmosphere' of ancient China. Some sense of feeling was romantic or poetic, such as WL089, who referenced vicariously drinking wine with two ancient scholars, and WL042, who was immersed in the romantic scene of the White Snake story. WL040's response was very emotional, his sense of feeling was deeply empathetic with Yue Fei's story and he actively engaged in a dialogue between past and present about 'good and evil.'

The sense of feeling is tied to memories, which are formed from the information we receive all our lives. As noted at the beginning of this chapter, '读万卷书，行万里路 Learn knowledge from thousands of books and accumulate experience by travelling thousands of miles.' However, the above examples,

Feeling a sense of place   125

and indeed all examples in this chapter, demonstrate that being in the site for reasons of tourism not only encouraged tourists' sense of feeling but also clearly magnified whatever that sense of feeling was. Tourism also helps to create a new layer of memories for generating a new sense of feeling. Heritage, therefore, was a place where people felt – and in particular felt connected to something vital, such as a connection to land or connection to their sense of place. In the next section, I will discuss local people's reactions to tourism and mass domestic tourists.

Local people's attitudes to tourism and tourists

A question was asked of residents about the reasons they visit West Lake. Only three local people (4.3%) came to West Lake for educational reasons, while 11 (15.9%) nominated cultural reasons. The majority of responses from local people (55 local people or 79.8%) considered they use West Lake as their 'city park,' a place for leisure. Those leisure activities include enjoying nature or aesthetic pleasure (22 local people or 31.8%), taking physical exercise (e.g. walking, playing Taiji and square dance – ten local people or 14.5%), strolling in the site from work (seven local people or 10.1%), nominating leisure (not specifying what kind of leisure activities – seven local people or 10.1%), reading (six local people or 8.7%) and to see a specific exhibition (three local people or 4.3%). Examples of local people's responses include:

> I usually read in 曲院风荷 *Breeze-ruffled Lotus at Winding Garden*. I remembered the time when I was not married when I passed through this place, it is interesting.
>
> (WL004, female, over 65, local)

> I come here for some fresh air. It is a nice place for reading; I usually read English here. When I get tired, it is interesting to watch visitors walk around.
>
> (WL006, male, 18–24, local)

> I come here because I want to have some fresh air and enjoy the view. When I was over pressured, sometimes, I would come to West Lake in order to release my pressure. You know, West Lake is a touristic attraction, however, it has been seen as a city park from Hangzhou citizen's [perspective]. Although we know everything about the culture of West Lake, and we are very proud of the Lake, we come to West Lake just like taking a walk in our own garden, for recreation.
>
> (WL069, male, 25–34, local)

WL069 simply nominated different leisure reasons they came to visit West Lake. However, their responses reflect their sense of belonging, which elicited a strong sense of pride. WL006 noted that the performances of tourists constituted his sense of place. WL004's sense of nostalgia was linked to her memories. The above responses demonstrated that senses of pride, nostalgia and belonging were very frequently elicited during the leisure process from local people. Local people's sense of pride is important, and is tied to their positive attitudes to mass tourists. This will be illustrated below.

Due to a large number of tourists coming to West Lake, particularly on public holidays, it is necessary to examine to what extent mass tourists influenced local people's leisure activities. A question was posed to them: 'do tourists have any impact on your daily life?' (Table 4.3). Twelve respondents (24.9%) did not think tourists have any impact on their daily life. The majority of local people (54.2%) were willing for tourists to come to West Lake. This included 31.2 % who considered tourists brought economic gain, and 23% of local people nominated tourists brought cultural gain such as enhanced nationalism, local identity and sense of pride, and they were happy to communicate with tourists. In terms of the economic gain, local people considered tourism and tourists to have raised funding that supported positive changes to their sites. Those changes include improvement to water quality, an enlarged lake area, and the creation of a new touristic area such as Xixi National Wetland Park and Jiang Yangfan Park, along with other infrastructural improvements (see Chapter 3, p. 95–98).

More importantly, there were cultural gains from tourism at the site. Local people mentioned that mass tourists come to the site which they were proud of. Some of them were proud of their cultural, historical and physical setting. Some of them were just simply proud to be a citizen of Hangzhou, a city receiving worldwide recognition; some of them hoped people could inherit and innovate intangible cultures such as the Longjin tea culture, silk skills and routines from the Southern Song Dynasty. Finally, some of them were proud of the new developments in the city.

Table 4.3 Do tourists have any impact on your daily life? (N=40)

	Local people (%)
Yes, but doesn't matter. Mass tourists bring economic growth – positive	31.2
No impact	24.9
Yes, represent local identity/proud/nationalism – positive	16.7
Yes, crowded weekend and public holiday- negative	10.4
Yes, happy to communicate with tourists – positive	6.3
Yes, bad traffic conditions – negative	6.3
Yes, mass tourists bring the increased price of food or housing estates – negative	4.2
Total	100.0

Some residents mentioned the negative effects that tourism has. This included increased prices for food or housing (4.2%), bad traffic conditions (6.3%) and crowding during weekends and public holidays (10.4%). The management literature has emphasised the pollution and physical damage to sites that tourism can cause and notes that these impacts can erode local heritage values (Harrison 1994; Swarbrooke 1995; Hall and McArthur 1998; Leask and Yeoman 1999; McKercher and du Cros 2002; Pedersen 2002). This research shows that, although local people at West Lake listed those negative impacts, which are not something that can be ignored, the majority of them nonetheless considered the benefits that tourists contributed to the site carried more weight than the negative impacts. They knew how to minimise those negative impacts. For instance, WL005 and WL058 mentioned that mass tourists had influenced their daily life, particularly during public holidays. However, they did not hate or curse mass tourists; rather they chose to leave the touristic places to the tourists and went to other places instead. The sense of pride that tourists brought to local people has influenced local people's attitudes and performances:

> Mass tourists come to our site, which means that Hangzhou is the best place in China. Everyone has the right to appreciate the culture and nature of West Lake. When they are visiting our site, I am always happy to tell them the stories and about the public transport systems of Hangzhou during their visiting. During the public holiday, we have left the touristic places to tourists. However, we know where to go around West Lake to avoid mass tourists, places such as Yuquan, Huapu and the botanical gardens which are not far from here.
>
> (WL005, female, over 65, local)

> As a Hangzhou citizen, I do not come to the touristic sites at West Lake during holiday seasons. We want to let tourists enjoy West Lake. I think most Hangzhou citizen have done the same thing as me. You know, there are 36 'West Lakes' in China, but our lake is no doubt the most famous one.
>
> (WL058, male, over 65, local)

Some local people want tourists to know about the general stories of Hangzhou, such as the White Snake story, and stories of Yue Fei, Yu Qian and Sun Dongpo etc. Some local people wanted tourists to explore some hidden stories, such as the histories of the Republic period that were ignored or excluded from the Communist harmony discourse. Many local people wanted tourists to be present at the physical sites and feel the poetic or romantic sense of West Lake:

> After their visiting, if tourists say to me 'Hangzhou is gorgeous,' I will be very happy and proud of that. Actually, many tourists told to me that

> 'Well, I want to buy an apartment and settle down around West Lake,' or 'Hangzhou is so beautiful.' At that time, I am heartfelt proud of my city. When some tourists came to ask me 'which places are worth visiting,' I always told them 'everywhere around West Lake.' If you come to West Lake during wintertime, you would understand what *Lingering Snow on Broken Bridge* means; if you arrive at spring, you would see the *Colourful Flower West Lake*, and many couples sitting around the Lake. There are also many activities in the evening around West Lake, tourists and local people were dancing together sometimes. All local people and tourists are happy.
>
> (WL076, female, 55–64, local)

WL076 nominated her sense of pride elicited by tourists who take their time to feel the *Ten Poetically Named Scenic Places of West Lake*, such as *Lingering Snow on Broken Bridge*. Indeed, the interview reveals that both local people and tourists can feel the poetic meaning of West Lake. In addition, the research also shows that tourism had changed the industry structure for local people who lived around West Lake from traditional agriculture to a service industry. These changes facilitated local people's sense of local identities:

> Hangzhou has become an international city because of tourism. Our tea farmers around West Lake used to live upon the traditional farm industry, however, most of us run restaurants and hostels instead. Therefore, we have more spare time to research traditional tea culture. Tourism has not only brought better living quality but also has enlightened us to explore and develop our traditional culture. Tourists coming to our village can be influenced by the tea culture or other cultures of Hangzhou. This is a virtuous circle.
>
> (WL097, female, 25–34, local)

Overall, the survey at the West Lake shows that the majority of local people thought that tourists had brought positive changes, not only the economic benefit or cultural gain as identified above but also a sense of bonding between tourists and local people. As WL051 (female, 18–24, local) states, tourists and tourism 'brought cultural diversity and vividness to the city.' The majority of local people I interviewed were explicitly aware that Hangzhou is an 'international touristic city,' are proud of this title and considered tourists to be significant for the identity of Hangzhou city. From the tourists' perspective, the level of engagement with a sense of contentment seems to appear when tourists feel they have made a connection with local people. For instance:

What I am interested in is the traditional songs from local people. I liked to sit aside West Lake and listened for hours. Their songs represent the characteristics of Hangzhou city.

(WL028, male, 18–24, tourist)

I was impressed by the local people of Hangzhou. They are very kind and give me the feeling that they truly welcome tourists to visit.

(WL078, female, 18–24, tourist)

I was very much enjoying the moment we were boating on the lake. A local was boating for us and told us about history, culture and stories of West Lake during the trip. He is such a good person, and he told us it is his honour to interpret the stories of West Lake and Hangzhou. I have learned about interesting stories and people from West Lake from his interpretation, including the stories of Su Xiaoxiao and Dao Ji monk.

(WL083, female, 25–34, tourist)

Compared to my hometown, Suzhou, Hangzhou is a city where the modern has merged into a traditional setting. The most memorable thing is local people, and they are so kind to me. For example, when we planned to set off, a retired lady came to tell us the best way of visiting. I appreciated this.

(WL118, male, 18–24, tourist)

The above examples reflect how the interactions between tourists and local people elicited a positive social connection between individual tourists and local people, which had a positive and active impact on the interpretation of West Lake (WL083), the city (WL028) or the daily lives of residents (WL118). The study shows the set of interactions or bonding that occur between local people and tourists at West Lake. Local people wanted tourists to 'feel' or experience their sites, and they hoped that the tourists' could invoke a sense of belonging or feeling for the site and engage in communication with local people. In return, tourists enjoyed communicating or connecting with local people as well. There is a strong sense of contentment that emerged when tourists feel they had made a connection with local people.

Dissonant

As part of the World Heritage listing process, a group of local communities were resettled during the development of West Lake. The group of residents was relocated to a residential quarter called '嘉绿苑 Jialvyuan' (Figure 4.4), as it was considered that their presence around the Lake influenced the integrity

Figure 4.4 Residential quarter '嘉绿苑 Jialvyuan' (photo by Rouran Zhang)

of the World Heritage values of the Lake (Yang 2007). There is no academic work concerned with these people, and during my interviews three government officials avoided my attempts to identify the places where they had been moved. Therefore, I had to use my personal relationships to find a vice director of Housing and Urban-Rural Development of Hangzhou who was in charge of this relocation project. However, when I told him I came from a Western university, and the interview was a part of my PhD research, he refused requests for an interview, but nevertheless gave me the address of the settlements the people had moved to, which is located in the city of Hangzhou, 6 kilometres away from the north side of West Lake.

I interviewed those local people (including four retired staff from two state-owned enterprises and one retired soldier) in order to identify the relationship between them and local governments and their attitude to tourists and WH listing. When I asked them about their perspective on the World Heritage nomination, they answered that they are very happy that West Lake was inscribed on the WH listing, as they considered it would mean more visitors would come to enjoy the beauty of the site. However, they did not think that the World Heritage application is the key reason for their being moved. They told me that staff from the local government had made a good offer for them to move, and the staff also complimented their support, which they thought was good for urban development and the World Heritage application. However, all of the interviewees were very unhappy after they moved. Firstly, they complained about the expensive cost of living in the urban area, which local governments had not talked to them about before they moved:

> I do not like it here. The living cost in this area is very expensive, and I have to pay more than 1000 Yuan (equal to 170 US$) per year for property management. My pensions are not sufficient for such an expensive cost of living, where I do not need to pay anything when we lived beside West Lake.
> (WL134, female, over 65, local)

Second, some of them talked about the inconvenience of the new neighbourhood, its lack of sports facilities and public leisure space. They were also very upset with the local government for forgetting them after they moved to this new settlement. For example:

> Local governments used to be very kind to us at the time they ask for our migration. After we settled down to this new place, they have never come back to check whether we were settled or not in the new environment. This area is the public space for us, without big trees and exercise facilities, just a boring playground with ugly sculptures. Another problem is private cars; it is unsafe for our elderly people to live in such a place.
> (WL135, female, 55–64, local)

Third, they complained about the poor public transport system, which means they have to transfer twice to West Lake, where they used to live, for exercise or leisure:

> You know, I am retired. My children are not living with us. My husband and I frequently go to West Lake to do some exercise and chat with our old friends. However, we have to take a bus and transfer once to our destination. It is very inconvenient. I miss my old house. Everything was perfect there.
> (WL138, female, over 65, local)

In addition, they also told me, very emotionally, that they have to build relationships with their new neighbours. It is very important for retired people to have a familiar neighbourhood. For example:

> You know, I had lived in my old place for more than 50 years, it is uneasy for us to move to a new place. I do not know my neighbour. It is very hard to build a new relationship because of high-rise housing. Some of them already have a circle of friendship.
> (WL135, female, over 65, local)

The interviews show that the tension was not caused by the development of tourism; rather the local government did not pay much attention to this group of people, particularly after they were moved. In this section, my interviews reveal that local people's attitudes towards World Heritage Listing and tourism were influenced by their relationship with the government. In contrast to the majority of responses from local people who have a great sense of pride, those marginal local people reflect some dissonance about the WH listing process. As per Ashworth and Tunbridge (1996: 21), the concept of 'dissonant heritage' implies that (see also Graham et al. 2000, 2005):

> all heritage is someone's heritage and therefore logically not someone else's: the original meaning of an inheritance [from which 'heritage' derives] implies the existence of disinheritance and by extension any creation of heritage from the past disinherits someone completely or partially, actively or potentially. This disinheritance may be unintentional, temporary, of trivial importance, limited in its effects and concealed; or it may be long-term, widespread, intentional, important and obvious.

Conclusion

As both Graburn and Barthel-Bouchier (2001: 149) and Ashworth (2009) have noted, tourists are often dismissed within heritage studies as a 'problem' that can only be resolved through the 'education' of visitors as to the meaning and value of heritage (see also Lowenthal 1992; Jokilehto 1995; Hall and McArthur 1998; McKercher and du Cros 2002). The first key theme of this chapter centres on the observation that the national and local Chinese governments, UNESCO experts, and national experts I interviewed reflected this view of tourists as a 'problem' to be resolved. However, officials from national authorities saw the need for tourists to come to sites, as otherwise what was the point of having such sites, suggesting that there is some discomfort or disjuncture with the UNESCO position. They have gone so far as to adopt UNESCO policy about tourism to ensure that they are 'playing the World Heritage game right.' One of the issues of playing the game by the rules of the AHD is that tourists and local communities are not given due consideration. Communities are overlooked, or are spoken for, by experts and tourists are seen as a management issue and not as constitutive of heritage.

International authorities such as UNESCO emphasise that education is one of the significant purposes of heritage tourism (see Pedersen 2002). The majority of tourists to West Lake were not there for education, but rather for the 'feel' of the site. As Coleman and Crang (2002:11) argue, 'tourism is a practice of ontological knowledge, an encounter with space that is both social and incorporates an embodied "feeling of doing".' Being at the heritage site invoked tourists' sense of feeling and was further tied to their various forms of agency, including a sense of empathy, sense of social or family connection and sense of pride, etc. Another dominant concern in international heritage policy is authenticity, in which unregulated heritage tourism is often defined as destructive of the authenticity of a material heritage site. As McKercher (1993) and McKercher and du Cros (2002, 2003) argue, tourists are marketing oriented, they come to heritage sites for cultural education or amusement and the presence of tourists threatens the authenticity of heritage. International authorities have promulgated policies to ensure that 'authentic' heritage can be recognised by tourists. As I mentioned in Chapter 1, ICOMOS promulgated The *Seoul Declaration on Tourism in Asia's Historic Towns and Areas* in 2005 and stresses the 'importance of accurate and aesthetic interpretation and presentation of heritage places for tourism' (Ashworth 2009: 80). Therefore, tourists have been defined as 'culturally inauthentic,' and as passive sightseers, with little or no agency in the meanings they construct at heritage sites. However, the interviews with domestic tourists at West Lake show that the performances of tourists at heritage sites can be mindful and complicated. The respondents often expressed their aspiration to experience authentic experiences. However, these authentic experiences were not only elicited by seeing or experiencing the 'authentic' objects or environment; rather they emerged from a sense of being emotionally engaged by the heritage site during their visit. The emotions and feelings were tied to their memories, and helped them to construct a sense of place and influenced their social experiences in the present. Bagnall (2003) has suggested the utility of the term 'emotional realism,' which reflects the active sense of tourists' engagement, based on her survey at heritage sites in the UK. The tourists who came to heritage sites were not simply 'touring;' they were undertaking 'cultural and social work,' and displaying an active feel for the sites (Poria et al. 2003), remembering and negotiating cultural meanings, as Smith (2006) points out. Therefore, heritage is not only a place with an inherent value derived from the material past, but rather a part of social and cultural processes people can feel at the site, and use to make sense of their identities.

In addition, this chapter also reveals that the majority of local respondents were willing for tourists to come to West Lake. The presence of mass tourists had elicited local people's sense of pride, tied to their local identities and nationalism. Some of them hoped that tourists would gain cultural experiences and enjoy the nature or landscape aesthetic. Some of them wanted tourists to 'feel' West Lake, and they expected tourists' sense of belonging could be invoked by communicating with local people or 'feeling' the site. This is counter to the mainstream of the heritage literature, which focusses on discussing the economic benefits/burdens that tourists bring to local communities (see Butcher 2003; Fisher et al. 2008; Su and Teo 2009; Hitchcock et al. 2010) and local agency in adapting to global tourism influences (see Oakes 1993; Cohen 2000, 2004; Erb 2000; Winter 2007; Su and Teo 2009). This study provides a new vision that residents have remained proud of tourism in their city, and it is because they became aware that tourists enjoyed their journey and 'felt the real West Lake,' which invoked a sense of contentment and further facilitated and magnified local people's sense of pride. Although local people at West Lake listed negative impacts such as inflation of food or housing prices, commercialisation, bad traffic conditions and crowding during weekends and public holidays, and these are not something that can be ignored, the majority of them nonetheless considered the benefits that tourists contributed to the site that are entangled with their sense of pride carried more weight than the negative impacts.

Some respondents considered tourists to have played a stimulating role in the new developments at West Lake. In their opinion, tourism or tourists have changed these sites for the better, not only bringing money to support preservation efforts and new infrastructure but also reinforcing local people's sense of traditional culture and encouraging them to create the new cultural experience of West Lake. In conclusion, this chapter shows that heritage discourse is not only constituted by heritage practice from international, national and local institutions, but also from tourists and local people's discourses and performances, which entangles active senses such as senses of place, feeling and pride.

There are, however, some issues I would like to address. West Lake is located in a prosperous area and represents a mature national tourist market. As I identified in this chapter, tourists come to visit for various reasons, and they are apparently familiar with the site because of history, stories, poetry and TV programmes etc. No tourists nominated that they come to West Lake because of the World Heritage brand. Therefore, the themes I identified may be different in sites located in relatively remote areas, where the World Heritage brand is one of the critical reasons attracting visitors. In the next two chapters, I will address this by analysing another case study, the Ancient Villages of Southern Anhui – Xidi and Hongcun.

Notes

1 Yu Qian (1398–1457), a native of Qiantang (modern-day Hangzhou, Zhejiang province), was a Chinese Defence Minister during the Ming dynasty.
2 Hu Xueyan (1823–1885) was a notable businessman in China during the latter Qing dynasty. He was active in banking, real estate, shipping and Chinese medicine. http://en.wikipedia.org/wiki/Hu_Xueyan

Chapter 5

Cultural moments at heritage sites

> One ordinary autumn morning in 2005, I was walking around Southern Lake. Looking at the peaceful lake, the white houses and their reflections in the water, I began to think that a few days ago, during the 'golden week,' hundreds of tourists were enjoying the view and shooting photos beside the lake. How wonderful was this! Suddenly, all my old memories were back. I still remembered that we were holding evening parties in Nanhu School during the Anti-Japanese War (1937–1945). I also have a strong memory of every villager gathered around the lake in order to produce steel in the winter, 1958.[1] During the Cultural Revolution period, all the houses were covered by Big-character posters, in particular the Nanhu School. Our village is just like a living book, it survives and keeps changing in the past, present and future. I started fantasising about the past and the future of Hongcun. What was the scene when our ancients were building Southern Lake 400 years ago? What was the scene at Southern Lake when children were going to Nanhu School when it just built 200 years ago? What will the scene of Southern Lake be in the future?
>
> (HC052, male, over 65, local scholar; see also Wang 2013:3)

From the perspective of most people, tourism in the 'golden week' means extremely crowded and horrible experiences. However, from this local interviewee's narrative, even the most 'evil' tourism moment became a precious memory and an important opportunity to remember and to speculate about not just the past, but also the future.

As Ashworth (2009) argues, the mainstream heritage tourism literature has tended to revile tourists, perceiving tourism as a product of economic commodification and a 'problem' that creates pollution and physical damage, obscuring or eroding the cultural values of heritage (see also Graburn and Barthel-Bouchier 2001; Smith 2006, 2012). Most importantly, the presence of tourists at sites have been perceived as making sites 'culturally inauthentic' (Sather-Wagstaff 2011; Shackel 2013). They are either characterised as being incapable of meaning-making or disregarded as active agents in the construction of meaning (Ashworth 2009; Hall 2009; Smith 2006, 2012). In this context, tourists are treated as one of the key problematic issues that dominate international authorities' attitudes in the heritage area. This chapter explores the interrelationship between tourism and heritage in a non-Western culture at a Chinese World Cultural Heritage site: the Ancient Villages in Southern Anhui – Xidi and Hongcun. Overall the chapter aims to extend understanding of the way Chinese domestic tourists and residents understand and use heritage sites, and map the interaction between them. Taking my cue from Ashworth (2009: 81), Hall (2009: 89) and Smith (2012:211), I argue that tourists are significant stakeholders in heritage issues, not only from an economic perspective but because they are actively undertaking cultural and social activities by visiting. My research also focusses on the reactions of local people to the intrusion of tourism in their home town. The performances of tourists are diverse and represent transformative 'cultural processes,' as Smith (2006, 2012) has argued, which influences residents' perspectives. Indeed, they sometimes find that interactions with tourists make them proud of their home and strengthens their sense of identity and connection to both material heritage and intangible heritage, which increases their awareness of issues of conservation. In addition, the performances of tourists also influence local governments and how companies from outside the area understand and use heritage sites. Therefore, this chapter discusses and maps the interrelations among tourists, residents, governments and external companies, and then reconstructs the meaning of heritage in this Chinese context.

Xidi and Hongcun – background and tourism development

The Ancient Villages of Southern Anhui – Xidi and Hongcun – are located in the northern and north-eastern part of Yi County in southern Anhui. Xidi is located at the foot of the mountains and built along three streams that enter from the centre, north and east of the village. The history of Xidi dates from 1047 when it was built based on a traditional geomantic theory to represent the shape of a ship that is constituted by 224 ancient traditional buildings (Figure 5.1). The layout of Xidi revolves around three ancestral halls. There is a memorial archway at the main entrance of Xidi, where I conducted most of the interviews with tourists. Four 3-metre-wide streets and three main open spaces in front of the Hall of Respect, the Hall of Reminiscence and the Memorial Archway constitute the framework of its road and public spaces (UNESCO 2000c).

Hongcun is situated at the foot of Leigang Mountain and faces two streams. There is a remarkable 400-year old artificial water system which determines the

Figure 5.1 The view of Xidi (photo by Rouran Zhang)

Figure 5.2 The view of Hongcun (photo by Rouran Zhang)

Cultural moments at heritage sites 139

Table 5.1 Statement and inscription reasons of Xidi and Hongcun

	Xidi	Hongcun
History	Began in 1047 AD (history of about 965 years)	Began in 1131 AD (history of about 875 years)
Population	About 420 households, more than 1300 residents (blood ties linked the inhabitants living in Xidi, and a single family name 'Hu' is shared by the majority of the residents of Xidi)	About 400 households, more than 1200 residents (blood ties linked the inhabitants living in Xidi, and a single family name 'Wang' is shared by the majority of the residents of Hongcun)
Area	12.96 hectares	19.11 hectares

Justification for inscription

(iii) 'The villages of Xidi and Hongcun are graphic illustrations of a type of human settlement created during a feudal period and based on a prosperous trading economy.

(vi) In their buildings and their street patterns, the two villages of southern Anhui reflect the socio-economic structure of a long-lived settled period of Chinese history.

(v) The traditional non-urban settlements of China, which have to a very large extent disappeared during the past century, are exceptionally well preserved in the villages of Xidi and Hongcun'

(UNESCO 2000b)

(Source: Data from the UNESCO website, official websites of Yixian County, (www.yixian.gov.cn) and Xidi (www.xidi.cn), and the author's interview data.)

layout of the village and is composed of water channels that flow through every household in the village, private water gardens, and two ponds called Moon Pond and the South Lake, inside and outside the village (Figure 5.2). Local people believe that Hongcun was built according to the traditional geomantic theory of bionics as an ox, with the water channels representing its intestines, the Moon Pond representing its stomach, the South Lake representing the ox's belly and the buildings the skin and muscle.

Xidi and Hongcun share many similarities in terms of their geographical setting and a similar cultural background, and the ancient buildings are defined as 'epitomes of the architectural style in the Anhui region, presenting strong local features in overall arrangement, style and techniques' (UNESCO 2000c:15). Table 5.1 outlines the characteristics held in common between the two villages.

The two villages were highly praised by the experts from ICOMOS and inscribed on the World Heritage list in 2000 at the 24th session of the World Heritage Committee meeting in Cairns, Australia. As I reviewed the nomination dossier of Xidi and Hongcun, I noted that the international authorities' interests focussed on the street patterns, the architecture and decorations, and the integration of houses with the comprehensive water systems (UNESCO 2000a; see also Ying and Zhou 2007: 99). This objective understanding of heritage is based, as Labadi and Long (2010: 74) argue, on a set of Eurocentric values which suggest that heritage represents the 'original – material, workmanship, design and setting of the site' (Labadi and Long 2010), which helps inform the development of the authorised heritage discourse. As Smith (2006, 2012) and Waterton (2010) argue, the AHD defines heritage as a material, finite, fragile and non-renewable resource that current generations must take care of for future generations, and it is a discourse that frames both Western national and international policies to protect and interpret sites. The limitations in defining heritage created by the Western AHD has been identified in a range of Asian contexts (Byrne 1991, 2009; Winter 2014; Dewi 2016 amongst others). In China, Ying and Zhou (2007), Gao and Woudstra (2011) and Xu et al. (2012, 2014) have pointed out that officials and experts have power over the decision making of heritage issues in Xidi and Hongcun and tend to neglect local participation. Therefore, according to Gao and Woudstra (2011), heritage objects and sites in Xidi are treated as if frozen in time and space, like museum objects, displayed behind glass, but not engaged with (see also Xu et al. 2012, 2014). Comparing the tourism process in Xidi and Hongcun, they criticise UNESCO's definition of 'authenticity,' which focusses on the original materials and designs, and support the management mode in Hongcun which sees local communities more actively engaged in the process of constructing heritage, even if it goes against international and national policies of authenticity. However, their arguments focus on how local communities are engaged in constructing material heritage objects in order to attract more tourists to the site. They omitted the issue of why local people actively engaged in rebuilding and innovating in their gardens in Xidi and Hongcun. This key issue is tourism, as shown below.

In terms of tourism, Xidi and Hongcun share many similarities in terms of population size, economic and socio-cultural conditions, as well as tourist attractions. However, there are dramatic differences between the processes of tourism development. In September 1986, a commercial tourism business started in Xidi, leading to steady growth in tourist numbers and income. The increasing tourist income led to local communities considering the question of how to develop a better plan for their own tourism business. In 1993, Xidi Village established the Xidi Tourism Service Company, run by a locally elected village committee to manage the entire tourism business (Liang and Wang, 2005; Chen 2005; Ying and Zhou 2007). The number of tourists increased from 147 in 1986 to 33,800 in 1993. The Tourism Bureau of Yixian County tried to take charge of Xidi's tourism authority; however, its efforts were strongly rejected by the local community (Liang and Wang, 2005; Ying and Zhou 2007). In 2000, World Heritage listing was seen as a major tourist attraction, with inscription of sites leading to increased visibility through newspaper, TV and other media, which led to the numbers of tourists dramatically increasing from 250,000 in 2000, to 300,000 with ticket-sale revenue of US$1.125 million in 2001 (Ying and Zhou 2007). Visitor numbers reached 800,000 and earned US$5.48 million from the sale of entrance tickets in 2012 (the Xidi government 2013a).

As the Tourism Service Company belongs solely to the Villagers' Committee of Xidi, local people share a large proportion of the tourism revenue (Liang and Wang 2005). According to Liang and Wang's research, the allocation of the ticket sale revenue to local people was nearly 80% in 2002 (Liang and Wang 2005: 29). However, my research shows that the figures for the allocation of the ticket sale revenue for local people were 4 million RMB (equal to US$64,000), which accounted for 11.7% of ticket sales revenue in Xidi in 2012. In 2012, there were 16 hostels, 36 restaurants and 143 shops and inns run by local people, and more than 70% of local people were engaged in tourism businesses (the Xidi government 2013b). In the year 2001, after Word Heritage listing, Xidi's average annual income per capita exceeded US$625, while the same figure for the whole of Yi County was only about US$210 (Zhai 2002). Local satisfaction with the benefits of tourism development at that time has been well documented (Zhai 2002; Liang and Wang 2005; Ying and Zhou 2007). However, since 2003, these tourists' numbers and revenue have been exceeded by Hongcun, although Xidi started tourist development much earlier (The Xidi Government 2013c).

In 2012, the revenue from the sale of entrance tickets in Hongcun was approximately US$12.9 million, which was more than twice that of Xidi.[2] Although the villagers in Xidi share a greater percentage of entrance ticket revenue than Honcun, local people in Xidi complained that compared to business opportunities that tourists have brought to Hongcun, ticket-sale revenue is just a small proportion of their annual income.[3] In addition, I was informed by officials from the county and local governments (see interviews with XD092 and XD093), staff from Co. Huihuang Ltd (see interview with XD094) and some local people (e.g. XD005 and XD036) that a state-owned enterprise, Co. Huihuang Ltd, has taken charge of tourism development in Xidi and was responsible for the promotion of the site. Conflicts emerged among local governments, the franchised company, local communities and tourists. The issues will be elaborated in the following management section.

Hongcun village shares many similarities with Xidi; however, its tourism development and operation are very different. The development of tourism in Xidi inspired other villages, including Hongcun, in the 1980s. The local community in Hongcun decided to follow the same route as Xidi, but the local government of Yi County in 1994 forced them to develop a franchise with Huangshan Tourism Development Co. Jingyi Ltd in 1998. This is the subsidiary company of a private Beijing-based tourism company, Beijing Zhongkun Investment Group (Chen 2005; Liang and Wang 2005). Zhang Xiao (2008: 42), the vice director of the Centre for Environment and Development of the Chinese Academy of Social Science, defines franchising as 'government in accordance with relevant laws and regulations, through the mechanism of market competition to choose a public investors or operator to operate and manage the cultural and natural heritage sites within a certain period.' The local government authorised Co. Jingyi Ltd to operate and manage Hongcun for 30 years. Although this company's instant investments in infrastructure and marketing, and professional management methods, resulted in Hongcun quickly becoming a popular tourist destination and exceeding the income of Xidi, conflict among local governments, the franchised company and local communities emerged. The original contract between the local governments and the external company meant that 'the company took away 95% of the ticket income with very limited investments. 4% was given to the local township government, while only 1% was left for the community' (Ying and Zhou 2007: 101). With the dramatic increase in the number of tourists, the local community considered the original contract was unfair, and they submitted a report to the Yi County government, requesting the tourism business ownership arrangement from 2000 be rejected by the county government (Ying and Zhou 2007). In 2001, the majority of local people (730 people, over 60% of the population) signed a further appeal to the Anhui Provincial Court in 2001, indicating that the county government's encroachment of their rights in tourism, which again failed (Ying and Zhou 2007). After several discussions, a final agreement was reached in 2002 that the Co. Jingyi Ltd took two-thirds of the ticket income, and the county government took 20%, the local township government 5%, and the community 8% (Liang and Wang 2005; Ying and Zhou 2007; Xu et al. 2012).

Since 2002, the Beijing Zhongkun Investment Group has kept up investments for tourism development in Hongcun. According to my interview with the head of the village and the managers of Co. Jingyi Ltd, the company built a new road directly linking the Huangshan World Heritage site with Hongcun. They considered that this was the most significant reason that Hongcun's tourism revenue exceeded Xidi's. The Zhongkun Investment Group has also invested money in advertisements for Hongcun. For example, more than US$37 million was paid for the living theatre production called *宏村阿菊 Hongcun A Ju*'. In addition, the company paid a great deal of money for advertising at airports and train stations, as well as through the internet, TV and other media. Furthermore, the Zhongkun Investment Group built some high-standard hotels, developed a new touring route and a business street of handicrafts and special local products (Figure 5.3), as well as upgraded tourism facilities and services. From my interview data, the investments and strategies of the Zhongkun Investment Group

Figure 5.3 Business street of handicrafts and special local products (photo by Rouran Zhang)

have been supported by a majority of local communities.[4] However, tensions still exist among local people, local and county governments, as well as the tourism company. I will further discuss the relations between stakeholders in the management section below.

Since World Heritage inscription, both villages have been the subject of research, most of which has examined the economic or physical impact of tourists on the heritage sites and local communities (Liu 2005; Su et al. 2005; Ying and Zhou 2007; Gao and Woudsra 2011), policy and management issues (Liang and Wang 2005), authenticity issues (Xu et al. 2012, 2014) and the physical and economic influences of WH listing (Chen 2005; Cheng and Morrison 2008). For example, Gu and Ryan (2010) have researched the local communities' attitudes and satisfaction with the intrusion of tourists in Hongcun. They concentrate on demonstrating the emotional linkage between local communities and the architecture and spatial organisation of the town, as well as relationships between neighbours. However, their research focusses only on local communities and does not examine the interaction between tourists and local communities, or how tourists may, or may not, facilitate constructing the local people's emotional links to the place. The research of Xu et al. (2012, 2014) suggested that the issue of authenticity is socially constructed and is an evolving concept. They criticised the way 'authenticity' is approached in Xidi and Hongcun as being object-related, static and with a superficial understanding of international policies, which 'mainly serves for the convenience of administration and reflects the will of community elites and tourists with the power of discourse' (Xu et al. 2014: 805). However, their argument still considered tourism to have a negative effect, which requires the management of authenticity to ensure pleasant or 'authentic' experiences for tourists. Therefore, the current literature considered that professionals, experts and local communities have the right to construct the meaning of heritage, but certainly not tourists, who were continually perceived as a 'problem' to be managed.

Fieldwork

The following research methods were used to produce the data on which this chapter and Chapter 6 are based. They included the following groups of interviews.

Interviews with domestic tourists and residents

Interviews with domestic tourists and residents at Xidi and Hongcun were undertaken during December 2013, with 154 people (Xidi 91 [with 69 tourists and 22 residents] and Hongcun 63 [with 45 tourists and 18 local residents]) interviewed at the sites. The interviews were structured, consisting of a number of demographic questions to determine, among other measures, age, gender, occupation, education and how far they had travelled. These were followed by open-ended questions designed to explore the types of identity and memory work that tourists undertook during their visits and their understanding of World Heritage and tourism. Open-ended questions were also designed for residents to identify local reactions to tourists (see Introduction, p. 15–16).

Interviews were conducted at the main entrances of the villages of Xidi and Hongcun. I also approached local people in Xidi and Hongcun by visiting their houses. I also facilitated my interviews with local people by living in locally run hostels in Xidi and Hongcun. In Xidi I stayed at five different local people's hostels, and four in Hongcun. At each site, I approached visitors and residents to ask if they could spare some time to go through an interview with me. The answers were recorded digitally (unless the visitor objected, then notes were taken). All interviews with visitors and residents were undertaken anonymously and no identifying information was collected. All those interviewed were handed an information sheet telling them about the research, reinforcing my verbal statement that the interview was anonymous and explaining how the information will be used. The rejection rate was about 10% in Xidi and Hongcun. The tendency was that I was rejected more often in crowded areas and busy times. I intended to undertake one-to-one interviews. Sometimes, interviews were also conducted where multiple people (e.g. family or visitor groups) desired to be interviewed collectively. In these cases, each individual was counted as a separate interview as separate points of view tended to be expressed.

Based on the open-ended questions, a random sample of transcripts was read through to define thematic responses. Codes were then devised by the researcher for each theme, and all transcripts were read through and coded. During the transcribing and coding process, the researcher can add new codes and alter codes when new themes emerged which were not covered by the sample, and some codes were collapsed. To create descriptive statistics, the demographic data and the coded open-ended questions were entered into the Statistical Package for the Social Sciences 22 (SPSS 22), which was used to derive descriptive statistics, and cross-tabulations were undertaken against the demographic variables to determine if variables such as gender and age influenced the interview results. Given the small size of the data such cross-tabulations returned no statistically significant results, nor were patterns in the variation of interview results identified. As such the results of the cross-tabulations are not discussed in this chapter.

Interviews with key local government officials from Xidi and Hongcun

Interviews were also conducted with the relevant local government officials who were in charge of the World Heritage nomination and management, which included the vice-head of Xidi town government (XD092), and the head of Xidi village[5] (XD093), on 14 and 16 December 2013, as well as the head and the vice-head of Hongcun Town (HC063) and the head of the Hongcun Village (HC064) on 23 December 2013.

Interview with tourism operators

Interviews were conducted with the vice-head (XD094) and the chief marketing officer (XD095) of the tourism company (Co. Huihuang Ltd) in Xidi on 16 December 2013. I also interviewed the vice-head of the Co. Jingyi Ltd in Hongcun, using the same questions, on 24 December 2013.

Interviews with the Chinese government officials and tourism operators were done confidentially, and material from the interviews has been cited anonymously. The people I proposed to interview were first approached by phone or email. An information sheet and consent form detailing the research, its aims, the ways in which the information from the interview was to be used, the questions to be asked etc, were emailed to the interviewee prior to the interview. A transcript of the interview was provided to the interviewee. Any material quoted in research publications has been verified before publication with the participating interviewees. The open-ended questions I asked in these interviews are listed in the Introduction, p. 15–16):

Observations

Observations of visitors were undertaken at the Xidi and Hongcun tourist sites to observe what tourists 'do' at these sites and to observe how local people and tourists interact. The data was recorded photographically and by note-taking. Observations were only undertaken in public open spaces at and around both heritage sites. This method was useful to map the interrelationship among different stakeholders. I also reviewed the tourists' messages in the message boards and message books in local. The data was recorded photographically (with 73 photos recorded).

In addition, I participated in three different tour groups in Xidi from 14 to 24 December 2013 (with 123 minutes of recorded data); I also joined five different tour groups in Hongcun from 20 to 22 December 2013 (with 204 minutes of recorded data). The aim of observing the tours was to identify the focus of the tourism company's interpretation and to observe tourists' interests and performances during the tour.

Tourists and cultural moments

A total of 69 tourists were interviewed in Xidi: 59.4% (41) were male and 41.6% (28) were female. Those aged 45–54 were the most frequent (33.3%) age group encountered followed by people over 25–34 (26.0%) and 35–44 (18.8%). The educational attainment of most visitors was high, with 69.4% of visitors having some level of university education. The majority (56 respondents or 81.2%) of tourists were visiting Xidi for the first time, while 13 (18.8%) were return visitors. Just over half, 56.7%, had travelled from a holiday address and just 43.3% from a home address. A total of 52 visitors (76.5%) travelled with their families/friends/tour groups and just 16 (23.5%) travelled by themselves. The majority (98.6%) of visitors had planned to visit in Xidi for less than three days. Only one (1.4 %) tourist had planned a longer visit of more than a week.

Of the 45 people interviewed in Hongcun, 23 (51.1%) were male and 22 (48.9%) were women. The frequency of age groups within the interview sample illustrates that age 25–34 were the most frequently interviewed group, followed by 18–24. More than three-quarters (75%) of visitors possessed some level of university education. The majority (86.7%) of tourists were on their first visit to Hongcun and only six (13.3%) were return visitors. A total of 21 respondents (46.7%) had travelled from a holiday address, slightly lower than those who had travelled from a home address (53.3%). Most of the tourists (86.7%) travelled with families/friends/tour group; only six people travelled alone. The majority (95.6%) of visitors had planned to visit Hongcun for less than three days. Only two (4.4 %) tourists had planned a longer visit of more than a week.

Cultural moments at heritage sites 147

Table 5.2 What are your reasons for visiting Xidi? (Total, N=113; Xidi, N=68; Hongcun, N=45)

	Xidi (%)	Hongcun (%)
Represent traditional architecture or landscape Feature of the Huizhou	47.1	24.4
Traditional Hui cultural reasons	17.6	20.0
Recreation/leisure	14.7	20.0
Aesthetic reasons	2.9	17.8
Come to visit Mount Huang Shan, just dropped by here.	7.4	8.9
Other	2.9	8.9
Total	100.0	100.0

In Chapter 4, I identified tourists as having agency in a way that is often not described in the literature, which tends to see tourists as superficial, inauthentic, destructive and culturally ignorant (Graburn and Barthel 2001). I also identified several themes, including a strong sense of feeling and connection between tourists and local people, which emerged at West Lake. However, West Lake is the most popular tourist destination in China and was well-known by most tourists before its World Heritage listing (Luo et al. 2018). The tourist experience in Xidi and Hongcun, and tourists' interactions with local people, might be entirely different. This chapter further explores those themes in the context of Xidi and Hongcun, which are relatively small and remote heritage sites compared to West Lake, where World Heritage listing has dramatically increased tourist numbers in both villages. A total of 12 open-ended questions were asked of tourists at Xidi and Hongcun. Given the wealth and complexity of the interview data generated, it is not possible to detail all the data; thus, what follows is necessarily a selective representation of the key themes and issues derived from analysing a few of the key open-end questions. Further details of the research findings appear elsewhere (Zhang 2017b).

The first key question I asked tourists is 'what are your reasons for visiting Xidi/Hongcun?' (Table 5.2). Only ten (14.7%) and nine (20%) tourists in Xidi and Hongcun respectively responded that they simply went for recreational reasons. Most frequently (47.1%) and (24.4%) tourists responded that they had come to visit the traditional architecture or landscape features of the Huizhou. For example:

> I am not here for touristic reasons. I come here to appreciate the traditional Hui architecture.
>
> (XD079, male, 45–54, tourist)

> I came here because of the traditional Hui buildings. They are original and in very good condition.
>
> (XD015, female, 25–34, tourist)

> It is the traditional Hui buildings. You know, the white wall and black roof have been deeply impressed in my memory. I like this kind of feeling.
>
> (HC018, female, 18–24, tourist)

> I am a website editor. Many tourists have uploaded their own travel experiences in Honcun online in our tourism section. I was attracted by many beautiful images of the landscape and buildings. I have always been interested in traditional Hui buildings. Therefore, I have come here.
>
> (HC026, female, 18–24, tourist)

HC018's interview shows that what brought her to Hongcun was her sense of feeling. Her aesthetic feeling about 'white wall and black roof' was embodied in her personal memories. HC026 indicated that many tourists wrote about their experiences of visiting a place and uploaded to Social Networking Services such as 微博 Weibo, 微信 We chat and 穷游 Qiongyou online. Each visitor has their own stories, experiences and inspirations during their visits, and construct cultural meanings at an individual level, which can, especially through social media, influence other visitors who have not been to the site. As indicated in Chapter 4, some local people (e.g. WL115) talked about tourists in the present who 'had written poems, their emotional message' on the message board, which is the same as ancient scholars writing poetry. Those ancient poems have become a significant part of Chinese culture. HC026 demonstrated that tourists have been using contemporary technologies to create new cultural meanings.

The second key question I asked was 'What experiences do you value on visiting this site?' (Table 5.3). In answering this, only 14.7% and 13.6% interviewees in Xidi and Hongcun considered that they were having a

Table 5.3 What experiences do you value on visiting this site? (Total, N=112; Xidi, N=68; Hongcun, N=44)

	Xidi (%)	Hongcun (%)
Immersion in local cultural, history and intangible heritage	35.3	20.5
Aesthetic (related to architectures/landscape)	20.6	20.5
Touristic/recreational/happy day out at the site	14.7	13.6
Identity/memory work	11.8	20.5
Social connection with local people/friends	4.4	6.8
Compare between Xidi and Hongcun	4.4	9.1
Don't know	2.9	2.3
Disappointed about commercialisation	2.9	4.5
Talking about general experiences in other Chinese heritage sites	2.9	2.3
Total	100.0	100.0

recreational or touristic experience. More than one-third of tourists (35.3%) in Xidi and a fifth (20.5%) in Hongcun considered that they were engaged in the recognition of culture/history/intangible heritage of the site/region. For example:

> I think for some people who are interested in traditional culture or have an abundant humanistic environment, just one or two hours' tour guide is not enough during the tour. For instance, I just received very superficial cultural messages about Xidi after the tour guide's interpretation. If you want to know more about the culture of Xidi, you should stay here at least one day.
> (XD019, male, 25–34, tourist)

> When I walked through these old buildings, I can imagine how grand this building used to be. At the moment, I cannot help but take my mind back to the old Xidi, where generations of Xidi people not only built the representative 'Hui building,' but created a glorious 'Hui culture' that has influenced the Southern Chinese cultural system.
> (XD028, female, 35–44, tourist)

> I have a very deep impression of traditional calligraphy couplets.
> (XD084, female, 45–54, tourist)

> I was impressed by the wood carvings and the decorations of each house, not only the magnificent skills but the implied meaning behind them. For example, the decorations of bats implied happiness. Local people arranged their tables with mirrors and porcelain vases meaning safety and happiness. Every detail of the houses has implied meaning.
> (HC042, male, 45–54, tourist)

These examples illustrate that tourists do not simply have fun during their visits, but have different cultural concerns and interests. XD028 linked the material buildings to the past Hui culture underlined by strong positive emotions. During his visit, his sense of feeling was an empathetic process that created an interesting cultural moment, with a dialogue between the present and the past. Both XD084 and HC042's concerns were about the intangible heritage of the site. HC042 linked the wood carvings and the decoration in a way that reflected China's traditional philosophy of attaching implied meanings to objects.

The next most frequent answer referred to aesthetics, 20.5% in both Xidi and Hongcun:

> Because of aesthetic reasons, I prefer Xidi over Hongcun. You know most of the buildings in Xidi are just like a small museum or art gallery. When you walk through a door, you can see hundred-year-old tree peony in the garden. The tile carving, the wood carving, and any details of the building are so delicate. Some houses may be small, but the contents they contain are abundant. I can feel the beauty of the four seasons, with the melting of snow in the spring, the clear water flowed freely in the summer, and the withered lotus in the autumn.
>
> (HC005, female, over 65, tourist)

> I have a very good memory of when I was at Hongcun thirteen years ago, that is was more natural and open to visitors. However, my experiences in Hongcun this time is just like the product I bought, very commercial. You know, there is a river outside Hongcun. Thirteen years ago it used to be very natural, with beautiful vegetation and soft sand on the riverbank. However, it has turned into an ugly concrete small dam. I think the reason the tourism company and local governments did this is to ensure the water yield inside the village during the dry season. It is stupid and wrong.
>
> (XD022, male, 25–34, tourist)

HC005 expressed her feeling of delight from enjoying the aesthetic view of Xidi. Physically being at the site generated in her a poetic sense of feeling that linked to her imagination of the four seasons. XD022 gave me a depressed emotional response that was linked to his memories of a previous visit. Although he criticised the commercial changes of Hongcun, it was an active process of remembering. Within this remembering process, new memories had been created as well. Indeed, many interviewees, such as HC005 and XD022, who discussed aesthetics, did not only simply nominate aesthetic appreciation, but made an in-depth connection to their feelings and/or personal memory. Their sense of feeling actively created 'live' cultural moments which interwove with the site, the present moment and their memories.

A further 11.8% and 20.5% of tourists in Xidi and Hongcun were doing identity or memory work. Many of them considered collective memories from their background by making physical contact with the heritage site or specific places, for instance:

> The buildings and landscape in my village were similar as they have Xidi and traditional Hui characteristics. However, they no longer exist. I can find my memories from when I was a boy visiting this similar environment.
>
> (XD024, male, 35–44, tourist)

Cultural moments at heritage sites 151

> During this trip, I feel that the landscape of the site represents the strong identity of the Hui culture. My understanding may be different from people who come from a similar cultural background. However, it still arouses my memory of what I used to know of such culture, and this influences my personal emotion.
>
> (XD029, male, 35–44, tourist)

> During my visit, I listened to the interpretation from a tour guide of the history of the ancestral temple of Mr Hu (胡家宗祠) (Figure 5.12), I was thinking that there are hundreds of tourists who walk through this building, but who will think about the stories that have happened in this place or how many memories of local people and tourists have been recorded by the building?
>
> (XD049, male, 45–54, tourist)

> The reason I come here is influenced by my mother, who fondly remembered travelling to Hongcun. And I did have a good time here. Indeed, I was kind of inspired by the conversation when I talked with the hostel owner where I stayed yesterday. I think it is remarkable that Hongcun has inherited its own culture for hundreds of years, even in this commercial environment. It is a very good example of the development of other Chinese old towns.
>
> (HC054, male, 18–24, tourist)

XD024 and XD029 came from different part of China. However, both of them have similar cultural affiliations to the site. Therefore, their sense of feeling had been aroused by seeing the landscape in Xidi that is linked to their personal memories, which invoked a similar sense of belonging. XD049 engaged an empathetic process when the cultural moments he created formed a dialogue between the past and present, between the physical building and tourists. The response from HC054 reflects the interaction between tourists and residents. The interactions I identified in Xidi and Hongcun are more complex than those I analysed at West Lake. I will further elaborate in this chapter and Chapter 6. As Smith (2012: 214) has also indicated, 'Reminiscing and remembering are often cited as important activities at heritage sites' (see also Nora 1989; Urry 1996; Davison 2005; Smith 2006; Anheier and Isar 2011). The four examples illustrate that tourists can have empathetic experiences during their visits, which creates their own cultural moments at the heritage site. Their emotional response reflects their deep engagement with constructing heritage meaning and with the heritage objects or landscape being the media that reinforces their sense of belonging and identities.

Table 5.4 What messages about the heritage or history of the site do you take away? (Total, N=101; Xidi, N=59; Hongcun, N=42)

	Xidi (%)	Hongcun (%)
Immersion in local cultural, history and intangible heritage	37.3	11.9
Aesthetic	15.3	26.2
Feeling/social connection between visitors and local people or visitors themselves	23.8	23.8
No message	13.6	26.1
Passive messages (include local cultural and history, intangible heritage, values, either natural or cultural preservation messages)	8.5	9.5
Other	1.7	2.4
Total	100.0	100.0

The third key question I asked was 'what messages about the heritage or history of the site do you take away?' (Table 5.4). More than one-third (35.6%) of the tourists in Xidi took away messages that demonstrated acknowledgement or recognition of the history and culture of the site or the region, while only 14.3% interviewees took away this message in Hongcun. For instance:

> I am interested in the traditional buildings of Xidi, which uses wood as the framework of a building rather than concrete. They also represent typical traditional Hui Chinese architecture. I am an architect. You know, many concrete buildings collapsed during the earthquake, however, this wooden framed traditional building survived for hundreds of years. Our ancients built these wood buildings with old technology and considered '风水 *Fengshui*'. I think I might be inspired by them.
>
> (XD046, male, 25–34, tourist)

> During the trip, I understand the profound traditional culture in Xidi. I think the traditional Confucianism was strongly influenced by their career choice, with the majority of the villagers' ancestors engaged in official careers.
>
> (XD012, female, 25–34, tourist)

> I come to Xidi and Hongcun just for recreational reason. I took many pictures and enjoyed the view in Hongcun. I did not shoot many photos today because the buildings and landscape in Xidi are similar to Hongcun. However, I was impressed by the cultural accumulations in Xidi. For example, the traditional calligraphy couplets implicate the philosophy of Chinese traditional culture.
>
> (XD020, female, 55–64, tourist)

XD012 and XD020's interests focus on traditional Chinese culture. While XD046 had taken messages relating to his architectural background and in-depth understanding when he uses the word inspired he shows his respect for the traditional culture or knowledge. In Hongcun, the most frequent response to the question (26.2 %) was aesthetic, while this represented only 15.3% of the response in Xidi. However, there are still more than a quarter of tourists (23.8%) in both Xidi and Hongcun who took away messages related to feeling or social connection. For examples:

> Just like I went back to ancient times.
>
> (HC016, male, 18–24, tourist)

> You know, many local people have run family hostels, restaurants and shops. I communicated with some of the shop owners what their concerns are, how to sell the local products such as bamboo and stone carving or local books which introduce the culture and intangible culture to me with a high price. I understand their living depends on tourism. However, I think there should be a good way to disseminate histories, culture, and intangible things to visitors rather trade culture like a commodity.
>
> (XD044, female, 18–24, tourist)

> Compared to Hongcun, which has already become a commercial place, Xidi is my preferred choice for visiting. I have a feeling that Xidi is alive. Local people are doing their own activities in their old houses which were built over 200 years ago. I can see many preserved ducks hanging under the roof, and I can feel the slight smoke curling up from kitchen chimneys.
>
> (XD047, female, 24–35, tourist)

> You know, when I communicated with local people, they are very proud of the achievements of their ancestors. I agree with that. However, times are changing. They are selling the culture that was created by their ancestors to visitors.
>
> (XD027, male, 45–64, tourist)

> There is a simple poster posted on the wall of a resident's house (Figure 5.4), which indicates that the house owner is going to butcher a pig and hopes that villagers will come to buy fresh meat at that time. It is funny, very alive. I walked into a villagers' house and I saw six big pumpkins. I asked the house owner whether he can give me the head of one big pumpkin that I want to use to make a seal. He was very generous and gave it to me.
>
> (HC005, female, over 65, tourist)

154 Cultural moments at heritage sites

Figure 5.4 Poster posted on the wall about 'butchering a pig' in Xidi (photo by Rouran Zhang)

Well, I met a local who took me to visit his house. I was impressed by the courtyard, the kitchen, and the fishing pond and the surroundings of the house. I said to him that I would come to stay for about two months when I have a vacation. I started to fantasise the scene when I would wake up on a quiet morning, and then go to the morning market to buy fresh vegetable and have a nice breakfast. After that, I take my drawing paper sitting in the courtyard to do some sketches. How wonderful it is!

(HC040, female, 25–34, tourist)

The responses from XD047 and HC005 illustrated the close interrelations among tourists, local people and the physical heritage site. Both XD005 and HC040 are deeply engaged in communicating with local people and they also listed unremarkable details such as 'preserved ducks hanging under the roof' and 'draft poster,' which influence their personal emotions. In this situation, both of them had actively created cultural moments, which represent close interaction among tourists, local people and the physical heritage site. XD044 and XD027 expressed depressed emotions because they were unsatisfied with the commodification of the site. HC016's response was simple but interesting: while they visited the site in the present his mind was connected to the past. The above responses show the different forms that tourists use to communicate or interact with local people. There is a strong sense of contentment that emerged when tourists feel the 'alive' things related to local people such as 'preserved ducks hanging under the roof, and I can feel the slight smoke curling up from kitchen chimneys,' the poster about the day and time the local people were going to butcher a pig, or just simply talked to local people.

Discussion – comparison of Xidi and Hongcun

It is worth remarking on the findings outlined above which show differences between the responses in the two villages. Recreation and aesthetics tend to be more frequently cited at Hongcun than Xidi, which in turn more frequently elicited a sense of cultural recognition and remembering. Why were tourists' responses distinct in these two villages, which share similarities of physical setting and cultural background? One of the significant reasons is the degree and intensity of how the concept of World Heritage and its management was used to frame tourism and heritage practices in the two villages. Both local governments and the tourism company in Hongcun considered heritage as aesthetically pleasing physical objects or/and landscape that is non-renewable, which required them to protect the site in order so it may be inherited by future generations. This is illustrated by my interview with the head (HC063) and the vice-head (HC064) of Hongcun on 12 December 2013. When I asked the question 'What does World Heritage mean to you?', he answered:

> The inheritance of objects from our ancestors. We have a responsibility to protect them for the future generation. In terms of Hongcun, we have to ensure the integrity of the building and the water system ... and obey relevant rules and regulations base on international standard.
>
> (HC064, vice-head of Hongcun)

In this sense, the local governments and the tourism company have constructed a systemic hierarchy of meaning-making in order to impose their understanding of heritage to tourists through narratives from tour guides and advertisements. In this sense, the local governments and the tourism company have constructed a systemic hierarchy of meaning-making in order to impose their understanding of heritage on tourists through narratives from tour guides and advertisements. I interviewed the head of the Co. Jingyi Ltd (HC065), which is the governments' authorised external tourism management company, and asked what changes Co. Jingyi Ltd brought to Hongcun. He answered:

> We have brought an advanced management mode since 1998. Firstly, village-based management did not have training systems for tour guides and other tourism management positions before our company took charge. After we had signed a 30 years' contract with County and local governments, we recruited a team of tour guides from Yi County with advanced training programmes. Second, in 1998 our company invested 20 million RMB (equal to US$3.22 million) in order to improve the water quality, repair or redecorate the traditional houses and build parking lots and hotels. Thirdly, we have kept advertising on TV, newspapers, internet. We also used an opportunity with the movie *Crouching Tiger, Hidden Dragon* directed by Ang Lee in 2000,[6] which shot in Hongcun to advertise the beautiful views of Hongcun to an international audience. In addition, our company also promoted Hongcun's inscription on the World Heritage list. During the listing process, we invited experts to help us to make a 40-year development plan, which provided a framework for the nomination dossier. We have also encouraged local people to inherit their traditional handicrafts. For example, we provided funds for the tourism office of the county government to organise a competition of tourism handcrafts in 2000.
>
> (HC065, head of Co. Jingyi Ltd)

His response shows that external capital has brought funds for the infrastructural improvements, improving tour guide systems and advertising and encouraging traditional handicraft. However, the primary aims of management were to enhance the aesthetics of the village. I attended five different tour groups from 20 to 22 December 2013 (with 204 minutes of recorded data). I observed that the interpretations from the company trained tour guides mainly focussed on describing the beauty of the landscape, the grand nature of the traditional buildings and identifying the metaphors of the decoration of buildings. Although tour guides did identify the history and customs of the village, their descriptions were nonetheless focussed on the material objects. I interviewed a local scholar (HC028) who has criticised the local governments and the external company, noting that:

I think the most important thing for World Cultural Heritage is how to develop sustainable use of the site, [rather than] old-style experts concerned about maintaining the physical objects. In my opinion, World Cultural Heritage is not a patient that needs to be taken care of by governments; rather it is a cultural product. This cultural product produces economic effects, which local people, local governments and tourism companies can benefit from. Culture is the soul of heritage. The tourism company can disseminate culture by advertising. However, no matter how much the company invests, it is just like your clothes, very superficial. In terms of Hongcun, I think … of course, it is important to protect our existing architecture which represents the milestones and the carriers of our culture. However, the protection is not simply for physical building or decorations that we can see. Intangible culture and customs also need to be considered. I am worrying that we are using the culture which was created by our ancestors for living. However, we are not developing our own culture. Fifty years later, there are just so-called 'old buildings' in Xidi without souls.

(HC028, male, 54–65, local scholar)

The local governments and the external capital in Hongcun ignored local perceptions of heritage and, in turn, these tourists focus on the material and aesthetics and tend not to mention culture. In Hongcun the management and interpretation of the World Heritage sites are framed by the AHD and tourists seem to be passive receivers of this framing. The management authorities in Hongcun, using the UNESCO influenced AHD, deliver strong messages about the aesthetic and object-related values of heritage, which influence the individual and collective remembering at the site.

The Xidi World Heritage site was run by local people for more than 20 years. Although in mid-2013 the state-owned enterprise Co. Huihuang Ltd took charge, the new tourism company had, at the time the interviews were undertaken, limited influence on existing tourism management. Tourists I interviewed more frequently elicited a sense of culture and remembering in Xidi than in Hongcun. For example, XD047 considered Hongcun a commercial place, while identifying Xidi as 'alive:' 'Compared to Hongcun, which had already become a commercial place, Xidi is my preferred choice for visiting. I have a feeling that Xidi is alive.' However, the understanding of heritage from local governments and external companies is similar to that of the authorities in Hongcun, as they still focus on material objects. The most important thing that has caused such differences between Xidi and Hongcun is that the AHD, in framing the management of Xidi, was not as successful as in Hongcun. Firstly, compared to Hongcun, the Xidi Tourism Service Company did not advertise as much as the Hongcun company. Many local people pointed out this issue, for example:

> Hongcun's tourism management is much better than us, which the private company has invested a lot of money on advertising. Many tourists who live in my hostel told me that they found many advertisements of Hongcun online, but few are about Xidi.
>
> (XD036, female, 35–44, local)

Secondly, Zhongkun Investment Group (Co. Jingyi Ltd) has developed a more efficient tour guide system than Xidi.[7] The influence of the AHD within the Xidi tours was not as explicitly identifiable, with slightly less emphasis placed on aesthetics, and thus the AHD was not as strongly present in the tour guide interpretations as at Hongcun. It is possible that this allowed tourists to have a more individually authentic response to visiting Xidi, and allowed greater space for them to develop observations of the site outside of the received AHD messages from authorities. As XD019 mentioned above, 'just one or two hours' tour guide interpretation is not enough during the tour,' and required more cultural engagement as they had experienced at Hongcun.[8]

The management authorities in both Xidi and Hongcun were primarily concerned with the protection of material objects. They also used their power to educate tourists to appreciate the aesthetic and cultural values of the sites. Dominant heritage tourism studies and practice consider tourism as inauthentic. This concept is derived from MacCannell's (1973, 1999) argument that 'tourism is the doomed search for the authentic' (Smith 2012: 211). Following from this conceptualisation literature on heritage tourism often defines tourists as mechanistic and tourism as market-oriented (Graburn and Barthel-Bouchier 2001; Smith 2006, 2012; Ashworth 2009). This difference between the two sites is interesting and shows the extent to which the intensity of marketing and interpretation can influence tourists' responses to a site. However, it also needs to be noted that while there was a difference between the two sites, there are similarities as well. It is also important to note that not all tourists were necessarily influenced by the management emphasis on the AHD and many constructed their own meanings – and that this happened at both sites.

Conclusion

This chapter reviewed previous scholars' research of Xidi and Hongcun after the World Heritage designation, in which they clearly identified that World Heritage designation brought dramatic increasing of tourism development in both villages (Zhai 2002; Chen 2005; Liang and Wang 2005; Ying and Zhou

2007; Chen and Morrison 2008; Gao and Woudstra 2011; and Xu et al. 2012, 2014). This research had focussed on the economic benefits or the negative effects of tourism. My interviews with domestic tourists in Xidi and Hongcun shows the majority of tourists have agency and they actively engaged in social and cultural work in the two villages.

A key issue that the interviews with tourists illustrates is that the cultural moments created by tourists are multi-dimensional. A large number of tourists are engaged in the recognition of the culture and history of the two villages or Anhui province, doing their own identity or memory work and are engaged in building social connections. For some visitors Xidi and Hongcun are associated with the depth and texture of the broader Chinese Southern identity and Confucianism. Compared to West Lake, as I discussed in Chapter 4, which is well-known by every Chinese person through school textbooks, stories, poetry, paintings and TV shows, many tourists are not very familiar with Xidi and Hongcun. However, my interview data in Xidi and Hongcun shows a similarity in their sense of feeling. Many tourists used the discourse of feeling very clearly, even explicitly using their sense of feeling to connect to physical places, landscape, local people and traditional Hui culture. The difference is that the sense of feeling tourists expressed in West Lake was about various places, culture in different periods, stories, TV shows and poetry which were tied to the memories related to West Lake they already knew. However, the sense of feeling tourists articulated in Xidi and Hongcun was about what they felt for the physical sites and the connections between local people. Another significant theme is the deep connection between tourists and local people. As I discussed above, there was a strong sense of contentment that emerged when tourists felt they had physical or spiritual connection to local people, as they described the villages as 'alive.' However, my interviews with both tourists and the local government officials demonstrated that the government-controlled or authorised tourism enterprise did not necessarily facilitate the sense of interaction between tourists and local people. In the next chapter, I will discuss the sense of contentment that local people gain from tourists and how government control influenced the interactions between tourists and local people.

Some visitors expressed their disappointment or provided some negative observations on commercialisation or pollution problems; nevertheless, they played an active role in the heritage site during their visit and were active in constructing their own meanings. As a World Heritage site, Xidi and Hongcun, in general, were places where people felt – and in particular felt connected to something vital such as a connection to land or connection to deep time (Poria et al. 2003; Byrne 2009, 2013a; Smith and Campbell 2015). My interviews reveal that tourists came to heritage sites to not just have a happy day out or conduct recreational activities; they were undertaking emotional and cultural work

(Smith 2006, 2012). Despite the apparent influences of the AHD employed by management at the two sites and discussed above, overall the work supports the sense of agency illustrated by Smith in her work with heritage visitors in European and Australian contexts (2006, 2011, 2012; see also Bagnall 2003; Byrne 2009, 2013a).

I identified that previous research on local–tourist interrelations focussed on economic benefits and marketing issues (Zhai 2002; Chen 2005; Liang and Wang 2005; Ying and Zhou 2007; Chen and Morrison 2008; Gao and Woudstra 2011 and Xu et al. 2012, 2014). In contrast to these researchers, I will analyse the cultural and social interrelations between local people and tourists, and how local governments and tourism companies relate to local–tourist interactions in the next chapter.

Notes

1 From 1958 to 1963, the campaign called the 'Great Leap Forward' was led by Mao Zedong and aimed to rapidly transform the country from an agrarian economy into a socialist society through rapid industrialisation and collectivisation. The production of steel was seen as one of the key pillars of the 'Great Leap Forward,' with most individuals in China involved in making steel. (Source: Chan 2001.)
2 Sourced from the interviews with managers of Co. Jingyi Ltd in Hongcun conducted by the author in December 2013.
3 Sourced from the interviews with local people in Xidi conducted by the author in December 2013.
4 Sourced from the interviews with 18 local people in Hongcun, as well as the head of the village and managers of Co. Jingyi Ltd in Hongcun conducted by the author in December 2013.
5 Xidi town is constituted by six villages with 6248 people. Xidi village is one of the villages in Xidi town, with about 1300 people. (Source: official web sites of Yixian County (www.yixian.gov.cn).)
6 Best Foreign Language Film Oscar award in 2001.
7 Based on my interview data with local people in Xidi. This observation is also based on my attendance of three different tour groups from 14 to 24 December, 2013 (with 123 minutes' of recorded data).
8 The tour guide service in both Xidi and Hongcun is about one hour.

Chapter 6

Local people's reactions to heritage tourism

Chapter 5 identified the active engagement of tourists with their visits to Xidi and Hongcun. They had agency and engaged in various activities in the two villages. Two significant themes have been identified. One theme is the sense of feeling, as many tourists were explicitly aware that they were seeking 'feeling' that linked to other senses, such as belonging, nostalgia and social connections. The other theme is the deep interaction between tourists and local people which is entangled with tourists' sense of feeling. When tourists felt they had a connection with local people, this evoked a sense of contentment. In this chapter, my focus turns to the local people. I will analyse local people's reactions to tourists at their sites and explore the interactions among local people, tourists, the local governments and tourism enterprises. As I discussed in Chapter 4, my interviews with local people at West Lake showed that a sense of pride was the key reason that the majority of local people at West Lake supported tourism. Local people's interactions with tourists also worked to sustain a sense of pride. However, Xidi and Hongcun represent a different type of heritage with different historical, political, economic and cultural backgrounds, nor are they nationally known sites that easily link to national narratives as West Lake does. Local people in West Lake are engaged in a range of occupations, while most of the local people in both Xidi and Hongcun base their living on tourism. Therefore, the interrelations among local people, tourists, local governments and tourism enterprises might be different to what I identified at West Lake. I will address these issues in this chapter.

The chapter finds that the interactions between tourists and local people are not only based on marketing and economic issues, as scholars such as Oakes (1993), Cohen (2000, 2004), and Su and Teo (2009) have identified, but are also underpinned by what are often deep cultural and social interactions. I also argue that tourist–local interactions can be constrained by the way various governments use heritage.

Local people's reactions to tourism

Interviews with residents at Xidi and Hongcun were undertaken during December 2013, with 40 people (Xidi 22 and Hongcun 18) interviewed at the sites. My interviews with residents of both villages show that local people in the 18–24 age group were not interviewed, as most local people of that age were working/searching for jobs outside the villages. Local people's educational attainment in Xidi is relatively low with 50% educated to year 9 or below, and 36.4% to year 12 or year 10 (with certificates). The low educational attainment of local people was due to the remote rural area and poverty of Xidi before tourism development. 86.4% local people in Hongcun have relatively low educational attainment (for the same reasons as in Xidi). The majority (63.6%) of local people in Xidi are small employers/own account workers engaged mainly in tourism businesses, while in Hongcun the local people's occupations are again similar to Xidi in that 70.6% are small employers/own account workers.

The question was asked of local people: 'Do you support tourism development in Xidi/Hongcun?' Two interviewees in Xidi and one in Hongcun did not answer this question. The remaining 37 local people I interviewed supported tourism development. However, the number is not surprising, as 70% of local people are engaged in tourism or tourism-related business in Xidi, and 90% in Hongcun (the Xidi government 2013c). Therefore, they have adequate reasons to support tourism. This result is consistent with other studies of local people's attitudes to tourism development in Xidi and Hongcun (see Su et al. 2005; Gu and Ryan 2010). However, local people do not only consider economic issues; there are also more in-depth cultural and social reasons for supporting it.

When I asked 'Do tourists have any impact on your daily life?' (Table 6.1), the majority of local people in Xidi (57.1%) and in Hongcun (62.5%) said that 'Yes, our living depends on tourism.' Some of them noted that their quality of life had been changed in positive ways because of tourism. Two villagers from Hongcun, who run a local hostel, responded as follows.

Table 6.1 Do tourists have any impact on your daily life? (Total, N=37; Xidi, N=21; Hongcun, N=16)

	Xidi (%)	Hongcun (%)
Yes, our living depends on tourism	57.1	62.5
Yes, represent local identity/proud – positive	19.0	0.0
Yes, mass tourists bring inflation (house/food, etc.) – negative	9.5	0.0
Yes, mass tourists bring economic growth – positive	9.5	12.5
Yes, happy to communicate with tourists – positive	4.8	0.0
Changes in industrial structure	0.0	25.0
Total	100.0	100.0

Locals' reactions to heritage tourism 163

HC061: Tourism is good. Our village used to be a very dirty place with cow dung and garbage before the development of tourism. Sometimes there are too many tourists coming to visit. Nevertheless, I do not mind, and I am hoping more tourists come.

HC062: I agree, we are living a better life because of tourism. You cannot imagine how hard the life we used to live was. Twenty years ago, we had to farm day and night. Even in winter, we had to cut down trees in the mountains in order to keep warm. Since the development of tourism, our share of the income from the sale of entrance tickets is 2800RMB [equal to 451 US$] per year. Elderly people can get an extra 200 RMB [equal to 32.2US$] per month. The numbers are increasing each year, which can ensure our basic living allowance even if we do not work.

HC061: Other neighbouring villages also benefit from tourism development in our village. They always bring their vegetable and other products to our market.

Author: I have interviewed a person in another village who argued that tourism development in Xidi and Hongcun brought price rises, which influenced their living quality.

HC061: Well, this is because they envy Hongcun has tourism resources which they do not have. However, without tourists coming to our village, no one would buy their products including vegetables, tea, and handiworks.

(HC061, female, 35–44 local; HC062, female, 45–54, local)

I interviewed two people who lived in a neighbouring village to Xidi. Their responses are similar, although they noted some drawbacks. One responded that:

Tourism is a sustainable and clean industry, and as a Huangshan citizen, I support it. However, except for villagers in Xidi and Hongcun, who have benefited from the World Heritage brand that attracted tourism investments, tourism also brought increasing food and product prices, which are unfair to the surrounding villages. Many of us prefer to migrate for work in Shanghai, Zhejiang and Jiangsu, and get a better income than staying in Huangshan city. You know the tourism income belongs to local governments, not local people.

(XD001, male, 25–34, local [from neighbouring village])

In terms of the increasing prices of food and other products that tourism development in Xidi and Hongcun caused by other villages, one of the villagers answered that:

HC053: Yes, more tourists come to our village, and our income is much better than before. We are busier than before during the tourism season.

Author: Do you think there are any negative impacts of World Heritage Listing or tourism development?

HC053: Well, some pollution ... I think mass tourists bring garbage and increase sanitary waste. I remembered there were many fish and crabs in the river beside the village. We used to wash dishes in the river, and fish gathered to eat the leftovers. The riverbank was very beautiful with white stones, which we used to dry quilts on. However, the government built a concrete riverbank; we cannot approach the river, and the water quality is no longer as clean as before.

Author: What do you think the impacts of tourism have been for other villages?

HC053: Some of my friends in other villages told me that they are envious of Hongcun, where everyone can share at least 2800RMB [equal to 451 US$] per year. They also complain that tourism development at Xidi and Hongcun has also brought increasing food prices to the region. However, most of them have brought their vegetables to sell in Hongcun.

(HC053, female, 25–34, local)

Although, as HC053 mentioned, tourism development has some negative effects, she nonetheless supports tourism. She also believed that other villages benefited from tourism development. As HC061 pointed out, the dissatisfaction of the communities surrounding Xidi and Hongcun is because they do not have such resources, but many of them depend on tourism as well by selling food and craft items. Wang (2013: 186) argues that tourism has brought a whole industry chain of tourism businesses to the region, and he also identified that the tourism development of Hongcun also boosted both economic and infrastructural development for the surrounding villages. Some local people have made active statements that tourism helps to reinforce local identity and pride. For example, a local tour guide from Hongcun told me that:

When I was a kid, nobody cared about the old buildings and the history of our village. Since the increasing number of tourists, I was curious why they wanted to come to our wrecked village. Elder villagers told me the reason they come is to visit our traditional architecture and water system. They also told me tourism is the reason that these traditional settings are still being taken care of. Therefore, I have been interested in our culture, not only the building but also more in-depth Hui culture which has been seen as a significant component of Chinese culture. One of the important reasons I am doing this guide job is that I am very proud to communicate with tourists about our culture.

(XD042, female, 25–34, local)

Locals' reactions to heritage tourism   165

Tourism also has saved the material form of the two villages. A local from Hongcun said that:

> You know, in our province, there were hundreds of towns or villages similar to Xidi and Hongcun, and even better 30 years ago; however, they had been demolished in order to build so-called 'new towns or villages.' Xidi and Hongcun still had the old setting at that time because of their remote location and poor traffic conditions, and we cannot afford to build a new village. After that, in the late 1980s, in order to develop tourism, we have to keep the old houses. Therefore, it is tourism that saved our villages [Xidi and Hongcun].
>
> (HC048, male, 35–44, local)

Furthermore, some local people reported that tourism has helped to reinforce or even save intangible heritage. A local who engaged in traditional wood carving in Xidi told me that:

> My family has engaged in this job for generations. These wood carvings used to be the most important decorations in traditional Hui buildings. However, the new type of building no longer needs it. Without tourists, who can we do this job for? Tourism is the most important reason that our family still inherits this skill. It is better than migrating for work.
>
> (XD090, female, 45–54, local)

A further four people (25%) in Hongcun nominated that tourism has changed the industrial structure of the village. For example:

> Well, I have thought about this question over the last ten years. The most significant impact changes to the industrial structure. 90% of local people are now engaged in tourism and relative occupations, they used to depend on farming. Tourism not only benefits Hongcun, but activates the economy and cultural innovation in the region.
>
> (HC052, male, over 65, local scholar)

However, a few local people nominated that tourism has brought negative things such as pollution (e.g. HC053), but the majority of local people considered tourism as an active factor that has done more than increase economic growth (e.g. HC053, HC061, HC062), and sustained the material sites (e.g. HC048). It also brought cultural gains (e.g. XD042 and XD090) tied to their sense of pride and facilitated their sense of local identity. A massive literature argues that tourism changing the industrial structure and labour market, and local people moving in to the hospitality industry, is usually seen as a negative thing, largely because of rampant commodification (Greenwood 1977; Handler and Saxton 1988; McCrone et al. 1995; Brett 1996; Handler and Gable 1997; Waitt 2000; Choay 2001; Greenspan 2002). As noted above, the majority of local people in both Xidi and Hongcun were engaged with the hospitality industry. Gu and Ryan (2010), based on their research on the resident–host relationships in Hongcun, criticise the changes to the local economic structure in this rural community, which they felt had negative effects when the old village feeling was replaced by a commercial or business ambience. However, my interviews reveal that some tourists identified the commercial feeling of both villages, particularly Hongcun. Tourism itself has been seen as a positive factor by local people in both Xidi and Hongcun, and most local people appear happy with the local industrial changes from farming to tourism. Some local people state that tourism has changed their villages for the better, and not only by bringing in funds that can support preservation and new infrastructure. More significantly, tourists aroused local people's public awareness and respect for their culture and were a positive factor in the protection of both material heritage and intangible heritage.

In addition, the tourist–local relationship is not only commercial or business activity, but it is also an active and complex series of bonds between tourism and local people. As I asked local people 'what are the messages or experiences that you hope visitors take away from the site?', the majority of local residents in both Xidi and Hongcun expressed active senses of what this meant. For example:

> The traditional Hui buildings, landscape, and culture of Xidi are unique, which you cannot find elsewhere in the world. Most of the tourists come from big cities such as Shanghai or Beijing where they share similar identities. They want to see something different. You know the former Secretary-General of the United Nations Kofi Atta Annan said 'Xidi is the most beautiful village of the World' during his visit to Xidi. I had made a lot of friends who used to visit Xidi. Some close friends have been coming to my hostel every year when they have a holiday. Each year, they have sent me postcards, I send them fresh tea during the tea season.
>
> (XD038, female, 45–54, local)

> I think it is natural that tourists want to pursue a feeling of freedom during their visit to a site. Tourist is the protagonist in the heritage scenario. Why I mean protagonist, you can find the answer in my book.
>
> (HC052, male, over 65, local scholar)

XD038 expressed her great sense of pride and wanted tourists to have a different experience from their daily lives. The sense of pride was widely reported as

Locals' reactions to heritage tourism 167

I conducted my interviews with local people at West Lake (see Chapter 4). However, the significant theme that Xidi and Hongcun reflects is a sense of emotional bonding between local people and tourists. XD038 further told me that she had made deep connections with tourists, and she considered some of these tourists to be her close friends. HC052 has pointed out that tourism is a key factor in heritage issues. He used the word 'freedom' to stress that tourists visit a site not only for recreation or receiving educational messages, but rather they are performing emotive and affective cultural practices. As I indicated in Chapter 4, tourists' sense of freedom was magnified when they feel they are not blocked by 'walls,' 'fences' or 'entrance gates.' In Xidi and Hongcun, tourists' sense of freedom was not only blocked by the physical boundaries, but also invisible boundaries of control from local governments and the tourism companies. I will further discuss this issue below. In HC052's book *Dream of Hongcun*, he designed a tour for his friend 阿萌 Ms Meng, with whom he had built a deep friendship. In his book, he engaged in an in-depth empathetic process through which he hoped Ms Meng could feel the contemporary life of Hongcun, to experience new and old local customs, and to remember this memorable journey (Wang 2013: 175–184). From his five-page narrative, he described the interplay between local people and tourists as having a different kind of emotional reaction. It is clear he does not see material objects as the key actor of tourism or heritage, rather the deep sense of bonding between local people and tourists construct the meaning of heritage.

The question 'do tourists have any impact on your daily life?' elicited different answers in the two villages. Most local people in Xidi would like tourists to gain cultural experiences or aesthetic appreciation. However, their responses were always accompanied by criticisms of the inefficient management model developed by local authorities. This particularly focussed on the lower tourist numbers in Xidi compared to Hongcun, although they thought that Xidi had better tourism resources. For example:

> Our village has a much better cultural background than Hongcun. However, the advertisement of Hongcun is much better than Xidi.
>
> (XD005, female, 35–44, local)

> I hope tourists can receive more cultural information about our Hui culture. I think the integrity of Hui buildings in Xidi is better than Hongcun. However, the tourism company in Hongcun has done a better job than local authorities in Xidi, in particular, the advertisements.
>
> (XD036, female, 35–44, local)

> Compared to Xidi, Hongcun has already turned into a commercial place. Most foreign people prefer Hongcun to Xidi, the layout and the

aesthetic view of Hongcun look better. If you want to gain more cultural experiences, Xidi is a better choice.

(XD082, female, 18–24, local)

Hongcun is a beautiful painting, while Xidi is a book. You can only enjoy superficial aesthetic value by watching a painting, but you can gain more cultural inspiration by reading a book. Visitors need to spend more time in Xidi to understand the culture of Xidi. Therefore, I told every guest who stayed in my hostel to advertise Xidi to their friends.

(XD090, female, 45–54, local)

Most interviewees in Xidi expressed dissatisfaction because the majority of tourists chose to visit Hongcun despite their view that Xidi provided better cultural experiences. The response from local people in Hongcun was quite different: most of them wanted tourists to recreate or use their leisure as a respite from their pressures at work, and unlike those from Xidi, did not reference cultural experiences. For instance:

I want visitors to enjoy the site, to totally relax by visiting Hongcun. No matter what reasons they come to our village initially, the most important is they can forget the pressure of their daily life, and pursue the feeling of freedom.

(HC052, male, over 65, local scholar)

Indeed, many local people had provided very sophisticated understandings of Hongcun. However, they do not mind if the messages tourists taken from Hongcun are shallow or banal. In their sense, the engagement process from each visitor that linked to the sense of freedom was emphasised as more important than particular messages. There are also the following examples:

The integrity of the traditional buildings in Xidi is better than Hongcun. However, the layout, the water, traditional buildings and people are perfectly merged in Hongcun. Therefore, you cannot simply say which village is better. Tourists come to our village for different reasons. I just want them to enjoy their journey.

(HC024, male, 25–34, local)

Hongcun represents the Chinese traditional ideology of '天人合一 harmony between man and nature.' Our water, our traditional buildings, our customs, our dialect system, and our people constitute this heritage site. In terms of Xidi, there are more traditional buildings than Hongcun. The stories that are carried by these old buildings are profound in Xidi.

However, Xidi does not have a representative building such as 承志堂 Chengzhitang in Hongcun. Hongcun's water system is much better [than Xidi], while Xidi has a better road system [than Hongcun]. It is unreasonable to say which village is better.

(HC028, male, over 65, local scholar)

The reason that local people's responses were distinct in these two villages may be linked to tourism development. As I discussed in Chapter 5, the successful World Heritage designation in 2000 has brought dramatic rises in tourist numbers to both Xidi and Hongcun, and facilitated industrial change from agriculture to the hospitality sector. Tourist numbers in Xidi had been much higher than in Hongcun, but have been exceeded by Hongcun since 2003, and the gap between the tourism revenue of the villages is becoming bigger and bigger. In 2013, as I conducted my interviews with local people in Xidi, ticket revenue in Hongcun was more than twice that of Xidi (the Xidi government 2013b). The majority of interviewees were extremely unhappy with the changes to tourism revenue compared to Hongcun, which they attributed to the inefficiency of the Xidi local government (discussed below). Local people's responses in Hongcun were more positive than Xidi, based on the fact that the number of tourists in Hongcun was more than twice that of Xidi. Nevertheless, tourism itself has been seen as a positive factor by local people in both Xidi and Hongcun, and most local people appear happy with the industrial changes from farming to tourism. Some local people state that tourism has changed their villages and made them better places. This is not just based on bringing in money that can support the preservation and new infrastructure. More significantly, tourists aroused the local people's public awareness of the need to respect their own culture and stimulated the protection of both material heritage and intangible heritage. Also, a sense of bonding has emerged where local people have a deep connection with tourists (discussed below). Chapter 5 also identified the sense of contentment tourists felt when they connect with local people. This is a significant positive change that tourism has brought to Xidi and Hongcun, and it has not been addressed in the heritage or tourism literature.

Local people's reactions to the government's policies and management mode

The above sections have outlined the views and aspirations of tourists, local people, local government and the tourism companies; this section explores the tensions between them by analysing several open-ended questions. The first question I asked of both local people and tourists was 'What do you think of the tourism management of the site?' (Tables 6.2 and 6.3). Tourists

170 Locals' reactions to heritage tourism

Table 6.2 What do you think about the tourism management of the site (for local people)? (Total, N=36; Xidi, N=21; Hongcun, N=15)

	Xidi (%)	Hongcun (%)
Negative about the management mode/policies/implementation	85.7	13.3
Positive about the management mode/policies/implementation	4.8	0.0
Don't know	4.8	0.0
Happy with improvements to the infrastructure	4.8	0.0
Better than Xidi, but still have weaknesses	11	73.4
Offers a management suggestion	4.8	13.3
Total	100	100

Table 6.3 What do you think about the tourism management of the site (for tourists)? (Total, N=36; Xidi, N=25; Hongcun, N=9)

	Xidi (%)	Hongcun (%)
Offers a management suggestion	52.0	55.6
High entrance ticket fee	28.0	33.3
Commercialisation – negative	12.0	11.1
Generally, positive	8.0	0.0
Total	100	100

nominated problems such as over-commercialisation and high entrance ticket fees or provided some management suggestions (Table 6.3). However, the local people's concerns were much more complex and in-depth, which reflected tensions in the relationship between local people, local governments and government authorised enterprises.

When I conducted my interviews with local people in Xidi, more than half of them expressed depressed or angry emotions about local governments and the state-owned enterprise (Co. Huihuang Ltd) which had just taken over their locally run tourism programme. As I asked their opinions about the management of the site, most local people (85.7%) complained about what they saw as a negative management model. Many of them even ignored other questions I asked and kept expressing their dissatisfaction with current management practices. Some of them criticised the current management policies that were seen as causing young people to move from Xidi. For example:

> Some villagers' houses are relatively far from touristic areas. Therefore, younger villagers from those houses prefer to search for work outside the village. However, most villagers whose homes are around the touristic site have stayed and lived dependent on tourism.
>
> (XD042, male, 35–44, local)

Locals' reactions to heritage tourism 171

> XD038: Firstly, Xidi is a World Heritage site. It is necessary to ensure the integrity of the old houses. However, our kids are growing up, and they have to move into new houses. According to the management policies, we cannot build new houses in the nomination area. In order to protect the integrity of the original layout of Xidi, we support such policies. The local governments had promised to build a new village which is located in the west of Xidi six years ago. However, it is still a wasteland. Secondly, the old houses are ours, and villagers have been taken good care of them for hundreds of years. We understand how to maintain our houses. With the tourists coming to our site, our sense of the place and buildings has been improved. However, the local governments' main concern is to repair the touristic areas or places that might be examined by international and national authorities. There are many cracks in the main walls of my old houses. It is very dangerous for both my family and tourists. I have reported the problems to local governments several times, and the officer told me to keep waiting.
>
> (XD038, local, female, 45–54)

The responses from XD042 reflect how tourism has caused positive economic growth, while it has also caused an unequal distribution of wealth. Local people whose houses are far from the touristic area had to work outside of the village. It seems that the competition that tourism brought to Xidi facilitated a sense of alienation within the local community. However, as I reviewed the statistical data of the Yi county government, the rate at which local people in both Xidi and Hongcun searched for jobs was dramatically lower than other villages in the county[1] (Yi County Government 2015; see also the Xidi Government 2013b). Indeed, there is a trend for the rural population to move to urban areas in recent decades because of urbanisation (Winter and Daly 2012). Therefore, tourism, in contrast, is the key factor keeping the population stable in both Xidi and Hongcun, as XD090, HC048 and HC053 mentioned above. XD038 nominated another issue, that the maintenance works conducted by local authorities were focussed on pleasing national or international authorities, rather than being concerned with the needs of local people. This sense of alienation was a primary concern over the state-run tourism company taking over the management of Xidi. In addition, many local people also complained that the focus of the existing management policies was primarily on material objects. For example, I interviewed a local who was repairing his old house (Figure 6.1). He said that:

> XD083: My house was built about 150 years ago. The framework of the building was broken and the main wall crushed. I have to rebuild it.
>
> Author: Did your repair work need to be approved by local governments?
>
> XD083: Yes!

172 Locals' reactions to heritage tourism

Figure 6.1 A resident was repairing his old house (photo by Rouran Zhang)

Author: Did the government pay the maintenance cost?

XD083: I already paid 60% of the repair cost, I am still waiting for 40% that the government should pay [angry].

Author: You mean according to the relevant policy they should pay you 40% of the costs of the maintenance project?

XD083: Well, local governments do not give the 40% money to me directly. Before the repair project started, local governments authorised a 'certificated' construction company to budget for the expenditure. The expenditure is always much more expensive than the local construction

Locals' reactions to heritage tourism 173

team we usually used before World Heritage inscription. I can use less than 60% of the budget to hire a local construction company to complete the job. I think the policy made by national governments is good, so that the maintenance cost expenditure is shared with a proportion of 40%–60% by the local governments and villagers. The problems have been the implementation of such policies by local governments.

Author: What kind of problems?

XD083: You know, World Heritage listing is supposed to be a good thing, it is Xidi's honour. However, it has become a burden for us. Firstly, the cost of repairing old houses is extremely high, and the huge repair costs have forced many of us give up repairing the broken houses. Secondly, the local governments' budget for the expenditure takes a long time, which delays the best time for repairing. In addition, there are strict requirements of the 'certificated' repair company made by local governments to restrain the reasonable development of our own house. It is my house, and I paid the maintenance fee, but I have to obey your unreasonable rules! [angry]

(XD083, male, 45–54, local)

In addition, local people such as XD007 pointed out the problem of corruption:

XD007: Corruption has been the most serious problem [angry]. There are two antithetical couplets our local people use for the irony of the corruption: '从里往外看，都是穷光蛋；从外往里看，都是贪污犯' [Translation: On the surface, officials appear to be poor and honest people; in effect, they are grafters]; and '劳动创业最可耻，贪污社会最光荣' [Translation: Labour (Working) is a shame, corruption is honour].

(XD007, female, 45–54, local)

Furthermore, local people residents from Xidi compared Xidi and Hongcun, and indicated the backwardness of the existing management system in Xidi. Examples are:

XD005: The tourism management in Hongcun has been operated by a private company, while Xidi used to be run by the village-based local company which was recently taken over by the local government […] Although the management of the village-based company was backward, we considered Xidi belonged to us. Since April 2013, the town's government based company has been in charge of tourism management. I did not see any difference in tourism management, but Xidi no longer belongs to us [distressed].

Author: Are there other problems with existing management?

XD005: Well, there are many restrictions on our regular life. For example, we are not allowed to hang washed clothes outside our old buildings [...] Before World Heritage inscription, Xidi was an impoverished village. The Xidi Tourism Service Company was established and gave local people a part of profit-sharing with conditions and restrictions, while most of us did not participate in the decision-making process. At that time, we were satisfied because our annual incomes were much better than Hongcun and other villages in Yi County. However, The Xidi Tourism Service Company had satisfied their achievement. Therefore, problems such as corruption and backward management concepts emerged.

(XD005, female, 35–44, local)

XD009: The tourists' numbers in Hongcun are much higher than us [...] because of a private company has been in charge of the tourism management in Hongcun, while the village-based company used to be responsible for tourism management in Xidi. The private company has efficient management ideas and experiences, and they have employed people with higher educational backgrounds and management experience. However, our village-based company used outdated management styles, which caused corruption problems. Many tourists come to Xidi do not know what to see. Recently, the village-based company has been replaced by a state-owned enterprise called Co. Huihuang Ltd.

Author: Did local people in Xidi agree with the local government decision?

XD009: Yes, we did. But we have to do that. If the local government have made a decision, there is no way we can change it.

(XD009, male, over 65, local)

The management in Hongcun is much better, and Beijing Zhongkun Investment Group has invested millions in tourism development.

(XD031, female, 25–34, local)

XD036: Our village company has been taken over by a state-owned enterprise run by the town government.

Author: I hear from other villagers that the majority of villagers voted to approve this management change.

XD036: Yes, we did. However, we had to do this. If not, there would be some troubles for my tourism business [angry].

(XD036, female, 35–44, local)

The above interviews show that the conflict between local people, the Xidi Tourism Service Company and the Xidi local government has existed for a long time. Economic benefits that local people gain from tourism, in particular the tourism revenue competition with Hongcun, has been the trigger for the conflict. The majority of local people I interviewed in Xidi considered that Xidi has better tourism resources, such as old traditional buildings and Hui culture than Hongcun (e.g. XD 005, XD036 and XD082 above). However, Hongcun's tourism revenue is much higher than Xidi's. They considered the Xidi Tourism Service Company and Xidi local government to be inefficient and corrupt. Ying and Zhou (2007) had praised the Xidi Tourism Service Company being elected by local villagers and standing for local people's interests when they conducted their research from 2001 to 2003. However, they also observed that Xidi's tourism management pattern 'has still been … resting on the benefit level' and there was a 'trend towards the centralization of decision-making right in tourism development to the minority of the community' (Ying and Zhou 2007: 105). My research verified Ying and Zhou (2007)'s prediction, as some local people, such as XD036, reflect that 'the Xidi Tourism Service Company has been controlled by a few villagers for many years, I doubt the sincerity of the tourism revenue they provided' (XD036, woman, 35–44, local). My research, conducted ten years after Ying and Zhou (2007), found that local people's attitudes to the local-run company were reversed. Although the county government took charge of tourism from the Xidi Tourism Service Company and established a new government-run company in early 2013, local people expressed deep distrust. While they were doubtful whether the new government-run company can improve tourism numbers and efficiency, they are very concerned and angry about the fact that Xidi no longer belongs to them – they feel alienated from their site. In terms of Hongcun, local people did not express distressed or angry emotions as the interviewees did in Xidi. For instance:

> The management of Xidi used to be run by a village committee and recently has been taken charge of by the local government. However, their management is chaotic, with a serious corruption problem.
>
> (HC049, female, 25–34, local)

> I understand why Xidi's villagers complained about their management. Local people in Hongcun share a much smaller proportion of the income from entrance tickets via the tourism company than Xidi does. However, the majority of people in both Xidi and Hongcun are more or less involved in the tourism business. Therefore, we would like more visitors to come to our site, which brings much more than just income than sharing the ticket sales.
>
> (HC024, male, 25–34, local)

Local people in Xidi expressed strong dissatisfaction or anger with both the local committee-run and state-owned enterprise's management practices. While local people in Hongcun considered the management of the franchised private company was better than at Xidi, it still had weaknesses. They did not express the same negative emotions as interviewees in Xidi. I reviewed the literature of Xidi and Hongcun in Chapter 5, and the work of scholars such as Chen (2005), Liang and Wang (2005) and Ying and Zhou (2007), who conducted their research before 2003, shows a different story. They identified that local people in Xidi used to be satisfied with their tourism development and management before 2003, when the tourists' numbers were much higher than at Hongcun. Hongcun's villagers were extremely unhappy with their tourism management, to the extent that some local people stopped maintaining their buildings and gardens and even damaged the physical setting to express their dissatisfaction with the franchised company (Ying and Zhou 2007). In 2000, the majority of Hongcun local people (730 villagers, over 60% of the local population) signed an appeal to the Anhui Provincial Court to request the tourism business rights back, though this appeal was rejected by the Anhui Provincial Court (Ying and Zhou 2007: 101). After negotiations between local people and the external company, a new agreement was made in 2002 (Ying and Zhou 2007). The literature shows that the resistance process in Hongcun before 2003 was much fiercer than my interviews showed the situation to be in Xidi. My interviews, conducted about ten years later than those of previous researchers, found a reversal of local attitudes towards management in Xidi and Hongcun. They revealed that tourism, in particular its economic value, was the key issue influencing the interrelation among local people, local governments and tourism companies, and government control caused a sense of estrangement of local people to the heritage site. The origin of the conflict between local people and the local governments is because the local communities in both Xidi and Hongcun have no right to participate in any decision-making about tourism management or the World Heritage listing process. I interviewed a local scholar, who provided a sophisticated answer about tourism management in Hongcun.

> In terms of management, the governments and Tourism Company assert that they have done great jobs of integrating and disseminating the culture of Hongcun. However, what they focus on are material objects or very superficial aspects of the culture of Hongcun. They do not care about the local customs and other intangible aspects of culture which are not listed in the nomination dossiers. For example, many local people in Hongcun used to sell Chinese style baked rolls, melon seeds or other food from a small basket to villagers and tourists. This custom had been seen as

'pollution' of the aesthetic value of the heritage site, and local governments have forbidden this custom to ensure the protection of the site [depressed emotion]. In addition, the authorised narratives by tour guides concentrate on interpreting great and profound antithetical couplets of culture in the past. However, we have used the computer printed couplets with advertisements of companies such as China Mobile Communications Corporation or Agricultural Bank of China instead of the traditional calligraphy couplets. Furthermore, our new generation has learnt Mandarin since primary school, and do not speak our dialect any more. The dialect is one of the significant aspects of identity in Hongcun, and it might disappear in this century. In my opinion, what belongs to the nation belongs to the world. However, local governments and Tourism Companies' concerns are conservation of the physical heritage objects and neglect of the intangible culture. For example, when the government and Tourism Company consider intangible culture it is used to perform so-called local customs for international or national authorities or tourists in order to entertain them. The problems are not from national governments but come from the corrupted and inefficient local governments.

(HC028, male, 54–65, local scholar)

From HC028's perspective, local authorities are only concerned to protect the historical and cultural appearance of heritage sites that are recognised by national or international authorities. However, some customs or aspects of contemporary culture mean more to local people in Hongcun than simply the physical site. He is reporting a sense of alienation from Hongcun's culture, a process which began at the point of developing the WH listing nomination. When I further asked him whether 'as a local expert, did you participate in the WH listing process?' he answered that 'the local governments never ask about my suggestions maybe. They are afraid the national and international authorities know the truth.' Another local scholar provided a similar answer:

I had not been invited to participate in any of the discussion of World Heritage listing. It is the local government's decision.

(HC052, male, over 65, local scholar)

The local people in both Xidi and Hongcun identified the key problem as being that local authorities have been controlling the management process. Therefore, local people's understanding of heritage, particularly their current use of heritage, has been ignored or even restricted by local authorities. In the next section, I will discuss how the local authorities used management policies to 'manage' the two villages.

The local management policies – 'Keep Old, Keep Authentic'

Interviews with the key officials and managers from local authorities and tourism companies in both Xidi and Hongcun show that their understanding of heritage is based on material objects and landscape, and they developed policies and regulations to ensure the authenticity of those precious and non-renewable resources can be protected. Both the Xidi and Hongcun government, 'strictly implement heritage management' (XD092) based on the international policies and local policy such as *Wannan Traditional Old Building Protection Regulation (安徽省皖南古民居保护条例)*. For instance:

> In 2003, the provincial government developed a regulation called *'Wannan Traditional Old Building Protection Regulation 安徽省皖南古民居保护条例.'* Over these ten years, this regulation has been seen as our management Bible, which local governments of Xidi strictly implemented for heritage management. From my view, these old traditional houses embodied the cream of Hui culture. Without the old houses, the culture only can be found in the literature. However, during the process of tourism development, local people required redecorating or enlarging their old houses into restaurants and hostels in order to satisfy tourists' demands. Any of their redecorating work or building a new house with traditional styles should be approved by local and county governments. Therefore, when you interview local people, some of them might reflect their dissatisfaction with governments. It is necessary to consider the local people's opinions. However, we have to consider site management at the macro level, and it is impossible to satisfy every local's requirements. I think it is significant that local people and governments should cooperate in order to protect our traditional buildings and bring more tourists to Xidi.
>
> (XD092, vice-head of Xidi town)

> I think the most valuable things in Xidi are the old traditional houses. Compared to Hongcun, local governments have done a lot to prevent commercialisation. The WH listing has brought a dramatic increase in local people's awareness of protection. Local governments have also established strict management policies […] local people wanted to redecorate their houses for tourism uses. However, their behaviour could influence the integrity of the old houses, even the entire layout of Xidi. Therefore, any redecoration work for old buildings should be approved by local governments. We will carefully design a suitable plan and send a certificated construction team to do the job. We also pay 40% of the repair fee.
>
> (XD093, head of Xidi village)

Compared to Hongcun, the protection of the traditional buildings and the integrity of the site layout in Xidi are much better. However, the tourism revenue in Hongcun is much higher. Therefore, our company has developed advanced tourism management methods, and we have also integrated most of the tourism resources at the county level. We are confident that the tourism development of Xidi will catch up with Hongcun soon. We always keep in mind that well-protected houses are our advantage that we will use to develop sustainable tourism.

(XD094, vice-head of Co. Huihuang Ltd)

From my perspective, World Heritage means protection. In terms of Xidi, villagers, and local governments have made a great effort to ensure the protection issues. Therefore, the integrity of our site is better than Hongcun […] The best protection of a site could bring the highest touristic recognition, while tourism could provide funding for protection, and increase local people's awareness of protection.

(XD095, chief marketing officer of Co. Huihuang Ltd)

XD092 and XD093 clearly talk about heritage as physical objects – to be specific, the traditional Hui buildings and landscape. They argued that the profound Hui culture can only be reflected by well-protected old buildings. Therefore, their management was primarily aimed to ensure the protection of old buildings. This, as identified above, caused local dissatisfaction, not simply in the transfer of management authority but also in the sense of alienation from the local culture. A situation was similarly noted by some in Hongcun (HC028 above). XD094 and XD095's considerations also focussed on ensuring the protection of material sites and upgrading tourism services.

Besides concern with the protection of the physical site, interviews conducted in Hongcun shows that the vice-head of Hongcun Town (HC063) and the head of the Hongcun Village[2] (HC064) praised the tourism management conducted by Beijing-based tourism company. Their consideration was focussed on developing tourism by protecting old traditional buildings and enhancing the infrastructure of Hongcun.

HC064: At the beginning of the tourism development, local people did not benefit from tourism, they wanted to rebuild their old houses in modern styles like in other villages. At that time, their living conditions were very poor, and redecorating the old houses was more expensive than building new buildings. Local governments had to make policies in order to protect the traditional buildings. After WH listing, in particular, the year 2005, local people realised the benefit of tourism development. The relationship among local people, Co. Jingyi Ltd [Beijing Zhongkun Investment Group] and our local governments have been positive.

HC063: If we did not sign the contract with them [Beijing Zhongkun Investment Group], we probably wouldn't have been inscribed on the WH list. During the process of WH listing, the Zhongkun Investment Group had used their networks to ensure that Hongcun was tied with Xidi for inscription. The company has invested millions to improve the infrastructure. They built a new road connecting to Huangshan Mountain in 2003, and Hongcun's tourism income exceeded Xidi's in the same year. They also helped to rebuild or redecorate some old buildings and pathways. In addition, the company has done an excellent job in advertising.

(HC063, vice-head of Hongcun Town; HC064, head of Hongcun Village)

In terms of the question 'are there any conflicts during the process of management since developing tourism?', HC064 stressed that local people's protection awareness had improved because of the increasing tourism revenue. I also asked the vice-head of the Co. Jingyi Ltd the same question on 24 December 2013. HC065 nominated the process of conflict, compromise and satisfying the local people's attitudes to Zhongkun Investment Group:

We do not have any conflict with the county or local government yet. The governments have taken charge of site conservation, while our company has been responsible for marketing and tourism operations. Therefore, the most important conservation works have been accounted for by governments, and we have provided funding support. In terms of local people, it was a complex process. In 1998, the first year Zhongkun Investment Group took charge of the tourism operation, our company offered to give 5% of ticket sales plus a fixed payment of about 180,000 RMB [equal to US$29,032] to local people. Local people were extremely happy with the contract because one year before the tourism management on the site was chaos and the ticket sales were only 170,000 RMB [equal to US$27,419]. As I mentioned, the company also invested an extra 20 million RMB [equal to US$3.22 million] for site conservation and tourism infrastructures. However, because of our investment and advanced tourism development plan, the tourist's numbers dramatically increased. Local people had been unsatisfied with the original contract and told us to get out of Hongcun, particularly from the year 2000 to 2002. In order to solve the problem, our company made a great compromise and signed a new agreement on revenue allocation with county governments and local representative in 2002, where 33% of the ticket income would be for local governments and local people. During these ten years, local people found their share of the ticket revenue to be only a small portion of their revenue; they gain far greater economic benefits from running restaurants, hostels or developing handicrafts. Compared to Xidi, they realised our company had used advanced management work and people networks that brought dramatic increases in tourist numbers. Tourism development also increased local people's sense of public awareness of site protection. Therefore, the relationship between the company and local people has been positive in recent years.

(HC065, head of Co. Jingyi Ltd)

Compare this to the interview I conducted with local authorities in West Lake (see Chapter 4), where the government officials were clearly aware of the need to recognise the AHD to ensure Western examiners were satisfied that the site can be a successful destination. While the Hangzhou government still used the local management policies to manage the site after WH listing, they were mindful to state that those local policies needed to not contradict the AHD. Therefore, the majority of interviewees praised heritage and tourism management in West Lake. However, the residents were clearly dissatisfied with the management models in both Xidi and Hongcun. Xu et al. (2014: 805) has analysed Hongcun's management policies, and emphasised that the principle of protection is to ensure the authenticity and integrity of the site for the 'convenience of administration and reflects the will of community elites and tourists with the power of discourse.' They summarised four aspects of those policies:

First, the authenticity of non-material culture is interpreted as 'non-commercialisation'; Second, to 'keep authentic' is interpreted purely as protecting the material appearance; Third, it gives a static and one-dimensional explanation of authenticity; Fourth, little attention has been paid to the residents' needs for life.

(Xu et al. 2014: 805)

My interview result support the observations of Xu et al. (2014). The local governments in both villages insisted on using the AHD to educate and even force local people to keep the appearance of the old houses. They were clearly aware of local people's dissatisfactions; however, they thought local people did not have an 'international vision' of protection, and what they did was for the benefit of local people. As HC065 points out, local people in Hongcun initially resisted the franchised company, as they thought the franchised company could not provide a good tourism development plan. When local people in

Hongcun gained great economic benefits from the tourism strategy formulated by the franchised company and compared it to Xidi's backwards management plan, Hongcun villagers were finally satisfied. Therefore, the local governments and external company in Hongcun considered they should make the decision for local people, and over time, the community would understand the advantages of their strategy. At Xidi, officials I interviewed considered the backwardness of tourism development was attributed to the village-based company who did not have the advantage of a tourism development plan as Hongcun did. Therefore, in order to catch up with Hongcun, 'we always keep in mind that well-protected houses are our advantage that we will use to develop sustainable tourism' (XD094). The similarity of the two villages is that the local governments both considered strictly following the precepts of the AHD and introduced external companies with the 'international advantage vision' of management for sustainable development of the site. They did not consider local people had agency and intended to ignore local people's voices.

However, my interviews with local people (see above) clearly show that they understood their sites and houses far more explicitly and in greater depth than governments and external companies. As XD038, XD083 and HC028 analysed the local authorities' implementation of top-down management policies that only focussed on 'material objects or very superficial aspects of the culture of Hongcun' (HC028), they showed that local people had no power to maintain their own houses and had to anticipate the longer-term, and what they saw as corrupt governments', assessment process (XD083). Local people also reflected that the local governments were being crafty, as their priority was to maintain the old houses located in touristic areas or 'places that might be examined by international and national authorities,' while houses that were not in the touristic area were ignored (XD038). A significant theme that HC028 mentioned is that the local authorities were only concerned about material authenticity that would be recognised by national or international authorities, and banned local customs such as local people who 'sell Chinese style baked rolls, melon seeds or other food from a small basket to villagers and tourists,' which had been seen as 'pollution' to the authenticity of the site.

The management practices from the local governments and tourism companies also influenced tourist experiences. Some tourists in both Xidi and Hongcun I interviewed felt their sense of feeling was blocked by the high entrance fee and commercialised environment: For instance:

> It is a theme park that I had to pay 104 RMB (equal to 16.8 USD) to enter. I felt the site has been managed.
>
> (HC038, male, 25–34, tourist)

> 104 RMB entrance fee! It is incredible. The village obviously has been managed. There is an organised touristic souvenir market in the village. It is funny.
>
> (HC042, male, 45–54, tourist)

> I had to pay 104 RMB to get thought. Although the ticket includes the tour guide fees, but I do not want to join it.
>
> (XD026, female, 45–54, tourist)

The three examples show that tourists at both sites had the feeling that the village 'has been managed.' Their sense of freedom was blocked by both physical boundaries of the site and the management of the local governments and tourism companies. In this sense, the local governments and tourism companies in both Xidi and Hongcun not only treated heritage as a static or dead material thing, but they also intended to block the 'live' elements and facilitate the sense that heritage should be 'frozen in time.' Therefore, the intervention of government control created invisible 'boundaries,' 'walls' or 'entrance gate' that not only blocked local people's sense of place but also disturbed tourists' sense of feeling. XD083 expressed his anger and explained his understanding of heritage:

> [...] World heritage belongs to who? Local people or governments? The local governments should improve their concept of management. In my opinion, there is a soul in our old houses, but it is not just materials. It is traditional technologies and other intangible things.
>
> (XD083, male, 45–54, local)

This chapter shows that the majority of residents in Xidi and Hongcun consider that tourism plays a positive role in the development and maintenance of heritage sites. Their responses reflect that it is not only economic increases or physical infrastructure which tourists have contributed to heritage sites; rather it is a social and cultural process where tourists play active roles in the construction, development and maintenance of heritage sites. Chapter 5 identified that many visitors considered tourism brought positive developments, but they also worried that tourism caused commercialisation and created protection problems. As Hall (2009: 80–90, quoted in Smith 2012: 213) points out, sometimes the negative effects that tourists brought to sites 'are consensual and normative understandings as new understandings of the past are created.' My research shows that the majority of local people nominated positive interconnections that tourism has facilitated at heritage sites, which include reinforcing local identity, pride and enthusiasm for protection, and the development and economic growth of villages. However, this is offset by the ways in which government and the tourism companies are alienating them from their sites and culture. This ultimately rests on differing understandings of not only heritage, but also the nature of tourism, and the failure of government and the tourism company to understand the complex relationship between then – a relationship that appears to be better understood by local people and tourists themselves.

Some visitors and local people provided very in-depth answers that recognise that tourism and heritage are linked with each other. Smith (2006, 2012) argues that the interrelation between heritage and tourism does not only occur at international or state level by the accumulation of heritage lists, or by developing management or protection policies and practices. Rather, the performance is the act of individuals visiting such heritage places. XD045 expressed it this way: 'If no one comes to visit a heritage site, it is a meaningless place.' This can be illustrated by the following two narratives from local people (XD033 and HC052), wherein tourism and heritage interplay with each other to create *'cultural moments'* which help both local people and tourists construct their memories, and make sense of their sense of place or identity.

> Well, the most important are the stories that happened or will happen in my old house, rather than the material or aesthetic things. I changed my house into a hostel more than ten years ago, and have served thousands of tourists. I always enjoy communicating with them. You know, they come here for learning traditional 'Hui culture,' enjoying the Confucianism that is carried forward by 朱熹 Zhu Xi, or for their own personal reasons. But all of these stories have become a part of the story of my house.
>
> (XD033, female, 35–44, local)

> […] Hongcun is composed of every segment of history, the stories are happening in the present and the future scenarios … I think people … both local people and tourists are key elements in a heritage site. People play active roles in the site. The old houses cannot survive without local people, while local people cannot live without tourists. Compared to Lijiang and Wuzhen, where many local people moved outside (or were forced to move outside) of the old town; Hongcun still has been [able to] keep the original local people. The new residents in Wuzhen were selected by tourism companies, they were not familiar with each other and had to do performances for tourists based on rules formulated by the tourism company. What both Lijiang and Wuzhen lost were the neighbourly relations and traditional customs. You know, most of the hostels in Hongcun are run by original villagers, and we have kept the neighbourly relations and customs. In this process, tourists play an active role in constructing the new neighbourhood, and local people have tried their best to enhance both the material

environment and build a connection with visitors. Therefore, the relation between tourism and heritage sites is a dynamic process. However, people are always the key to this process, which connects the past, present and future of Hongcun.

(HC052, male, over 65, local scholar)

Conclusion

This chapter discussed how tourism and tourists created economic benefits to Xidi and Hongcun but also brought cultural gains. The majority of local people in both villages have been engaged in the hospitality industry. This is counter to many arguments from the literature that suggest industry changing from traditional agriculture to tourism is usually seen as a negative thing, particularly in regard to commodification (Greenwood 1977; Handler and Saxton 1988; McCrone et al. 1995; Brett 1996; Handler and Gable 1997; Waitt 2000; Choay 2001; Greenspan 2002). The majority of local people were very happy and proud about the industrial transformation. They considered tourism to be an active factor that sustained the material sites (e.g. HC048), kept them out of poverty and provided more working opportunities (HC052, HC028), as well as arousing or enhancing local people's public awareness in regard to respecting their culture and inheriting and carrying forward their intangible heritage (e.g. XD042, XD090). More importantly, tourism facilitated cultural and social interactions between local people and tourists. My interviews with both tourists and local people reveal that in many cases there is a deep sense of emotional connection/bonding between local people and tourists when they felt they communicated or connected. There is a cultural and social impact of WH listing and increasing tourism. While some residents reported on the negative impacts of tourism found by other researchers, this was not the full story. Local people, particularly in Xidi, where they had greater control over tourism, reported a range of positive economic as well as cultural and social gains.

This chapter also discussed how the local governments of both villages used a so-called 'international standard' that resulted in maintaining the physical authenticity of the sites to legitimate their local management policies and impose those policies on local people through management practices. Contrary to Yan's (2015) research on Fujian Tulou World Heritage site, where the local government used the concept 'harmony' to legitimate their hegemonic values, the case of Xidi and Hongcun illustrates that the hegemonic process enjoyed by the local governments in both villages was still framed within the European AHD as represented by the 'international standard.' In addition, the majority of local people in both villages, and in particular in Xidi, expressed disappointment with those management policies and practices from governments and tourism companies, which they considered significant in blocking their sense of place and causing alienation for their villages. Tourists also felt the sites, and in particular Hongcun, 'had been managed' too much. Their sense of freedom was constrained by both the physical boundaries of the site and the management practices from the local governments and tourism companies. In this sense, the management policies and practices conducted by local governments and tourism companies caused dissonance in the two villages.

Chapters 5 and 6 analysed my interview data from the Ancient Villages of Southern Anhui – Xidi and Hongcun. Three significant intertwined themes emerged. Firstly, tourists visits to Xidi and Hongcun were tightly linked to their identities, and the meaning of visiting appears to be something simply felt. Comparatively (see Chapters 3 and 4), tourists in Xidi and Hongcun did not have such diverse feelings as my interviewees in West Lake. Many tourists showed that their sense of feeling was tied to the physical place or landscape and local people. However, those simple interactions among tourists, local people and site are very active and show strong emotional engagement. When tourists felt the site was 'alive,' such as XD047 identifying 'preserved ducks hang under the roof, and I can feel the slight smoke curling up from kitchen chimneys,' the sense of contentment emerged. The sense of contentment was identified with both local people and tourists, which links to the second theme of the two chapters.

The second theme to emerge is the in-depth interactions or bonding between tourists and local people, which is more complex and has the same very deep emotional engagement of both local people and tourists that I discovered in West Lake (see Chapter 4). In West Lake, the sense of contentment emerged when local people acknowledged that tourists enjoyed themselves and felt the beauty of the culture of West Lake. This sense of contentment was tied to their sense of pride. However, local people I interviewed in both Xidi and Hongcun not only wanted tourists to feel the physical site or the culture; sometimes they built a bond with tourists. For instance, XD038, had made a 'close friend' in her hostel, and they frequently communicated with each other and 'exchanged postcards' and 'fresh tea.' HC052, in his book *Dream of Hongcun*, engaged in a very deep empathetic process when he dreamed his friend Ms Meng came to visit and he showed her the contemporary life of Hongcun (Wang 2013: 175–184). When this sense of bonding had been built between residents and tourists, local people felt a great sense of contentment.

The final theme of the two chapters is that government control disturbed the interaction between local people and the site, tourists and the site, and local people and tourists. As I conducted my interviews at West Lake (see Chapter 4), the majority of local people and tourists strongly praised the heritage and tourism management of the Hangzhou governments. Both local people and tourists considered the Hangzhou governments' having demolished the 'walls' and 'fences,' and all fees at West Lake facilitated their sense of 'freedom.' However, as I interviewed local people and tourists, dissatisfaction with the heritage and tourism management of the local governments and tourism companies was apparent. From the tourists' perspective, they felt that the two villages are 'managed' (e.g. HC038, HC042 and XD026). Their sense of freedom was not only obstructed by 'gates,' 'walls' and 'high entrance fees,' it was also blocked by the government controls which adhered to the AHD to manage heritage as a static object. In terms of local people, they had a better understanding of their sites. However, the local governments and tourism companies not only marginalised the local residents in any decision-making process, they also set up rules and management strategies that 'followed the international criteria' to restrict local people's traditions and customs in order to keep the site 'authentic.' Thus, local people I interviewed felt a sense of alienation from their site. Ashworth and Tunbridge (1996) have put forward the concept of 'dissonant heritage' that encompasses the negative issues that tourism or tourists bring to the heritage site. However, in the case of Xidi and Hongcun, the 'dissonance' was not brought by tourists, but rather the local governments.

Notes

1 The government reports did not publish the exact demographic results of each village, only statements such as 'the population of the County has declined 13.85% from 2001 to 2000, because county residents were working outside the County.' In contrast, the population numbers were stable in Xidi and Hongcun.
2 Hongcun town is constituted by 13 villages with 13,900 people; Hongcun village is one of the villages in Hongcun town, with about 1200 people. (Source: official web sites of Yixian County (www.yixian.gov.cn).)

Chapter 7

Discussion
Emotion, tourist agency and heritage

This book reveals that the interrelationship between heritage, tourism and local communities is more complex than is generally assumed, both in Chinese and international heritage policy and practice. Several themes have emerged from the previous chapters. These are discussed here, as well as their implications for ongoing debates about World Heritage tourism in heritage studies and heritage management policy.

The first key theme is the identification of the set of complex interactions that occur between local people and tourists. The majority of local people at the two case study sites tended to have very positive views about tourists visiting their sites. Overall, the World Heritage listing and the presence of mass tourists had elicited a sense of pride in residents. Local people wanted tourists to 'feel' their sites, and they hoped that the tourists could invoke a sense of belonging or feeling for the site and engage in communication with local people. In return, tourists enjoyed communicating with the local people as well. Strong emotional contentment emerged when tourists felt they had made a connection with local people. This research also found that government control and authorised tourism enterprises do not necessarily facilitate what all the case studies have been showing people find valuable – cultural and emotional interaction between tourists and local people. What Xidi shows is that those cultural and emotional interactions between tourists and local people become magnified if local people control tourism. There is also a subtheme emerging from the second theme. My data reveals that the sense of metaphor that tourists used, and the emotional contentment they gained, were magnified when they felt they had 'freedom.' The sense of 'freedom' is one of the keys that tourists register as deep emotional and intellectual engagement when they connected to local people or connected to physical sites. However, the sense of 'freedom' was influenced by government management during the World Heritage listing process in my two case studies.

The second theme shows that heritage tourists visited sites that were tightly linked to their identities, and that the meaning of visiting appears to be something felt and not able to be clearly articulated. Poria et al. (2003) have argued that visitors' perceptions of places are linked to their personal feelings, which further influences their behaviours at heritage sites. They also noted that feeling was important; however, they use the term 'feeling' to describe a difficulty their interviewees had in putting their feelings into words or even acknowledging them (see also Smith 2006, 2012). Both of my two case studies show that many tourists' narratives present an aesthetic thought process with frequent use of metaphor in a self-conscious way. Some of them were far more overt about seeking a sense of 'feeling,' far more so than what Poria et al. (2003) recorded in Israel and Smith (2006, 2015) recorded in England, Australia and the United States. Heritage, therefore, was a place where people felt – and in particular felt connected to something vital, such as a connection to land or connection to their sense of place.

Finally, this research reveals that tourists at heritage sites did not necessarily passively accept the authorised messages or governments' interpretations. They were regularly undertaking in-depth and sophisticated cultural and social work, actively working out, remembering and negotiating cultural meanings. Despite the apparent influences of the AHD employed by management at the two sites and discussed above, overall the work supports the sense of agency illustrated by Smith in her work with heritage visitors in (2006, 2011, 2012), and other researchers such as Bagnall (2003), Palmer (2005), Byrne (2009), Sather-Wagstaff (2011) and Waterton and Watson (2012) in Western contexts. My research, using qualitative visitor interviews as previous research has done, has been carried out in a non-Western context. While there are similarities recorded in this data relating to agency there are also significant differences. Chinese visitors tended to employ metaphors far more frequently than is reported in similar research, and they are, on the whole, more explicitly aware they are constructing the meaning of heritage and utilising the past in the present. As I argue below, the sense of metaphor of Chinese visitors can link back to Han's (2006: 186) thesis, in which she demonstrated that traditional Chinese philosophy and the idea of 'oneness with nature' has influenced Chinese understanding of heritage. The task of this chapter is to synthesise the above three themes and reconceptualise the connection between heritage and tourism.

The influences of the authorised heritage discourse

As Smith (2006: 42) argues, the impact of the AHD has created a set of social and cultural practices which tend to marginalise non-expert stakeholders from decision making about heritage. At West Lake, the local government and experts attempted to educate local people and tourists about heritage through the international discourse of OUV and the national harmony discourse. However, my interviews reveal that many local people and tourists were constructing their ideas of heritage and the meanings of the sites without necessarily referencing the authorised discourse. For instance, the local government reformed the West Lake Museum in accordance with the OUV of West Lake in the nomination dossiers. As I conducted three days (including a weekend and a weekday) of observations at the West Lake Museum, the visitors (including local people) who came to the museum did not pay much attention to the 'OUV exhibition' area; certainly very few visitors mentioned or discussed their understanding of West in terms of the scientific values of the OUVs when I interviewed them. Rather, most visitors stressed or talked about their emotional experiences and interactions with West Lake, local people and other tourists. As I discussed in Chapter 3, both local people and tourists I interviewed were not influenced by the international discourse about the meaning of 'natural heritage' and 'cultural heritage;' they also did not make sense of the concept of 'cultural landscape.' It does not mean that local people and tourists do not understand the meaning of heritage; on the contrary, their sense of West Lake is far more active and complex than the AHD and the Chinese harmony discourse. Both local people and tourists I interviewed did not agree on the separation between nature and culture based on their understanding of West Lake. This demonstrated the arguments of Taylor (2009, 2012) and Inaba (2012), who argue that nature and culture are indivisible in Asia. For many local people and tourists, their understanding of nature, culture and heritage is based on their sense of feeling of being in a place. For instance, WL088 described the poetic meaning of 柳浪闻莺 *Orioles Singing in the Willows* to make his arguments about the combination of culture and nature:

> I was called by a friend to have a tea in the morning near 柳浪闻莺 *Orioles Singing in the Willows*. I realised that some of the scenic spots could change with the seasons and time. The swaying wicker in the mist is combined with the crisp bird songs, perfectly explaining the origin of the name 柳浪闻莺 *Orioles Singing in the Willows* from the audio-visual perspective.
>
> (WL088, female, 18–24, tourist)

From her perspective, and many other people's (see WL043, WL055) I interviewed in West Lake (see Chapters 3 and 4), the boundary between defining 'natural heritage,' 'cultural heritage' or 'cultural landscape' are meaningless. Despite this, many Chinese researchers have discussed and disseminated the discourse of cultural landscape with great enthusiasm (see Zhou et al. 2006; Shan 2009b, 2010b; Han 2010; Wu 2011). Both local people and tourists I interviewed were more concerned about their emotional feeling of heritage tied to personal memories and experiences, which further reflected their personal or collective identities. As I discussed in Chapter 3 and 4, local people's and tourists' senses of heritage were a combination of things evoked by physically being at the site and were influenced by their self-conscious pursuit of nature and culture in an inner world tied to their memories and experiences. Therefore, the sense of feeling about the aesthetic and poetic thought process demonstrated by tourists I interviewed at West Lake created a cultural moment that was a dialogue between their internal world and the outside world. To illustrate this, I note a story of sense of feeling from Wang Yangming,[1] who is one of the most influential Chinese idealist Neo-Confucians:

> The Teacher [Wang] was taking recreation at Nanchen. One of his friends pointed to the flowers and trees on a cliff and said: 'You say that there is nothing under heaven external to the mind. What relation to my mind have these flowers and trees on the high mountains, which blossom and drop of themselves?' The Teacher said: 'When you cease regarding these flowers, they become quiet with your mind. When you see them, their colours at once become clear. From this, you can know that these flowers are not external to your mind.' He further said: 'Perception has no structure upon which it depends: it uses the colour of all things as its structure. The ear has no structure upon which it depends: it uses the sounds of things as its structure. The nose has no structure: it uses the odours of things as its structure. The mouth has no structure: it uses the taste of things as its structure. The mind has no structure: it uses the right and wrong influences of heaven, earth, and things as structure.'
> (Wang and Henke 1964: 31–32, the text has been modernised by Prof. Arkenberg[2])

Many of the interviewees, such as WL043, expressed an explicit poetic sense of feeling when they talked about their understanding of nature and culture. Han (2006: 186) argues that the concept of 'oneness with nature' or 'harmony of man with nature'[3] are embodied in every Chinese person's personal or collective memories. The source of the 'harmony' concept can be found in school textbooks, poetry, traditional Chinese paintings and stories in everyday Chinese daily life, which facilitate the poetic thought process and sense of feeling I identified. The sense of 'harmony of man with nature' embodied in traditional Chinese culture is different from what Yan (2015) labelled the harmony discourse, which he argues is the Chinese hegemonic discourse and a Chinese version of the Western AHD. The sense of 'harmony of man with nature' that I identified linked to both local people and tourists' emotional feeling of the site, and is tied to their memories and experiences. The sense of feeling is active and complex. I will further discuss the issue of feeling in the following section.

At Xidi and Hongcun, as above noted, regardless of whether the local government misunderstood or misused the UNESCO standard, the policies implemented that reference UNESCO have caused local dissonance. My research demonstrates that the power relations underlying the discourse in the Chinese context are no different from that identified in the European context by Ashworth and Tunbridge (1996), Macdonald (2003), Graham et al. (2000) and Smith (2006). The national and local authorities and experts who represent the upper and ruling classes have the power to define the meaning and nature of heritage. Therefore, the consequences of the AHD marginalise the majority middle and lower classes' understanding of heritage.

Economic gain, cultural gain

The tension between tourism and heritage has existed for a long time. From a practical understanding of heritage, the literature has been concerned with managing tourism impacts on heritage sites. As Ashworth (2009) has argued, mainstream heritage tourism literature characterises tourists as a problem. Tourists are routinely defined as causing economic commodification (McCrone et al. 1995; Brett 1996; Lowenthal 1998; Choay 2001; Greenspan 2002), pollution and physical damage to sites, and they obscure or erode other values of heritage (Swarbrooke 1995; Hall and McArthur 1998; Leask and Yeoman 1999; McKercher and du Cros 2002). Moreover, these views tend to be embedded in international ICOMOS heritage policies and practices (Ashworth 2009). The interviews with national government officials revealed that they too followed this dominant negative perspective on tourism and tourists, in that they regarded tourists as a problem or threat that needs to be 'managed' in terms of their physical impact. They characterised tourism as one of the trickiest issues they needed to deal with both before and after World Heritage listing. The two experts (WL142 and WL143, see Chapter 4) told me that tourism problems would influence the World Heritage nomination. When they wrote the nomination dossiers, they avoided using the word 'tourism,' and substituted it with a new term, 'display and dissemination.' The economic effects of tourism were the only perceived benefit of tourism, and both the national governments' officials and experts admitted that they focussed on this in the dossiers.

While tourists may bring about the negative effects noted above, they may also have positive effects. The majority of local people I interviewed at the two case study sites considered that tourism and tourists caused them to have a great sense of pride. This sense of pride is constructed from both the economic and cultural gains received from tourism and tourists. In terms of the economic gain, local people in Hangzhou, no matter if they were a 'new Hangzhou citizen'[4] or an 'old Hangzhou citizen,' considered tourism and tourists to have raised funding that supported positive changes to their sites. Those changes include improvement to water quality, an enlarged lake area and the creation of a new touristic area such as Xixi National Wetland Park and Jiang Yangfan Park, along with other infrastructural improvements (see Chapter 3). The infrastructural improvements funded by tourism can also be witnessed in Xidi and Hongcun. The tourists' numbers in Xidi increased from 250,000, with ticket-sale revenue of US$0.7 million in 2000, to 800,000 with ticket-sale revenue of US$5.48 million in 2001, following the WH listing, while the ticket-sale revenue increased even more dramatically from US$0.15 million to US$12.9 million in Hongcun (Ying and Zhou 2007; The Xidi Government 2013b). The majority of local people believed that tourism is the most significant reason their villages still existed and were vital. My data also shows that the majority of local people were engaged in tourism or tourism-related business in the two villages. Tourism has caused an industrial transformation from traditional agricultural and tea farming to tourism services. Local people were very happy and proud of the industrial transformation, as they considered tourism development had saved them from poverty so that the young villagers could stay on to help the tourism business rather than search for jobs elsewhere, as occurred in many other surrounding villages (e.g. HC052, HC028 in Chapter 6).

More importantly, there were cultural gains from tourism at the sites of the two case studies. The majority of local people were very willing for tourists to come to their sites. At West Lake, local people mentioned that mass tourists come to the site, which they were proud of. Some of them were proud of their cultural, historical and physical setting (e.g. WL058, WL080, WL093 in Chapter 3 and 4). Some of them were just simply proud to be a citizen of Hangzhou in a city receiving worldwide recognition (e.g. WL076 in Chapter 4); some of them hoped people could inherit and innovate intangible cultures such as the Longjin tea culture, silk skills and routines from the Southern Song dynasty (e.g. WL094, WL097 in Chapter 3 and 4); and some of them are proud of the new developments in the city (e.g. WL032, WL033, WL080 in Chapter 3). Surveys conducted in Xidi and Hongcun revealed that tourism itself has been seen as a positive factor by villagers from a non-economic perspective. Some local people considered that tourists aroused local people's public awareness of the need to respect their culture and is a stimulating factor for the protection and improvement of intangible heritage (e.g. XD042, XD090 in Chapter 6).

Emotional engagement in cultural moments

Much of the heritage and tourism literature has defined tourists as 'culturally inauthentic,' passive sightseers, with little or no agency in the meanings they construct at heritage sites (see for example, McCrone et al. 1995; Brett 1996;

MacCannell 1999; Choay 2001: 4–5; Burton 2003; Mason 2004, 2005). A key issue that the interviews with tourists in the two case studies illustrates is that tourists have agency, and they are undertaking in-depth and sophisticated cultural work during their visits to heritage sites. At West Lake (see Chapter 4), a significant national icon, tourists were very familiar with the site and its meanings because of the history, stories, poetry and TV programmes etc. Many tourists came to West Lake not for the aesthetic reasons that dominate the criteria on which this site gained World Heritage status, but rather to gain cultural experiences, which link to histories, myth, stories, poetries, proverbs, the White Snake TV show and other intangible things (e.g. WL011, WL040, WL044, WL083 in Chapter 4). The reasons they were attracted to West Lake were linked to their personal or collective memories. They wanted to reminisce and remember those memories during their journey. Some of the tourists wanted to see the modern part of West Lake or how modern elements merged into the historical setting (e.g. WL072, WL129 Chapter 3). Ironically, those modern settlements are characterised by UNESCO and the Chinese governments as threatening the integrity and authenticity of the UNESCO criteria.

My research also reveals that there is a complex interrelation between tourists and heritage sites. The overall engagement of those interviewed at West Lake (Chapters 3 and 4) tended to be multi-dimensional, drawing on different aspects of emotional registers. Tourists' sense of nationalism (e.g. WL075), identities (e.g. WL064), belonging (e.g. WL048), nostalgia (e.g. WL129) and humility (e.g. WL078) were evoked by encounters with the physical sites or objects during their visit. With few exceptions, tourists' engagement facilitated a strong sense of emotional authenticity, based on the process of remembering and reminiscing that were entangled with their personal and collective memories. For instance: WL048 and WL082 compared Hangzhou to the city they were living in or used to live in, which represents their sense of belonging elicited by seeing another place with similar or interlinked historical or cultural backgrounds; WL064 engaged a powerful emotional register when he was reminiscing and searching for lost identity related to his family, as his grandparents moved from mainland China to Taiwan because of the Chinese Civil War from 1945 to 1950; and WL099's sense of place was linked to his religion, and he saw his visit as a 'pilgrimage.' In some cases, my survey shows a deep emotional engagement was linked to intellectual engagement. For example, WL040 demonstrated that physically being at the Yue Fei Temple made him deeply empathise with Yue Fei's experience in the past. During this empathetic process, he reflected on the meaning of 'good and evil' in the present, engaging in a dialogue between past and present.

In the case of Xidi and Hongcun (Chapter 5), the cultural and historical elements are not as complicated as those at West Lake. The World Heritage brand is one of the significant reasons people come to visit. A large number of tourists were engaged in acts of recognition of the culture and history of the two villages or Anhui province, doing their own identity or memory work, and were engaged in building social connections. For some visitors, the built environments of Xidi and Hongcun were associated with the depth and texture of wider Chinese Southern identity and Confucianism. For example, XD028 and XD049 linked the material buildings to the past Hui culture underlined by an emotion of adoration. Physical encounters with old buildings helped generate an interesting cultural moment with a dialogue between the present and the past. XD024 and XD029 were geographically separated, from different parts of China; however, both of them had a similar cultural affiliation to the site. Therefore, their memories had been aroused by seeing the landscape in Xidi, which invoked a similar sense of belonging. Although some tourists' perspectives of the two sites were impacted by the AHD, which focusses on aesthetic values, many tourists, however, were actively engaged in a complex aesthetic thought process rather than passively accepting the received messages of the AHD (e.g. XD057, HC005, HC040). For instance, XD057 used a metaphor to describe 'Hongcun is a woman, and Xidi is a man,' with an aesthetic view of Hongcun and the grand scale of buildings in Hongcun evoking his sense of feeling. HC005 was deeply engaged in the cultural moment she created, with physically being at the site eliciting her poetic sense of feeling linked to her imagination of the four seasons. Those tourists' aesthetic emotional expressions were invoked by a physical encounter with places, which linked to their personal or collective memories. My two case studies illustrate tourists' emotional engagement and reflect that, although some tourists offered formalistic or platitudinous responses in their interviews, the majority of them showed that tourists deeply engaged in constructing heritage meaning with registers of emotional engagement, sometimes positive with an active sense, sometimes negative with frustrated feeling. The heritage objects or landscape became a medium to reinforce their sense of belonging and identities. Some negative impacts of tourism, in particular, cultural commodification and commercial changes, were mentioned during my interview. For instance, WL021 expressed his disappointment about the commercial changes at West Lake. His sense of unpleasantness was linked to a sense of nostalgia, as he had had an enjoyable experience during his first visit to West Lake ten years ago; WL049 was disappointed with his journey because he felt commodification eroded other historical values which he had expected. Examples were also evident in Xidi and Hongcun; XD022 criticised the commercial changes of Hongcun, which also influenced his sense of nostalgia about a pleasant journey he had taken 13 years ago. Although some tourists were aware of the negative impacts of tourism, it was an engagement process of creating heritage. No matter the positive or negative memories created by the interaction between tourists and heritage, those memories make heritage meaningful and alive.

My interview reveals that tourists were not simply 'touring;' they were undertaking 'cultural and social work,' actively working out, remembering and negotiating cultural meanings. Despite the apparent influences of the AHD employed by management at the two sites and discussed above, overall the work supports the sense of agency illustrated by Smith (2006, 2011, 2012), Sather-Wagstaff (2011) and Byrne (2009) in their work with heritage visitors in England, the United States, Australia and Thailand. My research using qualitative visitor interviews was carried out in a Chinese context. There are two themes that emerged from Chinese tourists' discourse that are different from Western cultural contexts, which refer to the sense of feeling and the interactions between tourists and local people. In the following two sections, I will unpack these two themes.

Emotional expression of feeling

Poria et al. (2003) have argued that visitors' perception of places links to their personal feelings and further influences their behaviours at heritage sites. They acknowledged that this research, based on interviews with people visiting the heritage site the Wailing Wall, Israel, which has a strong association with tourists' feelings tied to their family or ethnicity. Cameron and Gatewood (2000, 2003) also identified a sense of feeling, which they called 'numinous,' that attempted to describe a visitor's sense of being spiritually linked to the past. They considered that some tourists at heritage sites are undertaking 'numen-seeking.' Smith (2006, 2015) observed that visitors often had strong emotional engagements; however, they tended not to talk explicitly about feeling anything. Smith based her research within Australia, England and US contexts, and reports (pers. comm.) that there is little overt acknowledgement that tourists were having or seeking certain feelings at sites, although their responses indicated that they were feeling something. Nonetheless, the degree of emotional authenticity that they felt was important in validating the meanings they were making.

Based on those scholars' research, my research further develops their arguments in the Chinese context. I have found that there is a more complex and multi-dimensional sense of feeling that emerges from my two case studies' interviews, which reveals that people talk about their feelings in a far more self-conscious way than the data Cameron and Gatewood (2000, 2003), Poria et al. (2003) or Smith (2006, 2015) have recorded. Firstly, some of the tourists were clearly aware they were seeking a sense of 'feeling' that tied to their sense of place. It is a dialogue between the personal and the physical site. Both of my two case studies showed that many tourists' narratives presented an aesthetic thought process with extensive use of metaphor. On the one hand, some of them were explicitly aware of the very subtle natural aesthetic beauty surrounding them. For instance, XD057 metaphorically thought that 'Hongcun is a woman and Xidi is a man' which '[t]he water view in Hongcun is so beautiful, which makes Hongcun like a woman. The old houses and ancestral temples in Xidi are larger and bigger than Hongcun, so I imagine Xidi is a man;' HC005 described her sense of place at Hongcun as being able to see that the four seasons were 'alive' there.

On the other hand, some of the tourists' sense of feeling evoked by their encounters with the physical sites revealed deeper emotional engagements. My research revealed a sense of the poetic that is tied to the idea of emotion and feeling which is more overt than Bagnall (2003), Poria et al. (2003) and Smith (2006, 2015) found in Western contexts. For instance, WL043 (see Chapter 3) when he vividly described the scene of 断桥残雪 *Lingering Snow on Broken Bridge* that 'reflects the scenery that on a sunny day after a heavy snow, the snow on the bridge melts and shows the brown floor, which gives people a feeling that the chain is broken.' I interviewed him in the autumn, and he easily described his aesthetic feeling in the winter season. In the interview with resident WL076 (see Chapter 4), he also understood the poetic meaning of the *Ten Poetically Named Scenic Places* such as 断桥残雪 *Lingering Snow on Broken Bridge*, and he wanted tourists to understand and feel these poetic meanings as well. My research reveals that the Chinese people (both tourists and local people) I interviewed seem to easily understand the poetic meaning of West Lake (e.g. see also WL093). Ironically, 断桥残雪 *Lingering Snow on Broken Bridge* was the place the local government and experts tried but failed, to explain the poetic meaning of to the ICOMOS experts in the WH listing process (Zhang 2017; Zhang and Taylor 2019). As the director from the Institute of Architectural History comments:

> When I prepared the World Heritage listing for West Lake, I studied the German psychologist Theodor Lippsor about his theory of aesthetics, particularly the concept of 'empathy.' I want to learn how to interpret nature from the perspective of 'human' for ICOMOS examination. However, I found that Chinese people's thoughts and ideas have never been divided into subject and object, rather a holistic idea of 'harmony between man nature' in Chinese philosophy.
>
> (WL144, director from the Institute of Architectural History)

The poetic or aesthetic thought process was embodied in Chinese traditional philosophy, and represents and speaks to Chinese identity and is easily made sense of by Chinese people. While Westerners were not influenced in this way, even the ICOMOS experts' expertise could not readily fill the gap of cultural differences. This gap supports Han Feng's (2006) thesis, where she demonstrated that the Chinese traditional philosophy precept of 'oneness with nature' (or harmony with nature as noted above) had influenced Chinese understanding of heritage (see also the essential spirit of traditional Chinese philosophies identified by Zhang 1986; Wang 1990; Xu 1996). Han (2006) argues that:

> Chinese philosophies are about human beings and their highest practices involve the aesthetic pursuit of life itself.
>
> (Han 2006:187)

> Nature, interpreted by Chinese philosophical, moral and aesthetic values, greatly contributed to the aesthetic construction of all aspects of traditional everyday life, from the ideal society to the ideal personality. Life, morals, politics, aesthetics everything could be interpreted by *Shanshui*, which had penetrated human ideology. Nature was spiritually and materially reconstructed by the Chinese when the boundary between human beings and nature disappeared.
>
> (Han 2006: 190) (see also Xu 1996; Peng 1998; Zhang 2005)

This poetic sense of feeling was also widely expressed by tourists quoting poetry from ancient scholars (e.g. WL083), some of them even creating poetry when they were visiting West Lake. For instant:

> I remember when I went to West Lake at mid-March, I just went to Shanghai for an interview at a university. At that time, I felt very anxious, lost hope for life, and desperately went to West Lake for recreation. At that time, 初春仍寒，阵雨初停，柳枝新绿，烟雾弥漫，绿水拍岸 the early spring was still cold, the shower stopped at the beginning, the willow branches were green, the smog was filled, and the green water flapping on the shore. I walked around the lake for more than 40,000 steps, sighing that there was such a beautiful scene in the world, and immediately restored the confidence and hope of life and revived.
>
> (WL042, female, 18–24, tourist)

Just like WL042, many other visitors, influenced by ancient scholars such as Bai Juyi and Sun Dongpo, actively express their feeling by composing poetry (see message board in Chapter 4). In this sense, the ancient scholars created the meaning of heritage in the past, while tourists in the present have been creating the contemporary meaning of heritage.

The sense of feeling was also expressed by some of the tourists metaphorically, though they are explicitly aware that they are constructing their meaning of heritage and utilising the past in the present. Some of those senses of feeling become entangled with the issue of authenticity. For instance, XD049's sense of feeling was tied to the physical authenticity of the building, and he considered that the physical authenticity of the old houses could invoke his sense of feeling and that his mind was drawing on the past to witness the memories of the building. WL040 had been aware that being in the Yue Fei Temple allowed him to have an emphatic emotional engagement with Yue Fei's stories in the past, and further influenced his view of the world in the present. The physical authenticity of the Yue Fei Temple triggered his feeling that he was engaging in a dialogue between past and present. However, sometimes visitors' sense of feeling does not link to the physical authenticity of the site. For example, WL043's and WL089's (see Chapter 3) senses of place were tied to what they felt was an empathetic process with romantic and poetic elements: WL089 who wanted to drink wine with two ancient scholars, and WL042 who was immersed in the romantic scene from The White Snake story. Their feelings were moving between the past and the present, and from the spiritual to the mundane. In their case, being in the physical place allowed them to be spiritually linked to the past in a quite poetic way. This deep intellectual engagement was not evoked by the physical authenticity of the site but was rather influenced by their memories and the experiences of their journeys. As Swarbrooke (1996: A69) states, 'the reality of a product or experience is probably less important … than the consumer's perception of it.' People's sense of emotional authenticity and those poetic thought processes can be traced back to Chinese Confucian philosophy and Wang Yangming, who considered that objects do not exist completely without the mind, because it is the mind that shapes them. He believed that what you see, hear, feel, think and all in your head is the world (Carsun 1962).

Therefore, I argue that sometimes visitors' emotional authenticity, at times influenced by physical authenticity and at other times not, but no matter in what circumstances, link to visitors' personal or collective memories and their social and cultural experiences. Hence, the importance of physical authenticity depends on the extent to which it elicits people's emotional engagement. My research has confirmed the arguments of emotional authenticity developed by Bagnall (2003), Smith (2006, 2012) and Zhu (2012). As Smith (2006: 70) states:

> This idea of emotional realism, or emotional authenticity in which visitors can validate or measure the legitimacy of their own social and cultural experiences outside of the heritage sites they are visiting, adds another layer of consequence to the idea of performativity.

There is a significant issue I would like to raise, which is that the questionnaire I used in my interviews was based on the questionnaire designed by Smith (2006, 2012, 2015) and used in her research in Australia, England and the US. There is a tendency that the differences that my research reveals in comparison to the Western findings are the sense of feeling Chinese visitors tend to employ; they are, on the whole, more explicitly aware of what they are feeling at and about the sites, and utilise the past in the present more than has been reported in other cultural contexts (see for example Smith 2006, 2012, 2015; Sather-Wagstaff 2011).

My interviews with tourists at both case study sites also reveal that the sense of feeling is not only tied to their sense of place but is also linked to their sense of interactions with local people. Poria et al. (2003) and Smith (2006, 2015) have discussed the issue of tourists' feeling connected to a site, and this was influencing their performances. My research further develops their argument by illustrating that there is an interplay of identity going on among tourists, local people and third parties (local governments and tourism companies) at Xidi and Hongcun. At Xidi, many tourists I interviewed had a feeling that Xidi is 'alive.' I also received some responses that visitors considered Hongcun to be alive as well (e.g. HC005, HC040); however, the general proportion was not as great as at Xidi. Some tourists had been to both places, but considered Xidi to be more alive and felt a sense of alienation at Hongcun. As noted above, there was a lot of interaction between tourists and local people in both villages. However, there were third party controls in both villages as well, and the third party's control in Hongcun was more effective than Xidi, which interrupted the interactions between local people and tourists. Therefore, tourists felt that the intimate relationship they felt when they were communicating with local people, without mediation by a third party, was typical of Xidi rather than Hongcun, where the interplay had been removed or influenced by third parties. The interactions that occur between tourists and local people is another significant theme and will be discussed in the next section.

There is a subtheme that links to tourists' sense of feeling, which I refer to as a sense of 'freedom.' Poria et al. (2003: 248) considered tourists who are motivated by the heritage attributes of the sites, and consider these attributes to be part of their heritage, have a deeper sense of emotional engagement and connection to the site than those tourists who are motivated by relaxation or entertainment. However, as I interviewed tourists at my two case study sites, no matter whether tourists' motivations to visit the site was for in-depth cultural and historical engagement, or just for relaxation or recreational reasons, they had expressed deep emotional engagement when they felt a sense of freedom during the journey. For instance, some tourists' motivation to visit West Lake was for recreation from working pressure (e.g. WL012), and experiencing a site with lots of natural features gave them a feeling of 'freedom.' There is a Chinese tradition that many travellers in ancient times, such as Bai Juyi and Su Dongpo, pursued the beauty of nature to forget reality. Han (2006: 90) used the term '*Shanshui Tour*' to argue that:

> In this travel, there was no bitterness at leaving home, no discontent with reality, no worries about life, and no burden of moral cultivation. The only thing it had was pure spiritual enjoyment obtained from beautiful destinations.

Thousands of poems describe the beauty of West Lake, which has been created by people who tried to engage themselves with nature and escaped from reality during their journey. Therefore, I argue that some tourists who come to heritage sites are not pursuing any other external things; rather, they are searching for the feeling of 'freedom.' However, sometimes their sense of freedom is blocked or restrained by physical and invisible boundaries. The physical boundaries include 'walls,' 'fences' and 'entrance gates,' while the invisible boundaries are 'entrance fees' and 'government control.' Some tourists I interviewed in the two case studies showed to some extent how their sense of freedom was influenced by those boundaries. At West Lake, some tourists I interviewed (see WL089, WL099 in Chapter 4) complimented the Hangzhou government for opening up the entire area around West Lake by removing the entrance fee. WL089, who actively engaged in a poetic and romantic cultural moment she created by imagining drinking wine with ancient scholars, as a return visitor considered that both the physical boundaries ('walls,' 'fences' or 'entrance gate') and the invisible boundaries ('entrance fee') interrupted her sense of feeling when she had last visited. While WL099 considered his sense of feeling 'was cut into several pieces by those walls and gates.' In terms of Xidi and Hongcun, visitors such as HC038, HC042 and XD028 were dissatisfied with the heritage and tourism management of the local governments and tourism companies, and they considered their sense of feeling 'has been managed' not only by the 'gates,' 'walls' and 'high entrance fees,' but rather constrained by the government controls drawing on the AHD to fossilise the two villages as a theme park. Therefore, the two case studies show that the sense of freedom is one of the keys that help tourists register deep emotions and facilitate their different kinds of sense of feeling; however, this can be obstructed by physical and intangible boundaries.

In this section, my interview results in both areas have reinforced and further developed the arguments that Poria et al. (2003) and Smith (2006, 2015) have made that tourists' motivations for visiting, their behaviour during their visits and the messages they had taken away were clearly linked to their sense of feeling. However, my interviews also show that not only do tourists have this sense of feeling; some residents also express a deep sense of feeling. This interrelationship with another significant theme was emerged from my research – the interaction between local people and tourists.

Emotional interactions between local people and tourists

The interviews in all of my case studies have shown the complex emotional interactions between local people and tourists. The sense of pride of local people was magnified when they had communicated with or made an emotional connection with tourists. In the case of West Lake (see Chapter 4), local people wanted tourists to experience or 'feel' their sites. Some of them hoped that tourists could gain cultural experiences, enjoy local customs or food from Hangzhou, some of them expect tourists could take their time to 'feel,' to enjoy or to 'taste' the poetic meaning of Hangzhou (e.g. WL076), and some of them hoped tourists could recognise or explore the culture and history beyond the authorised discourse. During my interviews with local people in West Lake, the majority of them were very engaged in the conversation we were having and displayed strong emotional registers of engagement. I easily related to the narratives they were relating, as they were very sincere. Against much of the heritage literature and policies made by international and national authorities, who criticise the destructive nature of mass tourists to local communities, my research clearly shows the majority of local people were willing for tourists to come to West Lake, which was tied to their strong sense of pride.

At Xidi and Hongcun, the majority of local people's livelihoods depend on tourists. Clearly, the dramatic development of tourism has been influenced by World Heritage designation (see Chapter 5 and 6). With the development of tourism, hostels operated by local people along with other tourism businesses have emerged. My survey reveals that nearly all of the residents I spoke to were willing for tourists to come to their villages. Apart from economic factors, a sense of protection of both tangible and intangible heritage, and the local people's pride as above noted, there is a sense of emotional connection between local people and tourists. The hostels (run by local people) were the places that magnified those emotional connections. Those types of hostels were normally traditional Huizhou dwellings renovated by the house owners (local people) to meet their personal needs. Many tourists frequently booked local hostels using social networking services such as

Figure 7.1 Message board in Hongcun's local hostel (photo by Rouran Zhang)

穷游 Qiongyou.com or 携程网 ctrip.com. They could write their own stories about their visit and detail their experiences and inspirations and compare them to other tourists' experiences before they set off. Therefore, the hostels provided places for communication or emotional engagements between local people and tourists or tourists themselves. Some of the communications or emotional engagements were shallow or banal. However, in many cases, the communications or emotional engagements were very deep, and some tourists had written down (or sketched) their experiences and feelings and posted them on the message board. Other tourists could be inspired, or have empathetic feelings during their visit (Figure 7.1).

I remembered the day I had a conversation as a tourist with HC051, who is the owner of a local hostel. She told me that interactions and communication with tourists could provide her with a great sense of pleasure and contentment:

> In the early morning, I saw my neighbour emerged out of the mist, with some dirt on her shoes. She was carrying a basket of fresh vegetables from her farm to the morning market. I smiled and said hi to her and then I went to Mr Wang's house, which is close to Moon Pool to have a cup of tea and some breakfast. From his house, I saw four women were washing clothes in the pool. They were chatting with each other, laughing. In the meantime, there were several elderly people who were drinking porridge at the opposite side of Moon Pool. Suddenly, I heard a large group of footstep getting closer, which I knew meant today's first group of guests

was coming. Some of these visitors were asking about the culture or the customs of the village from the local tour guide; and some of them were shooting photos of the pool, the houses, the reflections and the villagers. I like this kind of lifestyle.

(HC051, female, 45–54, local)

HC052, who is a local scholar, also operates a hostel, and wrote a book 古村有梦 *Dream of the Old Village*. In his book, he mentioned that he had built a deep relationship with a Beijing tourist, Ms Meng, who had been to Hongcun many times and witnessed and experienced the exceptional beauty of Hongcun, and 'spring's rape flowers, summer's lotus, autumn's red leaves and winter's "white village"' (Wang 2013: 175). The touristic places in Hongcun and surrounding areas did not attract her, 'the only reason she has come to Hongcun regularly is the deep interactions between the author and her' (Wang 2013: 176). In Mr Wang's book, he literally dreamed that he had an empathetic role as he turns into Ms Meng and dreamt how she would experience and enjoy contemporary life in Hongcun (Wang 2013: 175–184). In Xidi, XD038 experienced a deep bonding with tourists, as she made 'close friends' and 'exchanges postcards' and 'fresh tea' frequently (Chapter 6). Therefore, I argue that there is an emotional sense of pleasure and contentment, and even personal bonding occurred, when local people feel they had made a connection with tourists. Those interactions between local people and tourists keep the heritage alive, and it is an active process that creates memories between local people and tourists. As Smith (2006, 2012: 213) has argued, heritage is not 'frozen in time,' but rather is a performance, the act of which keeps the historical and heritage meanings and the values they represent relevant to society. In Smith's work (2006, 2012, 2015, 2017), she examined the relevance of this performance to tourists/visitors, and this research suggests that residents also engage in this performance, and that, moreover, they make meanings that reinforce their own identity and pride from witnessing the performances of visiting enacted by tourists. The interconnections and performances between tourists and local people construct the meaning of heritage. As I conducted my survey at West Lake, I also witnessed this relationship build between local people and tourists in hostels run by local people (e.g. WL097 in Chapter 4).

From the tourists' perspective, the level of emotional engagement with a sense of contentment seems magnified when tourists feel they had made a connection with local people and with the site. In the case of West Lake (see Chapter 4), communicating with the local people (e.g. WL078, WL083, WL118), enjoying or participating in local people's activities (e.g. WL028), listening to the stories of Hangzhou from local people, or watching the elder local people's performances such as Tai Ji or Square Dance were performances that elicited tourists' sense of belonging. At Xidi and Hongcun (see Chapter 5), my survey shows that the sense of contentment was also widely found when tourists are deeply engaged in communicating with local people. Some unremarkable details of the villages, such as 'preserved ducks hanging under the roof' (e.g. XD047), the busy morning market with fresh vegetables and food (e.g. HC040), and 'a simple poster posted on the wall of a resident's house, which indicates that the house owner is going to butcher a pig and hopes villagers will come to buy fresh meat at that time' (e.g. HC005), have made tourists feel that the heritage is alive. The sense of being 'alive' is what tourists found as they visited the two villages, which facilitated their sense of contentment.

Both studies reveal a similar process of interaction between local people and tourists. A sense of pleasure and contentment was generated between tourists and local people at nationally significant heritage sites such as West Lake and regionally significant sites such as Xidi and Hongcun. My research also finds that government control of authorised tourism enterprises interrupts the sense of contentment and bonding that both case studies have shown, stemming from the cultural interaction between tourists and local people. What Xidi shows is that those cultural interactions among tourists, local people and physical sites become magnified if local people control tourism. The reason is linked to who has the right to manage heritage. The tourism management in Hongcun is run by Co. Jingyi Ltd, which is the external company authorised by the local government. From the perspective of local communities, the tourism company was only concerned to protect the historical and cultural appearance of heritage sites, which was required by national or international policies. Therefore, some regulations and rules have been imposed since Hongcun was successfully inscribed on the WHL. For instance, local people had no right to maintain their own buildings unless approved by locally authorised so-called 'qualified' construction teams.[5] However, based on their traditions, traditional houses were normally maintained by local construction teams.

Therefore, those management strategies were the invisible 'boundaries' that had resulted in local people's sense of alienation from their own culture. In Xidi, tourism management was run by local people for more than 20 years. However, in mid-2013, the state-owned enterprise Co. Huihuang Ltd took charge, though the new tourism company had, at the time the interviews were undertaken, limited influence on existing tourism management. The local governments and tourism company intended to copy Hongcun's tourism management experiences in order to replicate Hongcun's tourism income. However, there were strong complaints and resistance from Xidi's villagers, as they feared both physical and cultural alienation from the state-run tourism company taking over management from local people. In Hongcun, local government, the tourism company and local people seem to have found a balance with each other and are aware that breaking the balance might negatively influence their income. Therefore, some tourists who went to both villages considered Hongcun to be more 'unified' than Xidi, while XD047 considered Hongcun a commercial place, yet identified Xidi as 'alive' (see Chapter 5).

Poria et al. (2003) argue that visitors engaged in an emotionally heightened register when they felt the heritage site relates to their family or ethnic connections. However, my research reveals that tourists with deep emotional registers and a poetic sensibility are responding to things that may not necessarily connect to their family or ethnic identity, but rather connect to their sense of place. My research also further identified the emotional feeling was not just in the tourists' connection to the site, but extended when there was an interplay of identity with local people. My interview results in Xidi and Hongcun show that local people in Xidi had a strong feeling of the sites belonging to them as a part of their identity. When the local governments took over the management from the locally run company, they expressed a deep, depressed emotion about their feeling of intimacy with their village. In essence, their sense of place was blocked by the 'boundaries' set up by the local government. While in Hongcun, apparently, local people did not express a depressed emotion because their income is higher than Xidi's. However, they also did not report the deep sense of place I recorded in Xidi. Scholars such as Chen (2005), Liang and Wang (2005) and Ying and Zhou (2007) have documented a fierce conflict among local people, the local government and the external company about the ownership of the management rights (see Chapters 5 and 6). However, local people failed twice with legal challenges, and in the end did not have any choice but to accept a situation they could not control. As I spoke to them about the management and ownership issues they became cynical; they tended to ignore or to complain about the management and then turned to compare tourism income with Xidi. In this sense, the income became a buffer zone among local people, the local government and the external company in Hongcun. Local people had no choice but to ignore their sense of place and put more emotional engagement into tourism. HC028 and HC052 are two local scholars I interviewed in Hongcun who did not participate in any decision making about tourism management or the World Heritage listing process. HC028 was sincerely worried about the way government control constrained both local people and tourists' sense of freedom. HC052 avoided considering the local government control; rather, he spent more than ten years writing his book, 古村有梦 *Dream of the Old Village*, which documents not only the history and customs of Hongcun but also the positive changes that tourism brought to the village.

Compared to Xidi and Hongcun, West Lake is much larger physically, as well as being of greater importance in terms of the depth and complexity of its cultural and historical layers. However, the sense of bonding between local people and tourists was not as strong as in the two villages. The reason is not that government control was stronger than in Xidi and Hongcun. Although the Hangzhou government intended to 'educate' tourists about the international and national discourse (Zhang 2017a), the example of the West Lake museum, as noted above, illustrated that tourists have agency, do not easily accept the imposed AHD and have their own understandings of heritage. The livelihoods of the majority of Hangzhou residents did not depend on tourism, so their interactions with tourists were primarily tied to a sense of pride. Some local people were engaged in hospitality, located around Maojiabu, the Linying Temple and the Longjin Tea Plantation Base, and I identified that they had similar experiences of emotional bonding between tourists and local people as I found in the two villages (e.g. WL097 in Chapter 4). However, because of the national significance of the cultural and historical layers of West Lake, tourists come to the site for a variety of reasons. The sense of contentment was not only elicited by the interaction between tourists and local people but also generated by the connection between the tourists and the physical sites. My survey shows that the relationship between tourists and physical sites at West Lake was multi-dimensional, and tied to their sense of feeling, and stronger than in the two villages (see Chapter 4 on feeling a sense of place).

Some local people in my two case studies mentioned the negative effects that tourism has. At West Lake, some local people considered that tourism inflated food or housing prices, and caused commercialisation, bad traffic conditions and crowding during weekends and public holidays. The management literature has emphasised the pollution and physical damage to sites that tourism can cause and notes that these impacts can erode local heritage values (see, for example, Harrison 1994; Swarbrooke 1995; Hall and McArthur 1998; Leask and Yeoman 1999; McKercher and du Cros 2002; Pedersen 2002 among others). My research shows that, although local people at West Lake listed those negative impacts, which are not something that can be ignored, the majority of them nonetheless considered the benefits that tourists contributed to the site carried more weight than the negative impacts. They knew how to minimise those negative impacts. For instance, WL005, WL058 and WL076 (see Chapter 4) mentioned that mass tourists had influenced their daily life, particularly during public holidays. However, they did not hate or curse mass tourists; rather, they chose to leave the touristic places to the tourists and went to other places instead. The sense of pride that tourists brought to local people has influenced local people's attitude and performances.

Some local people want tourists to know about the general stories of Hangzhou, such as the White Snake story, and stories of Yue Fei, Yu Qian and Su Dongpo, etc. Some local people wanted tourists to explore some hidden stories, such as the histories of the Republic period that were ignored or excluded from the Communist harmony discourse. Many local people wanted tourists to be present at the physical sites and feel the poetic or romantic sense of West Lake. WL076, WL088 and WL093 nominated their sense of pride elicited by tourists who take their time to feel the *Ten Poetically Named Scenic Places of West Lake*, such as 断桥残雪 *Lingering Snow on Broken Bridge* or 三潭印月 *Three Pools Mirroring the Moon*. Indeed, my interview reveals that both local people and tourists can feel the poetic meaning of West Lake (e.g. WL043 [tourist], WL009, WL033, WL076 and WL093 [local people] in Chapters 3 and 4, and WL088 in this chapter); however, being at the physical site did not elicit similar poetic feelings or thought processes from the ICOMOS experts (Zhang 2017a, Zhang and Taylor 2019).

From the dominating perspective of practitioners, the industrial transformation from tea farming to tourism services would change and erode the 'authenticity' of the site (SACH 2011). Ironically, my survey at West Lake and the two villages shows that the majority of local people thought that tourists had brought positive changes, not only the economic benefit or cultural gain as identified above, but also a sense of bonding between tourists and local people. As WL051 states, tourists and tourism 'brought cultural diversity and vividness to the city.' The majority of local people I interviewed were explicitly aware that Hangzhou is an 'international touristic city,' and are proud of this title, and considered tourists to be significant to the identity of Hangzhou city.

In addition, I was informed by local government officials and Co. Jingyi Ltd in Hongcun during my interviews that they planned to reform and unify the local hostels and handicraft shops in order to meet the World Heritage standards and provide a 'better' environment for tourists (Figure 7.2). I also received messages recently from my friend who operates a hostel at West Lake World Heritage area that the provincial government has held an international conference to discuss investment in and the development of local hostels. She (WL097) posted on WeChat[6] that:

> I am worried about the strategy that the provincial and local government is encouraged to bring external capital to local hostels. Those external companies only care for economic benefits, and the use of media and government resources to promote their business. The real local operators do not have any benefits from those government policies. The authenticity of the local hostel has been eroded.
>
> (WL097, female, 25–34, local)

WL097 is worried that 'the authenticity of the local hostel has been eroded.' The authenticity she references is not the physical authenticity of the site, rather an emotional authenticity that occurs between tourists and local people.

Figure 7.2 New handicraft shops in Hongcun (photo by Rouran Zhang)

This section has argued that the significant interaction between tourists and local people, and the individual and interlinked performances of both tourists and local people, construct the contemporary meaning of heritage. There is a tendency to ignore the interaction that occurs between host communities and tourists or to see it mainly as a problem, or as largely a result of the naturalising effects of the AHD. Heritage tourists tend to be defined in heritage policy as passive consumers who are to be educated about the meaning of heritage as framed by the AHD and used by local and national governments in response to UNESCO World Heritage requirements. Community participation in heritage management, interpretation and conservation work has been increasingly stressed in the heritage literature (see for example Hayden 1997; Newman and McLean 1998; Hodges and Watson 2000; Byrne et al. 2001; Smardz Frost 2004; Smith 2006, Smith and Waterton 2009a; Waterton and Watson 2010, among others), although the extent to which this is really addressed in relation to World Heritage sites is still very limited (Labadi 2013). However, the literature on community participation has paid little consideration to how the communities and tourists may interact. This gap in the literature is largely a result of the naturalising effects of the AHD, which considers heritage as an object frozen in time and space and displayed behind fences, rather than a changing process that tourists and local people may play an active role in.

Conclusion

Overall, the book argues that World Heritage Listing brought economic benefits, in particular for the two villages, and it is interwoven with the issue of tourism. These benefits are, however, counter-balanced by negative impacts such as pollution, crowding, increased food or housing costs, cultural commodification and commercial changes, which have been addressed in both case studies. However, it also brought positive impacts, such as improved infrastructure and funding for conservation. It offered opportunities for local–tourist dialogue that augment local and tourist heritage values. While there were some exceptions (particularly at West Lake where residents were relocated prior to listing), the majority of local people interviewed in the two case studies tended to have very positive views about tourists visiting their sites. Overall, the World Heritage listing and the presence of mass tourists had elicited a sense of pride in residents. Local people wanted tourists to 'feel' their sites, and they hoped that the tourists could invoke a sense of belonging or feeling for the site and communicate with local people. In return, tourists enjoyed communicating with local people. There is a strong sense of contentment that emerged when tourists felt that they had made a connection with local people. Third, the heritage tourists were very active during their visit; the values that they expressed about the sites they visited were often tightly linked to their identities. Tourists at heritage sites did not necessarily passively accept the authorised messages or governments' interpretations. They were actively working out, remembering and negotiating their own, often thoughtful and considered, cultural meanings. The fears of commodification and 'dumbing down' of culture and history often associated with mass tourism and associated changes to the value of WH sites (Hewison 1987; McCrone et al. 1995; Brett 1996; Handler and Gable 1997; Shackel 2013) were not supported by the interviews with tourists.

Therefore, my research supports Smith's (2006, 2012, 2017) observation that heritage is an emotional and cultural process. The meaning of heritage and tourism is interlinked in my two case studies. Smith (2006, 2012) argues that the process of visitation of each tourist constructs the meaning of heritage. My research reinforces her argument. I further argue that heritage is created not only by the 'cultural moment' from each visitation, but is a process of feeling, a dialogue between past and present, and a communication between personal internal worlds and the outside world; it is also created by the 'cultural moment' of the interplay of local people, tourists and government control.

Notes

1 Wang Yangming (31 October 1472–9 January 1529) was a Chinese idealist Neo-Confucian philosopher, official, educationist, calligraphist and general during the Ming dynasty. After Zhu Xi, he is commonly regarded as the most important Neo-Confucian thinker, with interpretations of Confucianism that denied the rationalist dualism of the orthodox philosophy of Zhu Xi. Wang was known as 'Yangming Xiansheng' and/or 'Yangming Zi' in literary circles: both mean 'Master Yangming.' (Source: https://en.wikipedia.org/wiki/Wang_Yangming.)
2 Source: http://sourcebooks.fordham.edu/eastasia/wangyang1.asp.
3 Chinese philosophy, by contrast with Western thinking, has from the start emphasised immanence and unity. Where Western dualism led to an opposition between man and nature, Chinese monism stresses the harmony between the two. Most Chinese philosophers share this unique view no matter how different their views on other issues may be. (Source: chinaculture.org.)
4 A total of 52% of local people I interviewed had lived in Hangzhou for less than five years, and many of this group of people defined themselves as 'New Hangzhou Citizens.'
5 From my interviews with local residents, there would seem to be corruption problems involved with getting the authority to use a 'qualified' construction company.
6 The most popular social networking service in China, similar to Twitter.

Conclusion

In this book based on research at two Chinese World Heritage sites, I have shown how tourism changes the values given to sites by local people. However, this is only in so far as existing values are augmented as local people gain pride and self-esteem, not simply through the World Heritage listing process, but more specifically and importantly through a process of sharing and communicating the values of the sites to domestic tourists. A sense of contentment emerged when both local communities and domestic tourists feel they are connected or bonded to each other. This is achieved more regularly and strongly when local people control local tourism operations. In broader global contexts, tourism, which is often devalued in heritage management policy and practice as a negative problem at World Heritage sites (Ashworth 2009), is revealed to be an integral and key value in and of itself to World Heritage sites. Tourists are revealed not as the main culprits in altering the values of heritage sites, but somewhat paradoxically it is UNESCO itself and the frameworks constructed through the concept of 'outstanding universal value' (OUV) that result in the changes feared by those operating within an 'official' or 'authorised heritage discourse' (AHD). However, the fears of commodification and erosion of culture and history often associated with mass tourism and associated changes to the value of World Heritage sites (McCrone et al. 1995; Brett 1996; Handler and Gable 1997; Shackel 2013) were not supported by my interviews with tourists and local people.

The idea that heritage is not a 'thing,' 'object' or 'cultural production,' but rather a social, cultural and emotional process (Smith 2006, 2012, 2015, 2017), underpins my research project. In this book, I have shown that heritage discourse is not only constituted by the AHD, but also from tourists' and local people's discourses and performances. Heritage is constructed at the international, national and local institutional scale partly via political, management and conservation practices and its discursive utility as an economic resource replete with marketable cultural meanings. However, I contend that equally important is the way in which the process of heritage is constituted by local people's and tourists' use of heritage, thereby subsuming a range of significant experiential themes, including sense of place, feeling, pride, contentment and freedom. I suggest that the expressions of such themes are most evident in 'cultural moments' – those tourists encounter with local people, place and practices that evoke different responses at different intensities. The macro process of government uses of heritage can become entangled with individual 'cultural moments' experienced by tourists and local people, and constitutes a dynamic, developing and negotiated heritage practice.

Book summary

Chapter 2 provides the background to and a Chinese perspective on the research project. First, the more than 2000 year-old feudal society of China was deeply influenced by Confucianism and Taoism. The idea of 'harmony between people and nature' is rooted in the collective memory, experience and knowledge of these Chinese belief systems. Therefore, this chapter reviews the origin and development of the idea of 'harmony between human and nature,' which lays a theoretical foundation for the emotional expression of 'feeling' in Chapters 3 and 4. In Chapter 2 I have also identified the development and performances of various levels of national governments that construct and are responsible for tourism and heritage. My arguments in Chapter 2 support Yan's (2012, 2018) observation that the Chinese government has used 'World Heritage' as a cultural tool to articulate and reshape the national heritage system. However, Yan's (2012, 2018) research only addressed the discursive influence of World Heritage issues (by analysing the State Administration of Cultural Heritage (SACH) policies and their influences), but did not acknowledge another significant national Chinese heritage authority – the Ministry of Housing and Urban-Rural Development (MHURD). Chapter 2 indentifies the significance of how the international authorised heritage discourse caused dissonance in the administration of World Heritage sites between the SACH and the MHURD.

In Chapters 3 and 6, my arguments also support Yan's (2015) identification of 'the Chinese harmony discourse,' a Chinese version of the AHD. Based on his research on the Fujian Tulou World Heritage site, Yan argued that the Chinese local government and the Chinese harmony discourse privilege the proficiency of experts and tend to ignore local voices. My two WH-focussed case studies, particularly in Xidi and Hongcun villages, revealed a similar local hegemonic process. The difference is that in Yan's (2012, 2015, 2018) research the local government used the traditional Chinese concept of 'harmony' to legitimate their hegemonic process, while in Xidi and Honcun, as illustrated in Chapter 6, the local government utilised the so-called 'international standard' to impose management policies on local people. Askew (2010:40) argues that the key role of UNESCO and its relevant international practice is as an 'iconic symbol' that serves 'to elaborate and organise an arena of status competition that centres on the multiple symbolic significance of its World Heritage List.' I argue against Askew's (2010) position; I agree that it is an iconic symbol, but also that it is more than a symbol and that its practices have real power to influence national and local policies. At the national level, World Heritage policies facilitate national policy transformation, and cause disorder and dissonance in the existing system. At a local levels, local governments use 'international standard' as a reason to disengage local people, causing alienation of local people's sense of place. As Smith (2006: 299) has identified:

> The AHD is also powerful, not simply because of its institutional position but also because of the cultural work it does in legitimizing certain experiences and identities – it is powerful because it is a form of 'heritage' itself. The existence of an AHD, whatever its particular nuances or various across time and space, is part of the cultural and social process of heritage, and is itself constitutive of 'heritage.'

In Chapters 3–6, I demonstrated that the process of heritage was not only constructed by the practice of governments, but is a dynamic interaction among tourists, local people and heritage sites. In Chapters 3 and 4, I illustrated that governments at different levels intend to disseminate the official heritage categories, such as the concept of cultural landscape, to tourists and local people. However, the majority of my interviewees did not passively accept the official discourses; rather, they expressed an active sense of individual understandings of heritage, and I stressed tourists and local people's discourses. Many of their discourses reflect an aesthetic thought process expressed with a poetic sense, which is firmly linked to Han's (2006: 216) argument about the Chinese traditional view of nature:

> Values of nature include intrinsic and instrumental values. These are determined and assigned by human ontological and epistemological positions. Nature is inescapably viewed through a cultural lens and the view of nature is filtered by a cultural lens. The view of nature is the nature presented in one's subjective consciousness. Values of nature differ between individuals, nations and cultures and are constantly and socially constructed. Contextual sensitivity, open-endedness, moral plurality and cultural diversity of values have been emphasised.

The Chinese sense of heritage is significantly different from the Western view, particularly with regard to the Chinese view of nature. My research identified a poetic sense and feeling that tourists experienced during their visits, influenced by this Chinese traditional cultural understanding, which is an essential element of Chinese identity. This sense of poetic expression is also widely linked to one of the significant themes of this book – an emotional feeling.

In Chapters 3 to 6, I discussed the active sense of engagement by Chinese domestic tourists at heritage sites. My observation, based on research in a Chinese context, supports the sense of agency illustrated by Smith in her work with heritage visitors (2006, 2011, 2012) and in Western contexts by other scholars (e.g. Coleman and Crang 2002; Bagnall 2003; Poria et al. 2003; Palmer 2005; Byrne 2009; Sather-Wagstaff 2011; and Waterton and Watson 2012, 2014). Chinese domestic tourists engaged with multi-dimensional and complex activities at heritage sites, and created a series of 'cultural moments' entangled with concepts such as identity, feeling, memory, remembering, place, performance and dissonance. The sense of feeling is one of the significant themes I documented, and the domestic tourists were much more overt in acknowledging that they were having or seeking feelings and they expressed their feelings in a more self-conscious way than has been typically recorded in Western contexts (see, for instance, Cameron and Gatewood 2000, 2003; Poria et al. 2003; Smith 2006, 2011, 2015). The sense of feeling was evoked in two ways – through an encounter with the physical and/or through connections and communications with local residents around heritage sites. Heritage sites, in this sense, were places where people felt – and in particular felt connected to something vital, such as a connection to land, their sense of place, or to local communities; it is also an engagement and a dialogue between the past and the present, and a communication between a personal internal world and the outside world. The sense of feeling also legitimated tourists' emotional authenticity and further influenced their performances at heritage sites. I observed that tourists' sense of emotional authenticity was sometimes influenced by the perceived physical authenticity of the site, sometimes not. I argue that perceived physical authenticity is meaningful because it serves to elicit people's emotional engagement. My argument supports the work of scholars such as Bagnall (2003), Smith (2006, 2012) and Zhu (2012), who have also identified emotional authenticity as legitimising tourists' performances, which for them makes heritage meaningful.

In Chapter 4 and 6, I observed a complex local–tourist dialogue which elicited 'cultural moments' at the heritage sites. As illustrated in Chapter 4, both the World Heritage listing and the presence of mass tourism had generated a sense of pride in local residents. The majority of local people were proud that Hangzhou was an 'International Tourism City,' and wanted tourists to enjoy their journey, feel connected to the sites and communicate with local people. Many of the domestic tourists I interviewed also told me that they enjoyed communicating with local people. The sense of contentment is overt, and both tourists and local people expressed this when local–tourist dialogue became sustained. In Chapter 6, I have shown how there can be a dimension to the local–tourist interactions in Xidi and Hongcun, where local people and tourists bonded with each other at a deep emotional level. This was particularly overt in the case of Xidi, as local people expressed a strong sense of place. In some cases, a sense of contentment emerged from both local people and tourists when they felt that bonds had been established with each other, no matter how fleeting or impermanent these bonds may have been. This is particularly expressed when local people were able to participate in local tourism operations. The interrelations between heritage and tourism is a cultural and social process constructed by the interplay of multiple stakeholders' use of heritage. The deep active sense of the local–tourist dialogue has not been adequately addressed in academic literature.

In addition, as illustrated in Chapters 4 and 6, governments' control obscured the local people's sense of place, tourists' sense of feeling and further interrupted the local–tourist dialogue. Both tourists and local people's sense of freedom was blocked by physical boundaries such as 'gates,' 'fences' and 'walls,' and many interviewees considered their aesthetic appreciation, thinking and feelings were interrupted. However, the deep sense is that the invisible boundaries such as 'high entrance fees' and government control obscured the local–tourist dialogue. As identified in Chapter 6, tourists in both Xidi and Hongcun considered the villages had 'been managed' or were 'too commercialised.' Local residents were also extremely unsatisfied with the local government and tourism company who forced them to follow the so-called 'international standard.' Nevertheless, the dissonance caused by the local governments is a part of the heritage process.

In Chapter 7, I drew out three themes that emerged from research, and examined these themes by comparing the two case studies and contrasting each stakeholders' perspective on heritage and tourism. I concluded my observations on the relationship between heritage and tourism with the observation that: heritage is a process not only constituted by the binary 'cultural moments' between tourist and heritage sites, or between tourists' internal world and the outside world; rather, the 'cultural moments' are multi-dimensional and created by the interactions between tourists, local people, governments, external companies and other active and passive stakeholders.

Some implications for World Heritage practice

There is tendency in the heritage and tourism literature to simplify and over generalise tourist behaviour and tourists' relationships with local people. Theoretically, I hope my work will contribute to current debates within heritage studies and studies of tourism by considering the social and cultural values and experiences of tourists. In terms of practice and policy, I think the ongoing and future development of policies and practices of the UNESCO World Heritage Programme and local and national management policies should continue to be re-evaluated. I am not suggesting that the UNESCO World Heritage Programme and its discursive practices are unnecessary, but rather that ongoing research and reflection are essential to an effective and relevant World Heritage system, particularly with regard to tourism and World Heritage.

In 2012, the 36th Session of the World Heritage Committee formally adopted a *World Heritage and Sustainable Tourism Programme (WH+ST)* and incorporated it into the *Strategic Action Plan for the Implementation of the World Heritage Convention 2012–2022* (UNESCO 2012a). One of the main concerns of the project is how to promote more effective participation of stakeholders. UNESCO also argues that the *WH+ST* can contribute to the realisation of the 17 sustainable development goals of the *2030 Agenda for Sustainable Development (UN SDGs)*, in particular goals 8, 12 and 14 which are directly related to tourism (United Nations 2015). As with many other researchers, I situate myself within the field of critical heritage studies to provide a considered and analytical understanding of heritage for both academic analysis and practice. If, as UNESCO states, World Heritage is constantly evolving (see Askew 2010), this book indicates that more bottom-up work needs to be undertaken from sociological and anthropological perspectives to more deeply understand tourists and local communities that are likely to be affected by World Heritage programmes, and what they do or feel at heritage sites. Such field-based studies can promote more active participation of stakeholders and contribute to *WH+ST* and goals 8, 12 and 14 of *UN SDGs*.

In September 2016, ICOMOS and IUCN members gathered at the IUCN World Conservation Congress in Hawaii, USA, to discuss improved approaches to the integration of culture and nature. At the event, the two organisations jointly proposed the Culture-Nature Journey project and launched a summary and action document – *Mālama Honua – to Care for Our Island Earth* (IUCN and ICOMOS 2016). This was one of the first times that ICOMOS and IUCN formally proposed a cooperative approach to finding a fusion of culture and nature in different cultural contexts. ICOMOS and IUCN then organised a team of 17 experts from different cultural backgrounds at the 19th ICOMOS General Assembly and Scientific Symposium held in Delhi, India on December 2017, drafting the action document *Yatra Statement*. *Yatra Statement* hopes to explore the ways in which culture and nature can be integrated under the global multiculturalism by listening to the voices of diverse communities (ICOMOS and IUCN 2017). The Culture-Nature Journey focusses on 'people' rather than traditional 'objects' and how to express cultural and natural cognition in the local context by studying 'people' of different cultural backgrounds. Therefore, researching the feelings and emotional expressions of tourists and local people is an effective way to explore the practical method for evaluating culture and nature integration value, contributing to the ongoing global work of the Culture–Nature Journey. For instance, the poetic sense of place that is tied to Chinese traditional culture, as Lin (1935), Zhang (1986), Wang (1990), Xu (1996) and Han (2006) have identified, was the issue that the ICOMOS experts could not make sense of within their expertise. This was replicated in ICOMOS's recommendations not to include the tea plantation within the listing for West Lake Cultural Landscape of Hangzhou. These instances are simply illustrative of a cultural divide between UNESCO/ICOMOS's understandings of heritage values and that of values expressed within China that need further consideration, research and integration. A process to document the views of tourists and local residents about their sense of place and feelings toward a site during the World Heritage listing is something that should be considered. Both tourists and local people's sense of feeling can be documented in the World Heritage nomination file and understood to be integral to how a site is valued. Values to tourists as well as to local people, and not just national values, need to be included in the value statements for World Heritage. Tourism is not something that can be defined as only happening after listing, but is integral to the values of World Heritage sites. Based on the existing World Heritage listing process documented in this research, it is clear that the Chinese experts understood the poetic meaning of West Lake to Chinese culture and history, but they are quite cynical about the listing process, in that they recognise they had to work within Eurocentric rules and terms, so they have to reframe values which can be 'edited out' or misrepresent Chinese values (for example, in the Longjing Tea plantation area), which could not be explained to Western experts, and utilised the discourses of international policy and expertise. For local governments, sometimes they should be inclusive and involve local people in the decision-making process of heritage management.

Further research

Winter and Daly (2012) identify what they define as the richness and distinctiveness of Chinese heritage practices, but it is impossible to consider and document all types of interrelations between tourism and heritage within one book. Further research needs to be undertaken to identify the influence of World Heritage listing and tourism at different types of Chinese heritage sites. As I conducted the research for this book, I interviewed 287 tourists and local people in two case study sites. Given the small size of the data, cross-tabulations returned no statistically significant results, nor were patterns in the variation of interview results identified against any of the interview demographic results.

Therefore, future research should conduct both qualitative interviews and quantitative questionnaires to map any statistically significant variations in tourists' and local people's responses to heritage in terms of gender, age and education. In addition, as I conducted research for this book, I observed that the World Heritage listing process of West Lake and Xidi and Hongcun caused significant changes to these sites. Therefore, further research also should be conducted at city or regional levels to identify how the relationship among tourists, local people and governments unfolds at these levels.

References

Aikawa, N. (2004) An Historical Overview of the Preparation of the UNESCO International Convention for the Safeguarding of the Intangible Heritage. *Museum International* 56 (1-2), 137–49.

Aikawa, N. (2009) From the Proclamation of Masterpieces to the Convention for the Safeguarding of Intangible Cultural Heritage, in L. Smith and N. Akagawa (eds), *Intangible Heritage*. Abingdon: Routledge, pp. 1–9.

Airey, D. (2008) *Tourism Education: Life Begins at 40*. University of Surry, School of Management: Tourism research. Available at: http://epubs.surrey.ac.uk/tourism/40 (accessed 19 January 2018).

Allerton, C. (2003) Authentic Housing, Authentic Culture? Transforming a Village into a 'Tourist Site' in Manggarai, Eastern Indonesia. *Indonesia and the Malay World* 31 (89): 119–128.

Anheier, H. and Isar, Y.R. (eds) (2011) *Heritage, Memory and Identity*. Los Angeles, CA: Sage.

Ap, J. and Crompton, J. (1993) Residents' Strategies for Responding to Tourism Impacts. *Journal of Travel Research* 32(1), 47–50.

Ap, J. and Crompton, J. (1998) Developing and Testing a Tourism Impact Scale. *Journal of Travel Research* 37(2), 120–130.

Araoz, G.F. (2008) World-Heritage Historic Urban Landscapes: Defining and Protecting Authenticity. *APT Bulletin* 39, 33–37.

Arizpe, L. (2000) Cultural Heritage and Globalisation, in E. Avrant, R. Mason and M. de La Torre (eds), *Value and Heritage Conservation*. Los Angeles: The Gerry Conservation Institute.

Ashworth, G.J. (2009) Do Tourists Destroy the Heritage They Have Come to Experience. *Tourism Recreation Research* 34(1), 79–83.

Ashworth, G.J. and Tunbridge, J. (1990) *The Tourist-historic City*. London: Belhaven Press.

Ashworth, G.J. and Tunbridge, J. (1996) *Dissonant Heritage: The Management of the Past as a Resource in Conflict*. Chichester: John Wiley and Sons.

Ashworth, G.J., Graham, B.J. and Tunbridge, J.E. (2007) *Pluralising Pasts: Heritage, Identity and Place in Multicultural Societies*. London: Pluto Press.

Askew, M. (2010) The Magic List of Global Status: UNESCO, World Heritage and the Agendas of States, in S. Labadi and C. Long (eds), *Heritage and Globalisation*. London: Routledge, pp. 19–44.

Aygen, Z. and Logan, W. (2016) Heritage in the 'Asian Century': Responding to geopolitical change, in W. Logan, M.N. Craith and U. Kockel (eds), *A Companion to Heritage Studies*. Chichester: Wiley Blackwell, pp. 410–425.

Bærenholdt, J., Haldrup, M., Larsen, J. and Urry, J. (2004) *Performing Tourist Places* Aldershot and Burlington. VA: Ashgate.

Bagnall, G. (2003) Performance and Performativity at Heritage Sites. *Museum and Society* 1(2), 87–103.

Bao, J. (2009) From Idealism to Realism to the Rational Return of Idealism – A Retrospective Review of 30 Years of China's Tourism Geography. *Acta Geographica Sinica* 64(10), 1184–1192.

Bao, J. (2010). Tourism Research: My Journey of Discovery, in S.L.J. Smith (ed.), *The Discovery of Tourism*. Bingley, UK: Emerald Group Publishing Ltd, pp. 69–78.

Bao, J. and Ma, L.J.C. (2011) Tourism Geography in China, 1978–2008: Whence, What and Whither? *Progress in Human Geography* 35(1), 3–20.

Bao, J., Chen, G. and Ma, L. (2014) Tourism Research in China: Insights from Insiders. *Annals of Tourism Research* 45, 167–181.

Barthel, D. (1996) *Historic Preservation: Collective Memory and Historical Identity*. Newark, NJ: Rutgers University Press.

Bauman, Z. (1987) *Legislators and Interpreters*. Cambridge: Polity Press.

Beazley, O. (2010) Politics and Power: The Hiroshima Peace Memorial (Genbaku Dome) as World Heritage, in S. Labadi and C. Colin (eds), *Heritage and Globalization*, New York: Routledge, pp. 45–65.

Belhassen, Y., Caton, K. and Stewart, W. P. (2008) The Search for Authenticity in the Pilgrim Experience. *Annals of Tourism Research* 35(3), 668–689.

Bendix, R. (2009) Heritage between Economy and Politics: An Assessment from the Perspective of Cultural Anthropology, in L. Smith and N. Akagawa (eds), *Intangible Heritage*. London: Routledge, pp. 253–269.

Biran, A., Poria, Y. and Oren, G. (2010) Sought Experiences at (Dark) Heritage Sites. *Annals of Tourism Research* 38(3), 820–841.

Blake, J. (2009) UNESCO's 2003 Convention on Intangible Cultural Heritage: The Implications of Community Involvement in 'Safeguarding', in L. Smith and N. Akagawa (eds), *Intangible Heritage*, London: Routledge, pp. 45–73.

Bortolotto, C. (2010) Globalizing Intangible Cultural Heritage?: Between International Arenas and Local Appropriations, in S. Labadi and C. Colin (eds), *Heritage and Globalization*. New York: Routledge, pp. 97–114.

Boswell, D. (ed.) (1999) *Representing the Nation: A Reader, Histories, Heritage and Museums*. London: Routledge.

Brett, D. (1966) *The Construction of Heritage*. Cork: Cork University Press.

Brown, J. and Hay-Edie, T., IUCN-WCPA Protected Landscapes Specialist Group, UNDP GEF Small Grants Programme (2014) *Engaging Local Communities in Stewardship of World Heritage: A Methodology Based on the COMPACT Experience (World Heritage Paper Series 40)*. Paris: UNESCO Press. Available at: http://unesdoc.unesco.org/images/0023/002303/230372e.pdf (accessed 10 January 2015).

Brunt, P. and Courtney, P. (1999) Host Perceptions of Sociocultural Impacts. *Annals of Tourism Research* 26, 493–515.

Buckley, K. (2014) The World Heritage Convention at 40: Challenges for the work of ICOMOS. *Historic Environment* 26(2), 38–52.

Burkett, I. (2001) Traversing the Swampy Terrain of Postmodern Communities: Towards Theoretical Revisionings of Community Development. *European Journal of Social Work* 4(3), 233–246.

Burton, A. (2003) When was Britain? Nostalgia for the Nation at the End of the 'American Century.' *Journal of Modern History* 75, 395–374.

Butcher, J. (2003) *The Moralisation of Tourism: Sun, Sand ... and Saving the World?* London: Routledge.

Byrne, D. (1991) Western Hegemony in Archaeological Heritage Management. *History and Anthropology* 5, 269–276.

Byrne, D. (2008)[1995] Western Hegemony in Archaeological Heritage Management, in G. Fairclough, R. Harrison, J.H. Jameson Jr and J. Schofield (eds), *The Heritage Reader*. New York: Routledge, pp. 229–234.

Byrne, D. (2009) A Critique of Unfeeling Heritage, in L. Smith and N. Akagawa (eds), *Intangible Heritage*. London: Routledge, pp. 229–252.

Byrne, D. (2012) Anti-superstition: Campaigns against Popular Religion and Its Heritage in Asia, in P. Daly and T. Winter (eds), *Routledge Handbook of Heritage in Asia*. London: Routledge, pp. 295–310.

Byrne, D. (2013a) Gateway and Garden: A Kind of Tourism in Bali, in R. Staiff and R. Bushell (eds), *Heritage Tourism: Place, Encounter, Engagement*. London: Routledge, pp. 26–44.

Byrne, D. (2013b) Love and Loss in the 1960s. *International Journal of Heritage Studies* 19(6), 596–609.

Byrne, D. (2014) *Counter Heritage: Critical Perspectives on Heritage Conservation in Asia*. New York and London: Routledge.

Byrne, D., Brayshaw, H. and Ireland, T. (2001) *Social Significance: A Discussion Paper*. Sydney: Department of Environment and Conservation NSW.

Cameron, C. (2005) *Evolution of the Application of 'Outstanding Universal Value' for Cultural and Natural Heritage*, Keynote speech by Ms Christina Cameron and presentations by the World Heritage Centre and Advisory Bodies, World Heritage Committee, 29th Session, Durban, South Africa, 10–17 July. WHC-05/29 COM/INF.9B.

Cameron, C. (2008) From Warsaw to Mostar: the World Heritage Committee and Authenticity. *APT Bulletin: Journal of Preservation Technology* 39(2–3), 19–24.

Cameron, C. and Gatewood, J. (2000) Excursions into the Unremembered Past: What People Want from Visits to Historical Sites. *Public Historian* 22(3), 107–127.

Cameron, C. and Gatewood, J. (2003) Seeking Numinous Experiences in the Unremembered Past. *Ethnology* 42(1), 55–71.

Cameron, C. and Gatewood, J. (2012) The Numen Experience in Heritage Tourism, in L. Smith, E. Waterton and S. Watson (eds), *The Cultural Moment in Tourism*. London: Routledge, pp. 235–251.

Campanella, T.J. (2008) *The Concrete Dragon: China's Urban Revolution and What It Means for the World*. New York: Princeton Architectural Press.

Cao, B. (2007) 中国文物与文化遗产概况及其保护的重要意义 (Overview of China's Cultural Relics and Cultural Heritage, and the Important Meaning of Preservation). 中国文化遗产保护成就通览 (Overview of the Achievements of China's Cultural Heritage Preservation). Beijing: Cultural Relics Press, pp. 1–8.

Carrier, P. (2005) *Holocaust Monuments and National Memory Cultures in France and Germany since 1989*. New York: Berghahn Books.

Carsun, C. (1962) *Wang Yang-ming: Idealist Philosopher of Sixteenth-century China*. New York: St. John's University Press.

Cassel, S.H. and Pashkevich, A. (2014) World Heritage and Tourism Innovation: Institutional Frameworks and Local Adaptation. *European Planning Studies*, 22(8): 1625–1640.

CCP (2015) *2015年中央一号文件《关于加大改革创新力度加快农业现代化建设的若干意见》* (2015 Central Document No. 1 'Several Opinions on Increasing

Reform and Innovation to Accelerate Agricultural Modernization Construction'), 2015-2-1.

Cfi.cn (2019). *San Te Cableways: A Summary of the 2018 Annual Report*(三特索道:2018年年度报告摘要). Available at: www.cfi.net.cn/p20190329002481.html (accessed 3 September 2019).

Chan, A.L. (2001) *Mao's Crusade: Politics and Policy Implementation in China's Great Leap Forward*. Oxford: Oxford University Press, pp. 71–74.

Chang, Q. (2009) 历史建筑修复的真实性判 (Debate of Authenticity in Historical Architectural Conservation). *Time Architecture* 3, 118.

Chen, G. and Bao, J. (2011) Progress on Oversea Studies on China's Tourism: A Review from the Perspective of Academic Contributions. *Tourism Tribune* 26(2), 28–35.

Chen, T., Fu, J. and Liu, J. (2012) The Outstanding Universal Value of West Lake Cultural Landscape of Hangzhou. *Landscape Architecture* (2), 68–71.

Chen, Y. (2005) '世界级遗产称号的决策和影响研究 (The Decision-Making and Influence of World Heritage Designation – A Case Study of Ancient Villages in Southern Anhui(Xidi and Hongcun) and Danxia Mountain in Guangdong). Masters Dissertation, Sun Yat-Sen University.

Cheng, Y. and Morrison, A.M. (2008) The Influence of Visitors' Awareness of World Heritage Listings: A Case Study of Huangshan, Xidi and Hongcun in Southern Anhui, China. *Journal of Heritage Tourism* 2(3), 184–195.

China Business Herald (2011) '西湖文化景观'成功申遗开启后申遗时代 (West Lake 'Cultural Landscape' after the Success of the Inscription on the Date of Opening). *China Business Herald*, July 19, pp. C01.

China.com (2004) '申遗热'背后有隐忧 (World Heritage Fever, There Are Hidden Behind). Available at: www.china.com.cn/chinese/zhuanti/28ycdh/601082.htm (accessed 6 September 2016).

China.com (2015) 杭蒋经国故居变身咖啡馆合理商业化应用未尝不可 (Chiangching Guo's House Used as a Cafe, Reasonable Commercial Application Is Not a Bad Idea). Available at: www.china.com.cn/cppcc/2015-11/16/content_37075941.htm (accessed 17 May 2016).

China.com (2018) 文化和旅游部：发展全域旅游共创美好生活 (Ministry of Culture and Tourism: Developing Global Tourism for a Better Life). Available at: http://travel.china.com.cn/txt/2018-05/19/content_51413126.htm (accessed 17 May 2016).

China Daily (2011) *Hangzhou's West Lake Makes the UNESCO List*. Available at: www.chinadaily.com.cn/interface/toutiao/1120783/2015-5-14/cd_20717622.html (accessed 3 January 2016).

China Daily (2015) *Ministry of Foreign Affairs: Anti-Japanese Declaration of Related Industrial Sites on the World Heritage List*. Available at: www.chinadaily.com.cn/interface/toutiao/1120783/2015-5-14/cd_20717622.html (accessed 25 August 2016).

China National Knowledge Infrastructure (2011) *Chinese Tourism Revenue Statistics*. Available at: http://number.cnki.net (accessed 21 August 2012).

China Today (2018) Communist Party of China. Available at: http://www.chinatoday.com/org/cpc (accessed 5 September 2018).

China Tourism Academy (2012) *Blue Book of China's Tourism Economy No. 4*. Beijing: China Travel and Tourism Press.

China Tourism News (2008) 新西湖能否更好展现杭州的根与魂 (New West Lake Can Better Show the Roots and Soul of Hangzhou). *China Tourism News*, 3 November, p. 001.

China Tourism News (2009) 杭州不停下西湖申遗的脚步 (Hangzhou Does Not Stop the Pace of West Lake Application). *China Tourism News*, 3 August, p. 008.

China.org.cn (2004) *UNESCO to Allow More Nominations for World Heritage,* Available at: www.china.org.cn/english/culture/100645.htm (accessed 12 September 2016).

Chinaculture.org (2014) *Harmony of Man with Nature.* Available at: http://history.cultural-china.com/en/167History13189.html (accessed 12 September 2016).

Chinadialogue.net (2007) *A Yellow Card for the Three Parallel Rivers.* Available at: www.chinadialogue.net/article/show/single/en/1200-A-yellow-card-for-the-Three-Parallel-Rivers (accessed 12 September 2016).

Chinanews.com (2011) 五大连池选择退出西湖"申遗"结果今日有望揭晓 (Wudalianchi Choose to Exit the West Lake "World Heritage" Results Are Expected to be Announced Today). Available at: www.chinanews.com/cul/2011/06-24/3133830.shtml (accessed 19 April 2016).

Chio, J. (2009a) A Critique of Unfeeling Heritage, in L. Smith and N. Akagawa (eds), *Intangible Heritage*. London: Routledge, pp. 229–252.

Chio, J. (2009b) The Internal Expansion of China: Tourism and the Production of Distance, in T. Winter, P. Teo and T. C. Chang (eds), *Asia on Tour: Exploring the Rise of Asian Tourism*. London: Routledge, pp. 207–220.

Choay, F. (2001) *The Invention of the Historic Monument*. Cambridge: Cambridge University Press.

Choi, H.S.C. and Sirakaya, E. (2005) Measuring Residents' Attitude toward Sustainable Tourism: Development of Sustainable Tourism Attitude Scale. *Journal of Travel Research* 43, 380–394.

Clark, K. (ed.) (1999) *Conservation Plans in Action: Proceedings of the Oxford Conference*. London: English Heritage.

Clark, K. (2005) The Bigger Picture: Archaeology and Values in Long Term Cultural Resource Management, in C. Mathers, T. Darvill and B.J. Little (eds), *Heritage of Value, Archaeology of Renown: Reshaping Archaeological Assessment and Significance*. Gainesville, FL: University Press of Florida.

Cleere, H. (2001) The Uneasy Bedfellows: Universality and Cultural Heritage, in R. Layton, P.G. Stone and J. Thomas (eds), *Destruction and Conservation of Cultural Property*. London: Routledge.

CNTA (2008) *The Yearbook of China Tourism Statistics 2007*. Beijing: China Tourism Press.

Cohen, B. (2004) Urban Growth in Developing Countries: A Review of Current Trends and a Caution Regarding Existing Forecasts. *World Development* 32, 23–51.

Cohen, E. (1988) Authenticity and Commoditization in Tourism. *Annals of Tourism Research* 15, 371–386.

Cohen, E. (2000) *The Commercialized Crafts of Thailand: Hill Tribes and Lowland Villages: Collected Articles*. Richmond, Surrey: Curzon.

Cohen, E. (2004) *Contemporary Tourism: Diversity and Change*. Boston: Elsevier.

Coleman, S. and Crang, M. (eds) (2002) *Tourism: Between Place and Performance*. New York: Berghahn Books.

Confucius (2002). *The Analects*. Beijing: Zhonghua Book Company.

Conran, M. (2006) Commentary: Beyond Authenticity: Exploring Intimacy in the Touristic Encounter in Thailand. *Tourism Geographies* 8 (3), 274–285.

Cook, C. and John, S. (2005) *The Routledge Companion to World History since 1914*. London: Routledge.

References

Cotter, M., Boyd, B. and Gardiner, J. (eds) (2001) *Heritage Landscapes: Understanding Place and Communities*. Lismore, NSW: Southern Cross University Press.

Crang, M. (2001) *Cultural Geography*. London: Routledge.

Crouch, D. (2010) The Perpetual Performance and Emergence of Heritage, in E. Waterton and S. Watson (eds), *Culture, Heritage and Representation: Perspectives on Visuality and the Past*. Farnham: Ashgate.

Crouch, D. (2012) Landscape, Land and Identity: A Performative Consideration. *Spatial Practices* 13, 43–65.

Crouch, D. and Parker, G. (2003) 'Digging-up' Utopia? Space, Practice and Landuse Heritage. *Geoforum* 34, 395–408.

Cultural Heritage Monitoring and Management Centre of West Lake, The (2012) *World Heritage Application of West Lake Cultural Landscape*. Available at: http://kpb.hz.gov.cn/showpage.aspx?nid=7497&id=701 (accessed 21 May 2015).

Dai, X. and Jue, W. (2012) Mining Heritage Research from the Perspective of World Heritage. *Geographical Science* 1, 31–38.

Daily Business (2011) 申遗成功西湖梦圆 (Dream Comes True, West Lake Inscribed on the World Heritage List). *Daily Business*, 25 June.

Daly, P. T. and Winter, T. (2012) *Routledge Handbook of Heritage in Asia*. Routledge, New York: London.

Davison, P. (2005) Museums and the Re-shaping of Memory, in G. Corsane (ed.), *Heritage, Museums and Galleries: An Introductory Reader*. London: Routledge.

Dean, M.C. (2000) Cutural Tourism. *Getty Conservation Institute Newsletter* 15(1), 2000. Available at: www.getty.edu/conservation/publications_resources/newsletters/15_1/feature1_7.html (accessed 10 August 2016).

Delamere, T.A. (2001) Development of a Scale to Measure Resident Attitudes Toward the Social Impacts of Community Festivals, Part II: Verification of the Scale. *Event Management* 7, 25–38.

Deng, H. (2007) Theory and Practice of the Nomination for the Inscription of the Silk Road on the World Heritage List. *Journal of Northwest Normal University (Social Sciences)* 06, 1–8.

Deng, M.Y. (2005) A Research on the Fundamental Issues of World Heritage Tourism. *Journal of Leshan Teachers College* 20(10), 97–101.

Dewi, C. (2016) *Iconic Architectural Heritage in Banda Aceh: Remembering and Conservation in Post-Disaster Contexts*. PhD thesis, The Australian National University.

Di Giovine, M. (2009) *The Heritage-Scape: UNESCO, World Heritage, and Tourism*. Lanham. MD: Lexington Books.

Díaz-Andreu, M. (2014) Nationalism and Archaeology, in C. Smith (ed.), *Encyclopedia of Global Archaeology*. New York: Springer, pp. 5144–5149.

Díaz-Andreu, M. (2015) Heritage and Migration in Barcelona, Building Constructive Citizenship, in P.F. Biehl et al. (eds), *Identity and Heritage*, Contemporary Challenges in a Globalized World. New York: Springer-Verlag.

Diaz-Andreu, M. and Champion, T. (eds) (1996) *Nationalism and Archaeology in Europe*. London: UCL Press.

Dicks, B. (1997) The Life and Times of Community – Spectacles of Collective Identity at the Rhondda Heritage Park. *Time and Society* 6(2–3), 195–212.

Dicks, B. (2000) *Heritage, Place and Community*. Cardiff: University of Wales Press.

Dicks, B. (2003) Heritage, Governance and Marketization: A Case Study from Wales. *Museum and Society* 1(1), 30–44.

Dove, M., Sajise, P.E. and Doolittle, A.A. (2011) *Beyond the Sacred Forest: Complicating Conservation in Southeast Asia*. Durham, NC: Duke University Press.

Du, X. and Zhou, M. (2019) 增强世界遗产视野下的文化自信 (Enhance Cultural Confidence in the World Heritage Perspective). *China Culture Daily*, 10 July 2019.

Du, Y. (2018) Four Major Development Stages of China's Tourism Industry. *China Youth Daily*, 2018-8-2. Available at: http://zqb.cyol.com/html/2018/08/02/nw.D110000zgqnb_20180802_3-08.htm (accessed 23 May 2019).

Du Cros, H. and Lee, Y.S.F. (2007) *Cultural Heritage Management in China: Preserving the Cities of the Pearl River Delta*. London: Róutledge.

Dubrow, G. (2003) Restoring Women's History through Historic Preservation: Recent Developments in Scholarship and Public Historical Practice, in G. Dubrow and J. Goodman (eds), *Restoring Women's History through Historic Preservation*. Baltimore, MD: Johns Hopkins University Press.

Economist, The (2010) *UNESCO's World Heritage Sites: A Danger List in Danger*. Available at: www.economist.com/node/16891951 (accessed 11 January 2016).

English Heritage (1997) *Sustaining the Historic Environment: New Perspectives on the Future, English Heritage Discussion Document*. London: English Heritage.

Erb, M. (2000) Understanding Tourists: Interpretations from Indonesia. *Annals of Tourism Research* 27, 709–736.

Erzberger, C. and Prein, G. (1997) Triangulation: Validity and Empirically-based Hypothesis Construction. *Quality and Quantity* 31(2), 141–54.

Fairclough, G. (1999) Protecting the Cultural Landscape: National Designation and Local Character, in J. Grenville (ed.), *Managing the Historic Rural Landscape*. London: Routledge.

Fairclough, G. and Rippon, S. (eds) (2002) *Europe's Cultural Landscape: Archaeologists and the Management of Change*. Brussels: Europe Archaeologies Concilium.

Fairclough, G., Lambrick, G. and McNab, A. (1999) *Yesterday's World, Tomorrow's Landscape: The English Heritage Historic Landscape Project 1992–94*. London: English Heritage.

Fan, Y. and Hu, Q. (2003) 中国旅游规划发展历程与研究进展 (Development History and Research Progress of China Tourism Planning). *Tourism Tribune* 18(6), 25–30.

Fang, B.S. and Dong, Y.M. (2001) Study on the compatible development between the construction of ropeway and the exploitation for landscape. *Geography and Territorial Research* 17(4), 39–43.

Fang, C. (2004) Tourism Impacts on Chinese World Heritage Sites. *Journal of Beijing International Studies University* (1), 64–70.

Feng, J. Z. (1990) 人与自然——从比较园林史看建筑发展趋势 (Human and Nature -- a Comparison of the History of Landscape Architecture). *Journal of Architecture* 5: 39–46.

Fengqi, Q. (2007) China's Burra Charter: The Formation and Implementation of the China Principles. *International Journal of Heritage Studies* 13(3), 255–264.

Filippucci, P. (2009) Heritage and Methodology: A View from Social Anthropology, in M.L.S. Sørensen and J. Carman (eds), *Heritage Studies: Methods and Approaches*. London: Routledge, pp. 319–325.

Fisher, R., Maginnis, S., Jackson, W., Barrow, E. and Jeanrenaud, S. (eds) (2008) *Linking Conservation and Poverty Reduction: Landscapes, People and Power*. London: Earthscan.

Francis, F. (1995) Confucianism and Democracy. *Journal of Democracy* 6 (2), 20–33.

Franklin, A. and Crang, M. (2001) The Trouble with Tourism and Travel Theory? *Tourist Studies* I, 5–22.

Frey, B.S., Pamini, P. and Steiner, L. (2013) Explaining the World Heritage List: An Empirical Study. *International Review of Economics* 60(1), 1–19.

Fu, H. (2004) 杭州旅游国际化之路如何走(How to Take the International Road of Hangzhou Tourism). *Observation and Ponderation* 19, 28–30.

Fung, C. and Allen, H. (1984) Perceptions of the Past and New Zealand Archaeology. *New Zealand Archaeological Association Newsletter* 27(4), 209–220.

Gable, E. and Handler, R. (2003) After Authenticity at an American Heritage Site, in S.M. Low and D. Lawrence-Zúñiga (eds), *The Anthology of Space and Place: Locating Culture*. Malden: Blackwell.

Gao, J. (1998) 避暑山庄与承德市的城市生态环境 (The Urban Ecological Environment of Mountain Resort and Chengde City). *Territory & Natural Resources Study* (2), 36–39.

Gao, L. and Woudstra, J. (2011) Repairing Broken Continuity: Garden Heritage In the Historic Villages Xidi And Hongcun, China. *Historic Environment* 23, 48–55.

Gao, M. (2014) 丝路入遗33遗迹22处在中国 *(22 of 33 Sites of Silk Roads Property in China)*. Available at: http://finance.people.com.cn/n/2014/0623/c1004-25185125.html (accessed 10 February 2016).

Gao, X. (1989) *The Tree of Life and the Tree of Knowledge: Comparison of Chinese Culture and Western Culture*. Shijiazhuang: Hebei People's Publishing House.

Gao, Z. and Guo, X. (2017) Consuming Revolution: The Politics of Red Tourism in China. *Journal of Macromarketing* 37(3), 240–254.

Gentry, K. and Smith, L. (2019) Critical Heritage Studies and the Legacies of the Late-Twentieth Century Heritage Canon. *International Journal of Heritage Studies*. DOI: 10.1080/13527258.2019.1570964

Gong, P. (2001) *Cultural History of the Spirit of Travel*. Shijiazhuang: Hebei Education Press.

Goodall, B. and Ashworth, G.J. (1988) *Marketing in the Tourism Industry: The Promotion of Destination Regions*. New York: Croom Helm.

Gov.cn (2009) '促进文化与旅游结合发展的指导意见' 发布会召开 *(The 'Guiding Opinions on Promoting the Combination of Culture and Tourism' was held)*. Available at: www.gov.cn/gzdt/2009-09/24/content_1425087.htm (accessed 15 August 2019).

Gov.cn (2019) 国情 *(National Conditions)*. Available at: www.gov.cn/guoqing/ (accessed 15 August 2019).

Graburn, N.H.H. and Barthel-Bouchier, D. (2001) Relocating the Tourist. *International Sociology* 16, 147–58.

Graham, B. (2001) Blame it on Maureen O'Hara: Ireland and the Trope of Authenticity. *Cultural Studies* 15(1), 58–75.

Graham, B.J., Ashworth, G. and Tunbridge, J. (2000) *A Geography of Heritage: Power, Culture and Economy*. London: Routledge.

Graham, B.J., Ashworth, G. and Tunbridge, J. (2005) The Uses and Abuses of Heritage, in G. Corsane (ed.), *Heritage, Museums and Galleries: An Introductory Reader*. London: Routledge.

Greene, J., Benjamin, L. and Goodyear, L. (2001) The Merits of Mixing Methods in Evaluation. *Evaluation* 7(1), 25–44.

Greenspan, A. (2002) *Creating Colonial Williamsburg*. Washington, DC: Smithsonian Institution Press.

Greenwood, D. (1977) Culture by the Pound: An Anthropological Perspective Tourism as Cultural Commoditization, in V.L. Smith (ed.), *Hosts and Guests: The Anthropology of Tourism*. Philadelphia, PA: University of Pennsylvania Press, pp. 129–137.

Gregory, K. and Witcomb, A. (2007) Beyond Nostalgia: The Role of Affecting Generating Historical Understanding at Heritage Sites, in S.J. Knell, S. Macleod and S. Watson (eds), *Museum Revolutions: How Museums Change and Are Changed*. Abingdon: Routledge, pp. 263–275.

Grenville, J. (ed.) (1999) *Managing the Historic Rural Landscape*. London: Routledge.

Gu, H. and Ryan, C. (2010) Hongcun, China – Residents' Perceptions of the Impacts of Tourism on a Rural Community: A Mixed Methods Approach. *Journal of China Tourism Research* 6(3), 216–244.

Guizhou Daily (2007) *The Inspiration of Libo Karst Successful Inscribed on the World Heritage List*. Available at: www.gog.com.cn (accessed 8 September 2016).

Hafstein, V. (2009) Intangible Heritage as a List: from Master Pieces to Representation, in L. Smith and N. Akagawa (eds), *Intangible Heritage*. London: Routledge, pp. 93–111.

Hall, C.M. (1994) *Tourism and Politics: Policy, Power and Place*. Chichester: Wiley.

Hall, C.M. (2001) Cape Town's District Six and the Archaeology of Memory, in R. Layton, P.G. Scone and J. Thomas (eds), *Destruction and Conservation of Cultural Property*. London: Routledge.

Hall, C.M. (2009) Tourist and Heritage: All Things Must Come to Pass. *Tourism Recreation Research* 34 (1), 88–90.

Hall, C.M. and McArthur, S. (1998) *Integrated Heritage Management*. London: Stationery Office.

Hall, D. and Leslie, D. (1995) *Eastern Europe: Tourism/Leisure Perspectives – An Introduction*. Leeds: Leisure Studies Association, pp. 3–10.

Hall, M. and McArthur, S. (1998) *Integrated Heritage Management*. London: Stationery Office.

Han, F. (2006) *The Chinese View of Nature: Tourism in China's Scenic and Historic Interest Areas*. PhD thesis, Queensland University of Technology.

Han, F. (2008) The West Lake of Hangzhou A National Cultural Icon of China and the Spirit of Place. Paper presented at *16th General Assembly and Scientific Symposium* Quebec, Canada, September. Available at: <www.icomos.org/quebec2008/cd/toindex/77_pdf/77-u9Vo-112.pdf> (accessed 25 August 2016).

Han, F. (2010) 文化景观——填补自然和文化之间的空白 (Cultural Landscape—Filling the Gaps between Nature and Culture). *Chinese Landscape Architecture* 9, 7–11.

Han, F. (2012) 'Cultural Landscape: A Chinese Way of Seeing Nature', in K. Taylor and J. Lennon (eds), *Managing Culture Landscape*. London: Routledge, pp. 90–108.

Hancock, M. (2008) *The Politics of Heritage from Madras to Chennai*. Indianapolis, IN: Indiana University Press.

Handler, R. and Gable, E. (1997) *The New History in an Old Museum: Creating the Past at Colonial Williamsburg*. Durham, NC: Duke University Press.

Handler, R. and Saxton, W. (1988) Dissimulation: Reflexivity, Narrative, and the Quest for Authenticity in 'Living History'. *Cultural Anthropology* 3(3), 242–260.

Hangzhou.com (2011) 申遗成功西湖圆梦 *(Dream Comes True, West Lake Successfully Inscribed on the World Heritage List)*. Available at: http://jrsh.hangzhou.com.cn/sale/content/2011-06/25/content_3778129.htm (accessed 29 August 2016).

Hangzhou Government (2002) *Master Plan for the West Lake Scenic Area 2002–2020*. Unpublished document in Local Government Archive.

Harrison, R. (ed.) (1994) *Manual of Heritage Management*. London: Butterworth Heinemann.

Harrison, R. (2010) The Politics of Heritage, in R. Harrison (eds), *Understanding the Politics of Heritage*. Manchester: Manchester University Press.

Harrison, R. (2013) *Heritage: Critical Approaches*. Abingdon: Routledge.

Harvey, D. (2001) Heritage Pasts and Heritage Presents: Temporality, Meaning and the Scope of Heritage Studies. *International Journal of Heritage Studies* 7(4), 319–338.

Hayden, D. (1997) *The Power of Place*. Cambridge, MA: MIT Press.

Head, L. (2000) *Cultural Landscapes and Environmental Change*. London: Arnold.

Heike, C.A. and Helen, D.H. (2010) Maintaining Authenticity and Integrity at Cultural World Heritage Sites. *Geographical Review* 100, 56.

Hevia, J.L. (2001) World Heritage, National Culture and the Restoration of Chengde. *Positions: East Asia Cultures Critique* 9(1), 219–243.

Hewison, R. (1981) *In Anger: British Culture and the Cold War, 1945–60*. New York: Oxford University Press.

Hewison, R. (1987) *The Heritage Industry: Britain in a Climate of Decline*. London: Methuen.

Heywood, A. (2003) *Political Ideologies: An Introduction* (3rd edn). Basingstoke: Palgrave.

Hitchcock, M., King, V.T. and Pamwell, M. (2010) *Heritage Tourism in Southeast Asia*. Honolulu, HI: University of Hawai'i Press.

Hobsbawm, E. (1992) Mass Producing Traditions: Europe, 1870–1914, in E. Hobsbawm and T. Ranger (eds), *The Invention of Tradition*. New York: Cambridge University Press, pp. 263–308.

Hodges, A. and Warson, S. (2000) Community-based Heritage Management: A Case Study and Agenda for Research. *International Journal of Heritage Studies* 6(3), 231–243.

Hoggart, R. (2011) *An Idea and Its Servants: UNESCO from Within*. Piscataway, NJ: Transaction.

Howard, P. (2003) *Heritage: Management, Interpretation and Identity*. London: Continuum.

Hu, X. and Lu, Q. (2007) Research in Medium Texts on the Event of 'Starbucks located in the Forbidden City'. *Journal of Advertising Study* 5, 75–84.

Hu, Z. (2005) 旅游的现代生活含义——关于杭州旅游特色和优势的思考 (The Modern Meaning of Tourism – Thoughts on the Characteristics and Advantages of Tourism in Hangzhou). *Policy Outlook* 11, 26–28.

Huang, Y. (2006) Research on Residents' Attitude and Perceptions on Tourism Impacts at Chinese World Heritage Sites – A Case Study of Pingyao Ancient City. *Journal of Guilin Institute of Tourism* 17(1), 124–127.

ICOMOS (1979 [revised 1981, 1988, 1999]) *The Australia ICOMOS Charter for the Conservation of Places of Cultural Significance (the Burra Charter)*. Canberra: Australia ICOMOS.

ICOMOS (1999) *Cultural Tourism Charter*. Paris: ICOMOS. Available at: www.icomos.org (accessed 11 August 2016).

ICOMOS (2001) *Heritage at Risk from Tourism*. Available at: www.icomos.org/risk/2001/tourism.htm (accessed 14 August 2016).

ICOMOS (2005) *Managing Tourism in Historic Towns in Asia. Seoul Declaration (Recommendation 3)*. Available at: www.icomos.org/xian2005/seoul-declaration.pdf (accessed 22 February 2012).

ICOMOS (2011) *Evaluations of Nominations of Cultural and Mixed Properties*. ICOMOS Report for the World Heritage Committee, 35th Ordinary Session UNESCO, June 2011.

ICOMOS China (2002[2000]) *Principles for the Conservation of Heritage Sites in China*. ICOMOS, Retrieved 29 September 2009. Available at: www.getty.edu/conservation/publications_resources/pdf_publications/pdf/china_prin_heritage_sites.pdf (accessed 9 May 2014).

ICOMOS and IUCN (2017) *Yatra Statement*. Available at: www.icomos.org/images/DOCUMENTS/General_Assemblies/19th_Delhi_2017/19th_GA_Outcomes/ICOMOS_GA2017_CNJ_YatraStatement_final_EN_20180207circ.pdf (accessed 15 August 2018).

Inaba, N. (2009) Authenticity and Heritage Concepts: Tangible and Intangible – Discussions in Japan, in N. Stanley-Price, and J. King (eds), *Conserving the Authentic: Essays in Honour of Jukka Jokilehto, ICCROM Conservation Studies 10*. Rome: ICCROM, pp. 153–162.

Inaba, N. (2012) Cultural Landscapes in Japan: A Century of Concept Development and Management Challenges, in K. Taylor and J.L. Lennon (eds), *Managing Cultural Landscapes*. London: Routledge, pp. 109–129.

Ingerson, A.E. (2000) *Changing Approaches to Cultural Landscapes*. Institute for Cultural Landscape Studies, The Arnold Arboretum, Harvard University. Available at: www.icls.harvard.edu/language/hist1.html (accessed 14 August 2011).

IUCN and ICOMOS (2016) *Mālama Honua – to Care for Our Island Earth*. Available at: www.iucn.org/sites/dev/files/malama-honua-cn.pdf (accessed 15 August 2018).

Jafari, J. (1996) *Tourism and Culture: An Inquiry into Paradoxes. Proceedings of the Round Table Debate on Culture, Tourism, Development: Crucial Issues for the 21st Century*. Paris: UNESCO, pp. 43–47.

James, T.C.L. (1972) Yueh Fei (1103–41) and China's Heritage of Loyalty. *The Journal of Asian Studies* 31(2), 291–297.

Jenkins, T.N. (1998) Economics and the Environment: A Case of Ethical Neglect. *Ecological Economics* 26 (2), 151–163.

Jiang, H., Yang, Y. and Bai, Y. (2018) Evaluation of All-for-One Tourism in Mountain Areas Using Multi-source Data. *Sustainability* 10(11).

Jing, F. (2019) 我亲历的首次跨境申遗 (I Have Witnessed the First Cross-border World Heritage Application). *People's Daily*, 8 June 2019.

Johnston, C. (1992) *What Is Social Value*. Canberra: Australian Government Publishing Service.

Jokilehto, J. (1995) Authenticity: A General Framework for the Concept, in K. Larsen (ed.), *Proceedings of the Nara Conference on Authenticity in Relation to the World Heritage Convention*, UNESCO World Heritage Centre (France), Agency for Cultural Affairs (Japan), ICCROM (Italy) and ICOMOS (France), pp. 17–36.

Jokilehto, J. (2011) World Heritage: Observations on Decisions Related to Cultural Heritage. *Journal of Cultural Heritage Management and Sustainable Development* 1(1), 61–74.

Jokilehto, J. and Cameron, C. (2008) *The World Heritage List: What Is OUV?: Defining the Outstanding Universal Value of Cultural World Heritage Properties*. Berlin: Bässler Verlag.

Keightley, E. and Pickering, M. (2012) *The Mnemonic Imagination: Remembering as Creative Practice*. Basingstoke: Palgrave Macmillan.

Kim, K., Uysal, M. and Sirgy, M.J. (2013) How Does Tourism in a Community Impact the Quality of Life of Community Residents? *Tourism Management* 1(36), 527–540.

Kirshenblatt-Gimblett, B. (1998) *Destination Culture: Tourism, Museums, and Heritage*. Berkeley, CA: University of California Press.

Kirshenblatt-Gimblett, B. (2004) Intangible Heritage as Metacultural Production. *Museum International* 56 (1–2), 52–64.

Kreps, C. (2009) Indigenous Curation, Museums, and Intangible Cultural Heritage, in L. Smith and N. Akagawa (eds), *Intangible Heritage*. Abingdon: Routledge, pp. 193–209.

Kurin, R. (2004) Safeguarding Intangible Cultural Heritage in the 2003 UNESCO Convention: Acritical Appraisal. *Museum International* 56 (1–2), 66–76.

Labadi, S. (2007) Representations of the Nation and Cultural Diversity in Discourses on World Heritage. *Journal of Social Archaeology* 7, 147–170.

Labadi, S. (2010) World Heritage, Authenticity and Post-authenticity: International and National Perspectives, in S. Labadi and C. Long (eds), *Heritage and Globalisation*. London and New York: Routledge, pp. 66–84.

Labadi, S. (2013) *UNESCO Cultural Heritage and Outstanding Universal Value*. Walnut Creek, CA: AltaMira Press.

Labadi, S. and Long, C. (eds) (2010) *Heritage and Globalisation*. London and New York: Routledge.

Lafrenz Samuels, K. (2009) Trajectories of Development: International Heritage Management of Archaeology in the Middle East and North Africa. *Archaeologies* 5(1), 68–91.

Landsberg, A. (2004). *Prosthetic Memory: The Transformation of American Remembrance in the Age of Mass Culture*. New York: Columbia University Press.

Lane, R. and Waitt, G. (2001) Authenticity in Tourism and Native Title: Place, Time, and Spatial Politics in the East Kimberley. *Social and Cultural Geography* 2(4), 381–405.

Larsen, K.E. (1995) 'The Test of Authenticity' and National Heritage Legislation, in K.E. Larsen (ed.), *Proceedings of the Nara Conference on Authenticity in Relation to the World Heritage Convention, Nara, Japan, 1–6 November 1994*. Paris: UNESCO World Heritage Centre, pp. 363–364.

Leask, A. and Yeoman, I. (1999) *Heritage Visitor Attractions: An Operations Management Perspective*. London: Cassel.

Leng, Z. and Zhang, T. (2009) 我国世界遗产地的旅游研究进展及展望 (Development and Prospect of Tourism Research on World Heritage Sites in China). *Human Geography* (6), 111–115.

Lennon, J.L. (2003) Values as the Basis for Management of World Heritage Cultural Landscapes, *Cultural Landscapes: The Challenges of Conservation, World Heritage Papers 7*. Paris: UNESCO World Heritage Centre.

Lennon, J.L. (2012) Cultural Landscape Management International Influences, in K. Taylor and J. Lennon (eds), *Managing Culture Landscapes*. London: Routlege, pp. 45–69.

Li, C. (2011) 现代世界视角下的儒学人文主义 (Confucian Humanism from the Perspective of Modern World). *Group of Heaven and Earth* (20), 93–93.

Li, F. and Jin, Z. (2002) The Comparative Study of the Tourist Impact on Ancient Villages in Southern Anhui: A Case Study of Xidi, Hongcun and Nanping. *Human Geography* 17(5), 17–21.

Li, H. (2012) 西湖世界遗产与杭州旅游发展的实践与思考 (West Lake World Heritage and Hangzhou Tourism Development Practice and Thinking). *Tourism Tribune* 27(5), 12–13.

Li, J. (2007) Six World Heritage Sites Being Warned. *China Daily* (chinadaily.com.cn). Available at: www.chinadaily.com.cn/ezine/2007-06/29/content_905721_2.htm (accessed 3 January 2016).

Li, J. (2016) The Value and the Way to the 'All-for-One Tourism' (全域旅游的价值和途径). *People's Daily*, 2016-3-4.

Li, J. (2018) 推进文旅融合发展全域旅游共创美好生活 (Promotes the Integration of Cultural Tourism and Travel to Develop a Better Life). Available at: http://travel.china.com.cn/txt/2018-05/19/content_51413126.htm (accessed 1 June 2019).

Li, J.L., Zhang, X.L. and Zheng, S.J. (2006) A Preliminary Discussion on the Way out for World Heritages. *Tourism Tribune* 9 (21), 86–91.

Li, J.Q. (2007) 把《印象西湖》打造成杭州旅游的金名片 (The 'Impression of the West Lake' to Create a Gold Medal in Hangzhou Tourism). *Hangzhou Newsletter*, pp. 10.

Li, K. (2017) 政府工作报告——2017年3月5日在第十二届全国人民代表大会第五次会议上 (Government Work Report – 5 March 2017 at the Fifth Session of the 12th National People's Congress). Available at: www.gov.cn/premier/2017-03/16/content_5177940.htm (accessed 1 June 2019).

Li, M., Wu, B. and Cai, L. (2008) Tourism Development of World Heritage Sites in China: A Geographic Perspective. *Tourism Management* 29, 308–319.

Li, R. (2011) 中国世界遗产保护的现状、问题与对策 (Current State, Problems and Countermeasures of the World Heritage Protection in China). *City Planning Review* (5), 38–44.

Li, S.X. (2005) 书画文化和杭州旅游 (Calligraphy and Painting Culture and Hangzhou Tourism). *Daily Zhejiang* 24, 45–46.

Li, X.K. (2005) Breaking Through 'Keynes', Promoting the World Heritage to Develop in Harmony. *Urban and Rural Development* 2, 27–30.

Li, Y. (2007b) 中国的世界遗产保护视野概述 (Overview of China's World Heritage Conservation). 中国文化遗产保护成就统览 (Overview of the Achievements of China's Cultural Heritage Conservation). Beijing: Cultural Relics Press, pp. 38–44.

Liang, D. and Wang, B. (2005) Exploring Operation and Management of World Heritage Xidi and Hongcun (I). *Journal of Hefei University (Social Sciences)* 22(1), 28–33.

Liang, X. (2006) An Analysis of the Tourism Value of World Heritages and Study of Their Exploring Model. *Tourism Tribune* 6, 16–22.

Libo Government, The (2013) *Research of Protection and Sustainable Use of Nature Heritage, Libo*. Unpublished document, Libo Government.

Light, D. (2000) Gazing on Communism: Heritage Tourism and Post-communist Identities in Germany, Hungary and Romania. *Tourism Geographies* 2, 157–176.

Light, D., Prentice, R., Ashworth, G. and Larkham, P. (1994) Who Consumes the Heritage Product? Implications for European Heritage Tourism, in P.J. Larkham and G.J. Ashworth (eds), *Building a New Heritage: Tourism, Culture and Identity in the New Europe*. London: Routledge, pp. 90–116.

Lin, Y. (1935) *The Little Critic: Essays, Satires and Sketches on China* (1st ser. 1930–1932, 2nd ser. 1933–1935). Shanghai: Commercial Press.

Lin, Y. (2001) *The Importance of Living*. Beijing: Foreign Language Teaching and Research Press.

Lin, Y. (2002) *My Country and My People*. Beijing: Foreign Language Teaching and Research Press.

Lipe, W.D. (1977) A Conservation Model for American Archaeology, in M.B. Schiffer (ed.), *Advances in Archaeological Method and Theory*, Volume 5. New York: Academic Press.

Little, B.J. and Shackel, P. A. (2014) *Archaeology, Heritage and Civic Engagement: Working toward the Public Good*. Walnut Creek, CA: Left Coast Press.

Liu, B. (1994). 风景名胜区资源开发以及保护与旅游开发的矛盾和对策 (The Conflicts and Countermeasures of Resource Development and Protection and Tourism Development in Scenic Spots). *Tourism Tribune* (6), 39–42.

Liu, C. (2005) 世界遗产地旅游推力—引力因素研究-以西递和宏村为例 (A Study of Push and Pull Factors at World Heritage Sites: A Case of Vernacular Villages Xidi and Hongcun in Southern Anhui). *Tourism Tribune* 20(5), 15–20.

Logan, W. (2001) Globalising Heritage: World Heritage as a Manifestation of Modernism and Challenges from the Periphery, in L. William (ed.), *Proceedings of the Australia ICOMOS National Conference 2001, 20th Century Heritage – Our Recent Cultural Legacy, Adelaide, 28 November–1 December 2001*. Burwood, Australia: ICOMOS Australia, pp. 51–57.

Logan, W. (2012) States, Governance and the Politics of Culture: World Heritage in Asia, in P. Daly and T. Winter (eds), *Routledge Handbook of Heritage in Asia*. London: Routledge, pp. 113–128.

Long, C. and Labadi, S. (2010) Introduction, in S. Labadi and C. Long (eds), *Heritage and Globalisation*. London and New York: Routledge, pp. 1–16.

Long, C. and Reeves, K. (2009) 'Dig a Hole and Bury It': Reconciliation and the Heritage of Genocide in Cambodia, in W. Logan and K. Reeves (eds), *Places of Pain and Shame: Dealing with 'Difficult' Heritage*. Abingdon: Routledge.

Lowenthal, D. (1985) *The Past is a Foreign Country*. Cambridge: Cambridge University Press.

Lowenthal, D. (1992) Authenticity? The Dogma of Self-delusion, in M. Jones (ed.), *Why Fakes Matter: Essays on the Problems of Authenticity*. London: British Museum Press, pp. 184–192.

Lowenthal, D. (1994) Identity, Heritage, and History, in J. Gillis, *The Politics of National Identity*. Princeton, NJ: Princeton University Press, pp. 41–60.

Lowenthal, D. (1998) *Possessed by the Past: The Heritage Crusade and the Spoils of History*. New York: The Free Press.

Lowenthal, D. (1999) Authenticity: Rock of Faith or Quicksand Quagmire? *Getty Conservation Institute Newsletter* 14(3). Available at: www.getty.edu/conservation/publications_resources/newsletters/14_3/feature1_2.html (accessed 10 August 2016).

Lowenthal, D. (2005) Natural and Cultural Heritage. *International Journal of Heritage Studies* 11(1), 81–92.

Lu, Z. and Zhou, H. (2004) A Study on the Overall Protection of World Heritage and on Tourism Development – with Hongcun Village, Yixian County in South Anhui as an Example. *Planners* 4, 53–55.

Luke, C. and Kersel, M.M. (2012) *Soft Power, Hard Heritage: U.S. Cultural Diplomacy and Archaeology*. London: Routledge.

Luo, Z. (1999) 文物保护五十年回眸 (Retrospection of the Fifty Years' Cultural Relics Protection). *Outlook Weekly*, Issue 36.

Luo, Z. (2008) *World Heritage Collections*. Beijing: China Intercontinental Press.

Luo, C. (2010) 世博年杭州旅游收入取得巨大成绩 (Hangzhou Tourism Revenue in the World Expo Has Made Great Achievements). *Hangzhou* 12, 67.

Luo, Y., Wang, F., and Song, X. (2018) 我国世界文化遗产保护管理状况及趋势分析——中国世界文化遗产2017年度总报告 (China's World Cultural Heritage Protection

Management Status and Trend Analysis – China World Cultural Heritage 2017 Annual Report). *Chinese Cultural Heritage* 88(06), 6–30.

Lv, H. (2006) 杭州旅游做大做强"水文章"的构想 (The Conception of 'Water Articles' in Hangzhou Tourism). *Hangzhou Newsletter* 3, 16–19.

Lv, Z. (2008) 中国文化遗产保护三十年 (Thirty Years of Chinese Cultural Heritage Protection). *Architecture Journal* 12, 1–5.

Lv, Z. (2014) 文化遗产保护国际原则和地方实践"国际研讨会在清华大学召开 (International Symposium on International Principles and Local Practices of Cultural Heritage Protection Was Held in Tsinghua University). *World Heritage* (6), 112–112.

Lv, Z (2019) 从苏州到福州：中国遗产保护的不平凡之路 (From Suzhou to Fuzhou: An Extraordinary Way to Protect Chinese Heritage). *People's Daily*, 21 July.

MacCannell, D. (1973) Staged Authenticity: Arrangements of Social Space in Tourist Settings. *American Journal of Sociology* 79(3), 589–603.

MacCannell, D. (1999) *The Tourist: A New Theory of the Leisure Class*. Berkeley, CA: University of California Press.

Macdonald, S. (2003) Museums, National, Postnational and Transcultural Identities. *Museum and Society* 1, 1–16.

Malcolm-Davies, J. (2004) Borrowed Robes: The Educational Value of Costumed Interpretation at Historic Sites. *International Journal of Heritage Studies* 10(3), 277–293.

Mao, L. (2015) 中国加入《世界遗产公约》30周年 (*The 30th Anniversary of China's Accession to the World Heritage Convention*). Beijing: Social Sciences in China Press.

Mason, J. (2006) Mixing Methods in a Qualitatively Driven Way. *Qualitative Research* 6(1), 9–25.

Mason, R. (2002) Assessing Value in Conservation Planning: Methodological Issues and Choices, in M. de la Torre (ed.), *Assessing the Values of Cultural Heritage, Research Report*, Los Angeles, CA: The Getty Conservation Institute.

Mason, R. (2004) Conflict and Complement: An Exploration of the Discourses Informing the Concept of the Socially Inclusive Museum in Contemporary Britain. *International Journal of Heritage Studies* 10(1), 49–73.

Mason, R. (2005) Museums, Galleries and Heritage: Sires of Meaning-making and Communication, in G. Corsane (ed.), *Heritage, Museums and Galleries: An Introductory Reader*. London: Routledge.

McCrone, D., Morris, A. and Kiely, R. (1995) *Scotland – The Brand: The Making of Scottish Heritage*. Edinburgh: Edinburgh University Press.

McGimsey, C. R. (1972) *Public Archaeology*. New York: Seminar Press.

McKercher, B. (1993) Some Fundamental Truths about Tourism: Understanding Tourism's Social and Environmental Impacts. *Journal of Sustainable Tourism* 1 (1), 6–16.

McKercher, B. and Du Cros, H. (2002) *Cultural Tourism: The Partnership between Tourism and Cultural Heritage Management*. New York: The Haworth Hospitality Press.

McKercher, B. and Du Cros, H. (2003) Testing a Cultural Tourism Typology. *International Journal of Tourism Research* 5(1), 45–58.

McKercher, B., Ho, P. S. Y. and Du Cros, H. (2004) Relationship between Tourism and Cultural Heritage Management: Evidence from Hong Kong. *Tourism Management* 26, 539–548.

Meskell, L.M. (2002) The Intersections of Identity and Politics in Archaeology. *Annual Review of Anthropology* 31, 279–301.

Meskell, L.M. (2014). States of Conservation: Protection, Politics and Pacting within UNESCO's World Heritage Committee. *Anthropological Quarterly* 87(1), 217–244.

Meskell, L.M., Liuzza, C., Bertacchini, E. and Saccone, D. (2015) Multilateralism and UNESCO World Heritage: Decision-making, States Parties and Political Processes. *International Journal of Heritage Studies* 21(5), 423–440.

Meyer, J. (2009) Globalization: Sources and Effects on National States and Societies, in J.W. Burton (ed.), *World Society*. New York: Oxford University Press, pp. 156–169.

Meyer, M. (2008) *The Last Days of Old Beijing: Life in the Vanishing Backstreets of a City Transformed*. New York: Walker and Company.

Michael, I. (1995) Walk on the Wild Side. *The Independent on Sunday*, 9 April, pp. 36–37.

Misztal, B. (2003) *Theories of Social Remembering*. Berkshire: McGraw-Hill.

Mitchell, W.J.T. (1994) *Landscape and Power*. Chicago, IL: University of Chicago Press.

Moran-Ellis, J., Alexander, V.D., Cronin, A., Dickinson, M., Fielding, J., Sleney, J. and Thomas, H. (2006) Triangulation and Integration: Processes, Claims and Implications. *Qualitative Research* 6(1), 45–59.

Morgan, D., Dean, A. and Tan, T.E. (2002) Service Quality and Customers' Willingness to Pay More for Travel Services. *Journal of Travel and Tourism Marketing* 12, 95–110.

Morton, A. (2013). *Emotion and Imagination*. Cambridge: Polity.

Musitelli, J. (2002) World Heritage, between Universalism and Globalization. *International Journal of Cultural Property* 11(2), 323–336.

Natchitoches Declaration on Heritage Landscapes (2004) *USA: 7th International US ICOMOS Symposium. Learning from World Heritage: Lessons from International Preservation and Stewardship of Cultural and Ecological Landscape of Global Significance*. Available at: www.heritagelandscapes.com/cl/Natchitoches Declaration.pdf (accessed 21 May 2015).

National Bureau of Statistics of China (2016) *China Statistical Yearbook*. Beijing: China Statistics Press.

National People's Congress Standing Committee (2002 [1982,1991]) *Law on Protection of Cultural Relics*. Beijing: China Legal Publishing House.

NDRC (2018) 《促进乡村旅游发展提质升级行动方案（2018年—2020年）》发布 (The Action Plan for Improving and Upgrading Rural Tourism (2018–2020) Was Released). Available at: www.gov.cn/xinwen/2018-10/17/content_5331694.htm (accessed 29 July 2019).

Newman, A. and Mclean, F. (1998) Heritage Builds Communities: The Application of Heritage Resources to the Problems of Social Exclusion. *International Journal of Heritage Studies* 4(4-3), 143–153.

Ni, Q. and Xu, P. (2012) 杭州西湖世界文化景观遗产的物质表象与精神内涵 (The Material Manifestation and Spiritual Connotation of the West Lake as a World Cultural Landscape Heritage). *Chinese Landscape Architecture* 8, 86–88.

Nora, P. (1989) Between Memory and History: Les Lieux de Memoire. *Representations* 26, 7–24.

Norwegian Delegation (2010) *Report to the UNESCO World Heritage Committee 34th Session*, Brasilia, 25 July–August 3.

Nuryanti, W. (1996). Heritage and Postmodern Tourism. *Annals of Tourism Research*, 23(2), 249–260.

Nyaupane, G.P. and Poudel, S. (2012). Application of Appreciative Inquiry in Tourism Research in Rural Communities. *Tourism Management* 33(4), 978–987.

Oakes, T. (1993) The Cultural Space of Modernity: Ethnic Tourism and Place Identity in China Tourism. *Environment and Planning D: Society and Space* 1(1), 47–66.

O'Connor, B. (1993) Myths and Mirrors: Tourist Images and National Identity, in M. Cronin and B. O'Connor (eds), *Tourism in Ireland: A Critical Analysis*. Cork: Cork University Press, pp. 68–85.

Page, S.J. and Hall, M. (2003) *Managing Urban Tourism*. London: Prentice Hall.

Palmer, C. (2005) An Ethnography of Englishness: Experiencing Identity through Tourism. *Annals of Tourism Research* 32, 7–27.

Pearson, M. and Sullivan, S. (1995) *Looking after Heritage Places*. Melbourne: Melbourne University Press.

Pedersen, A. (2002) *Managing Tourism at World Heritage Sites: A Practical Manual for World Heritage Site Managers (World Hertiage Paper Serise No.1)*. UNESCO World Heritage Centre.

Peng, F. (1998). The Aesthetic Interpretation of 'Tao'. *The Eastern Forum* 4.

People.cn (2014) 谈"申遗热"：重申报轻保护得不偿失 (Reconsider World Heritage Fever, World Heritage Application Carries More Weight than Protection Is Not Worth the Candle). Available at: http://culture.people.com.cn/n/2014/0211/c172318-24321123.html (accessed 8 September 2016).

People.com (2011a) 2011年中国文化遗产日主场城市活动侧记 (Sidelights on the Main City Activities of China's Cultural Heritage in 2011). Available at: http://culture.people.com.cn/GB/14906282.html (accessed 21 July 2015).

People.com (2011b) 让世界读懂西湖：湖光山色中不只有风花雪月 (How to Translate the Meaning of West Lake to World). Available at: www.people.com.cn/h/2011/0705/c25408-1740990265.html (accessed 18 July 2015).

People.com (2018) People's Daily Public Opinion Monitoring Office released '2017 Red Tourism Impact Report' (人民网舆情监测室发布《2017年红色旅游影响力报告》). Available at: http://yuqing.people.com.cn/n1/2018/0131/c394872-29798399.html (accessed 29 July 2019).

People's Daily (2019). "中国为世界遗产保护作出重要贡献"——访联合国教科文组织世界遗产中心亚太部主任景峰 (China Makes an Important Contribution to the Protection of World Heritage – Interview with Jing Feng, Director of the Asia-Pacific Department of the UNESCO World Heritage Centre). Available at: www.gov.cn/xinwen/2019-07/27/content_5415759.htm (accessed 7 August 2019).

Petzet, M. (1995) 'In the Full Richness of Their Authenticity': The Test of Authenticity and the New Cult of Monuments, in K. Larsen (ed.), *Proceedings of the Nara Conference on Authenticity in Relation to the World Heritage Convention*. Paris: UNESCO, pp. 85–100.

Pocock, D. (1997) Some Reflections on World Heritage. *Area* 29 (3), 260–8.

Poria, Y, Butler, R. and Airey, D. (2003) The Core of Heritage Tourism. *Annals of Tourism Research* 30(1), 238–254.

Prentice, R. (1993) *Tourism and Heritage Attractions*. London: Routledge.

Prentice, R. (1998) Recollections of Museum Visits: A Case Study of Remembered Cultural Attraction Visiting on the Isle of Man. *Museum Management and Curatorship* 17(1), 41–64.

Prentice, R. (2001) Experiential Cultural Tourism: Museums and the Marketing of the New Romanticism of Evoked Authenticity. *Museum Management and Curatorship* 19(1), 5–26.

Pretes, M. (2003) Tourism and Nationalism. *Annals of Tourism Research* 30, 125–142.

Qian, F. (2007) China's Burra Charter: The Formation and Implementation of the China Principles. *International Journal of Heritage Studies* 13(3), 255–264.

Quan, H. (1994) 从武陵源看自然风景开发区的区域社会效应 (A Study on the Regional Social Effects of Natural Landscape Development Zone from Wulingyuan). *Economic Geography* 1994(4), 89–96.

Rakic, T. and Chambers, D. (2008) World Heritage: Exploring the Tension between the National and the 'Universal'. *Journal of Heritage Tourism* 2(3), 145–155.

Reichel, A., Cohen, R. and Poria, Y. (2011) World Heritage Site – Is It an Effective Brand Name?: A Case Study of a Religious Heritage Site. *Journal of Travel Research* 50, 482–495.

Reyes, V. (2014) The Production of Cultural and Natural Wealth: An Examination of World Heritage Sites. *Poetics* 44, 42–63.

Ribeiro, M.A., Pinto, P., Silva, J.A., and Woosnam, K.M. (2017) Residents' Attitudes and the Adoption of Pro-tourism Behaviours: The Case of Developing Island Countries. *Tourism Management* 61, 523–537.

Riegl, A. (1996)[1903] The Modern Cult of Monuments: Its Essence and Its Development, in N. Stanley-Price, M. Kirby Talley, Jr and A. Mellucco Vaccaro (eds), *Historical and Philosophical Issues in the Conservation of Cultural Heritage*. Los Angeles, CA: The Getty Conservation Institute, pp. 69–83.

Robinson, M. and Boniface, P. (1999) *Tourism and Cultural Conflicts*. Oxford: CABI.

Rössler, M. (2008) Applying Authenticity to Cultural Landscapes. *APT Bulletin* 39, 47–52.

Ruan, Y. and Li, H. (2008) 原真性视角下的中国建筑遗产保护 (Architectural Heritage Conservation in China from View of Authenticity). *Hua Zhong Architecture* 26(4), 144–148.

Russell, L. (2012) Remembering Places Never Visited: Connections and Context in Imagined and Imaginary Landscapes. *International Journal of Historical Archaeology* 16(2), 401–417.

SACH (2009[2002]) 关于加强和改善世界遗产保护管理工作的意见 (Suggestions on Strengthening and Promoting the Protection and Management of World Heritage), in 中国文化遗产事业法规文件汇编1949–2009 (Collection of Legal Documents on China's Cultural Heritage Enterprises) Beijing: Cultural Relics Press.

SACH (2011). *West Lake Cultural Landscape of Hangzhou (West Lake Nomination Document)*. Available at http://whc.unesco.org/en/list/1334 (accessed 16 August 2014).

SACH (2019a) The State Administration of Cultural Heritage Issued a Notice on the Issuance of the Work Guidelines of the State Administration of Cultural Heritage in 2019 *(国家文物局关于印发《国家文物局2019年工作要点》的通知)*. Available at: www.sach.gov.cn/art/2019/2/3/art_2234_42558.html (accessed 10 August 2019).

SACH (2019b) 申遗成功意味着更大的责任——国家文物局局长刘玉珠谈良渚古城遗址成功列入《世界遗产名录》(Success Means Greater Responsibility – Liu Yuzhu, Director of the State Administration of Cultural Heritage, Talked about Successfully Listed Liangzhu Ancient City as a World Heritage Site). Available at: www.sach.gov.cn/art/2019/7/9/art_722_155896.html (accessed 10 August 2019).

Samuel, R. (1994). *Theatres of Memory. Volume 1: Past and Present in Contemporary Culture*. London: Verso.

Sather-Wagstaff, J. (2011) *Heritage that Hurts: Tourists in the Memory Scapes of September 11*. Walnut Creek, CA: Left Coast Press.

Schama, S. (1995) *Landscape and Memory*. London: Harper Collins.

Schouten, F.F.J. (1995) Heritage as Historical Reality, in D. Herbert (ed.), *Heritage, Tourism and Society*. London: Pinter.

Scio.gov.cn (2018) *Party and State Institution Reform Helps China Modernize*. Available at: www.scio.gov.cn/32618/Document/1625741/1625741.htm (accessed 13 February 2019).

Selby, M. (2004) Consuming the City: Conceptualizing and Researching Urban Tourist Knowledge. *Tourism Geographies* 6, 186–207.

Shackel, P. (2001) Public Memory and the Search for Power in American Historical Archaeology. *American Anthropologist* 103(3), 655–670.

Shackel, P. (2013) 'Where We Need to Go': Comments on Decennial Reflections on a 'Geography of Heritage'. *International Journal of Heritage Studies* 19(4), 384–387.

Shackley, M. (1998) Visitor Management at Cultural World Heritage Sites, in M. Shackley (ed.), *Visitor Management: Case Studies from World Heritage Sites*. Oxford: Butterworth Heinemann.

Shan, J.X. (2008) New Type of Cultural Heritage – Protection of Cultural Routes. *China Cultural Heritage Scientific Research* 03, 12–23.

Shan, J.X. (2009a) 文化遗产保护与城市文化建设 (Cultural Heritage Conservation and Urban Culture Renaissance). Beijing: China Architecture and Industry Press.

Shan, J.X. (2009b) 走进文化景观遗产的世界 (Insight the Cultural Landscape Heritage). Tianjin: Tianjin University Press.

Shan, J.X. (2010a) 提案背后的故事—"文化遗产日"的诞生 (The Story behind the Proposal – The Born of the 'Cultural Heritage Day'). *China Cultural Relics*, 10 March, p. 3.

Shan, J.X. (2010b) 从"文化景观"到"文化景观遗产"（上）(From the Cultural Landscape to the Cultural Landscape Heritage (Part One)). *Southeast Culture* 2, 7–28.

Sharpley, R. (2011). *The Study of Tourism: Past Trends and Future Directions*. London: Routledge.

Shen, Y. and Yan, H. (2018) 申遗背景下的中国海上丝绸之路史迹研究 (Historical Relics of China's Maritime Silk Road under the Background of World Heritage Application). *Chinese Cultural Heritage* (2), 74–79.

Shi, Q. (2012) 西湖申遗成功的深层解读 (A Deep Interpretation of the Success of the West Lake). *Journal of Changsha University* 26(1), 19–21.

Sina.com (2013) 申遗热是否可以降降温？ (World Heritage Fever, Good or Bad?). Available at: http://news.sina.com.cn/c/2013-11-22/064028778279.shtml (accessed 8 September 2015).

Sina.com (2015) 杭州蒋经国故居主楼变麦当劳副楼开星巴克 (Chiangching Guo's House Turned into a McDonald's, and the Adjacent Building Turned into a Starbucks). Available at: http://news.sina.com.cn/c/nd/2015-11-16/doc-ifxkszhk0278004.shtml (accessed 21 May 2015).

Skounti, C. (2009) The Authentic Illusion: Humanity's Intangible Cultural Heritage, the Moroccan Experience, in L. Smith and N. Akagawa (eds), *Intangible Heritage*. Abingdon: Routledge, pp. 74–92.

Smardz Frost, K.H. (2004) Archaeology and Public Education in North America, in N. Merriman (ed.), *Public Archaeology*. London: Routledge.

Smith, L. (1993) Towards a Theoretical Overview for Heritage Management. *Archaeological Review from Cambridge* 12, 55–75.

Smith, L. (2006) *Uses of Heritage*. Abingdon: Routledge.

Smith, L. (2008) Heritage, Gender and Identity, in B. Graham and P. Howard (eds), *The Ashgate Research Companion to Heritage and Identity*. Aldershot: Ashgate Publishing Ltd, pp. 159–178.

Smith, L. (2011) Affect and Registers of Engagement: Navigating Emotional Responses to Dissonant Heritage, in L. Smith, G. Cubitt, R. Wilson and K. Fouseki (eds), *Representing Enslavement and Abolition in Museums: Ambiguous Engagements*. New York: Routledge, pp. 260–303.

Smith, L. (2012) The Cultural 'Work' of Tourism, in L. Smith, E. Waterton and S. Watson (eds), *The Cultural Moment in Tourism*. Abingdon: Routledge, pp. 210–234.

Smith, L. (2014a) Travellers' Emotion and Heritage Production. *GuiZhou Social Sciences* 12, 11–16.

Smith, L. (2014b) Changing Views? Emotional Intelligence, Registers of Engagement and the Museum Visit, in V. Gosselin and P. Livingstone (eds), *Museums as Sites of Historical Consciousness Perspectives on Museum Theory and Practice in Canada*. Vancouver: UBC Press.

Smith, L. (2015) Theorizing Museum and Heritage Visiting, in K. Message and A. Witcomb (eds), *The International Handbooks of Museum Studies: Museum Theory*. Chichester: Wiley-Blackwell, pp. 459–484.

Smith, L. (2016) Changing Views? Emotional Intelligence, Registers of Engagement and the Museum Visit, in V. Gosselin and P. Livingstone (eds), *Museums and the Past – Constructing Historical Consciousness*. Toronto: UBC Press, pp. 101–121.

Smith, L. (2017) Explorations in Banality: Prison Tourism of the Old Melbourne Gaol, in J.Z. Wilson, S. Hodgkinson, J. Piche, and K. Walby (eds), *The Palgrave Handbook of Prison Tourism*. London: Palgrave Macmillan, pp. 763–786.

Smith, L and Akagawa, N. (2009) Introduction, in L. Smith and N. Akagawa (eds), *Intangible Heritage*. Abingdon: Routledge, pp. 1–9.

Smith, L and Campbell, G. (2015) The Elephant in the Room: Heritage, Affect and Emotion, in W. Logan, M.N. Craith and U. Kockel (eds), *A Companion to Heritage Studies*. Oxford: Wiley-Blackwell, pp. 443–460.

Smith, L. and Waterton, E. (2009a) *Heritage, Communities and Archaeology*. London: Duckworth Academic.

Smith, L. and Waterton, E. (2009b) Constrained by Commonsense: the Authorised Heritage Discourse in Contemporary Debates, in J. Carman, R. Skeates and C. McDavid (eds), *The Oxford Handbook of Public Archaeology*. Oxford: Oxford University Press.

Smith, L., Shackel, P. and Campbell, G. (eds) (2011) *Heritage, Labour and the Working Classes*. Abingdon: Routledge.

Soren, B.J. (2009) Museum Experiences that Change Visitors. *Museum Management and Curatorship* 24(3), 233–251.

Sørensen, M.L.S. (2009) Between the Lines and in the Margins: Interviewing People about Attitudes to Heritage and Identity, in M.L.S. Sørensen and J. Carman (eds), *Heritage Studies: Methods and Approaches*. London: Routledge, pp. 164–177.

Spillman, L. (1997) *Nation and Commemoration*. Cambridge: Cambridge University Press.

Staiff, R. (2003) Cultural and Heritage Tourism: Whose Agenda, *Journal of Hospitality and Tourism Management* 2(10), 142–156.

Starn, R. (2002) Authenticity and Historic Preservation: Towards an Authentic History. *History of the Human Sciences* 15(1), 1–16.

Starr, F. (2010) The Business of Heritage and the Private Sector, in S. Labadi and C. Long (eds), *Heritage and Globalisation*, London and New York: Routledge, pp. 147–69.

State Council of PRC (2006a) 中华人民共和国国务院令第474号 *(Order of the State Council of the People's Republic of China No. 474)*. Available at: www.gov.cn/flfg/2006-09/29/content_402774.htm (accessed 1 May 2015).

State Council of PRC (2006b) 国务院关于核定并公布第六批全国重点文物保护单位的通知 (Notice of the State Council on Approving and Announcing the Sixth Batch of National Key Cultural Relics Protection Units). Available at: www.gov.cn/zwgk/2006-06/02/content_297818.htm (accessed 1 May 2015).

State Council of PRC (2009[2005]) 关于加强文化遗产保护的通知 (Circular on Strengthening the Protection for Cultural Heritage), in *Zhongguo Wenhua Yichan Shiye Fagui Wenxian Huibian 1949–2009 (Collection of Legal Documents on China's Cultural Heritage Enterprises)*. Beijing: Cultural Relics Press.

State Council of PRC (2016) 国务院关于同意设立"文化和自然遗产日"的批复 (Reply of the State Council to the Establishment of 'Cultural and Natural Heritage Day'). Available at: www.gov.cn/zhengce/content/2016-09/29/content_5113289.htm (accessed 1 May 2015).

State Council of PRC (2017) 国务院关于发布第九批国家级风景名胜区名单的通知 (Notice of the State Council Concerning the Issuance of the List of the 9th Batch of National Scenic Sites). Available at: www.gov.cn/zhengce/content/2017-03/29/content_5181770.htm (accessed 4 June 2019).

State Council of PRC (2018) 国务院办公厅关于促进全域旅游发展的指导意见 *(Guiding Opinions on Promoting the Development of 'All-for-One Tourism')*. Available at: www.gov.cn/zhengce/content/2018-03/22/content_5276447.htm (accessed 15 June 2019).

Su, M. and Li, B. (2012) Resource Management at World Heritage Sites in China. *Procedia Environmental Sciences* 12 Part A (0), 293–297.

Su, M. and Wall, G. (2011) Chinese Research on World Heritage Tourism. *Asia Pacific Journal of Tourism Research* 16(1), 75–88.

Su, Q., Cao, Y.H. and Lin, B.Y. (2005) Comparative Study on Residents' Perception of Tourism Impact at Tourist Places – A Case Study of Xidi, Zhouzhang and Jiuhua Mountain. *Chinese Geographical Science* 15(1), 70–79.

Su, X. and Teo, P. (2009) *The Politics of Heritage Tourism in China: A View from Lijiang*. London: Routledge.

Su, Y. (2018) The Relationship between National Parks and Existing Natural Reserve System – an Interpretation of General Plan for Establishing National Park System (Part One) (大部制后三说国家公园和既有自然保护地体系的关系——解读《建立国家公园体制总体方案》之五（上)). *China Development Observation* 189(09), 46–49.

Sullivan, S. (2004) Local Involvement and Traditional Practices in the World Heritage System, in E. de Merode, R. Smeers and C. Wesrrik (eds), *Linking Universal and Local Value J: Managing a Sustainable Future for World Heritage,* Paris: World Heritage Centre.

Sullivan, S. and Bowdler, S. (eds) (1984) *Site Surveys and Significance Assessments in Australian Archaeology*. Canberra: Department of Prehistory, Research School of Pacific Studies, Australian National University.

Susan, D. (2000) Authenticity in World Heritage Cultural Landscapes: Continuity and Change, in *New Views on Authenticity and Integrity in the World Heritage of the Americas*. Paris: ICIMOS.

Swarbrooke, J. (1995) *The Development and Management of Visitor Attractions*. Oxford: Butterworth Heinemann.

Swarbrooke, J. (1996) Towards the Development of Sustainable Tourism in Eastern Europe, in G. Richards (ed.), *Tourism in Central and Eastern Europe: Educating for Quality*, Tilburg, Netherlands: ATLAS Tilburg University Press.

Tan, C. (1971) *Chinese Political Thought in the Twentieth Century*. Garden City, NY: Doubleday.

Tang, Y. (1991) *Confucianism, Buddhism, Daoism, Christianity, and Chinese Culture*. Washington, DC: Council for Research in Values and Philosophy.

Tang, Y. (1994) 武陵源旅游开发研究 (Study on Tourism Development of Wulingyuan). *Journal of Hengyang Teachers College* (5), 73–76.

Tao, W. and Luca, Z. (2011) Management and Presentation of Chinese Sites for UNESCO World Heritage List (UWHL). *Facilities* 29, 313–325.

Taylor, K. (2004) Cultural Heritage Management: A Possible Role for Charters and Principles in Asia. *International Journal of Heritage Studies* 10(5), 417–433.

Taylor, K. (2009) Cultural Landscapes and Asia: Reconciling International and Southeast Asian Regional Values. *Landscape Research* 34(1), 7–31.

Taylor, K. (2010) International Practice and Regional Applications in Cultural Heritage Management: Whose Values?, at *Çannakal eOnsekiz Mart University 2010 World Universities Congress Proceedings II*, 20–24 October, Çannakale, Turkey.

Taylor, K. (2012) Landscape and Meaning: Context for a Global Discourse on Cultural Landscape Values, in K. Taylor and J. Lennon (eds), *Managing Culture Landscape*. London: Routledge, pp. 21–44.

Taylor, K. (2017) *Landscape, Culture and Heritage, Changing perspectives in an Asian Context*. PhD thesis, Deakin University.

Thomas, J. (2000) Introduction: The Polarities of Post-Processual Archaeology, in J. Thomas (ed.), *Interpretive Archaeology: A Reader*. London: Leicester University Press, pp. 1–22.

Timothy, D.J. and Nyaupane, G.P. (2008) *Cultural Heritage and Tourism in the Developing World*. London: Routledge.

Tribe, J. and Xiao, H. (2011) Developments in Tourism Social Science. *Annals of Tourism Research* 38(1), 7–26.

Trigger, B.G. (1989) *A History of Archaeological Thought*. Cambridge: Cambridge University Press.

Trofanenko, B.M. (2014) Affective Emotions: The Pedagogical Challenges of Knowing War. *Review of Education, Pedagogy and Cultural Studies* 36 (1), 22–39.

Turtinen, J. (2000) *Globalising Heritage: On UNESCO and the Transnational Construction of a World Heritage*. Stockholm: Stockholm Center for Organizational Research Stockholm.

UNESCO (1972) *Convention Concerning the Protection of the World Cultural and Natural Heritage*. Available at http://whc.unesco.org/archive/convention-en.pdf (accessed 23 June 2012).

UNESCO (1987) *The Great Wall*. Available at: http://whc.unesco.org/en/list/438 (accessed 6 November 2015).

UNESCO (2000a) *Cairns Decisions – Work of The World Heritage Reform Groups*. Available at: http://whc.unesco.org/en/decisions/1218 (accessed 12 March 2015).

UNESCO (2000b) *Ancient Villages in Southern Anhui- Xidi and Hongcun*. Available at: https://whc.unesco.org/en/list/1002 (accessed 19 November 2011).

UNESCO (2000c) *Ancient Villages in Southern Anhui- Xidi and Hongcun (nomination file)*. Available at: http://whc.unesco.org/uploads/nominations/1002.pdf (accessed 19 November 2011).

UNESCO (2000d) *Report of the 24th Session of the Committee*. Available at: http://whc.unesco.org/archive/repcom00.pdf (accessed 15 May 2016).

UNESCO (2003) *Convention for the Safeguarding of the Intangible Cultural Heritage*. Available at: http://unesdoc.unesco.org/images//0013/001325/132540e.pdf (accessed 11 June 2018).

UNESCO (2004) *Comments and Proposals by States Parties on the Cairns Decision*. Paris, 11 March 2004.

UNESCO (2007) *Global Strategy: Evaluation of the Cairns-Suzhou Decision*. Paris, 8 June 2007.

UNESCO (2010) *Preparing World Heritage Nominations*. Available at: http://whc.unesco.org/uploads/activities/documents/activity-643-1.pdf (accessed 10 December 2018).

UNESCO (2011a) *World Heritage Committee: Thirty-fifth Session*. Paris, 6 May 2011.

UNESCO (2011b) *West Lake Cultural Landscape of Hangzhou*. Available at: http://whc.unesco.org/en/list/1334 (accessed 19 November 2018).

UNESCO (2012a) *Community Development through World Heritage (World Heritage Paper Series 31)*. Available at: http://unesdoc.unesco.org/images/0023/002303/230372e.pdf (accessed 9 May 2014).

UNESCO (2012b) *Sustainable Tourism: UNESCO World Heritage and Sustainable Tourism Programme*. Available at: https://whc.unesco.org/en/tourism/ (accessed 11 May 2018).

UNESCO (2014a) *Human Origin Sites and the World Heritage Convention in Asia Experience (World Heritage Paper Series 39)*. Available at: http://unesdoc.unesco.org/images/0023/002303/230372e.pdf (accessed 12 May 2015).

UNESCO (2014b) *South China Karst*. Available at: http://whc.unesco.org/en/list/1248 (accessed 8 September 2016).

UNESCO (2015) *Word Heritage Tantative List*. Available at http://whc.unesco.org/en/tentativelists/ (accessed 12 October 2015).

UNESCO (2016) *Tentative Lists (China): Historic Monuments and Sites of Ancient Quanzhou (Zayton)*. Available at: http://whc.unesco.org/en/tentativelists/6073/ (accessed 11 January 2019).

UNESCO (2017) *Operational Guidelines for the Implementation of the World Heritage Convention*. Available at: http://whc.unesco.org/archive/opguide17-en.pdf (accessed 21 November 2018).

UNESCO (2018a) *Lists of Intangible Cultural Heritage*. Available at: www.unesco.org/culture/ich/en/lists (accessed 1 May 2018).

UNESCO (2018b) *World Heritage Tentative List (China)*. Available at: http://whc.unesco.org/en/tentativelists/state=cn (accessed 23 May 2018).

UNESCO (2019) *World Heritage List*. Available at: http://whc.unesco.org/en/list/ (accessed 1 May 2019).

United Nations (2008) *The State of the World's Cities 2008/9: Harmonious Cities*. London: Earthscan.

United Nations (2015) *Transforming our world: The 2030 Agenda for Sustainable Development*. Available at: www.un.org/sustainabledevelopment/development-agenda (accessed 16 May 2019).

Urry, J. (1990) *The Tourist Gaze*. London: Sage.

Urry, J. (1996) How Societies Remember the Past, in S. Macdonald and G. Fyfe (eds), *Theorising Museums*. Oxford: Blackwell.

Uysal, M., Woo, E. and Singal, M. (2012) The Tourist Area Life Cycle (TALC) and its Effect on the Quality-Of-Life (QOL) of Destination Community, in M. Uysal, R. Perdue and M.J. Sirgy (eds), *Handbook of Tourism and Quality-Of-Life Research*. Dordrecht, Netherlands: Springer, pp. 423–443.

Waitt, G. (2000) Consuming Heritage: Perceived Historical Authenticity. *Annals of Tourism Research* 27(4), 835–862.

Wall, G. and Su, M.M. (2011) Chinese Research on World Heritage Tourism. *Asia Pacific Journal of Tourism Research* 16, 75–88.

Wan, K.F. (2004) Tourism Policy Making at World Heritage Sites in China. *Guangxi Social Sciences* 9, 75–77.

Wang, G.P. (2008) 以培育发展十大特色潜力行业为突破口推动杭州旅游实现新一轮跨越式大发展 (To Promote the Development of the Top Ten Characteristics of the Industry as a Breakthrough to Promote Tourism in Hangzhou to Achieve a New Round of Great Development by Leaps and Bounds). *Hangzhou Newsletter* 9, 4–17.

Wang, J. (2009) 原真性和真实性 (Authenticity). *Urban Planning* 11 (2009), 87.

Wang, N. (1999) Rethinking Authenticity in Tourism Experience. *Annals of Tourism Research* 26, 349–370.

Wang, S. (2013) 古村有梦 *(Dream of the Old Village)*. Jiangsu: Jiangsu Fine Arts Publishing House Press.

Wang, S.L. (1998) *Chinese Tourism History*. Beijing: Tourism Education Press.

Wang, Y. (1990) *Gardens and Chinese Culture*. Shanghai: Shanghai People's Press.

Wang, Y.C. (2007) *A Yellow Card for the Three Parallel Rivers*. Available at: www.chinadialogue.net/article/show/single/en/1200-A-yellow-card-for-the-Three-Parallel-Rivers (accessed 1 July 2016).

Wang, Y. and Bramwell, B. (2011). Heritage Protection and Tourism Development Priorities in Hangzhou, China: A Political Economy and Governance Perspective. *Tourism Management* 33(4), 988–998.

Wang, Y. and Henke, F.G. (1964) *The Philosophy of Wang Yang-ming (2d edn)*. Paragon Book Reprint Corp, New York.

Wang, Y.Y. and Fan, X. (2005). Opinions on Uprising Problem of World Heritage Admission in China. *Tourism Science* 19(3), 70–73.

The Washington Post (2006) China's Party Leadership Declares New Priority: 'Harmonious Society', *The Washington Post*, 12 October 2006.

Waterton, E. (2005) Whose Sense of Place? Reconciling Archaeological Perspectives with Community Values: Cultural Landscapes in England. *International Journal of Heritage Studies* 11(4), 309–326.

Waterton, E. (2010) *Politics, Policy and the Discourses of Heritage in Britain*. Basingstoke: Palgrave Macmillan.

Waterton, E. and Smith, L. (2010) The Recognition and Misrecognition of Community Heritage. *International Journal of Heritage Studies* 16(1–2), 4–15.

Waterton, E and Watson, S. (2010) *Heritage and Community Engagement: Collaboration or Contestation?* London: Routledge.

Waterton, E and Watson, S. (2012) Shades of the Caliphate: the Cultural Moment in Southern Spain, in L. Smith, E. Waterton and S. Watson (eds), *The Cultural Moment in Tourism*. London: Routledge, pp. 161–181.

Waterton, E and Watson, S. (2014) *The Semiotics of Heritage Tourism (Vol. 35)*. Bristol: Channel View Publications.

Watkins, J. (2003) Beyond the Margin: American Indians, First Nations, and Archaeology in North America. *American Antiquity* 68(2), 273–285.

Watson, S. and Waterton, E. (2010) Heritage and Community Engagement. *International Journal of Heritage Studies* 16(1–2), 1–3.

Wei, L. (2015) A Brief Analysis of the Role of Rural Tourism in Regional Economic Development. *Cuide to Business* (15), 18–18.

Wei, X. (2012) 杭州旅游:新城市新模式新发展 (Hangzhou Tourism: New City, New Model and New Development). *Tourism Tribune* 27(4), 48–56.

Wertsch, J. and Billingsley, D.M. (2011) The Role of Narrative in Commemoration: Remembering as Mediated Action, in H. Anheier and Y.R. Isar (eds), *Heritage, Memory and Identity*. Los Angeles, CA: Sage.

Wertsch, J.V. (2002) *Voices of Collective Remembering*. Cambridge: Cambridge University Press.

Wetherell, M. (2012) *Affect and Emotion: A New Social Science Understanding*. London: Sage.

Whiteley, P. (2011) UNESCO Honor to Attract More Global Tourists to Hangzhou's West Lake. *China Daily*, 7 July.

Williams, R. (1977) *Marxism and Literature*. Oxford: Oxford University Press.

Wills, J.E. Jr. (1994) *Mountains of Fame: Portraits in Chinese History*. Princeton, NJ: Princeton University Press, pp. 168–180.

Winter, T. (2007) Rethinking Tourism in Asia. *Annals of Tourism Research* 34(1), 27–44.

Winter, T. (2009) Destination Asia: Rethinking Material Culture, in T. Winter, P. Teo and T.C. Chang (eds), *Asia on Tour: Exploring the Rise of Asian Tourism*. New York: Routledge.

Winter, T. (2014) Beyond Eurocentrism? Heritage Conservation and the Politics of Difference. *International Journal of Heritage Studies* 20(2), 123–137.

Winter, T. (2015) Heritage Diplomacy. *International Journal of Heritage Studies* 21(10), 997–1015.

Winter, T. and Daly, P.T. (2012) Introduction, in Daly, P.T. and Winter, T. (eds), *Routledge Handbook of Heritage in Asia*. New York: Routledge, pp. 1–36.

Winter, T., Teo, P. and Chang, T.C. (2009) *Asia on Tour: Exploring the Rise of Asian Tourism*. New York: Routledge.

Witcomb, A. (2012) On Memory, Affect and Atonement: The Long Tan Memorial Cross(es). *Historic Environment* 24(3), 35–42.

World Heritage Committee (1979) *Report of the Rapporteur on the Third Session of the World Heritage Committee in Cairo and Luxor, 22–26 October 1979*. Available at: http://whc.unesco.org/en/statutorydoc/?searchDocuments=&title=&file_name=&meeting=&unit=&years=1979&category= (accessed 11 April 2016).

World Heritage Committee (1980) *Operational Guidelines for the Implementation of the World Heritage Convention*. Intergovernmental Committee for the Protection of the World Cultural and Natural Heritage (Paris, October 1980), WHC/2/ Rev., 5, para. 18. Available at: http://whc.unesco.org/archive/opguide80.pdf (accessed 1 July 2016).

World Tourism Organization (2009 [1995]) *UNWTO Technical Manual: Collection of Tourism Expenditure Statistics*. Madrid: UNWTO.

Wright, P. (1985) *On Living in an Old Country*. London: Verso.

WTO (2011) *UNWTO World Tourism Highlights*. Available at: http://mkt.unwto.org/sites/all/files/docpdf/unwtohighlights11enlr.pdf (accessed 1 July 2016).

Wu, B.H., Li, M.M. and Huang, G.P. (2002) A Study on Relationship of Conservation and Tourism Demand of World Heritage Sites in China. *Geographical Research* 21(5), 617–626.

Wu, C., Funck, C. and Hayashi, Y. (2014) The Impact of Host Community on Destination (Re)branding: A Case Study of Hiroshima. *International Journal of Tourism Research* 16(6), 546–555.

Wu, D. (2011) 议文化景观遗产及其景观文化的保护 (Discussing on Cultural Landscape Heritage and Its Landscape Culture's Conservation). *Chinese Landscape Architecture* 4, 1–3.

Wu, J. (2015) *One Belt and One Road*. Far-reaching Initiative. Available at: www.chinausfocus.com/finance-economy/one-belt-and-one-road-far-reaching-initiative/ (accessed 3 July 2016).

Xidi Government, The (2013a) *Allocation of the Total Tourism Revenue (2007–2013)*. Unpublished document, Xidi Government.

Xidi Government, The (2013b) *Develop a Town with Characteristics, Establish New Rural Environment*. Unpublished document, Xidi Government.

Xidi Government, The (2013c) Introduction of Xidi. Unpublished report, Xidi Government.

Xie, H., Bao, J.G. and Kerstetter, D.L. (2014) Examining the Effects of Tourism Impacts on Satisfaction with Tourism between Native and Non-native Residents. *International Journal of Tourism Research* 16(3), 241–249.

Xinhuanet.com (2010) 我国出现"申遗"热西湖等35个项目排队备战 (World Heritage Fever in China, West Lake and other 35 Projects Line up for Preparation). Available at: http://news.xinhuanet.com/society/2010-08/11/c_12431554_2.htm (accessed 29 July 2016).

Xinhuanet.com (2011) 西湖申遗全程参与者揭秘申遗路：让世界"读懂"湖 (A Participant of World Heritage Listing Process of West Lake Illustrating the Process of How to Translate the Meaning of West Lake to World). Available at http://news.xinhuanet.com/local/2011-12/04/c_122372799.htm (accessed 29 July 2016).

Xinhuanet.com (2018) 王晨作关于《中华人民共和国宪法修正案（草案）》的说明（摘要） (Wang Chen's Description of the 'A Constitutional Amendment [Draft] of the People's Republic of China' [Summary]). Available at www.xinhuanet.com/politics/2018lh/2018-03/06/c_1122496003.htm (accessed 25 July 2019).

Xu, F. (1996) *Elaboration and Promotion of Traditional Chinese Humanity*. Beijing: Broadcasting and TV Publishing.

Xu, H., Wan, X. and Fan, X. (2012) 从"原真性"实践反思中国遗产保护 - 以宏村为例 (Rethinking Authenticity in the Implementation of China's Heritage Conservation: The Case of Hongcun Village). *Human Geography* 27(1), 107–112.

Xu, H., Wan, X. and Fan, X. (2014) Rethinking Authenticity in the Implementation of China's Heritage Conservation: The Case of Hongcun Village. *Tourism Geographies: An International Journal of Tourism Space, Place and Environment* 16:5, 799–811.

Xu, Q., Wang, L. and Pan, J. (2006) 西递村民不能擅自整修古寨 (Xidi Villagers Can Not Unauthorised Restore Their Ancient House). *Xihua News Agency*.

Yan, H. (2012) *World Heritage in China: Universal Discourse and National Culture*. PhD thesis, University of Virginia.

Yan, H. (2015) World Heritage as Discourse: Knowledge, Discipline and Dissonance in Fujian Tulou Sites. *International Journal of Heritage Studies* 21(1), 65–80.

Yan, H. (2017) *Heritage Tourism in China: Modernity, Identity and Sustainability*. Bristol: Channel View Publications.

Yan, H. (2018) *World Heritage Craze in China*. New York: Berghahn.

Yang, D. (2003) 杨典琴论之三："乱"声 *(About Chinese Music: the Voice of 'Mess')*. Available at: www.china.com.cn/chinese/zhuanti/282248.htm (accessed 23 June 2012).

Yang, X.R. (2007) The Blend of the Nature and Humanity – Exploring the Protection and Renovation Approach for the Sustainable Development of West Lake Scenic Area. *Chinese Landscape Architecture* 12, 29–36.

Yao, X. (2000) *An Introduction to Confucianism*. Cambridge: Cambridge University Press.

Ye, J. (2004) 论战国百家争鸣对专制主义的孵化作用及其历史影响 (On the Incubation of the Authoritarianism in the Warring States and Its Historical Influence). *Journal of Hubei Institute of Socialism* 4, 68–70.

Yi County Government (2015) 黟县2015年国民经济和社会发展统计公报 *(The National Economic and Social Development Statistical Bulletin in Yi County, 2015)*. Available at: www.yixian.gov.cn/DocHtml/1/16/04/00161037.html (accessed 29 July 2016).

Yin, X., Zhu, H. and Gan, M. (2005) 红色旅游产品特点和发展模式研究 (Research on the Characteristics and Development Mode of Red Tourism Products). *Human Geography* 20(2), 34–37.

Ying, T. and Zhou, Y. (2007) Community, Governments and External Capitals in China's Rural Cultural Tourism: A Comparative Study of Two Adjacent Villages. *Tourism Management* 28(1), 96–107.

Yoshida, K. (2004) The Museum and The Intangible Cultural Heritage. *Museum International* 56(1–2), 108–12.

Zeng B. (2018) *40 Years of Reform and Opening Up: The Evolution of China's Tourism Development Orientation*. China Travel News. Available at: www.ctnews.com.cn/art/2018/10/9/art_113_26255.html (accessed 2 June 2016).

Zhai, M. (2002) The Pain of Hongcun Village. *Southern Weekend*, 21 March.

Zhang, B. (1992) *Chinese Tourism History*. Yunnan: Yunnan People's Publisher.

Zhang, C. (2006) 世界遗产地管理体制之争及其理论实质 (The Disputes of World Heritage Management System and Its Theoretical Essence). *Commercial Research* 340(8), 175–179.

Zhang, C. (2010) 真实性和原真性辨析 (The Discussion about Two Translations of Authenticity). *Journal of Architecture* 2, 55–59.

Zhang, C. (2018a) 究竟谁影响谁？遗产保护与旅游利用关系的时空演化 (Who Influences Whom? The Temporal and Spatial Evolution of the Relationship between Heritage Protection and Tourism Utilization). *Chinese Cultural Heritage News*, 22 December.

Zhang, C. (2018b) The Integration of Culture and Tourism: Understanding from Perspective of Identity. *Social Sciences in Nanjing* 374(12), 168–172.

Zhang, C. and Li, W. (2016) 遗产旅游研究：从遗产地的旅游到遗产旅游 (Heritage Tourism Research: From Tourism in Heritage Sites to Heritage Tourism). *Tourism Science* 30(1), 37–47.

Zhang, C., Zhou, X. and Song, X. (2018) 我国世界文化遗产旅游发展现状分析报告 (China's World Cultural Heritage Tourism Development Status Analysis Report). *Chinese Cultural Heritage* 88(06), 37–41.

Zhang, J. (1986) *History of Chinese Gardens*. Haerbing: Heilongjiang People's Publisher.

Zhang, J. (2003) Research on Ancient Village Residents' Perceptions of Tourism Impact – A Case of Village Yixian-Xidi. *Geography and Geo-Information Science* 19(2), 105–109.

Zhang, J. (2007) 旧城遗产保护制度中"原真性"的谬误与真理 (Authenticity in Heritage Conservation Institution in Old City: Truth or Error). *City Planning Review* 11/ 20, 79–83.

Zhang, J., Xu, H. G. and Xing, W. (2016) The Host–Guest Interactions in Ethnic Tourism, Lijiang, China. *Current Issues in Tourism* 20(7), 1–16.

Zhang, R. (2012) 让南宋文化融进杭州旅游中 (Let the Southern Song Dynasty Culture into Hangzhou Tourism). *Hangzhou* 6, 79.

Zhang, R. (2017a) World Heritage Listing and Changes of Political Values: A Case Study in West Lake Cultural Landscape in Hangzhou, China. *International Journal of Heritage Studies* 23(3), 215–233.

Zhang, R. (2017b) *'Value in Change': What Do World Heritage Nominations Bring to Chinese World Heritage Sites?* (PhD thesis). Australian National University.

Zhang, R. and Smith, L. (2019) Bonding and Dissonance: Rethinking the Interrelations among Stakeholders in Heritage Tourism. *Tourism Management* 74, 212–223.

Zhang, R. and Taylor, K. (2020) Cultural Landscape Meanings. The Case of West Lake, Hangzhou, China. *Landscape Research* 45(2),164–178.

Zhang, S. and Ma, X. (2006) Reflections on Wannan Ancient Village Development and Tourism – A Case Study of World Heritage Site of Hongcun Village. *Journal of the Party College of C.P.C. Hefei Municipal Committee* 3, 50–52.

Zhang, X. (2008) 政府特许经营与商业特许经营含义辨析 (An Analysis of the Connotation of Government Franchising and Commercial Franchising). *China Terminology* 3, 42–43.

Zhang, Y. (2005) On 'Naturalization of Man' and Appreciation of Beauty. Fujian Tribune. *The Humanities & Social Sciences Monthly* 8, 76–81.

Zhao, D. (2002) An Angle on Nationalism in China Today: Attitudes among Beijing Students after Belgrade 1999. *The China Quarterly* 172, 885–905.

Zhao, S. and Timothy, D. (2017) Tourists' Consumption and Perceptions of Red Heritage. *Annals of Tourism Research* 63, 97–111.

Zhao, X. (2018) 乡村何以振兴？——自然与文化对立与交互作用的维度 (How Can a Village Be Revitalized? – Dimensions of Confrontation and Interaction between Nature and Culture). *Journal of China Agricultural University (Social Science Edition)* (3), 29–37.

Zhe Jiang Zai Xian (2013) *2013年杭州市游客满意度调查报告* (A Survey of Hangzhou's Tourist Satisfaction Survey in 2003). Available at: http://gotrip.zjol.com.cn/system/2014/03/17/019914071.shtml (accessed 2 June 2016).

Zhejiang Daily (2010) 西湖要申遗还靠老十景 (Ten Poetically Named Scenic Places of West Lake are the Key for Applying World Heritage Site). *Zhejiang Daily*, 16 September, p. 3.

Zhejiang Daily (2011) 西湖申遗后专家话传承 (After the West Lake Inscription, Experts Perception for Inheriting Culture). *Zhejiang Daily*, 12 August, p. 17.

Zhejiang Daily (2013) "全民旅游"时代——免费西湖：怎样扛住人潮 ('National Tourism'era, How to Deal with Mass Tourists in West Lake). *Zhejiang Daily*, 21 October, p. 3.

Zhejiang Government (2015) 杭州人均GDP接近富裕国家临界水平 (Hangzhou's per Capita GDP is Close to the Critical Level of Rich Countries). Available at: http://news.zj.com/detail/2015/03/20/1570881.html (accessed 2 June 2016).

Zheng, J.N. (2008) 杭州旅游从西湖走向钱塘江之有利条件分析 (An Analysis of the Favourable Conditions of Hangzhou Tourism from West Lake to Qiantang River). *Ecological Economy* (2), 123–126.

Zheng, S. (2017) The Present Situation, Problems and Countermeasures of Rural Tourism in China. New Countryside (我国乡村旅游的现状、问题与对策. 新农村). *Heilongjiang* (33), 12–13.

Zhong, W. (2006) China Yearns for Hu's 'Harmonious Society'. *Asia Times*, Last Modified 11 October 2006.

Zhou, J. (2003) *Remaking China's Public Philosophy for the Twenty-First Century*. Westport, CT: Praeger.

Zhou, M. (1999) *Exceeding and Transcending*. Chengdu: Sichuan People's Publisher.

Zhou, N.X., Yu, K.J. and Huang, Z.F. (2006) 关注遗产保护的新动向：文化景观 (New Challenges of World Heritage Conservation: Cultural Landscape). *Human Geography* 21(5), 61–65.

Zhou, W. (1999) *The History of Classical Chinese Gardens*. Beijing: Tsinghua University Press.

Zhu, Y. (2012) Performing Heritage: Rethinking Authenticity in Global Tourism. *Annals of Tourism Research* 39(3), 1495–1513.

Zhu, Y. (2013) Authenticity and Heritage Conservation in China: Translation, Interpretation and Practices, in K. Weiler (ed.), *Aspects of Authenticity in Architectural Heritage Conservation*. Heidelberg: Springer, pp. 250–260.

Zhuangzi and Lin, Y. (1957) *Zhuangzi*. Taibei: Shi jie shu ju.

Zou, T., Huang, S.S. and Ding, P. (2014) Toward a Community-Driven Development Model of Rural Tourism: The Chinese Experience. *International Journal of Tourism Research* 16(3), 261–271.

Index

advertising *see* marketing
aesthetics 189, 197–198, 214; West Lake 91, 92, 101, 102, 124, 191; Xidi and Hongcun 148, 149–150, 153, 155–158, 167, 168, 177, 195
agency 3, 5–7, 42, 189, 207; emotional engagement in cultural moments 193–196; West Lake 107, 133; Xidi and Hongcun 159, 160
Aikawa, N. 33
Akagawa, N. 27, 33
Allen, H. 70
all-for-one tourism 54–55
Ancient Villages in Southern Anhui *see* Hongcun; Xidi
Anheier, H. 151
Annan, K.A. 166
Ap, J. 3, 105
Araoz, G.F. 25
Arizpe, L. 24
Ashworth, G.J. 5, 20, 24, 30, 34, 36, 37, 41, 104, 106, 132, 133, 136, 137, 158, 187, 192, 212
Askew, M. 21, 22, 31, 32, 57, 213, 214, 217
authenticity 10, 11, 136, 215; *China Principle* 65; emotional 44, 199–200, 208, 215; emotional engagement in cultural moments 194; emotional expression of feeling 196, 199–200; heritage tourism 37; international debate 22, 23, 24, 31–32; West Lake 97, 109, 133, 208; Xidi and Hongcun 140, 143–144, 158, 178–184, 185
authorised heritage discourse (AHD) 6, 69, 189, 212; China's heritage development 58, 60, 73; China's heritage management systems 68; educational aspect 107; heritage tourism 35–36, 37, 41; influences 189–192; international debate 27–30, 32, 33–34, 35, 40, 41; local–tourist interactions 209; memory 43; power 213; West Lake 77, 81–83, 86–89, 91, 102; 104–105, 107–109, 117, 133, 181, 189–191, 207; Xidi and Hongcun 140, 157–158, 160, 181–182, 185, 192, 195
Aygen, Z. 5, 8

Bærenholdt, J. 41
Bagnall, G. 6, 7, 12, 27, 41, 42, 44, 45, 113, 134, 160, 189, 197, 199, 215
Bai Juyi 78, 96, 103n2, 121, 123, 198, 201
Bao, J. 39, 40, 54
Barthel-Bouchier, D. 5, 36, 104, 132, 136, 147, 158
Bauman, Z. 36
Beazley, O. 29
Belhassen, Y. 44
Billingsley, D. M. 43
Biran, A. 41
Blake, J. 33
Boniface, P. 36
Boswell, D. 27
boundaries 201, 205, 206, 216; West Lake 122–3, 201; Xidi and Hongcun 167, 183, 186–187
Bowdler, S. 70
Bramwell, B. 38
Brett, D. 2, 11, 36, 41, 166, 185, 192, 193, 210
Brown, J. 35
Brunt, P. 105
Buckley, K. 21
Buddhism 91, 94, 95

Burkett, I. 28
Burra Charter 75n16
Burton, A. 2, 36, 194
Butcher, J. 6, 134
Byrne, D. 5, 6, 7, 8, 12, 20, 23, 27, 32, 33, 34, 40, 42, 45, 68, 70, 73, 140, 159, 160, 189, 196, 209, 215

Cameron, C. 8, 12, 22, 31, 42, 45, 102, 117, 123, 124, 196, 215
Campanella, T. J. 31–32
Campbell, G. 32, 44, 45, 124, 159
Cao, B. 70
Carrier, P. 27, 28
Chambers, D. 38
Champion, T. 27
Chan, A.L. 160n1
Chen, G. 39
Chen, T. 7
Chen, Y. 11, 140, 142, 143, 158, 160, 176, 206
Cheng, Y. 143, 159, 160
China 47, 68–73; heritage development 56–63; heritage management systems 63–68; heritage tourism 38–40; historical and philosophical context 47–51; tourism development 51–56
China Principles 64, 65, 68, 71
Chinese Communist Party (CCP) 47–48, 69, 71, 72–73; heritage development 75n15; heritage management systems 64; red tourism 55, 56; rural tourism 56
Chinese harmony discourse *see* harmony discourse
Choay, F. 2, 11, 21, 36, 37, 41, 166, 185, 192, 194
Clark, K. 70
Cleere, H. 20, 24, 27, 32
Cohen, B. 6, 8, 134, 161
Cohen, E. 6, 8, 37, 134, 161
Co. Huihang Ltd 141, 145, 157, 170, 174–176, 205
Co. Jingyi Ltd (Zhongkun Investment Group) 141–143, 145, 156, 158, 174, 176, 180, 181, 205–206, 208
Coleman, S. 6, 37, 133, 215
community *see* local residents
Confucius/Confucianism 48, 49–50, 51, 52, 72, 90–91, 159, 184, 195, 199
contentment 3, 212; local–tourist interactions 203–205, 207, 210; West Lake 128, 129; Xidi and Hongcun 155, 159, 169, 186, 212

Cotter, M. 25
Courtney, P. 105
Crang, M. 6, 37, 133, 215
Crompton, J. 3, 105
Crouch, D. 42, 43
cultural heritage 48, 71, 73, 76, 190; 58, 62; China's heritage management systems 63–68; international debate 23, 25, 30–33, 38; West Lake 78, 81, 86, 90, 91, 96; Xidi and Hongcun 137, 157
cultural landscape 59, 62, 66, 76–77, 190, 214; international debate 25–6, 31, 39; tourists' and locals' discourses 85–91, 101; *see also* West Lake
cultural routes 59–60

Daly, P.T. 3, 5, 8, 10, 31, 32, 40, 69, 171, 218
Daoism *see* Taoism
Davison, P. 151
Deng, M.Y. 5
Deng, X. 52–53
Dewi, C. 70, 140
Díaz-Andreu, M. 27, 28
Dicks, B. 34, 37, 42, 45
Di Giovine, M. 21
dissonant heritage 129–132, 187
Dong, Q. 104
Dong, Y.M. 39
Dong, Z. 49
Dove, M. 35
Du, X. 62
Du, Y. 52, 53, 54
Dubrow, G. 34
du Cros, H. 3, 4, 35, 36, 37, 40, 127, 133, 129, 207

economics of tourism: active sense of tourists 40–1; China's heritage development 58; China's tourism development 53; and culture 192–193; heritage tourism 37; local–tourist interactions 206; red tourism 56; World Heritage sites 4, 5; Xidi and Hongcun 141–142, 157, 162–165, 169, 175–176, 179–181, 185
education 107, 111, 117, 125, 133
emotion 3, 7–8, 43–44, 188, 215; authenticity 44, 199–200, 208, 215; in cultural moments 193–196; expression of feeling 196–202; heritage 210; local people–tourist interactions 200, 202–210; West Lake

Index

98, 117, 121, 123, 124, 190; Xidi and Hongcun 150–151, 158, 167, 185; *see also* feelings
empathy: emotional expression of feeling 199; local–tourist interactions 203, 204; West Lake 119, 123, 124, 133, 194; Xidi and Hongcun 149, 151, 167, 186
engagement *see* emotion
Erb, M. 6, 134
Erzberger, C. 9

Fairclough, G. 25
Fan, X. 39
Fan, Ye. 53
Fang, B. S. 39
feelings 3, 7–8, 189, 191, 210, 215; emotional expression of 196–202; West Lake 87, 88, 91, 98–101, 102; 113, 117–125, 133, 134; Xidi and Hongcun 148, 150, 151, 159, 182; *see also* emotion
Feng, J.Z. 27
fieldwork 1–3, 9–17, 83–85, 144–146
Filippucci, P. 9
Fisher, R. 4, 6, 134
Francis, F. 50
Franklin, A. 37
freedom 188, 200–201, 216; West Lake 121–123, 201; Xidi and Hongcun 166, 167, 168, 182–183, 186
Frey, B. S. 24
Fu, H. 11, 82
Fung, C. 70

Gable, E. 11, 37, 41, 166, 185, 210, 212
Gao, J. 38
Gao, L. 10, 64, 140, 143, 159, 160
Gao, M. 60
Gao, X. 27
Gao, Z. 55
Gatewood, J. 8, 12, 42, 45, 102, 117, 123, 124, 196, 215
Gentry, K. 27, 45
Gong, P. 27, 52, 90
government 69, 73, 188–189, 216, 218; China's heritage development 57–63; China's tourism development 52–56; fieldwork 10–11, 13–14, 16–17; heritage management systems 63–68; local–tourist interactions 205, 206–207, 208; West Lake 81, 82–83, 84, 95, 122–123, 130–133; World Heritage meaning 5; Xidi and Hongcun 137, 141–143, 145, 155–159, 167, 169–184, 186–187; *see also* Ministry of Housing and Urban–Rural Development; State Administration of Cultural Heritage
Graburn, N.H.H. 5, 36, 104, 132, 136, 147, 158
Graham, B.J. 9, 20, 24, 27, 34, 132, 192
Great Leap Forward 160n1
Great Wall of China 58
Greenspan, A. 11, 166, 185, 192
Greenwood, D. 11, 166, 185
Grenville, J. 25
Gu, H. 55, 143, 162, 166
Guo, X. 55

Hafstein, V. 33
Hall, C.M. 41, 43, 106, 137, 183
Hall, M. 3, 4, 36, 127, 133, 192, 207
Han, F. 7, 11, 18, 25, 26, 27, 29, 50, 51, 52, 63, 66, 70, 76, 78, 90, 91, 122, 189, 190, 191, 198, 201, 214, 218
Hancock, M. 27
Handler, R. 11, 37, 41, 166, 185, 210, 212
Hani Rice Terraces 59
harmony discourse 7, 71–72, 72, 76, 191, 213, 217; emotional expression of feeling 197–198; heritage development 58, 62; international debate 26–30, 34; philosophical context 50, 51, 72; West Lake 78, 81–83, 90–91, 98, 102, 105, 190; Xidi and Hongcun 168
harmony with culture *see* harmony discourse
Harrison, R. 4, 21, 36, 77, 127, 207
Harvey, D. 7, 21, 27, 28, 33, 34, 41, 42, 45, 68, 76
Hayden, D. 6, 34, 209
Head, L. 26
Henke, F.G. 191
heritage 189, 212; boundedness 24–27; Chinese view of 214–215; and community 34–35; as cultural process 41–45; dissonant 129–132, 187; as emotional and cultural process 210; emotional expression of feeling 198–199; local–tourist interactions 204, 205, 209; meaning 22–23; natural 25, 190; nature–culture journey 76–103; tourism 35–40; Xidi and Hongcun 166, 169, 177, 183–185; *see also* cultural heritage; intangible heritage
Hevia, J.L. 30, 57
Hewison, R. 3, 5, 37, 210

252 Index

Heywood, A. 48
Hitchcock, M. 6, 134
Hobsbawm, E. 27
Hockney, D. 102
Hodges, A. 6, 34, 209
Hongcun 137, 158–162, 184–187, 210, 216; authorised heritage discourse 140, 157–158, 160, 181–182, 185, 192, 195; background and tourism development 137–144; comparison with Xidi 155–158; emotional engagement in cultural moments 194–195; emotional expression of feeling 197, 200, 201; emotional interactions between local people and tourists 202–204, 205–206; fieldwork 1–2, 3, 9, 10–17, 144–146; local management policies 178–184; local people's reactions to governments' policies and management mode 169–177; local people's reactions to tourism 162–169, 193; tourists and cultural moments 146–155
Howard, P. 76
Hu, J. 30
Hu, Q. 53
Hu, X. 39, 115, 135n2
Hu, Z. 83
Hua, C. 71
Huang, Y. 5

identity 188–189, 191; cultural 69; emotional engagement in cultural moments 195; heritage discourse 34; international debate 27; local–tourist interactions 204, 206; national 27, 28, 69, 116, 197, 215; tourists 43–44; West Lake 112–113, 117, 128, 134; World Heritage 87; Xidi and Hongcun 150–151, 159, 165, 183, 186
Inaba, N. 25, 190
Intangible Cultural Heritage Convention (ICHC) 32–33
intangible heritage 32–33, 63, 193; Xidi and Hongcun 149, 157, 165, 166, 169, 177
integrity 22; West Lake 91–95, 97, 109, 130; Xidi and Hongcun 155, 167, 168, 171, 178–179, 181
International Centre for the Study of the Preservation and the Restoration of Cultural Property (ICCROM) 22, 61
International Council on Monuments and Sites (ICOMOS): authorised heritage discourse 27, 29; China's relations with 61, 67; community and heritage 35; Culture–Nature Journey 217–218; heritage meaning 1; *Nara Document on Authenticity* 31; negative effects of tourism 192; outstanding universal value 23; *Seoul Declaration on Tourism* 36, 133; West Lake 77, 91–93, 95, 98–99, 101, 124, 208; World Heritage Committee 22; Xidi and Hongcun 139; *Yatra Statement* 217
international debate 20–1, 45–46; active sense of tourists 40–41; authorised heritage discourse 27–38; boundedness of heritage 24–27; community and heritage 35–38; heritage as cultural process 41–45; heritage tourism, China's 38–40; heritage tourism, issue of 35–38; World Heritage Programme, Eurocentricity 21–24; World Heritage Programme, evolution 31–34; West Lake 82
International Union for Conservation of Nature (IUCN): China's relations with 61; Culture–Nature Journey 217–218; national park system 63; outstanding universal value 23; World Heritage Committee 22; *Yatra Statement* 217
Isar, Y.R. 151

Jenkins, T. N. 51
Jiang, H. 54
Jing, F. 60–61
Johnston, C. 70
Jokilehto, J. 22, 133

Kim, K. 3
Kirshenblatt-Gimblett, B. 33, 40, 45
Kreps, C. 33
Kurin, R. 33

Labadi, S. 3, 20, 22, 23, 24, 31, 32, 68, 69, 140, 209
Lafrenz Samuels, K. 22
Lao, Z. 50
Laozi 48–49, 50
Leask, A. 3, 4, 36, 127, 192, 207
Lee, Y.S.F. 35
Leng, Z. 4, 38, 58
Lennon, J.L. 25
Li, B. 39
Li, C. 49
Li, H. 11, 32, 82

Index

Li, J. 54, 55
Li, J.L. 66
Li, J.Q. 70, 83
Li, K. 54
Li, M. 4, 39
Li, R. 39
Li, S.X. 83
Li, W. 38, 39
Li, X.K. 66
Li, Y. 66, 68, 73
Liang, D. 140, 141, 142, 143, 158, 160, 176, 206
Liang, X. 5
Lin, Y. 7, 26, 51, 78, 102, 218
Lipe, W. D. 70
Lippsor, T. 197
Little, B.J. 6
Liu, B. 38
Liu, C. 143
Liu, J.T.C. 113
local government *see* government
local residents 8; attitudes to tourism/tourists 125–132, 134, 141, 162–169, 183, 185, 192–193, 207; authorised heritage discourse 28; fieldwork 10–11, 13, 14–17; and heritage 34–35; reactions to governments' policies and management mode 169–177; relocation 129–132; West Lake 77–78, 82, 85–91, 93–94, 96, 99–102, 105, 121, 124, 125–133, 134; World Heritage and cultural landscape discourses 85–91, 209; Xidi and Hongcun 137, 140–146, 157–158, 161–187; *see also* local–tourist interactions
local–tourist interactions 1–3, 6, 8, 188, 210, 212, 216; and emotions 200, 202–210; fieldwork 11; West Lake 88, 128–129; Xidi and Hongcun 153–155, 159, 161, 167, 169, 185–186
Logan, W. 5, 8, 22, 23, 29, 31, 32, 68
Long, C. 20, 24, 140
Lowenthal, D. 3, 21, 25, 27, 30, 36, 41, 69, 133, 192
Lu, Q. 39
Lu, Y. 94
Lu, Z. 5
Luca, Z. 4
Luo, C. 11, 82
Luo, Y. 5, 147
Luo, Z. 30, 57, 70
Lv, H. 11, 83
Lv, Z. 57, 58, 59, 60, 65, 71

Ma, X. 5
MacCannell, D. 11, 37, 158, 194
Macdonald, S. 27, 192
Mao, Z. 160n1
Maritime Silk Road 60, 61, 73, 74n12
marketing 8, 37; Hongcun 142, 156, 167, 180; Xidi 158, 167
Mason, J. 9
Mason, R. 2, 36, 107, 194
McArthur, S. 3, 4, 36, 127, 133, 192, 207
McCrone, D. 2, 11, 36, 37, 41, 166, 185, 192, 193, 210, 212
McGimsey, C.R. 70
McKercher, B. 3, 4, 36, 37, 38, 40, 127, 133, 192, 207
McLean, F. 6, 34, 209
memory 190; Chinese paintings 102; emotional engagement in cultural moments 195; international debate 27, 43; local–tourist interactions 204; West Lake 112–117, 119, 121, 124–125, 126, 194; World Heritage 87, 88; Xidi and Hongcun 148, 150–151, 159
Mencius 48
Meskell, L.M. 20, 21, 22, 24, 29, 60, 68
Meyer, J. 69
Meyer, M. 30, 69
Ministry of Housing and Urban–Rural Development (MHURD) 72; fieldwork 11–12; heritage development 59, 62; heritage management system 63, 64, 65–66, 67; West Lake 84
Misztal, B. 43
Mitchell, W.J.T. 76
Moran-Ellis, J. 9
Morrison, A.M. 143, 159, 160
Morton, A. 44
Musitelli, J. 23

National Cultural Heritage 64–65
natural heritage 25, 190
nature: Chinese sense of 90–91, 124, 214; West Lake 77–103, 121–122, 127
Newman, A. 6, 34, 209
Ni, Q. 82
Nora, P. 151
Nuryanti, W. 36
Nyaupane, G.P. 8

Oakes, T. 6, 8, 40, 134, 161
Obama, M.L. 104
One Belt, One Road initiative 60–61, 73

Outstanding Universal Value (OUV) 10, 68, 212; evolution 31; harmony discourse 30; international debate 21–23, 24, 28; West Lake 77, 82, 90, 91–93, 95–96, 109, 111, 189–190

Palmer, C. 6, 7, 12, 41, 42, 45, 189, 215
Pamini, P. 24
Parker, G. 43
Pearson, M. 70
Pedersen, A. 3, 36, 127, 133, 207
Peng, F. 198
Pocock, D. 24
poetic sentiment 7, 214–215, 218; emotional expression of feeling 197, 198, 199; local–tourist interactions 206, 208; West Lake 99–101, 112, 119–121, 122, 124, 127–128, 191, 197, 198, 208; Xidi and Hongcun 148, 150, 195
Poria, Y. 6, 7, 8, 12, 18, 41, 42, 43, 45, 102, 118, 121, 124, 134, 159, 189, 196, 197, 200, 201, 206, 215
Poudel, S. 8
Prein, G. 9
Prentice, R. 36, 44
pride 8, 188, 192, 210, 212; local–tourist interactions 202, 204, 207, 208; West Lake 126, 127–128, 133, 134; Xidi and Hongcun 153, 164, 165, 166–167, 183

Qian, F. 68
Quan, H. 38

Rakic, T. 38
red tourism 55–56
Reeves, K. 24
Reichel, A. 3
Reyes, V. 24
Ribeiro, M. A. 6
Rippon, S. 25
Robinson, M. 36
Rössler, M. 25
Ruan, Y. 32
rural tourism 56
Russell, L. 25
Ryan, C. 55, 143, 162, 166

Samuel, R. 116
Sather-Wagstaff, J. 6, 7, 11, 41, 107, 136, 189, 196, 200, 215
Saxton, W. 11, 37, 166, 185
Scenic and Historic Interest Areas 63–64, 65

Schouten, F.F.J. 41
Selby, M. 12, 42, 45
Shackel, P.A. 6, 34, 136, 210, 212
Shackley, M. 3
Shan, J.X. 26, 48, 49, 58, 60, 64, 67, 70, 76, 190
Sharpley, R. 39
Shen, Y. 61
Shi, Q. 82
Silk Road 60–61, 62, 73, 74n10
Skounti, C. 33
Smardz Frost, K.H. 6, 34, 209
Smith, L. 5, 6, 7, 8, 11, 12, 13, 18, 20, 21, 23, 20, 24, 27, 28, 29, 32, 33, 34, 35, 36, 37, 38, 40, 41, 42, 43, 44, 45, 68, 69, 70, 77, 101, 102, 107, 108, 113, 116, 117, 118, 124, 134, 136, 137, 140, 151, 158, 159, 160, 183, 189, 192, 196, 197, 199–200, 201, 204, 209, 210, 212, 214, 215
Sørensen, M.L.S. 9, 12
Spillman, L. 27
Staiff, R. 7
Starn, R. 31
Starr, F. 4
State Administration of Cultural Heritage (SACH) 69, 72; heritage development 59, 61, 62; heritage management system 63, 64–68; West Lake 84
State Forestry and Grassland Administration (SFGA) 62, 64, 72
Steiner, L. 24
Su, D. 78, 96, 103n3, 112, 113, 118, 119, 120, 121, 123, 198, 207
Su, M. 39, 58, 62
Su, Q. 143, 162
Su, X. 4, 6, 8, 37, 40, 57, 134, 161
Su, Y. 64
Sullivan, S. 24, 32, 70
sustainable development goals 217
Swarbrooke, J. 4, 36, 127, 192, 199, 207

Tan, C. 49
Tang, Y. 38, 50
Tao, W. 4
Taoism 48–49, 50–51, 52, 72, 90–91, 94
Taylor, K. 5, 6, 23, 25, 26, 30, 32, 40, 60, 76, 77, 78, 99, 124, 190, 197, 208
Teo, P. 4, 6, 8, 37, 40, 57, 134, 161
Timothy, D. 55, 56
Tong, M. 5
tourist companies 216; fieldwork 13–14; local–tourist interactions 205, 206,

208; Xidi and Hongcun 137, 140–143, 145–146, 155–156, 157–159, 167, 170, 173–184, 186–187
tourists/tourism: active sense of heritage 40–41, 111–117; definitions 40; development in China 51–56; emotional engagement in cultural moments 193–196; emotional expression of feeling 196–202; engagement with heritage 1–3; fieldwork 10–12, 13, 14–17; heritage as cultural process 41, 42–44; local people's attitudes to 125–132, 134, 141, 162–169, 183, 185, 192–193, 207; negative aspects 105–111, 127, 136–137, 143–144, 164, 165–166, 183, 185, 192, 195, 207; West Lake 77–78, 82–83, 85–91, 94, 97–98, 99–102, 105–134; World Heritage and cultural landscape discourses 85–91; World Heritage sites 3–5; Xidi and Hongcun 137, 140–171; *see also* agency; economics of tourism; local–tourist interactions
Tribe, J. 39
Trigger, B.G. 27, 28
Tunbridge, J. 20, 24, 30, 37, 132, 187, 192
Turtinen, J. 21, 22, 23, 30, 68

United Nations Education, Scientific and Cultural Organization (UNESCO): authorised heritage discourse 27, 28, 29; China's relations with 61, 62; community and heritage 35; cultural landscape 25, 26; emotional engagement in cultural moments 194; expectations 8; fieldwork 12; heritage, meaning of 1, 23; Intangible Cultural Heritage list 33; *Nara Document on Authenticity* 31; *see also* World Heritage Programme
United Nations Sustainable Development Goals 217
Urry, J. 37, 42, 151

Venice Charter 69

Waitt, G. 11, 166, 185
Wall, G. 39, 58, 62
Wang, B. 140, 141, 142, 143, 158, 160, 176, 206
Wang, G.P. 11, 83
Wang, N. 32
Wang, S.L. 91, 97, 164, 167, 186, 204
Wang, Y. 7, 27, 29, 38, 78, 191, 198, 199, 218, 211n1

Wang, Y.C. 4
Wang, Y.Y. 39
Waterton, E. 5, 6, 12, 20, 23, 26, 28, 29, 33, 34, 35, 41, 42, 45, 68, 71, 140, 189, 209
Watkins, J. 34
Watson, S. 5, 6, 12, 34, 41, 42, 45, 189, 209, 215
Wei, X. 11, 82
Wertsch, J. 43
West Lake 77, 101–102, 104–105, 132–135, 210, 215–216; authorised heritage discourse 77, 81–83, 86–89, 91, 102, 104–105, 107–109, 117, 133, 181, 189–191, 207; case study background 78–80; comparison with Xidi and Hongcun 147, 151, 159, 161, 181, 186; continually changing landscape 95–98; cultural diversity and integrity 91–95; emotional engagement in cultural moments 194; emotional expression of feeling 197, 198, 201; emotional interactions between local people and tourists 202, 204–205, 206–207; feelings 117–125; fieldwork 3, 9–17, 83–85; heritage development 59; locals' attitudes to tourism 125–132, 192–193; Longjing Tea Plantation 92–94, 218; ten poetically named scenic places 98–101, 197, 208; tourism as a problem 105–111; tourists' active sense of heritage 111–117; World Heritage and cultural landscapes 85–91
Wetherell, M. 44
Williams, R. 44
Winter, T. 3, 5, 6, 8, 10, 27, 31, 32, 35, 37, 40, 69, 134, 140, 171, 218
World Heritage, tourists' and locals' discourses 85–91, 101
World Heritage Centre 22
World Heritage Committee: authorised heritage discourse 29; *Cairns Decision* 58, 60, 65–68; cultural landscape 25; Suzhou (2004) 58–59, 66; West Lake 77, 95, 98; *World Heritage and Sustainable Tourism Programme* 217
World Heritage Convention (WHC): China's ratification 57, 65, 68, 85; Chinese government responses 69, 70, 71, 72; Eurocentricity 77; international debate 21, 22, 23, 24, 32

World Heritage Programme (WHP) 1–5, 8, 68–72, 73; authorised heritage discourse 28, 30; benefits 210; China's heritage development 56–63; China's heritage management systems 63, 65–66, 68; community participation 209; cultural landscape 25, 76–77; devaluation of tourism 212; Eurocentricity 21–24; evolution 31–34; further research 218–219; implications for 216–218; role 213–214; *see also* Hongcun; West Lake; World Heritage Committee; World Heritage Convention; Xidi
World Tourism Organization (WTO) 40
Woudstra, J. 10, 64, 140, 143, 159, 160
Wright, P. 37
Wu, B.H. 4, 5, 58
Wu, C. 6
Wu, D. 26, 76, 190
Wu, J. 60

Xi, J. 54, 74n12
Xiao, H. 39
Xidi 137, 158–162, 185–187, 210, 216; authorised heritage discourse 140, 157–158, 160, 181–182, 185, 192, 195; background and tourism development 137–144; comparison with Hongcun 155–158; emotional engagement in cultural moments 194–195; emotional expression of feeling 197, 200, 201; emotional interactions between local people and tourists 202–203, 204, 205–206; fieldwork 3, 9, 10–17, 144–146; local management policies 178–183; local people's reactions to governments' policies and management mode 169–177; local people's reactions to tourism 162–169, 193; local–tourist interactions 188; tourists and cultural moments 146–155
Xie, H. 6
Xijin, P. 60
Xu, F. 7, 29, 50, 78, 198, 218
Xu, H. 10, 140, 142, 143, 159, 160, 181
Xu, P. 82

Yan, H. 18, 28, 29, 30, 34, 39, 45, 49, 50, 51, 57, 61, 62, 64, 67, 68, 69, 70, 71–72, 73, 81, 185, 191, 213
Yang, G. 96
Yang, W. 112
Yang, X.R. 82, 102, 130
Yao, X. 50, 74n4
Yeoman, I. 3, 4, 36, 127, 192, 207
Ying, T. 8, 10, 139, 140, 141, 142, 143, 158, 160, 175, 176, 193, 206
Yoshida, K. 24
Yu, Q. 135n1, 207
Yue, F. 94, 112–113, 115, 116, 120–121, 124, 194, 199, 207
Yuqian 115
Yuzhi, L. 62

Zeng, B. 52, 53, 54
Zhai, M. 141, 158, 160
Zhang, B. 91
Zhang, C. 5, 32, 38, 39, 58, 59, 61, 72
Zhang, J. 6, 7, 29, 32, 78, 99, 198, 218
Zhang, R. 5, 6, 9, 11, 23, 25, 30, 32, 60, 69, 70, 73, 77, 78, 82, 89, 99, 110, 124, 147, 197, 207, 208
Zhang, S. 5
Zhang, T. 4, 38, 58
Zhang, X. 142
Zhang, Y. 198
Zhao, D. 57
Zhao, S. 55, 56
Zhao, X. 7
Zheng, J.N. 11, 83
Zheng, S. 56
Zhong, W. 30
Zhongkun Investment Group (Co. Jingyi Ltd) 141–143, 145, 156, 158, 174, 176, 180, 205–206, 208
Zhou, H. 5
Zhou, J. 7, 27, 48, 49
Zhou, M. 29, 48, 62, 98
Zhou, N.X. 32, 190
Zhou, W. 102
Zhou, Y. 8, 10, 139, 140, 141, 142, 143, 158, 160, 175, 176, 193, 206
Zhu, X. 211n1
Zhu, Y. 6, 12, 32, 44, 199, 215
Zhuangzi 26, 48, 50
Zou, T. 6